MS-DOS® 6.2 QuickStart

Steve Konicki

DiskPack by Bradley F. Shimmin

MS-DOS 6.2 QuickStart

Library of Congress Catalog No.: 94-65319

ISBN: 1-56529-754-7

97 96 95 94 4 3 2 1

Interpretation of the printing code: the rightmost double-digit number is the year of the book's printing; the rightmost single-digit number, the number of the book's printing. For example, a printing code of 94-1 shows that the first printing of the book occurred in 1994.

Publisher: David P. Ewing

Associate Publisher: Michael Miller

Publishing Director: Joseph B. Wikert

Managing Editor: Michael Cunningham

Marketing Manager: Ray Robinson

Dedication

To Joe and Joey Bohan, my personal target audience for this book. It's hard to describe the unbridled joy in little Joey's eyes when he learns something new on the computer. At age 3, he's already becoming a DOS and Windows master. Joey's joy at the keyboard is equalled only by the surprise in his father Joe's eyes, when dad sits down with Joey at the computer and the boy teaches dad something new.

Credits

Publishing Manager
Brad R. Koch

Acquisitions Editor
Angela J. Lee

Product Director
Robin Drake

Production Editors
Christine Prakel
Thomas F. Hayes

Copy Editors
Danielle Bird
Susan Shaw Dunn

Technical Editor
Danny Kusnierz

Acquisitions Coordinator
Patricia J. Brooks

Book Designer
Amy Peppler-Adams

Cover Designer
Dan Armstrong

Production Team
Steve Adams
Angela Bannan
Karen Dodson
Terri Edwards
Brook Farling
Teresa Forrester
Joelynn Gifford
Carla Hall
Bob LaRoche
Tim Montgomery
Nanci Sears Perry
Dennis Sheehan
Rebecca Tapley
Michael Thomas
Marcella Thompson
Suzanne Tully
Sue VandeWalle
Mary Beth Wakefield
Donna Winter
Robert Wolf

Composed in *Stone Serif* and *MCPdigital* by Que Corporation.

About the Authors

MS-DOS 6.2 QuickStart is **Steve Konicki's** ninth book effort for Que Corporation. He recently authored *Killer PC Utilities,* which provides in-depth coverage of computer hardware and software, and includes two disks of important software utilities for speeding up and optimizing your computer.

Konicki also is the primary author of *Killer Windows Utilities,* a book on getting the most from Windows. Konicki also authored *Windows Hot Tips,* a book of advanced techniques for intermediate to advanced users of Microsoft Windows 3.1; was primary author of *Tuning Windows 3.1,* an easy-to-use technical reference on Windows for advanced users or those who want to become quite knowledgeable; and was co-author of *Upgrading to Windows 3.1,* a step-by-step guide to installing and using Windows for users of previous versions. He also contributed to *Upgrading and Repairing PCs,* Third Edition; *Using WordPerfect 6 for DOS,* Special Edition; and *Using WordPerfect 5.2 for Windows,* Special Edition.

Konicki works as a computer consultant based in Miami, Florida, and writes for computer magazines, particularly on Windows and Windows software. Konicki worked for many years as a newspaper reporter and editor. His first exposure to computers was nearly two decades ago on a newspaper newsroom mainframe that crashed so often, reporters would make printouts of their work every 10 minutes and often spend entire afternoons retyping stories that had been lost in that day's crash. Nevertheless, Konicki still likes computers. He can be reached on CompuServe at 71640,3311.

As an associate reviews editor for McGraw-Hill's *LAN Times* magazine and as a former local area network administrator, **Bradley F. Shimmin** has had extensive experience with and written many articles about PC hardware and software. He lives in Salt Lake City, Utah.

Trademarks

All terms mentioned in this book that are known to be trademarks or service marks have been appropriately capitalized. Que cannot attest to the accuracy of this information. Use of a term in this book should not be regarded as affecting the validity of any trademark or service mark. Trademarks indicated below were derived from various sources.

MS-DOS is a registered trademark and Microsoft Windows is a trademark of Microsoft Corporation.

WordPerfect is a registered trademark of WordPerfect Corporation.

Contents at a Glance

Table of Contents

V Appendix 437

Introduction

Everyone who uses a personal computer needs to know at least a little about the disk operating system (DOS) that runs the computer. Although your computer manages many of its functions without commands from you, you often will need to know how to work with DOS to accomplish specific objectives. For example, suppose that you want to copy a file from your hard drive to a floppy disk. You use DOS to format the floppy disk, and you use DOS to copy the file. This book teaches you the commands for these actions and how to use the commands appropriately.

This book covers what DOS is, what it does, and the basics of how to use DOS. This book explains to beginning users the most frequently used DOS commands, and it serves as a quick reference to DOS commands for more experienced users. Although this book primarily covers commonly used commands like COPY and FORMAT, it also covers important MS-DOS 6.2 utilities like MSAV, the virus-checking utility, and DoubleSpace, a utility that can nearly double the amount of data you can store on your hard drive.

Who Should Use This Book?

If you are a new computer user, *MS-DOS 6.2 QuickStart* can help you become productive quickly with your computer. If you are experienced with MS-DOS or other versions of DOS, you can use this book to learn how to use the new advanced features of MS-DOS 6.2. For all levels of users, this book teaches you how to work safely and efficiently with the powerful DOS commands, how to configure your computer system for maximum performance, how to work with Windows, and many other important topics that can save time and improve your computing skills.

How This Book Is Organized

DOS becomes much easier to understand after you become aware that DOS is mostly a collection of small programs, or utilities, each of which enables you to perform a particular action on your computer. For most computer users, a small, essential set of commands (such as COPY, FORMAT, and ERASE) are important to learn right away. This book begins by exploring the most essential DOS commands and functions and how to use them. After you are comfortable with the most commonly used DOS commands, this book acquaints you with more advanced DOS utilities, such as DEFRAG, which speeds up your system's access to files on your hard drive.

MS-DOS 6.2 QuickStart is a tutorial developed with easy-to-follow, step-by-step instructions. Most lessons follow the same format. First, new commands or procedures are described briefly. Next, the lesson presents procedures in numbered steps to guide you through the required actions or keystrokes. In most cases, illustrations show how the screen appears during and after taking a certain action.

Throughout each lesson, notes and cautions provide shortcuts, additional information, and warnings about possible pitfalls. Sections called "If You Have Problems" alert you to possible problems and provide suggestions for solving them. Key terms in the margin clarify terminology.

A summary table appears at the end of the lesson, with instructions for executing commands covered in the lesson. Also included at the end of the lesson is an optional exercise to reinforce your understanding of the concepts presented in the lesson.

The lessons and appendixes are organized into five parts.

Part I: DOS Basics

Part I introduces you to the basic terminology of computer hardware, software, and DOS, and helps you begin understanding how to use DOS commands.

Lesson 1, "Understanding Hardware, Software, and DOS," begins the book by describing the components of personal computer systems: the display, the keyboard, the system unit, and so on. The last part of this lesson explains the way that computers handle data. In this lesson, you learn the fundamental concepts of how a computer works, including its operating system.

Lesson 2, "Making a Quick Start with DOS 6.2," covers the new features in DOS 6.2, as well as the changes in DOS since version 4.0 and the basic DOS commands a novice should learn immediately.

Lesson 3, "Starting DOS," covers how to start, or boot, the computer.

Lesson 4, "Working from the DOS Command Line," teaches you how to work with DOS from the command line, including the way you must enter DOS commands.

Part II: Files and Directories

The lessons in this part describe the organization of data on disks and teach you how to set up your computer to make your data easy to find.

Lesson 5, "Understanding and Using Directories," introduces you to the way directories and subdirectories organize files on your system and how to move around in your systems directory structure.

Lesson 6, "Maintaining Files," shows you the fundamentals of copying, moving, deleting, and renaming files. You also learn how to copy an entire disk.

Part III: Using DOS Commands

Part III covers useful commands that can help give your system more flexibility and power and provide important system information for maintenance purposes.

Lesson 7, "Formatting Disks," teaches you how to use the FORMAT command to prepare disks for storing data.

Lesson 8, "DOS Command Reference," provides a command reference to the most commonly used DOS commands.

Lesson 9, "Basic DOS Commands," introduces you to some of DOS's basic yet less-used commands, such as MEM, CHKDSK, and CLS. Although you don't use commands such as these as often as COPY or DEL, they are important to learn.

Lesson 10, "Advanced DOS Commands," describes the more advanced DOS commands. You learn about the Microsoft System Diagnostics (MSD) utility, how to use it to troubleshoot your system, and many of your systems internal components. This lesson also covers redirection, piping, and DOS filters.

Part IV: Customizing Your Setup

This part describes how to change the way DOS works for you—to make the system more responsive to your needs.

Lesson 11, "Customizing DOS," covers how to customize DOS by using the PATH and PROMPT commands and by using SmartDrive to speed up your system. The lesson also covers using the extended memory and expanded memory device drivers provided with DOS 6.2 and better managing the memory in your computer. Lesson 11 also introduces you to batch files—small computer programs you can write to perform many DOS functions.

Lesson 12, "Protecting Your PC's Data," shows you how to protect your valuable data with backups and virus-prevention software.

Lesson 13, "Using DoubleSpace, SCANDISK, and DEFRAG" explores how to use the MS-DOS 6.2 utility DoubleSpace to increase the storage capacity of your hard drive and floppy disks.

Lesson 14, "Configuring DOS 6.2 for Windows," covers the best way to configure DOS if you run Windows and how to optimize your system to get the best Windows performance possible.

Part V: Appendix

The Appendix, "Setup and Installation," covers DOS setup and installation for both floppy and hard disk systems.

Conventions Used in This Book

MS-DOS 6.2 QuickStart uses certain conventions throughout the text and graphics to help you better understand the uses of DOS. The following sections provide examples of these conventions.

Command Syntax and Examples

When you type DOS commands, various ways of typing the command can be correct. When this book provides examples, you can type them exactly as shown. Some parts of a command are *mandatory*, required by DOS to perform an action. Other command parts are *optional*. The way of correctly typing the mandatory and optional parts of commands is known as the *command syntax*. This book illustrates command syntax by using symbols to represent possible entries. When you enter a command, you substitute real values for the symbols.

When an entry appearing in this book is capitalized, you type those exact characters. When an entry appears in boldface type, the entry is mandatory if you want to use that command. For example, when you see **DIR** in this book, you need to type those exact letters. In other words, this mandatory text, typed exactly the way you see it in the book, prompts DOS to perform the particular action you want. For example, typing the command **DIR** prompts DOS to show you the contents of a directory or provide information about a particular file. But typing any other combination of letters obtains a different result.

When an entry in this book appears in plain italic type, you can *optionally* substitute a real value. When an entry appears in bold italic type, you *must* substitute a real value.

Spaces separate some parts of the command line. The forward slash (/) or backslash (\) separate other parts. These separators, or *delimiters*, are important to DOS because they help DOS break apart the command. For example, typing the following command is correct:

DIR A:

But typing this command is not correct:

DIRA:

If you want to use a command line parameter or switch, you must include the appropriate separator.

The syntax for the DIR command appears this way in this book:

DIR *d\filename.ext /W /P*

As you can see, **DIR** is boldface and capitalized because you must type those exact characters to use the DIR command. In the syntax example, the lowercase *d* represents the disk drive the command uses for its action. If you want the command to perform its action on a particular drive, you must replace *d* with the appropriate drive, for example, A:, B:, or C:. As mentioned, the *filename.ext* stands for the name of a file, including its extension. If you want the command to perform its action on a particular file, you must substitute the correct file name and extension.

The entry for drive, file name and extension, and the two possible switches appear in plain italic type because you are not required to make entries for these parts of the syntax. Only the DIR is mandatory. The other parts of the command, *d\filename.ext /W /P*, are optional. Entering the command DIR alone produces a file listing similar to the partial listing shown in the following example:

```
Volume in drive C is DRIVE_C
 Volume Serial Number is 1B6A-9B34
 Directory of C:\DOS

.            <DIR>          09-30-92   3:41p
..           <DIR>          09-30-92   3:41p
DBLSPACE BIN         64,246 09-30-93   6:20a
DBLSPACE EXE        177,034 09-30-93   6:20a
ANSI     SYS          9,065 09-30-93   6:20a
APPEND   EXE         10,774 09-30-93   6:20a
ATTRIB   EXE         11,208 09-30-93   6:20a
CHKDSK   EXE         12,241 09-30-93   6:20a
COUNTRY  SYS         19,546 09-30-93   6:20a
DBLSPACE HLP         80,724 09-30-93   6:20a
DBLSPACE SYS         22,502 09-30-93   6:20a
DBLSPACE INF          2,620 09-30-93   6:20a
```

The special `monospace` typeface in this example and others throughout the book indicates what you see on-screen in error messages and prompts.

If you want to have the DIR command operate on a particular disk drive, you enter that drive letter. The following is an example of properly entering the command for the A: drive:

DIR A:

If you want to have the DIR command operate on a particular file, you enter the file name and extension of that file. The following is an example of properly entering this command to obtain information about the file COMMAND.COM located in the C:\DOS directory:

DIR C:\DOS\COMMAND.COM

To obtain a wide listing of files in the current directory (more file names fit across the screen), you use the W/ switch, as in this example:

DIR /W

Note: *Although this book displays mandatory text in uppercase, you can type the text in uppercase or lowercase. DOS understands commands typed either way.*

Key Combinations

In this book, a key combination is joined by a hyphen. For example, Ctrl-Break means that you hold down the Ctrl key, press the Break key, and then release both keys. If the keys are not connected with a hyphen, press the first key and release it before pressing the second key. For example, the text may instruct you to press End Down; in this case, you press and release the End key before pressing the Down key.

Icons

When a numbered step has an icon next to it, you can click the button that the icon represents on the appropriate toolbar in Windows or other programs instead of using the command in the step.

MS-DOS 6.2 System Requirements

Many companies manufacture or market MS-DOS-based personal computers, including IBM, COMPAQ, Zeos, Gateway, Dell, Toshiba, Leading Edge, Hewlett-Packard, Zenith Data Systems, NCR, Tandy, Advanced Logic Research, AT&T, AST, EPSON, Wang, NEC, Sharp, and others.

You cannot use MS-DOS on most computers made by Apple Computer Inc., Commodore (except the new Amiga computers, when equipped with additional hardware), or Atari. These computers use operating systems sometimes referred to as DOS, but their operating systems are not MS-DOS compatible.

Your computer should have at least 256 kilobytes (256K) of system random-access memory (RAM), at least one floppy disk drive, a display (screen), and a keyboard. These suggestions are minimal; most MS-DOS PCs sold today include at least 1M of system memory, a second floppy disk drive, and a color graphics display.

To make even the most minimal use of DOS, your computer should have a hard disk with at least 20M of storage capacity. (You need at least 4M of hard disk space to set up DOS 6.2.) To install the three optional programs, you need additional hard drive space: 2M for Anti-Virus for Windows and DOS, 1.7M for Backup for Windows and DOS, and about 300K for Undelete for Windows and DOS.

Where To Find More Help

After you have learned the DOS basics covered in this book, you may want to explore more of the capabilities of MS-DOS 6.2. Que Corporation has a complete line of books designed to meet the needs of all MS-DOS computer users. Other books include *Using MS-DOS 6.2*, Special Edition; *Upgrading to MS-DOS 6*; *Turbocharging MS-DOS;* and *MS-DOS 6.2 Quick Reference*.

Que wishes you good computing!

Part I
DOS Basics

Lesson 1

Understanding Hardware, Software, and DOS

This lesson explains the standard components of the IBM PC and compatibles, and how DOS works with these components. Although you don't need to know all this information to work with your computer, you may find that understanding these concepts helps you understand what DOS is doing when you run a program or execute a command in subsequent lessons.

You probably do not want to memorize all the terms in this lesson, but if you are a novice to PCs you may need to refer to this lesson later. This information may help when you read about making the most of system memory and hard drive space as well as other system optimization issues.

This lesson covers the following topics:

- Definition of MS-DOS
- Hardware and software basics
- The way computers use data
- Networked PCs

Review of MS-DOS

Operating system
Software that starts when you turn on your computer. The operating system is the working base for all other programs and includes utilities you use to manage your system.

MS-DOS 6.2—the common *operating system* for IBM PCs and compatibles—is the focus of this book. MS-DOS is short for *Microsoft Disk Operating System*. This book covers MS-DOS 6.2 and earlier versions.

The different versions of Microsoft Corporation's DOS and the IBM versions of DOS are highly compatible. Actually, the versions are nearly identical, except that IBM calls its version *PC-DOS* and Microsoft calls its version *MS-DOS*. This text uses *DOS* as the generic term when referring to both packages. If you need specific information about PC-DOS and its capabilities, refer to Que's *Using PC-DOS 6.1*.

Computer Technology Basics

In 1981, International Business Machines (IBM) introduced the IBM Personal Computer, or PC. Although this first PC was a primitive device compared with the PCs on today's desktop, this simple machine was responsible for creating a computing revolution that continues to dominate technology to this day.

Previous business computers had been large, expensive machines generally available only to large corporations that could afford them. Today's desktop PC systems often are as powerful as the huge mainframes that were available in 1981 and cost only a fraction as much. Modern PCs are common not only in business, but also in the home.

Originally, PCs by other manufacturers were called *clones*, but some systems were only partially compatible with the IBM PC. Today, personal computers manufactured by companies other than IBM adhere strictly to what has become known as the *IBM standard*, although many manufacturers produce computers that are in many ways superior to the IBM product line. Rapid technical developments in new companies are raising microcomputer technology to astounding heights. Even the venerable IBM uses much of this technology in its newest PCs.

Note: *Although the Apple II and Macintosh also are personal computers, the term* PC *has come to distinguish computers made by IBM and other manufacturers that run DOS.*

Hardware
The physical components of your computer—the chips, circuit boards, electronics, metal and plastic moving parts, and other components.

Software
Word processing, spreadsheet, graphics, and database programs, and other application software that enables you to do your work.

The disk operating system for the first IBM PC was produced by Microsoft, at that time a small company with few employees. This operating system, containing some very simple computer programming, was the first version of MS-DOS. Microsoft parlayed this first version of DOS into a multi-billion dollar computer software empire, due in large part to the fact that since 1981, nearly every one of the millions of IBM-compatible computers manufactured has included a copy of MS-DOS.

All DOS computers operate in essentially the same manner, despite the wide variety of sizes, shapes, and installed components. Desktop and tower computers are developed to be large enough to contain disk drives and other devices. The laptop is small and light, perfect for computing while on the road. The major difference is that laptops are not as expandable as desktop and tower computers, and therefore laptops are not as versatile or powerful.

Hardware and *software* make up the two main segments of a computer system. Both segments must be present for a computer to work. Table 1.1 illustrates the variety of software available for a computer.

Table 1.1 Computer Software

Type of Software	Examples
Operating systems	MS-DOS, OS/2, UNIX
Databases	dBASE, Paradox, PC-FILE
Spreadsheets	Lotus 1-2-3, Excel, Quattro Pro
Word processing	Microsoft Word, WordPerfect, Ami Pro
Utilities	Norton Utilities, FastBack Plus, PC Tools
Graphics	CorelDRAW!, Lotus Freelance, Harvard Graphics
Integrated programs	Symphony, Microsoft Works, Q&A
Games	Flight Simulator, Tetris, SimCity
Home finance	Quicken, Managing Your Money
Desktop publishing	Aldus PageMaker, Microsoft Publisher, Ventura Publisher

Displays

Display
The computer screen or monitor.

Personal computers are *interactive*, which means that the PC reacts to any action you take and displays the results. The video display is the normal, or *default*, location the computer uses to communicate with you. The video *display* (also called the *monitor* or *screen*) is the part of the computer's hardware that produces visual images.

Note: *On the display, a blinking symbol (box, underscore, or other character) shows where the next character will appear. This symbol is the* cursor.

Output
Information produced from your computer.

Because the video display exhibits the results of your work, the display is called an *output device*. To date, the cathode ray tube (CRT) type of monitor, which operates on the same principle as a television set, provides the most crisp and easiest-to-read image.

Manufacturers sometimes use other types of technology in computer displays. For example, to build flatter, more lightweight displays, some manufacturers use a technology known as *gas plasma*. Gas plasma displays produce an orange color against a dark background. You find this type of display primarily in portable computers, where a TV-type display would be heavy and cumbersome.

Another technology adapted to computer displays is liquid crystal. *Liquid crystal displays* (LCDs) work on the same principle as today's digital watch displays. Most LCDs produce dark characters against a lighter background. LCDs work well in brightly lit rooms, because the light striking the display increases the contrast of the display image. Some LCDs also use a backlight to increase the display's contrast. This type of display appears primarily on laptop computers.

Regardless of the display type, all computer screens take electrical signals and translate them into patterns of tiny dots, or *pixels*. Pixel is an acronym coined from the phrase *picture element*. You can recognize pixels as characters or figures. The more pixels a display contains, the sharper the visual image. The number of pixels in the image multiplied by the number of lines on the display determines the image's *resolution*.

The resolution of the visual image is a function of both the display and the *display adapter*. The display adapter controls the computer display. The display adapter often resides on a separate circuit board that fits into a slot in the computer. In some PCs, the display circuitry is a part of the motherboard (see this lesson's section "The System Unit and

Peripherals"). Display adapters come in different types, including the monochrome display adapter (MDA), Hercules monochrome graphics adapter (MGA), color graphics adapter (CGA), enhanced graphics adapter (EGA), video graphics array adapter (VGA), extended graphics array adapter (XGA), super video graphics array (SVGA), or a less common display adapter.

Monochrome display adapters, and the monitors designed to work with them, can display only text characters, as described in the following section. MDAs cannot display graphics characters. MDA cards and monitors are all but obsolete technology. Most computers produced in the past 8 to 10 years have graphics displays because so much software today is graphically oriented.

Text Displays

When you see letters, numbers, or punctuation on your display, you recognize these images as text. This text comes from your computer's display adapter, which stores the text under the standard that most computers recognize, the *American Standard Code for Information Interchange* (abbreviated *ASCII* and pronounced to rhyme with *passkey).*

Each ASCII code represents a letter or a symbol. Your computer sends these codes to the display adapter so you can see the characters on-screen. The display adapter has a built-in electronic table from which the adapter can take the correct pixel pattern for any letter, number, or punctuation symbol.

Although only 128 standard ASCII codes exist, a single computer character can contain 256 different codes. The upper codes are known as IBM *extended ASCII codes*. These additional codes are used for patterns of foreign language letters, mathematical symbols, lines, corners, and special images, such as musical notes.

Text displays and text display adapters cannot generate graphics. To display graphics, you need a graphics display, as described in the next section.

Graphics Displays

Graphics displays enable you to view, on-screen, complex figures with curves and fine detail. Your computer works harder to create graphics images than text because images are painted on-screen pixel-by-pixel. To display the correct image on-screen, the display adapter must find the screen coordinate points for each pixel. Unlike the ASCII codes in text mode, no table of predetermined pixels exists for graphics mode.

Graphics displays vary in the number of pixels available. The greater the number of pixels, the finer the detail of the display. Each pixel contains characteristics that describe to the graphics adapter what the color or intensity of the pixel should be. Likewise, graphics displays present a varying number of colors on-screen. For example, CGA displays offer four colors. Many Super VGA displays offer millions of colors. The greater the number of colors and intensities, the more storage space you need in memory. Graphics adapters offer varying combinations of pixel density, number of colors, and intensity.

Table 1.2 lists the most common display adapters, showing the maximum resolution and colors available with each display adapter.

Table 1.2 Resolution and Colors for Display Adapters

Adapter	Graphics Mode	Resolution	Colors
CGA	Medium resolution	320x200	4
CGA	High resolution	640x200	2
EGA	CGA high resolution	640x200	16
EGA	EGA high resolution	640x350	16
MGA	Monochrome graphics	720x348	2
MDA	Text characters only	80x25	2
VGA	Monochrome	640x480	2
VGA	VGA high resolution	640x480	16
VGA	VGA medium resolution	320x200	256
Super VGA	Super VGA	800x600	256 – 16 million
Super VGA	1024 Super VGA	1024x768	256 – 16 million
XGA	Standard mode	1024x768	256
XGA	16-bit color	640x480	65,536

The number of colors available on the display depends on the capabilities of your display adapter and the software program you are using. For example, a Super VGA adapter with 2M of video memory can display up to 16 million colors, but a particular software application may take advantage of only 16 colors. On the other hand, certain software applications may be capable of displaying images using 16 million colors, but this capability is lost on a display adapter that can display only 16 colors.

Keyboards

Input
Any information you enter into your computer.

Using the *keyboard* is the most basic way to enter information into the computer. The computer converts every character you type into code the machine can understand. The keyboard is therefore an *input device.*

Like a typewriter, a computer keyboard contains all the letters of the alphabet. The numbers, symbols, and punctuation characters are virtually the same. The common computer keyboard has the familiar QWERTY layout. (The letters *QWERTY* come from left side of the top row of letter keys on a standard typewriter.) However, a computer keyboard differs from a typewriter keyboard in several important ways.

The most notable differences of the computer keyboard are the extra keys that do not appear on a typewriter. These keys and their standard functions are described in table 1.3. Some of these keys have different functions when used with different programs. Also, depending on the type of computer and keyboard you use, you see 10 or 12 special *function keys* marked F1 through F10 or F12.

Table 1.3 Special Keys on the Computer Keyboard

Key	Function
Enter	Signals the computer to respond to the commands you type. Also functions as a carriage return in programs that simulate the operation of a typewriter.
Cursor keys	Changes the location of the cursor on-screen. Cursor keys include the arrow keys, PgUp, PgDn, Home, and End keys.
Backspace	Moves the cursor backward one space at a time, deleting any character in that space.
Delete	Deletes, or erases, any character at the location of the cursor.

(continues)

Table 1.3 Continued

Key	Function
Insert	After you press this key, any character you type inserts at the location of the cursor.
Shift	Capitalizes letters when you hold down Shift as you press another letter key. When pressed in combination with another key, Shift can change the standard function of that key.
Caps Lock	Enables you to enter all capital letters when the key is pressed down in the locked position. Caps Lock doesn't shift the numbered keys, however. To release Caps Lock, press the key again.
Control (Ctrl)	Changes the standard function of a key when pressed in combination with another key.
Alternate (Alt)	Changes the standard function of a key when pressed in combination with another key.
Escape (Esc)	Enables you to escape from a current operation to a previous one in some situations. Sometimes Esc has no effect on the current operation.
Number Lock	Changes the numeric keypad from cursor-movement to numeric-function mode.
Print Screen	Sends the displayed characters to the printer. Enhanced keyboards provide this key.
Scroll Lock	Locks the scrolling function to the cursor-movement keys so they scroll the screen instead of moving the cursor.
Pause	Suspends display activity until you press another key. (Not provided with standard keyboards.)
Break	Stops a program in progress from running.
Numeric keypad	A cluster of numbered keys at the far right of the standard keyboard.

Note: *On your keyboard, some keys in table 1.3 may be spelled or abbreviated differently.*

Many keys are designed for use in combination with other keys (see table 1.4). For example, holding down the Ctrl key as you press the Print Screen key causes DOS to continuously print what you type after you have pressed this *key combination*. Pressing Ctrl and Print Screen a second time turns off the printing. You do not use the Break key as a separate key. On most keyboards, you must press the Ctrl and Break keys together to produce a break. With some keyboards, pressing the Ctrl and Scroll Lock keys together causes a break. With other keyboards, pressing the Ctrl and Pause keys together causes a break.

Table 1.4 DOS Key Combinations

Key Combination	Function
Ctrl-S	Freezes the display. Pressing any other key restarts the display.
Ctrl-Print Screen	Sends output to both the screen and printer. Pressing this sequence a second time turns off this function.
Ctrl-C or Ctrl-Break	Stops the execution of a program.
Ctrl-Alt-Del	Restarts DOS (system reset).

The function keys, the row of keys marked F1 through F10 or F12, are above and/or beside the alphanumeric keys. Depending on the software application you are running, you can use the function keys as shortcuts or command keys. Not all programs use these keys, and some programs use only a few of them. When used, however, these keys automatically carry out certain operations for you. For example, programs often use the F1 key for *on-line help*. On-line help displays instructions to help you understand a particular operation.

When your computer is booting-up with DOS 6.2, you can bypass the CONFIG.SYS and AUTOEXEC.BAT files by pressing F5. For example, you may want to bypass CONFIG.SYS and AUTOEXEC.BAT if a change you made recently to these two system configuration files has caused your computer to malfunction. Using a text editor, you can edit CONFIG.SYS and AUTOEXEC.BAT to remove the problem, then reboot your system for the changes to take effect. Only knowledgeable computer users should edit CONFIG.SYS and AUTOEXEC.BAT.

A better way of protecting your system against changes made to CONFIG.SYS and AUTOEXEC.BAT is to make backup copies of these important files before you install new software. Then you can restore the original copies if changes made by software-install programs cause problems on your system.

Standard Keyboards

The original standard keyboard contains the function keys F1 through F10 on the left side. The standard Extended keyboard offers keys F1 through F12 across the top of the keyboard. The Extended keyboard offers a major improvement over the original keyboard: a cursor-control keypad separate from the numeric keypad. Many current computer systems offer function keys on the left side of the keyboard as well as across the top for convenience.

AT and Enhanced Keyboards

Many early PC-compatible computers used a standard keyboard design similar to that of the IBM PC. Other machines used a personal computer AT-style keyboard. The IBM PS/2 computers and almost all other personal computers today use a 101-key Enhanced keyboard. Some users prefer the layout of the standard keyboard, and others prefer the Enhanced keyboard.

You can determine whether your computer has a standard keyboard, a personal computer AT-style keyboard, or an Enhanced keyboard. You find certain keys only on specific keyboards. For example, you find separate Print Screen and Pause keys only on the Enhanced keyboard. You can, however, simulate these keys by using a combination of keys on the standard keyboard.

Special Keyboards

Some new keyboards try to provide the advantages of both the older and newer keyboards. Such keyboards enable you to change key caps and switch key definitions for the Caps Lock, Ctrl, Esc, and tilde (~) keys. Some keyboards provide the Enhanced layout but locate the function keys on the left side of the keyboard rather than at the top. In addition, some systems offer keyboards with the separate cursor keys arranged exactly as they are on the numeric keypad. Some people think this arrangement makes the cursor keys easier to use with most software.

Keyboards for Portables

Laptop and notebook computers employ nonstandard keyboards, usually to conserve space. A *space-saver keyboard* is small enough to fit in a portable computer, but often the trade-off for its smaller size is fewer keys and less functionality. A few of these computers have so little keyboard space that you may need to add an external numeric keypad for software that manipulates numbers.

System Unit and Peripherals

CPU (central processing unit)
The processor in which the actual computing takes place. The CPU is the brain of the computer.

Peripheral
A device such as a printer, separate from the computer, that enables you to do some work or display results.

Industry engineers designed the standard desktop PC around a box-shaped cabinet that connects to all other parts of the computer including disk drives and disks. This box is called the *system unit*. The brain of the computer, the *central processing unit* (*CPU*), is contained in the system unit. The CPU is located on the main circuit board of the computer, the *motherboard*. Any devices attached to the system unit are *peripherals*. The system unit and peripherals complete the hardware portion of the computer system.

The system unit houses all but a few parts of a PC. Included are the disk drives, various circuit boards, a power supply, and even a small speaker.

The system units on today's PCs come in many variations of the original design. Desktop models are smaller to conserve desk space. Larger models with room for larger, multiple hard disks and other peripherals often use a floor-standing tower design that requires no desk space at all.

The *motherboard* is a large circuit board that holds the main electronic components of the computer. The CPU chip, also called the *microprocessor*, the chips that support it, and various other circuits are the primary parts on the motherboard. The motherboard contains *expansion slots*, electrical sockets where you can plug various adapter circuit boards. The number of available expansion slots varies with each PC builder.

RAM (Random-Access Memory)
The silicon chips that store data temporarily. When you start your computer, DOS loads into RAM. When you start an application, the program code loads into RAM.

Data
A broad term meaning words, numbers, symbols, graphics, or sounds—any information stored in the computer.

Chips that provide the computer with its *random-access memory* (*RAM*) are on the motherboard. You can plug additional memory chips into most system motherboards to increase the system's memory. On some motherboards, you may need to plug an adapter card into an available expansion slot to increase memory.

An important point to remember is that as you type *data* into a software program, your information is stored only temporarily in RAM and is lost when you shut off your computer. To keep the information you have entered into a program, you must use your software applications *Save* function to store the information on your hard drive or a floppy disk.

Most motherboards have a socket for a *math coprocessor*, which helps speed up programs that manipulate large volumes of graphics or math equations. Spreadsheet programs and desktop publishing software, for example, benefit from the addition of a math coprocessor chip.

Disk Drives and Disks

Disk drive
The equipment that records and reads back information on disks.

Disk
A circular plastic or metal platter with magnetized surfaces used to store files.

Disk drives are complex mechanisms that carry out a fairly simple function: they rotate *disks*. As the disk rotates, the drive converts electrical signals from the computer and places the information into magnetic fields or retrieves information from magnetic fields on the disk. The storage process is called *writing* data to the disk.

Disk drives also recover, or *read*, magnetically stored data and present the data to the computer as electrical signals. You do not lose magnetically stored data when you turn off the computer.

The components of a disk drive are similar to those of a phonograph or a CD player. The disk rotates like a record. A positioner arm, like a toner arm, moves across the radius of the disk. A head, like a pickup cartridge, translates information into electrical signals. Unlike a record, however, the disk's surface does not have spiral grooves. The disk's surface is recorded in magnetic, concentric rings, or *tracks*. The tighter these tracks are packed on the disk, the greater the storage capacity of the disk.

File
A named group of data in electronic form. In word processing, a file might contain a proposal. In a database, a file might be an address listing.

When writing to a disk, the computer stores data in groups that the operating system identifies as *files*. For example, when you save information entered into a word processing program, the computer saves this information as a file.

Two types of disks are available and come in a variety of data storage capacities. Disks are either *floppy* or *hard*, as described in the following sections.

Floppy Disks

Floppy disks come in two common sizes—flexible 5 1/4-inch and rigid 3 1/2-inch. The measurement refers to the size of the disk's jacket. Originally, 5 1/4-inch floppy disks were called *minifloppies* to distinguish them from 8-inch disks used on very early personal computers. (The 3 1/2-inch disks sometimes are called *microfloppies* because of their size compared to 5 1/4-inch disks; often, 3 1/2-inch disks are called *disks* because their rigid shells no longer make them "floppy.") Unless size is important, this book refers to both disk types as *floppies*.

In almost all cases, the disk drive uses both sides of a disk for encoding information; therefore, the disk drives and the floppy disks are called *double-sided*.

1

Floppy drive
A disk drive that handles floppy disks.

K (kilobyte)
1,024 bytes, used to show size or capacity in computer systems.

M (megabyte)
1,024 kilobytes.

A *floppy drive* can handle only one size disk. You cannot read a 5 1/4-inch floppy disk in a 3 1/2-inch disk drive or vice versa. The storage capability of various disks is termed *capacity*. Throughout this book, disk capacities are shown in *kilobytes (K)* or *megabytes (M)*. Floppy disks store from 360K to 2.88M of data. The 5 1/4-inch disks are available in two capacities: 360K and 1.2M. The 3 1/2-inch disks are available in three capacities: 720K, 1.44M, and 2.88M. The 1.2M and 1.44M disks are called *high-density*, or *extended density*. The 2.88M disks are termed *extra high-density*.

A high-density disk drive can format, read, and write to both high-density and double-density floppy disks. A double-density disk drive can use only double-density disks. Make sure that you know the specification of your drive before you buy or interchange floppies. Floppies of the same size but with different capacities may be incompatible with a particular disk drive. For example, a 360K disk formatted in a 1.2M drive may not work on a system with a 360K floppy disk drive.

You can tell that a drive is reading or writing to a floppy disk when the small light on the front of the disk drive glows. Never open a drive door or eject a disk until the light goes out, unless the computer specifically instructs you to do so.

Hard Disks

Hard drive
A drive with non-removable disks, generally installed as a permanent part of a computer and used to store computer programs and data files.

Hard disks, also called *fixed* disks, often consist of multiple, high-capacity rigid platters that you cannot remove as you can floppies. Hard disks are sealed inside the hard disk drive (also called *hard drive*). When a hard drive is reading or writing data, a light may glow on the front of the drive or a separate disk-drive light may glow on the front of the system unit.

Each side of each hard disk platter has a separate head. The platters spin at a minimum of 3,600 RPM, much faster than a floppy disk drive spins. As the platters spin within the drive, the head positioners make small, precise movements above the tracks of the disk. Because of this precision, hard disks can store large quantities of data—from 10M to hundreds of megabytes. Hard disks are reasonably rugged devices. Factory sealing prevents contamination of the housing.

Peripherals

Besides the display, keyboard, and disk drives, a variety of peripherals can be useful to you. Peripherals such as a printer, mouse, modem, and joystick enable you to control your computer more easily. For example, using a mouse with a modern computer program like WordPerfect 6.0 or Word 6.0 takes best advantage of the program's features.

The *mouse* gets its name from the small wire that sticks out the back, like a mouse's tail. Moving the mouse on your desktop or on a mouse pad rolls a ball on the underside, sending electronic signals to the screen. These signals control the position of a special cursor, called the *mouse pointer*. Your mouse probably has two buttons, although some have three, and a few have only one button. Pressing the left mouse button, the *primary button*, causes an action similar to pressing the Enter key on your keyboard.

When used in combination, the movement of the mouse and the clicking of its buttons enable you to make program selections. For example, moving the mouse pointer onto the Word 6.0 File menu and clicking the primary mouse button opens the File menu, enabling you to make selections. Moving the mouse pointer to the Open command and clicking produces a dialog box in which you can open an existing word processing document.

You also can use the mouse to move the keyboard cursor swiftly, to select sections of your work to manipulate, and even to draw with graphics programs. Although mouse functions vary in different programs, the standard mouse techniques are based on Microsoft Windows. Not all software supports a mouse, but many popular programs do.

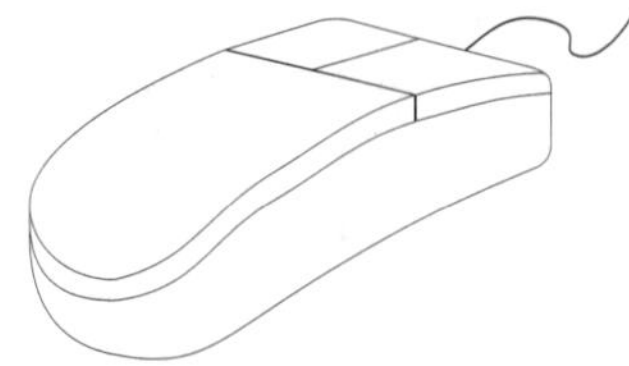

You use a mouse with programs offering a graphical interface, such as WordPerfect 6.0 or Word 6.0, and with Microsoft Windows.

The *joystick*, a popular peripheral in games, is used to enter information into the computer. Sometimes you can use joysticks in place of keyboard operations. Moving a joystick forward, backward, or side-to-side moves a pointer on-screen. Pressing one of the joystick's buttons causes an action, often similar to pressing the Enter key on your keyboard.

Joysticks are used most often with game programs such as Flight Simulator or Wing Commander.

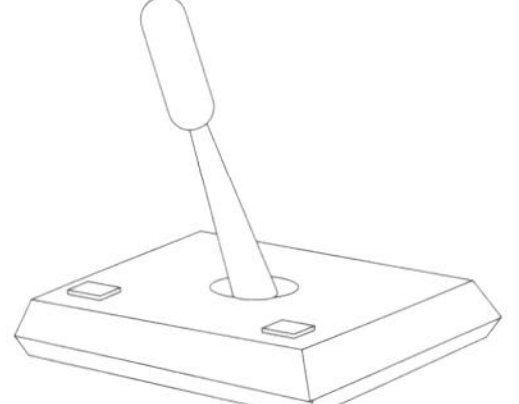

Printers. Printers produce output by accepting signals from your computer and converting those signals to characters imprinted on paper. This output often is text, but the output also can be graphics images. You can classify printers in two ways:

- How the printer receives input from the computer
- How the printer produces output

A printer accepts data from the computer and renders the data as text and images on paper.

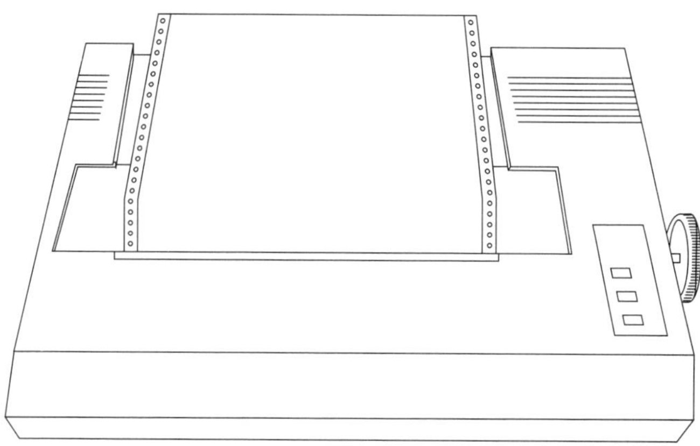

You connect printers to the system unit through a *port.* A port is an electrical connection through which data flows between the system unit and an outside peripheral. A port has its own expansion adapter or shares an expansion adapter with other ports or circuits, such as a multifunction card.

Byte
A collection of eight bits that a computer stores and manipulates as a single character (letter, number, or symbol). A bit can be 0 or 1. A byte is made up of a sequence of 0s and 1s.

The terms *parallel* and *serial* describe two types of ports that send output from personal computers to printers. A *parallel port* continuously sends all the bits of data *synchronously*, through separate wires in the cable, one character at a time. Parallel printer connections are more common than serial connections. A *serial port* delivers the data one bit after another, in single-file fashion. Although sending one complete *byte* using serial communications takes longer, serial ports require fewer wires in the cable. Serial printers also can communicate with the port over longer distances than parallel printers.

Printers usually are rated by their printing speed and the quality of the finished print. Some printers print by using all the addressable points on the screen, much as a graphics display adapter does. Some printers even produce color prints. Four major classifications of printers exist, and each printer type produces characters in unique ways:

- The *laser printer* uses a technology that closely resembles photocopying. Instead of a light-sensitive drum picking up the image of an original, the drum is painted with the light of a laser diode. The image on the drum transfers to the paper in a high dot-density output. With high dot density, the printed characters look fully formed. Laser printers also can produce graphics image output. The high-quality text and graphics combination is useful for desktop publishing as well as general business correspondence.

- The *inkjet printer* literally sprays words and graphics on a page in near silence. The print quality rivals that of a laser printer; of all the printers, only a laser printer is faster and sharper than this high-resolution, moderately priced printer.

- The *dot-matrix printer*, a common printer type, uses a print head that contains a row of pins or wires to produce the characters. A motor moves the print head horizontally across the paper. As the print head moves, a vertical slice of each character forms as the printer's controlling circuits fire the proper pins. The wires press corresponding small dots of the ribbon against the paper, leaving an ink dot impression. After several tiny horizontal steps, the print head leaves the dot image of a complete character. The process continues for each character on the line. Dot-matrix printers are inexpensive but slow. With the print quality close to that of a typewriter, this type of printer is commonly used for internal reports.

- The *daisywheel printer* steps, or moves incrementally, a print head across the page and produces a complete character for each step. The characters of the alphabet are arranged at the ends of petals that resemble spokes on a wheel. The visual effect of this wheel is similar to a daisy's petals arranged around the flower head. Because the daisywheel prints fully formed characters, the quality of daisywheel printing is about the same as a typewriter. Daisywheel printers are far slower than the other printers and are virtually obsolete.

Modems. A *modem* is a peripheral that helps your PC communicate with other computers over standard telephone lines. Modems are serial communications peripherals; they send or receive characters or data one bit at a time. Most modems communicate with other modems at speeds from 300 to 14,400 bits per second (bps). New modem technology, called V-Fast, communicates with other V-Fast modems at 28,800 bps. At one time, the most common modem speed was 2400 bps, but in recent years, inexpensive high-quality 14,400-bps modems have replaced a great number of the older 2400-bps modems.

Modems are available in external types and internal types. *External modems* connect to a serial port on the back of your computer and require you to plug in their power supply. *Internal modems* plug into an expansion slot on your motherboard and are powered by the motherboard.

A modem transfers signals between computers using telephone lines.

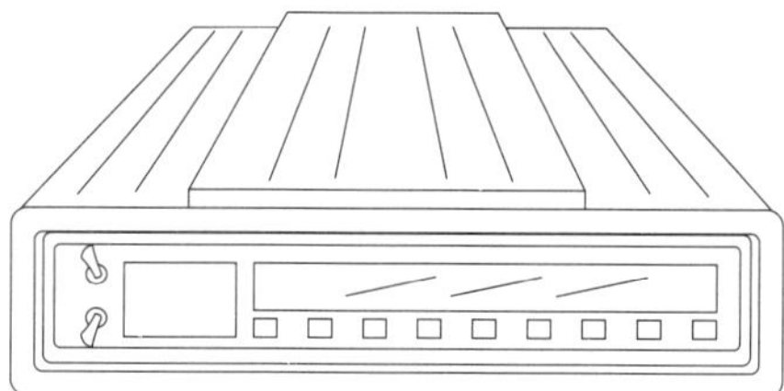

You use a modem to send or receive files to another computer, to use a computerized *bulletin board system* (BBS), or to access an on-line service such as Prodigy or CompuServe. Modems need special communications software to coordinate data exchanges with other modems.

How Computers Work with Data

Now that you have learned about the essential parts of the computer system, you are ready for an overview of how all these parts carry out the job of computing. You do not absolutely need to know the details of a computer's operation to produce finished work. But if you explore a little bit, you adjust more quickly to using your computer.

Computers perform many useful tasks by accepting data as input, processing it, and releasing the data as output. Data is information. It can be a set of numbers, a memo, an arrow key that moves a game symbol, or anything you can imagine.

The computer translates input into electrical signals that move through a set of electronic controls. You can think of output in four ways:

- Characters the computer displays on-screen
- Information the computer holds in RAM
- Codes stored magnetically on disk
- Permanent images and graphics printed on paper

Bit
The smallest discrete representation of a value a computer can manipulate.

Computers receive and send output in the form of electrical signals. These signals are actually processed in two states: on and off. Think of these states as you would electricity to a light switch that you can turn on and off. Computers contain millions of electronic switches that can be on or off. All input and output follow this two-state principle. The computer name for the two-state principle is *binary*. Computers interpret data as two binary digits, or *bits*—0 and 1. A computer thinks only in numbers. Several numbers make up a character, such as a digit or letter. In short, bits are similar to the dot/dash concept used in Morse code.

Before your PC can perform any useful function, you must load a set of instructions in the form of a *program*. A program is a set of binary-coded instructions that produce a desired result. The microprocessor decodes the binary information and carries out the instruction from the program. Of course, the instructions in a word processing application are different from the instructions in a graphics design program. The differences between the many thousands of available computer programs, all designed to run on the same type of computer, is what makes the modern PC so useful. One device can perform almost unlimited functions.

On most modern PCs, the hard drive stores program instructions, although floppy disks also can store programs. When you run one of the programs on the hard drive or a floppy disk by entering the command that starts the program, DOS loads the program into system memory, enabling you to use the program's instructions. Programs are stored on disk in binary form.

Stand-Alone versus Networked PCs

Network
Two or more computers linked together by cables so they can share data, files, and peripherals.

Until the mid 1980s, most personal computers served only a single user. Today, PCs in a corporate environment often are linked by cables into *networks* or *workgroups*. For a business that relies on its workers sharing data, network capability translates into increased productivity. Networking ensures that employees are using the same tools and can communicate easily, and networking decreases spending because fewer peripherals and software programs are needed.

In a PC network, each user still has a PC on his or her desktop. To the individual user, the PC looks and acts like a stand-alone system. But networked PCs can share files, applications, and peripherals such as printers. Users on a network can communicate with each other on-line. They can use electronic mail (*e-mail*) to send and receive messages. In some cases, users can communicate in *real time*, which means that the information entered at one user's keyboard immediately appears on another user's display.

On some networks, an individual *workstation* may not have all the components, such as disk drives, of a stand-alone. On such networks, a more powerful PC called a *server* manages the individual PCs. The server stores the software and controls the data input and output. Because more than one user may be running programs or accessing files at the same time, workstation-server networks require software that can support multiple users. Instead of using a single-user operating system, networks must use a *network operating system*, such as Novell's NetWare. Even the application programs that run on these networks must be designed for multiple users.

On other types of networks, often termed *peer* or *peer-to-peer* networks, each computer is a complete system connected to the other computers on the network. The connection is more for the ability to share messages and files than to use a single copy of software stored on a server. Peer-to-peer networks often are considerably faster than workstation-server systems because programs can load more quickly from the hard drive on the individual computer than they can from a distant server.

Lesson 2

Making a Quick Start with DOS 6.2

This lesson covers the new features in DOS 6.2, as well as important improvements in DOS since version 4.0. The lesson also describes commands the DOS novice should learn immediately—commands that enable you to make the most of your system more quickly.

The first part of this lesson explains how DOS serves as the basic link between hardware, other software, and you. The final sections help you understand more about DOS and how to make it work for you. Experts estimate that a typical computer user spends about 20 percent of his or her time using DOS functions. These functions serve as building blocks to operating your system in the most efficient, useful way.

The following topics are covered in this lesson:

- Improvements and new functions in DOS 6.2
- File, directory, and disk management
- Important commands to learn
- The DOS Help utility
- Command parameters and switches

New Features in DOS 6.2

Command
An instruction you give the computer to perform a task. To use a DOS command, type its name at the DOS prompt and press Enter.

DOS 6.2 is considered a major upgrade to DOS 6.0, because it makes existing features of DOS easier to use and more reliable and because it introduces important new utilities to help you keep your data safe. The following sections cover the improvements and new utilities and *commands* in DOS 6.2.

Changes in the COPY Command

When you use the COPY command to copy a file from one directory to another or to a floppy disk, the COPY command now detects if a file with the same name already exists in the destination directory or disk. If a file of the same name exists, COPY asks whether you want to replace the file. For example, if you try to copy a file named MR1.DOC into the C:\TEMP directory and a file named MR1.DOC already exists in that directory, the following message appears:

```
Overwrite C:\TEMP\MR1.DOC (Yes/No/All)?
```

If you want to replace the existing file, enter **Y** for yes. If you do not want to replace the file, enter **N** for no. If you are copying more than one file to the destination directory or disk and you want to replace all existing files, enter **A** for all.

Changes in the DIR Command

The DIR command now provides commas in file lengths, so you don't need to count from right to left to determine the size of a file. For example, if you are in the directory C:\TEMP and use the DIR command to view the contents of that directory, a read-out similar to the following appears:

```
Volume in drive C is C_DRIVE
 Volume Serial Number is 1B6A-9B34
 Directory of C:\TEMP

.             <DIR>          07-27-93   1:44p
..            <DIR>          07-27-93   1:44p
DESKSCAN HL_         155,557 08-20-93  12:00a
DESKSCAN IN_           1,074 08-20-93  12:00a
DS2      IN_           1,492 08-25-93  10:27a
DS2UTIL  IN_             892 08-20-93  12:00a
MSDETECT IN_           4,726 03-10-92  12:00a
SETUPAPI IN_          13,459 03-10-92  12:00a
SETUP    LST             653 08-20-93  12:00a
```

```
DS2      MS_        8,985 08-20-93  12:00a
MINI400I SY_       13,774 08-20-93  12:00a
SJDRIVER SY_        2,074 06-29-92  12:00a
SJII     SY_        5,086 06-29-92  12:00a
SJIIX    SY_        4,874 08-20-93  12:00a
README   TXT        5,611 08-20-93  12:00a
UNINSTAL TXT        1,402 08-20-93  12:00a
~MF0214  TMP            0 01-03-94  10:11a
~WRF0000 TMP            0 01-03-94  10:11a
~WRF0001 TMP        1,536 01-03-94  10:11a
~DFT0D37 TMP            0 01-03-94  10:11a
~WRS0003 TMP            0 01-03-94  10:12a
~DFT1208 TMP            0 01-03-94  10:37a
MR1      1        552,190 08-01-93   2:00p
        66 file(s)      1,695,053 bytes
                      162,627,584 bytes free
```

The DIR command is described in more detail later in this lesson in the section titled "DOS Commands To Learn Immediately," and in Lesson 9, "Basic DOS Commands."

Changes in DoubleSpace

DOS 6.2 provides a number of important enhancements to DoubleSpace, the utility that compresses programs and data on your hard drive or floppies, enabling you to nearly double the data you can pack onto a disk. These enhancements include the following:

- The ability to bypass DoubleSpace when you start, or *boot*, your system so you can work on your uncompressed drive.
- The ability to uncompress a DoubleSpace drive, rather than have to back up your system, delete the compressed drive, and restore the backup, as DOS 6.0 DoubleSpace required.

DoubleSpace is covered in detail in Lesson 13, "Using DoubleSpace, SCANDISK, and DEFRAG."

DoubleGuard

DoubleGuard constantly monitors the region of memory that DoubleSpace uses to keep track of file information and its own programming code. This feature also guards against any other program intruding on that region of memory. DoubleGuard disables any program that attempts to corrupt the DoubleSpace region of memory before damage is done, making the use of DoubleSpace much safer. DoubleGuard is covered in Lesson 13, "Using DoubleSpace, SCANDISK, and DEFRAG."

2

Automount

With DOS 6.0, if you were using DoubleSpace to increase the capacity of removable media like a Bernoulli Drive, you had to issue a MOUNT command to access the data on the removable drive. The DOS 6.2 Automount capability automatically mounts such drives, saving you the bother of issuing the MOUNT command. This new feature is an important improvement, making such removable media perform more as a transparent part of a system rather than making the media seem like an add-on. Automount is covered in Lesson 13, "Using DoubleSpace, SCANDISK, and DEFRAG."

The SCANDISK Command

The new DOS 6.2 utility, *SCANDISK*, checks your drive for errors, whether or not you are using DoubleSpace. The integrity of your hard drive's file structure is vitally important, and that importance only increases when you are using DoubleSpace. If the file structure becomes corrupted when using DoubleSpace, data recovery can be much more difficult and much less reliable.

On compressed or uncompressed drives, SCANDISK checks and repairs the MS-DOS boot sector, the File Allocation Table, the directory tree structure, the file system structure (lost clusters, crosslinked files), and the physical surface of the drive (bad clusters). On DoubleSpace drives, SCANDISK checks and repairs the DoubleSpace compression structure, the DoubleSpace volume file structure (MDFAT), and the DoubleSpace volume signatures.

You should use SCANDISK rather than the old CHKDSK command because SCANDISK does a much more thorough job of testing your disk, and it makes repairs more carefully than the CHKDSK /F command did.

If SCANDISK finds errors on your drive, the program gives you the option of creating an Undo disk, which enables you to undo repairs SCANDISK makes to your drive. The Undo disk contains information that specifies which drive the disk applies to as well as information on every change SCANDISK made to that drive. The use of SCANDISK is covered in detail in Lesson 13, "Using DoubleSpace, SCANDISK, and DEFRAG."

Improvements in SmartDrive

The SmartDrive disk caching software has been an important part of Windows and DOS since the introduction of Windows 3.0 and DOS 5.0. Disk-caching software reads into memory sectors of your hard drive and floppies that your system is likely to need next, speeding up access to programming code and data and thus speeding up the performance of your system. The DOS 6.2 version of SmartDrive fixes a problem that some users experienced with earlier versions of this utility and adds some new capabilities that help increase the speed of a CD-ROM drive.

In DOS 6.0, SmartDrive by default held data in memory for a short time when you used your software applications Save command, instead of writing the data immediately to your hard drive. Holding data in memory until your system was less busy provided a performance boost. But for many users, the data SmartDrive held in memory did not always write to the hard drive. For example, during a sudden power outage, a user would lose information not yet written to disk. The DOS 6.2 version of SmartDrive by default immediately writes all saved data to disk, safeguarding your work against power outages and other problems.

If you prefer the speed boost that caching provides, the DOS 6.2 SmartDrive enables you to use this capability. Lesson 11, "Customizing DOS," details the use of SmartDrive.

Changes in DOS since Version 4.0

For the first two-thirds of its life, DOS changed surprisingly little, as far as the commands and command structure were concerned. DOS versions 1-4 focused mostly on internal changes, including the way DOS controlled your hard drive and the maximum size of hard drive partitions. However, to the user, DOS remained the same difficult interface—a `C:\>` prompt sitting on your monitor, telling you nothing about what to do next to make your computer work.

That situation changed a great deal with DOS 5.0. This section provides information on the capabilities added to DOS in versions 5.0 and 6.0 to help users of previous versions—for example, 3.3 or 4.01—get a quick start using DOS 6.2. If you already are familiar with DOS 6.0, you may want to move ahead to the section "The Role of an Operating System." Advanced users may want to skip the rest of this lesson and move ahead.

Capabilities Introduced in DOS 5.0

DOS 5.0 added new utilities that enable you to care for your hard drive and files more easily. For example, the UNFORMAT command enables you to undo the formatting of a floppy disk, and the UNDELETE command enables you to recover a file you have deleted. This version also added other utilities described in the following sections.

On-Line Help

One of the most important additions to DOS in version 5.0 was on-line help for DOS. Typing HELP at the `C:\>` prompt provides a screen that lists DOS commands. Using the arrow keys, you can move from topic to topic and press Enter when you have highlighted the command for which you need information. The Help command, which is covered later in this lesson and in Lesson 4, "Working from the DOS Command Line," can save you the trouble of looking through a DOS manual for an obscure command reference.

The DOS 6.2 version of Help.

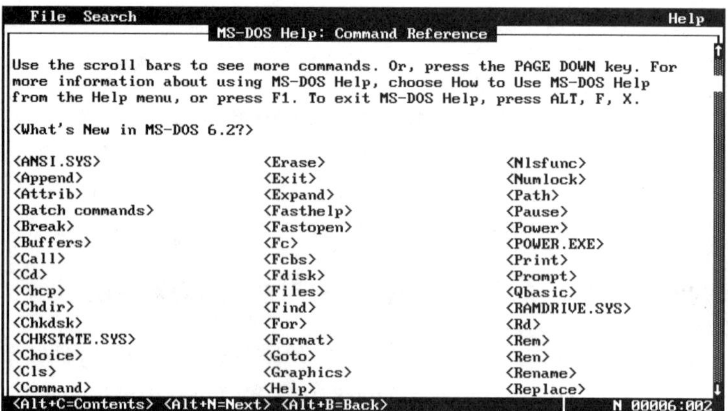

DOS Editor

DOS 5.0 provided for the first time a full-screen editor you can use to modify your startup files, AUTOEXEC.BAT and CONFIG.SYS. (These files are covered in Lesson 11, "Customizing DOS.") The following figure shows the editor provided with DOS 6.2 and the edit of a simple AUTOEXEC.BAT file.

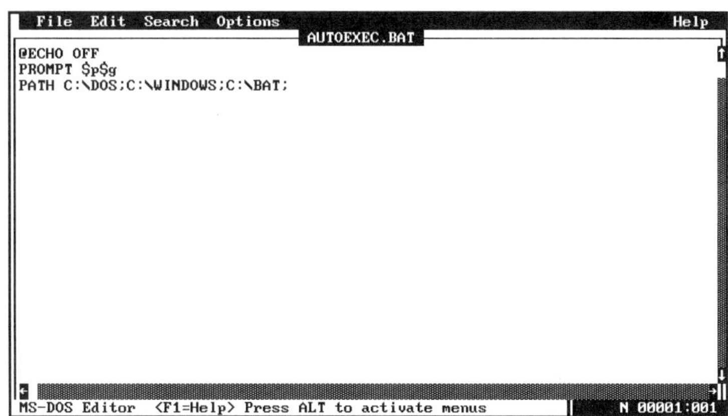

The DOS 6.2 Editor.

2

Memory Management

DOS 5.0 introduced memory management utilities and capabilities that enable you to move device drivers and memory-resident programs (which customize your system to work the way you want) into unused regions of *upper memory*—the area of memory above 640K and below 1M. Among the breakthroughs in DOS 5.0 was the capability of 386 or 486 processor-based systems to reduce the memory requirements of DOS by moving part the DOS code into upper memory. Using the DOS 6.2 memory management capabilities is detailed in Lesson 10, "Advanced DOS Commands."

Capabilities Introduced in DOS 6.0

The functions and capabilities added to DOS in version 6.0 prompted a great deal of excitement among computer users. For one reason, DOS 6.0 provided for the first time the basic capabilities of many high-priced utility packages like QEMM, 386MAX, Stacker, PCTools, and Norton Utilities. Although DOS 6.0 didn't replace these utility packages for most users who depended on them, the new capabilities in DOS 6.0 did provide much of the functionality of these packages for merely the price of a DOS upgrade, benefiting users who had not already invested hundreds of dollars in other utilities. The following sections describe the important capabilities added in DOS 6.0.

DoubleSpace

This utility can double the amount of data and programs that you can store on a hard disk or floppy disk. DoubleSpace is covered in Lesson 13, "Using DoubleSpace, SCANDISK, and DEFRAG."

MemMaker

This program increases the amount of conventional memory available to programs by moving device drivers like ANSI.SYS and memory-resident programs like MOUSE.EXE into unused upper memory. Unlike DOS 5.0 memory management, MemMaker tries all possible combinations of these device drivers and memory-resident programs to maximize the amount of available conventional memory, and MemMaker makes all changes to your AUTOEXEC.BAT and CONFIG.SYS files for you. MemMaker is covered in Lesson 10, "Advanced DOS Commands."

Multiple Boot Configurations

DOS 6.0 introduced the capability for you to create numerous boot configurations by defining a startup menu in CONFIG.SYS and then choosing, each time you boot, which device drivers and memory-resident programs you want loaded. Multiple boot configurations enable you to customize the way your system works each time you start it without having to maintain multiple copies of AUTOEXEC.BAT and CONFIG.SYS.

For example, if you have a program that needs a great deal of expanded memory, you can configure your system on boot-up to load an expanded memory driver and allocate memory as expanded memory. If you have another program, such as Microsoft Windows, that operates better with memory configured as extended, you can configure your system on boot-up to load an extended memory driver. Using the DOS 6.2 multiple boot configuration capability is covered in Lesson 11, "Customizing DOS."

To bypass your AUTOEXEC.BAT and CONFIG.SYS files for a "clean" boot-up of your system, press F5 when the words `Starting MS-DOS` appear after you turn on your system or reboot. To step through the device drivers and memory-resident programs in your CONFIG.SYS and AUTOEXEC.BAT files one at a time (so you can choose to load only the files you want), press F8 when you see the words `Starting MS-DOS`. As it processes CONFIG.SYS, DOS prompts you for confirmation before loading each device driver. DOS then prompts you for whether to process the AUTOEXEC.BAT file in the same manner.

Anti-Virus

Microsoft Anti-Virus and V-Safe are two very potent virus-detection and prevention utilities. Microsoft Anti-Virus scans your system for any of hundreds of viruses in case your system has become infected. V-Safe is a memory-resident utility that prevents virus infection. These two utilities are covered in Lesson 12, "Protecting Your PC's Data."

Disk Defragmentation

The *DEFRAG* utility solves a problem that can slow down your system considerably—fragmentation of files on your hard drive. Over time, the files on your hard drive can become so fragmented that the hard drive mechanism that reads files has to jump all over the drive to find all the pieces of even a single file. DEFRAG solves this problem by grouping together all the pieces of each file, end-to-end, and by moving files on your hard drive so all unused space is together. The DOS 6.2 DEFRAG utility is covered in Lesson 12, "Protecting Your PC's Data."

Backup Utilities

The program MSBACKUP replaces the arcane and complicated BACKUP and RESTORE utilities in previous versions of DOS with a convenient menu-based interface you can use with a mouse. MSBACKUP is covered in Lesson 12, "Protecting Your PC's Data."

System Troubleshooting and Diagnostics

You can use the Microsoft Diagnostics (MSD) utility to find out the exact components of your system, including these elements: CPU type (for example, 386, 486, etc.), the amount of memory installed on your computer, the type of video on your computer (for example, EGA or VGA), the DOS and Windows versions, installed disk drives (for example, A:, B:, and C:), and installed printer and serial ports. You also can use MSD to find memory conflicts and troubleshoot other problems, such as IRQ and DMA channel conflicts. The use of the DOS 6.2 MSD utility is covered in Lesson 10, "Advanced DOS Commands."

The Role of an Operating System

The first job of an operating system is to get your computer hardware components working together properly so that later you can run the software you need to do your work. DOS configures your computer using the startup files AUTOEXEC.BAT and CONFIG.SYS. For example, if you have a mouse, which is a hardware device, it will not work until DOS loads the mouse driver program from AUTOEXEC.BAT or CONFIG.SYS.

The second job of the operating system is to provide special services to other programs and to the computer user.

Program
Files that contain computer instructions.

When you boot your computer, the operating system acts as an interface between your hardware and the software you run later. You or a *program* tell DOS what action you want to take, and DOS directs the hardware to carry out your requests.

DOS Prompt
The symbol onscreen, such as `C:\>`, that indicates DOS has loaded successfully and is ready for you to enter commands.

Application or application program
Instructions that tell the computer to perform a specific type of task. Applications include word processing programs, spreadsheets, databases, and so on.

When you enter commands at the *DOS prompt*, the information you type is known as the *command line*. DOS uses your commands to translate into action your desire to manipulate data.

Because operating systems already contain instructions, you or a program can call on DOS to control your computer. The operating system software performs all the services that bridge the gap between the hardware and an *application program* so the program is not burdened with routine details. If a computer's operating system did not supply these services, you would need to deal directly with the details of controlling the hardware. Without the disk operating system, for example, every computer program would hold instructions telling the hardware each step to do its job.

IBM PC-compatible computers use MS-DOS, the disk operating system developed by Microsoft Corporation. Some PC manufacturers, such as Zenith, IBM, and COMPAQ, modify MS-DOS for their computers. These firms place their own names on the disks and include different manuals with the DOS packages they provide. Some firms add one or two modified utility programs as an improvement. All DOS versions are similar—the commands are the same and you operate them in the same way.

Note: *If you have a computer that requires a version of DOS from the manufacturer, you should not attempt to use generic MS-DOS on that computer. For example, do not use MS-DOS 6.2 on a Compaq computer unless you first contact Compaq and determine that MS-DOS 6.2 will work with your system.*

DOS's many activities fall into several general categories. The following sections describe the services that DOS performs most frequently.

Managing Files

One of DOS's main functions is to keep track of files you store on your disks. The smallest-capacity floppy disk can hold the equivalent of 100 letter-sized pages of information. Suppose that each sheet of information makes up one file; you have 100 files to track. DOS keeps track of those files and keeps the data from one file separate from the other files.

Besides its own internal housekeeping functions, DOS gives you the tools to be a good computer housekeeper. DOS lists files, tells their names and sizes, and gives the dates when the files were created or last modified. You can use this information for many organizational purposes. In addition to organizing files, DOS provides commands to duplicate files, discard outdated files, and replace files whose file names match. If you use disks that can hold more information than a standard floppy (such as a hard disk), these housekeeping tools are crucial.

Managing Directories

When you work with a hard disk, you can have thousands of files. To help you keep track of all these files, you can group them into *directories*. The use of directories is one of the basic concepts you need to know if you have a hard disk. The manner in which you set up directories on your disk is the most important method you have to help you keep track of all the files on your disk.

Think of the hard disk as a file cabinet and the directories as folders. You can look into one folder at a time. Each folder can contain any number of programs and data files. When you use the DIR command to have DOS list the files on your disk, you are asking DOS to list the files in a single directory.

The first directory on a disk is called the *root directory*. The root directory contains both files and other directories. You can have *subdirectories* under each directory, which is like having smaller folders inside a larger folder. Unlike a real folder, a directory expands automatically. You generally can put as many files and subdirectories into a directory as will physically fit on the disk. You learn the details of using directories in Lesson 5, "Understanding and Using Directories."

Directories have names, like DOS, WORD, or DATA. When you install DOS on your hard disk, the Install program creates a directory with the name DOS and copies all the DOS files that you need from the floppy disks into this directory. When you install other programs, the installation program should create a directory to hold the program files, or the program documentation may tell you to create a new directory before you run the installation program. A complete listing of a drive and directory is called a *directory path*. After you install DOS on a hard disk, the complete directory path to the DOS files is `C:\DOS`.

DOS provides commands you can issue to create and name directories. You also can use DOS commands to change from one directory to another when you want to work with a different set of files. The directory you are working in is called the *current directory*. The particular disk you are using is called the *current disk*.

Managing Disks

Certain DOS functions are essential to all computer users. For example, you must prepare all disks before you can use them in your computer. This preparation is called *formatting*. (You learn about formatting disks in Lesson 7, "Formatting Disks.") Following are some other ways DOS helps you manage disks:

- Labeling disks electronically
- Making backup copies of files
- Restoring damaged files on disk
- Copying disks
- Checking a disk for errors

Handling Miscellaneous Tasks

Some DOS functions fall into the category of miscellaneous tasks. One example is maintaining the computer's clock and calendar so files and application programs have access to dates and times. Or you may need to use DOS's text editor to create text files, such as memos or notes. You can even use DOS to see the amount of computer memory available for application programs.

DOS Files

File name
The unique name that identifies a particular file on disk.

A *file name* has two parts, the first of which can be as long as eight characters or as short as one character. The second part of a file name is a three-character *extension* to the file name. For example, a file name for a business report on the month of April might have the file name APRIL.DOC (where DOC is short for *document*).

When running software applications, in many cases, you specify the file name, and the program adds the file extension. Over the years, a universal shorthand has evolved that uses the file extension to simplify identification of computer files, as described in the following sections.

Many other file extensions and file formats exist in addition to those described here. Application programs often have their own special file extensions for particular types of files used by the program.

COM, EXE, and BAT Files

COM, EXE, and BAT files are termed *executable files* because typing the file name and pressing the Enter key causes the file to *run*, or load program instructions into system memory and begin to *execute* those instructions. For example, typing FORMAT or FORMAT.COM and pressing Enter causes the Format program in DOS to execute.

The COM extension is found on what are sometimes called *command files*. Examples of command files are FORMAT.COM and EDIT.COM.

The EXE extension comes from the term *executable file*. Examples of executable files are MSAV.EXE (the DOS 6.2 anti-virus utility) and SCANDISK.EXE, the new disk repair utility.

The BAT extension comes from the term *batch file*, which describes a computer program you can write with a text editor; the program loads DOS commands into memory and causes them to run. A good example of a batch file is AUTOEXEC.BAT, which you use to configure your hardware so your system runs the way you want.

SYS, HLP, and CPI Files

Files whose extension is SYS are *system files*; they also are called *device drivers*. Examples include KEYBOARD.SYS, ANSI.SYS, and CONFIG.SYS.

The data files used by the DOS 6.2 Help utility, or other programs, to display on-screen assistance have an HLP extension.

Files with the CPI extension operate the display screen. Examples are EGA.CPI and LCD.CPI.

BAS Files

Files with the BAS extension are written in the BASIC programming language and require you to use QBASIC.EXE to run them. Some games are written in BASIC, including GORILLA.BAS, MONEY.BAS, and NIBBLES.BAS, which are included with DOS 6.2.

INI Files

Files with the extension INI are *initialization files*, which means they contain information used by a program to determine its default startup configuration. Examples include MSAV.INI and QBASIC.INI.

TXT and DOC Files

A text editing program creates a *text file*, which often has a TXT or DOC file extension. Text editors, as opposed to word processing programs, do not add formatting codes to documents. For this reason, if you edit your CONFIG.SYS or AUTOEXEC.BAT files, use only a plain text editor, like the MS-DOS EDIT program. A word processor, such as WordPerfect, may add formatting codes that could spoil your CONFIG.SYS or AUTOEXEC.BAT files and cause your computer not to boot. An example of a text file is a letter written to a friend.

Another kind of text file is an information file that comes with most software. This file, often titled README.DOC, README.TXT, or just READ.ME, usually supplies additional program instructions that were not included in the printed manual.

Internal and External Commands

DOS commands come in two varieties: internal commands and external commands. For most users, knowing which commands are internal or external is necessary only if you are trying to find the executable files for particular commands. Following are the distinctions between the two types of commands:

- *Internal commands* are programs that automatically load into memory each time you start your computer. The DIR command is a good example. Internal commands get their name because their programming instructions are in DOS itself, not in a separate utility. For example, DOS has no DIR.COM or DIR.EXE file, like it has a FORMAT.COM file. Automatically loading internal commands into memory speeds up their operation.

- *External commands* are programs that exist as separate utilities in your DOS directory. For example, the Format program loads into memory only when you run the file FORMAT.COM. The DOS utilities, like FORMAT.COM, are command programs not built into DOS. These DOS utilities carry out useful housekeeping tasks, such as preparing disks, comparing disks and files, determining the memory and free space on a disk, and printing in the background.

COMMAND.COM

The file COMMAND.COM is one of the most important files on your system. This file loads into memory each time you start your computer, and it interacts with you through the keyboard and screen when you operate your computer. When COMMAND.COM displays the DOS prompt, your computer is ready to receive a command. When you enter a command, you are telling COMMAND.COM to interpret what you type and to process your input so DOS can take the appropriate action. COMMAND.COM contains the most commonly used commands, such as DIR, COPY, DEL, DATE, and TIME.

MSDOS.SYS and IO.SYS

When you start a computer, the DOS system files MSDOS.SYS and IO.SYS load into system memory. Your computer cannot run without these special *hidden files*; they define the hardware to the software, providing a link (*interface*) between you and your computer hardware. Combined, the files provide a unified set of routines for controlling and directing the operation of the computer's hardware. These files are known as the *input/output system*.

Hidden files do not appear on a normal directory listing or other lists of files, and you cannot delete or copy them. These files are hidden to protect you from deleting or changing them accidentally.

The hidden files interact with programs stored in a special read-only memory (ROM) chip that is part of your computer's hardware. The special ROM is called the ROM *basic input/output system*, or *BIOS*.

Responding to a program's request for service, the system files translate the request and pass it to the ROM BIOS. The BIOS provides a further translation of the request that links the request to the hardware.

DOS Commands To Learn Immediately

DOS contains more than 100 commands and functions. This section focuses on the commands you should learn immediately. After you know how to use these commands, you not only will be able to perform the functions you need most often in DOS, but you will have a much better idea of how DOS commands work. The following commands are covered in this section:

- DIR
- COPY
- ERASE (DEL)
- CD
- MD
- FORMAT
- DISKCOPY
- HELP

The examples in this section show you how to issue commands on your system using files and directories you probably already have.

Following are some important rules to remember when working with most DOS commands:

1. First type the command you want to use (COPY or DIR, for example).
2. Then type the file name, extension, directory, or disk you want the command to affect.
3. Then type any other information important to making the command work right.

4. After you type all the necessary information, press Enter to make the command run.

Listing Directories and Files with DIR

The DIR command, which stands for *directory*, is important because you can use it to learn a great deal about the files on your computer. You can determine the amount of space these files take, the amount of space still available on your system, and even the name of the file you need to run to start a computer program on your system. In a sense, the DIR command offers you the kind of information a building directory beside an elevator offers about who occupies the offices on the various floors.

Determining the Current Directory

If you want to find out quickly which directory you are in, follow these steps:

1. Type **DIR** at the DOS prompt (C:\>)
2. Press Enter.

The third line of the resulting listing indicates the directory. For example, a partial read-out might look like the following:

```
Volume in drive D is D_DRIVE
 Volume Serial Number is 3A30-1DCE
 Directory of D:\

SIERRA       <DIR>          12-24-93  11:47a
SHOW         <DIR>          12-15-93  10:17p
ZIPSNEW      <DIR>          12-15-93  10:22p
ARCADE       <DIR>          12-17-93  10:49a
PSTYLER      <DIR>          12-20-93   7:41p
WINWORD      <DIR>          12-17-93  11:51p
```

The DIR command shows that the *current directory*, or the directory where you are right now, is `D:\`. The directory `D:\` also is termed the *root directory*, because `D:\` contains all the other directories on the drive.

You can see from this example that SIERRA is the name of a directory within the root directory. When you use the DIR command, any entry followed by the word *DIR* in angle brackets (`<DIR>`) is a directory. Remember that directories contain files, and directories also may contain other directories, or subdirectories.

Listing the Files in a Directory

The DIR command is useful for determining what's in a directory on your system. For example, to see the contents of the current directory, follow these steps:

1. Type **DIR** at the DOS prompt.

2. Press Enter.

You may notice that this command is the same as the command in the preceding section's example. When you use the DIR command with no other specific instructions to DOS, the operating system lists all files *and* directories in the current directory.

The complete readout you receive from executing the DIR command in this way looks something like the following:

```
Volume in drive D is D_DRIVE
 Volume Serial Number is 3A30-1DCE
 Directory of D:\

SIERRA       <DIR>          12-24-93  11:47a
SHOW         <DIR>          12-15-93  10:17p
ZIPSNEW      <DIR>          12-15-93  10:22p
ARCADE       <DIR>          12-17-93  10:49a
PSTYLER      <DIR>          12-20-93   7:41p
WINWORD      <DIR>          12-17-93  11:51p
HURRICA3 WK1          7,768 12-18-92  10:46p
KEEN         <DIR>          12-27-93   1:48a
DUKE2        <DIR>          12-27-93   2:06a
BSTONE       <DIR>          12-29-93   8:48p
HURRICAN WK1          8,535 12-18-92  12:43a
PREVIEW  XLM        149,832 12-09-90  12:00p
TRANS123 XLM         18,930 04-01-92  12:00p
TRANSMP  XLM         17,309 04-01-92  12:00p
EXPENSES XLS         24,414 12-09-90  12:00p
HURRICA3 XLS         21,494 12-18-92  11:30p
HURRICAN XLS         18,324 12-20-92   1:27a
RECVABLS XLS          1,518 01-03-93   4:12a
DIR      TXT              0 01-03-94   4:52p
SHIHDAO      <DIR>          12-24-93  12:49p
       20 file(s)         268,124 bytes
                      380,264,448 bytes free
```

Look at the line for the file PREVIEW.XLM; the size of the file is 149,832 bytes or roughly 149K. The file is dated Dec. 9, 1990, and the time on the file is 12:00 p.m.—the actual date and time this file was last saved.

The readout also shows the amount of total space that the files in the directory use. In this example, the amount of space used is 268,124 bytes, or roughly 268K.

When you use the DIR command to obtain a listing of files contained on a disk or directory, the dot for the file name extension does not appear. Notice in the preceding example that the file name PREVIEW.XLM appears as PREVIEW XLM.

Finding Information about a File

You can use the DIR command to obtain information about a particular file. For example, if the directory you are in contains a file named BOX.TXT, you can find details about this file by following these steps:

1. Type **DIR BOX.TXT** at the DOS prompt.

2. Press Enter.

The results might look like the following listing:

```
Volume in drive D is D_DRIVE
 Volume Serial Number is 3A30-1DCE
 Directory of D:\

BOX      TXT         1,079 01-03-94   4:52p
        1 file(s)          1,079 bytes
                     371,867,648 bytes free
```

In the preceding read-out, you see that the file BOX.TXT is 1,079 bytes in size and was created on Jan 3, 1994, at 4:52 p.m.

Finding a Particular File

Another valuable use of the DIR command is its capability to find a particular file. For example, if you have a directory containing dozens or hundreds of files and you want to find a particular file, follow these steps:

1. At the DOS prompt, type **DIR** followed by the name of the file you want to find. For example, type **DIR COLUMN.DOC** to find a file named COLUMN.DOC in the current directory.

2. Press Enter.

Your read-out looks much like the following:

```
Volume in drive C is C_DRIVE
 Volume Serial Number is 1B6A-9B34
 Directory of C:\WINWORD\DOCS

COLUMN   DOC         4,251 01-27-93   8:08a
        1 file(s)          4,251 bytes
                     162,004,992 bytes free
```

You can use the DIR command in this same way to find files that start application programs. For example, if you have a word processing program installed on your system but you forget the command that runs the program, the DIR command can help. Because you type the name of a file that ends in COM, EXE, or BAT to run a program (EXE commands are most common), use the DIR command in this way:

1. Change to the directory where the word processing program is installed (see the explanation of the CD command below if you do not know how to change directories).

2. Type the DIR command this way (make sure that you enter the * character and the period, or dot, as shown):

   DIR *.EXE

3. Press Enter.

If the program is Microsoft Word for DOS, for example, and you are listing the EXE files in the C:\WORD directory, the results of the DIR command might look like the following:

```
Volume in drive C is ABCDEFG
 Volume Serial Number is 1B6A-9B34
 Directory of C:\WORD

WORD    EXE          344,251 01-27-91   5:00a
         1 file(s)         344,251 bytes
                       162,004,992 bytes free
```

Seeing the read-out of the DIR command reminds you that to run your word processing program, you type WORD at the DOS prompt and press Enter.

The files you use to run some programs have the extension COM. So if you don't find an EXE file, search for COM files. You also run some programs with a file having a BAT extension. You can find a COM or BAT file by substituting those extensions where the example shows you typing EXE.

Using Switches with DIR

If you use the DIR command in a directory that contains dozens or hundreds of files, the listing shoots by so quickly you cannot read any of the file names. The DIR command offers *switches* you can use to control the display of information about files. You type these switches as **/P** and **/W**.

Pausing the Listing with /P. The /P switch *pauses* the display after the screen fills up, enabling you to read the file names and information one screen at a time. For example, follow these steps to list the directory C:\WINDOWS one screen at a time:

1. Type **DIR /P** at the DOS prompt in the C:\WINDOWS directory.
2. Press Enter. The results look much like the following:

```
Volume in drive C is C_DRIVE
 Volume Serial Number is 1B6A-9B34
 Directory of C:\WINDOWS

.            <DIR>          03-11-93   8:23a
..           <DIR>          03-11-93   8:23a
GAMES        <DIR>          07-30-93  11:48p
ICON         <DIR>          07-27-93   1:18p
MSAPPS       <DIR>          07-27-93   1:23p
SOUND        <DIR>          07-27-93   1:23p
SYSTEM       <DIR>          07-27-93   1:24p
TWAIN        <DIR>          07-27-93   1:30p
ADXPL100 DLL        243,092 10-06-93   4:15p
256COLOR PAL            162 01-16-93   5:15p
AD       CFG             94 01-04-94  12:01p
AD       HLP         35,871 10-05-93   3:16p
AD-DOS   COM         20,080 03-29-93  12:00a
ADMODULE ADS          4,851 11-22-93   2:47p
AD_AILAN RTL            733 07-22-92  12:00a
AD_MESG  ADS          1,968 07-22-92  12:00a
AD_MOD   DLL        209,040 11-16-92  12:00a
AD_NSTLL INI          4,022 07-27-93   9:50a
AD_NVLNW RTL          3,166 07-22-92  12:00a

Press any key to continue . . .
```

   Notice that DOS displays a prompt at the bottom of the screen to tell you what to do next.

3. When you want to go on to the next screen of information about the files in the directory, press any key on your keyboard.

   The screen displays the next screen of files and a status message telling you that the display is continuing. The status message looks much like the following:

```
(continuing C:\WINDOWS)
```

4. Continue pressing keys and viewing screens of files until DOS finishes scrolling the entire list.

   or

   To stop viewing the list and return to the prompt, press Ctrl-C or Ctrl-Break.

Viewing the List in a Wide Format with /W. The /W switch causes the DIR command to display file and directory information in a *wide* format, packing more file names onto the screen. However, the listing does not show the size, date, and time information you see when you use the DIR command alone or with the /P switch. To display a directory listing in wide format, follow these steps:

1. Type **DIR /W** at the DOS prompt.
2. Press Enter.

Using the /W switch produces a read-out much like the following:

```
[.]             [..]            [GAMES]         [ICON]          [MSAPPS]
[SOUND]         [SYSTEM]        [TWAIN]         ADXPL100.DLL    256COLOR.PAL
AD.CFG          AD.HLP          AD-DOS.COM      ADMODULE.ADS    AD_AILAN.RTL
AD_MESG.ADS     AD_MOD.DLL      AD_NSTLL.INI    AD_NVLNW.RTL    AD_PREFS.INI
AD_RSRC.DLL     AD_SND.DLL      AD_WRAP.COM     AFTER.PIF       AGDO.FON
AGDO.PFM        AGD.FON         AGD.PFM         AGWO.PFM        AGWO.FON
AGW.FON         AGW.PFM         ALMANAC.INI     ALSETUP.EXE     AMAZE.INI
AMWSAVER.SCR    APPLICAT.GRP    APPLICAT.QAG    APPLICAT.QAB    APPS.HLP
```

If you have problems...

If you have problems running the DIR command, make sure that you correctly type the command. If you have problems using DIR to obtain file information, make sure that you correctly type the DIR command, that you place a space between the DIR command and the file name, and that you correctly type the file name.

Copying Files with COPY

The COPY command is another important tool to master immediately. With the COPY command, you can duplicate any file on your hard drive or a floppy, enabling you to make backup copies of your work. For example, you can make copies of a file on your hard drive to a floppy so you can carry work from one computer to another.

The basic use of the COPY command is easy. You tell the command what you want to copy and where you want to copy it.

Copying a File from the Current Directory to a Floppy Disk

A good example of the COPY command is to copy the file COLUMN.DOC from its hard drive directory to a floppy disk, so you have a safe backup copy of COLUMN.DOC. Follow these steps to copy the file to a floppy disk in the A: drive:

1. Make sure that you are in the directory where COLUMN.DOC is located.
2. Insert a formatted floppy disk into the A: drive.
3. Type **COPY COLUMN.DOC A:**
4. Press Enter.

You must enter the command exactly this way, including the spaces, the full file name and DOS extension (in this case DOC), and the destination drive (in this case, A:).

Copying a File from a Different Directory to a Floppy Disk

The preceding example assumes that you are in the directory where COLUMN.DOC is located. If that is not the case, for example, if you are in the directory C:\ and want to copy COLUMN.DOC from the directory C:\WINWORD\DOCS to the A: drive, you can follow these steps:

1. Insert a floppy disk into the A: drive.
2. Type **COPY C:\WINWORD\DOCS\COLUMN.DOC A:**
3. Press Enter.

Copying a File to a Specified Directory

The COPY command enables you to specify a directory where you want a file copied. For example, if you are in the directory where COLUMN.DOC is located and you want to copy COLUMN.DOC to the subdirectory A:\DOCS, follow these instructions:

1. Insert a floppy disk into the A: drive.
2. Type **COPY COLUMN.DOC A:\DOCS**
3. Press Enter.

If you are not in the directory where COLUMN.DOC is located, follow these instructions:

1. Insert a floppy disk into the A: drive.
2. Type **COPY C:\WINWORD\DOCS\COLUMN.DOC A:\DOCS**
3. Press Enter.

Note: *You use most DOS commands much like the COPY command. First you enter the command you want to execute, then you enter the file, directory, or disk you want the command to affect, and then you enter other important information (like the destination directory as in the preceding example, or command switches like /P or /W).*

If you have problems...

If you have problems using the COPY command, make sure that you correctly type the COPY command itself. Then check to ensure that you specify a destination for the copy operation. Then make sure that you correctly type the name of the file you want to copy.

Removing Files with ERASE and DEL

You use the ERASE command and the delete (DEL) command for only one purpose: to permanently remove data from a disk. Never use either of these commands unless you are sure you do not want a particular file any more.

Note: *DOS 6.2 provides emergency data recovery tools that you can use, under some circumstances, to recover erased files. The UNDELETE command, the simplest of these tools, is covered in Lesson 4, "Working from the DOS Command Line." But the best practice is to use the ERASE and DEL commands very carefully, and only after you have made a backup copy of all important data. (Making backup copies of your files is easy using the COPY command.)*

The ERASE command and the DEL command essentially are identical; you use both commands in the same way. For sake of simplicity, this section focuses on the ERASE command.

Erasing a Single File

Suppose that you have a file named OLD.TXT in the current directory and you no longer want that file. Use these steps to remove the file permanently from your disk:

1. Type **ERASE OLD.TXT**
2. Press Enter.

The ERASE command operates without producing a read-out so the file simply disappears and no longer takes up space on your disk.

Confirming Erasures

If you want the ERASE command to prompt you for confirmation to remove the designated file, you need to use switches. For example, to have the ERASE command prompt you to confirm the removal of the OLD.TXT file, perform these steps:

1. Type **ERASE OLD.TXT /P**
2. Press Enter.

   The erase command produces the following read-out:

   ```
   D:\OLD.TXT,    Delete (Y/N)?
   ```

3. If you want to delete the file, press the Y key (for yes). If you do not want to erase the file, press the N key (for no).

Erasing a File in a Different Directory

Like the COPY command, the ERASE command enables you to enter the drive and directory of the file you want to remove. For example, to remove the file BUNGEE.DOC in the C:\WINWORD\DOCS directory, follow these steps:

1. Type **ERASE C:\WINWORD\DOCS\BUNGEE.DOC**
2. Press Enter.

If you add the /P switch to the end of the line in the preceding example, the ERASE command prompts you to confirm the removal of the file.

If you have problems...

If you have problems with the ERASE or delete (DEL) command, make sure that you correctly type the command. Then check to ensure that you correctly type the file name and extension of the file you want to erase.

Changing the Current Directory with CD

The CD command is a very important tool for a newcomer to DOS to learn because it is the basic navigation tool to get from one directory to another. CD stands for *change directory*, and its use is easy to understand.

The following example shows you how to navigate through the three branches of a directory tree:

1. To move from the root directory (C:\) to the WORD directory, type **CD\WORD**
2. To move from the root directory or the C:\WORD directory into the subdirectory C:\WORD\DOCS, type **CD\WORD\DOCS**
3. To move from the root directory or the subdirectory C:\WORD\DOCS to the subdirectory C:\WORD\DOCS\BOSS, type **CD\WORD\DOCS\BOSS**

Other ways to use the CD command are explored in Lesson 5, "Understanding and Using Directories."

Switching from the Root Directory to a Subdirectory

To move from the root directory of the C: drive to the DOS directory (also on drive C:) you enter the following:

CD\DOS

If you enter the command exactly as shown, including the backslash, you change from the root directory to the DOS directory.

Switching from One Directory to Another

You use the CD command in exactly the same way when you want to move from one directory to another. Suppose that the current directory is the DOS directory and you want to change to the WORD directory; you enter the following:

CD\WORD

Switching from a Subdirectory to Its Parent Directory

If you are in a subdirectory, like C:\WINDOWS\SYSTEM, and want to move back to the WINDOWS directory, use the CD command in the following way:

1. Type **CD\WINDOWS**
2. Press Enter.

   The prompt now appears as C:\WINDOWS>.

Switching from a Subdirectory to the Root Directory

To move quickly from the WINDOWS directory (or any other directory) back to the root directory, you use the CD command in the following way:

1. Type **CD**
2. Press Enter.

   The prompt now appears as `C:\>`

If you have problems... If you have problems with the CD command, make sure that you correctly type the command. Then check to ensure that you correctly type the backslash character and that you type the name of a directory that exists. Also don't forget that when you want to change to a subdirectory, you need to type in the entire name of the subdirectory.

Adding Directories with MD

Another command that's important for newcomers to DOS is the MD command, short for *make directory*. You use this command to create a new directory.

The major reason you should learn this command is that sometime you may receive a floppy disk of files from another computer. The easiest and safest way to manage the files is to create a new directory and then use the COPY command to make copies of the floppy disk files on your hard drive. You then can work with the copies and store the original floppy disk in case you need it.

Note: *Keep the number of files in a root directory to a minimum, perhaps only three or four (including the required AUTOEXEC.BAT and CONFIG.SYS files) so you have plenty of room in the root directory for directories. You can have a total of only 512 files and directories in the root directory of the C: drive.*

Creating a Directory in the Root Directory

The MD command, like other DOS commands, is straightforward. To create a new directory, make sure you are in the root directory of the disk where you want to create the new directory (the DOS prompt should read `A:\>` or `B:\>` or `C:\>` or `D:\>` or the disk name where you want to create the directory). If you are in a subdirectory, use the CD\ command to move back to the root directory. These steps explain how to create a subdirectory named BOSS:

1. At the DOS prompt, type **MD BOSS**
2. Press Enter.

This command creates the directory C:\BOSS (assuming that you created the new directory on the C: drive).

Creating a Subdirectory

Suppose that you store your documents in a subdirectory such as C:\WORD\DOCS. You want to create another subdirectory for your boss' files, but rather than a directory under the root directory, you want a new subdirectory under C:\WORD\DOCS. Follow these steps:

1. Type **MD C:\WORD\DOCS\BOSS**
2. Press Enter.

When you want to act on a file in the new directory, you need to remember that the subdirectory name is

C:\WORD\DOCS\BOSS

If you have problems...

If you have problems creating directories, remember to correctly type the MD command. Also make sure you enter the proper name for the new directory. The section on the RD command, "Working from the DOS Command Line," covers how to remove a directory or subdirectory.

Preparing Disks for Data with FORMAT

The FORMAT command is important to know because you cannot use new floppy disks without it. Floppy disks, of course, are valuable for making backup copies of important data and transferring files from one computer to another.

Formatting a floppy disk prepares it for use by DOS. Before a disk is formatted, it is simply a plastic disk covered with magnetic media. Formatting the disk creates a root directory and a structure in which DOS can store and keep track of files.

Like the COPY and ERASE commands covered earlier in this lesson, you can use the FORMAT command with a number of switches. However, this section starts by explaining the easiest way to format floppy disks.

You first must find out the capacity of the floppy drives on your system. If you have both a 5 1/4- and a 3 1/2-inch floppy drive, these capacities are possible:

- 5 1/4—360K or 1.2M
- 3 1/2—720K, 1.44M, or 2.88M

If you are not sure of the capacity of your floppy drives, your system documentation contains this information. If the documentation is not available for your system, have someone familiar with IBM-compatible PCs help you.

Formatting without Switches

After you have determined the maximum capacity of your floppy drives, the easiest approach to formatting disks is to use *only* the highest capacity disks your drives can handle. For example, if you have a 3 1/2-inch drive with a 1.44M capacity, buy only 1.44M floppy disks for that drive. If you have a 1.2M capacity 5 1/2-inch floppy drive, buy only 1.2M floppy disks for use in that drive. If you use only the maximum capacity disks that work in the drive, formatting disks is as simple as entering the FORMAT command along with the drive you want to format.

For example, to format a disk of maximum capacity in the A: drive, perform these steps:

1. Insert a disk in the A: drive.
2. Type **FORMAT A:**
3. Press Enter.

To format a disk in the B: drive, perform these steps:

1. Insert a disk in the B: drive.
2. Type **FORMAT B:**
3. Press Enter.

When you use floppy disks with a lower capacity than the drive, you need to use switches. These switches are explained fully in Lesson 7, "Formatting Disks."

Specifying the Disk Capacity

You can use only 360K and 1.2M disks in a 5 1/4-inch drive. The 360K disks are often termed *double-density*. The 1.2M disks are often termed *high-density*. To format a double-density (360K) floppy disk in a high-density 5 1/4-inch drive (assuming the drive is A:), follow these steps:

1. Insert a 360K disk in the A: drive.
2. Type **FORMAT A: /F:360**
3. Press Enter.

Because the capacity of 3 1/2-inch disks can be 720K, 1.44M, or 2.88M, you must deal carefully with formatting. You can use 2.88M floppy disks only in a 2.88M capacity drive, but you also can use 1.44M and 720K disks in that drive. If you have a 1.44M capacity drive, you can use 1.44M and 720K disks. If you have a 720K capacity drive, you can use only 720K disks.

You use the following switches with the FORMAT command to format a 3 1/2-inch disk with a lower capacity than the drive (assuming the 3 1/2-inch drive is B:):

FORMAT B: /F:1.44
(used to format a 1.44M disk in a 2.88M drive)

FORMAT B: /F:720
(used to format a 720K disk in a 2.88M or 1.44M drive)

Note: *Do not attempt to format a double-density (360K) floppy disk as a 1.2M disk, or a 720K or 1.44M disk at a higher capacity. If you try to use a lower density disk formatted at a higher capacity, you will lose your data. If you use different capacity disks in your drives, label the disks so you do not get them mixed up.*

If you have problems... If you have problems with the FORMAT command, make sure that you have placed the disk in the drive right-side up. Also make sure you close the drive door (if the drive has one) before attempting to format a disk in that drive. If the FORMAT command informs you the disk is write-protected, the write-protect notch on a 5 1/4-inch disk is covered by tape or the write-protect shutter on a 3 1/2-inch disk is open. For help on write protecting disks, refer to Lesson 7, "Formatting Disks."

Duplicating Disks with DISKCOPY

Occasionally you may need an exact duplicate of a floppy disk. DOS 6.2 provides a simple command, DISKCOPY, that enables you to make a perfect duplicate of any floppy disk. When copying disks with the DISKCOPY command, you need to ensure that you are copying to the same capacity floppy disk as the original. In other words, you cannot diskcopy a 1.44M disk to a 720K disk. Nor can you diskcopy a 720K disk to a 1.44M disk.

To make an exact copy of a disk, assuming the disk you want to copy is in the A: drive, take these steps:

1. At the DOS prompt, type **DISKCOPY A: A:**
2. Press Enter.

   This command tells DISKCOPY to copy the disk in drive A: to a second disk that you will insert in the A: drive. DISKCOPY produces this read-out:

   ```
   Insert SOURCE diskette in drive A:

   Press any key to continue . . .
   ```

3. Press a key to begin the copy process.

   DISKCOPY examines the original disk and produces a read-out that looks like the following:

   ```
   Copying 80 tracks, 18 sectors per track, 2 side(s)

   Reading from source diskette . . .
   ```

   When DISKCOPY finishes the operation, this read-out appears:

   ```
   Insert TARGET diskette in drive A:

   Press any key to continue . . .
   ```

4. Take the original disk out of the A: drive and insert a formatted destination disk.

5. Press any key.

   If you forgot to format the disk, DISKCOPY formats the disk for you. Then DISKCOPY continues the copy process, as the read-out indicates:

   ```
   Writing to target diskette . . .
   ```

   After DISKCOPY finishes the copy process, it displays this read-out:

   ```
   Do you wish to write another duplicate of this disk (Y/N)?
   ```

6. Press **Y** for yes if you need another copy of the disk or press **N** for no if you do not want an additional copy.

   After you finish making all the disk copies you want (and press N), DISKCOPY asks whether you want to copy another disk:

   ```
   Copy another diskette (Y/N)?
   ```

7. Press **Y** for yes or **N** for no.

   After you finish copying all your disks (and press N), DISKCOPY exits.

If you have problems... If you have problems with the DISKCOPY command, make sure the capacity of the original disk is the same as the capacity of the disk to which you are making the copy. Also make sure you correctly type the DISKCOPY command and the source and destination drives. To avoid mistakes, make sure the original disk is write-protected (see Lesson 7, "Formatting Disks"). And make sure you do not confuse the original disk and the disk to which you are making the copy.

The DOS Help Utility

Another important command a new DOS user should learn is the HELP command. This section describes how to use the Help utility and how to understand the somewhat cryptic way the Help utility explains the syntax of DOS commands.

Typing HELP at the `C:\>` prompt runs the Help utility and produces the screen shown in the following figure. At the top of the Help screen is a menu with three choices: File, Search, and Help. On the bottom line of the screen are shortcut key combinations in brackets that you can use to navigate the Help utility. The rest of the screen shows a wide alphabetical listing of the common DOS commands.

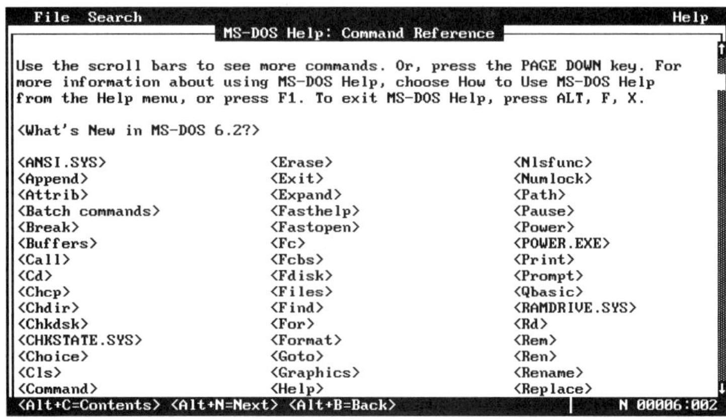

The Help utility screen.

Using the Mouse in the Help Utility

If you have a mouse, you can use it to perform several functions in the Help utility:

- Choose a menu option using these steps:

  1. Click File, Search, or Help to open the menu you want.
  2. Choose from the menu by moving your mouse pointer to a command and clicking the primary button.

     For example, to exit the Help utility, click the File menu then click Exit. You return to the DOS prompt.

- Select a shortcut key combination. Click a shortcut selection at the bottom of the Help utility screen to execute the associated action. For example, clicking Alt-N=Next cycles through the Help topics one after the other.

- Select a DOS command for which you want help. For example, clicking the DIR command produces the screen shown in the next figure.

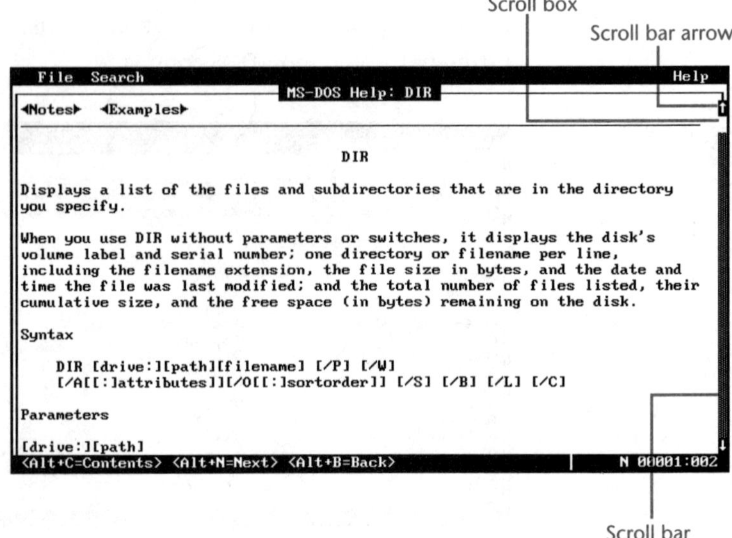
Scroll box
Scroll bar arrow
File Search
Help
MS-DOS Help: DIR
◄Notes► ◄Examples►
DIR
Displays a list of the files and subdirectories that are in the directory you specify.
When you use DIR without parameters or switches, it displays the disk's volume label and serial number; one directory or filename per line, including the filename extension, the file size in bytes, and the date and time the file was last modified; and the total number of files listed, their cumulative size, and the free space (in bytes) remaining on the disk.
Syntax
DIR [drive:][path][filename] [/P] [/W]
[/A[[:]attributes]][/O[[:]sortorder]] [/S] [/B] [/L] [/C]
Parameters
[drive:][path]
<Alt+C=Contents> <Alt+N=Next> <Alt+B=Back>
N 00001:002
Scroll bar

The Help display for the DIR command.

- Move the scroll bar on the right side of the Help screen. Use the scroll bar to move to commands on the next screen. The easiest way to use the scroll bar is to click the up arrow to move up a line in the help screen or click the down arrow to move down a line in the help screen. You can click above the scroll box to move up one screen or click below the scroll box to move down one screen. You can drag the scroll box up or down to move quickly from one part of the help screen to another.

Using the Keyboard in the Help Utility

You can perform the same functions in the Help utility using the keyboard rather than the mouse. The following sections explain these functions.

Choosing a Menu Option

Use these steps to choose a menu option:

1. Press the Alt key in combination with the first letter of the menu you want to open. For example, pressing Alt-F opens the File menu.

2. Use your arrow keys to move to the menu option you want.

3. Press Enter.

   or

   Press the highlighted letter in the menu option to execute your choice. For example, in the File menu, the highlighted letter in the Exit command is the X. You can exit the Help utility by pressing Alt-F to open the File menu and then pressing the X key for Exit. You return to the DOS prompt.

Using the Shortcut Keys

To select a shortcut key combination at the bottom of the Help screen, press the Alt key in combination with the corresponding shortcut key. For example, when viewing help on the DIR command, pressing Alt-N moves to the DIR-Notes screen, which provides additional information on the DIR command. Pressing Alt-N again moves to the DIR-Examples screen, which provides examples of the DIR command.

Switching between Topics and Fields

The following steps explain how to switch between topics and fields using the keyboard:

1. Use the Tab key and the up and down arrow keys (*cursor keys*) to move from topic to topic or field to field within the Help utility.

   For example, to move from the ANSI.SYS topic to the ERASE topic, press the Tab key. To move from the ANSI.SYS topic to the APPEND command, use the down arrow key.

2. Press the Enter key to execute your selection.

Using the Help Utility Menus

The Help utility menus contain several commands that enable you to make the most of the utility. The menu selections are File, Search, and Help. The following sections cover the options in each menu.

The File Menu

This menu contains the Print and Exit menu commands as shown in the next figure.

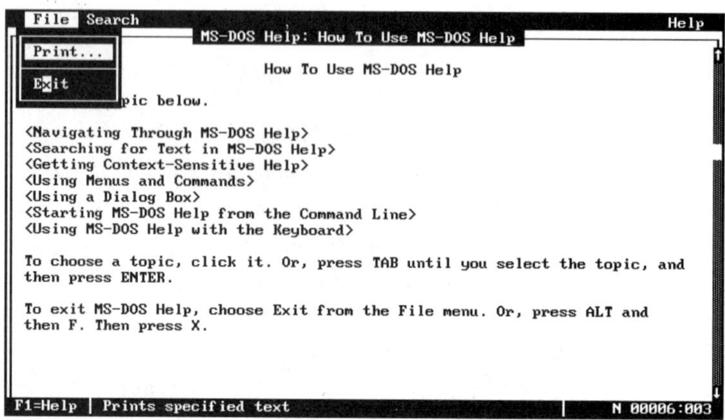

The Help utility's File menu.

Printing Help Selections. Using the Print command on the File menu, you can print the Help information currently displayed in the Help utility, or you can save the information to a file on disk that you can read or edit. For example, if you are reading help on the DIR command, choosing Print enables you to print this DIR information. These steps describe how to use the Print command:

1. Choose the Print command from the File menu to open the Print dialog box.

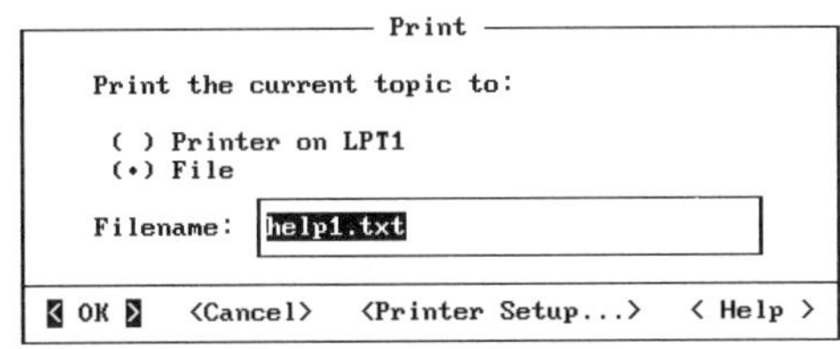

The Print dialog box.

2. Choose the Print to LPT*x* option to print to your printer.

   If the entry for your printer is incorrect—for example, if the selection shows your printer on LPT1 and your printer is actually on LPT2—choose Printer Setup to produce the Printer Setup dialog box. Choose the proper port for your printer (LPT1, LPT2, LPT3, COM1, or COM2). If you are unsure which port your printer is on, consult your computer's documentation.

3. Click OK.

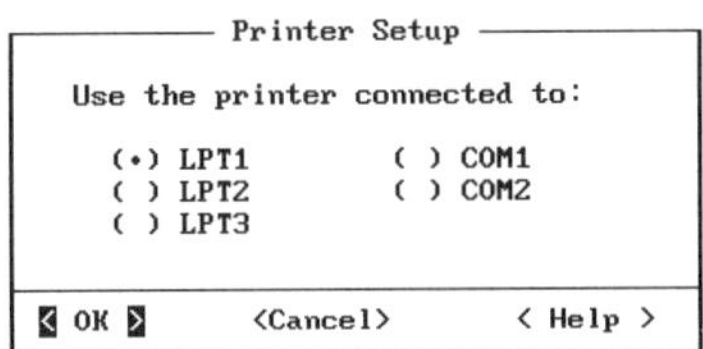

The Printer Setup dialog box.

Saving Help Text to a File. Use these steps to save Help text to a file:

1. Choose the Print command from the File menu to open the Print dialog box.
2. Choose the File option.
3. Type a name for the Help text, such as HELP1.TXT. The help utility defaults to the file name HELP.TXT.
4. Choose OK.

   If you need help on printing the Help topic, choose the Help button.

The Search Menu

You can quickly find the DOS command for which you want help by following these steps:

1. Choose the Find command from the Search menu to open the Find dialog box.

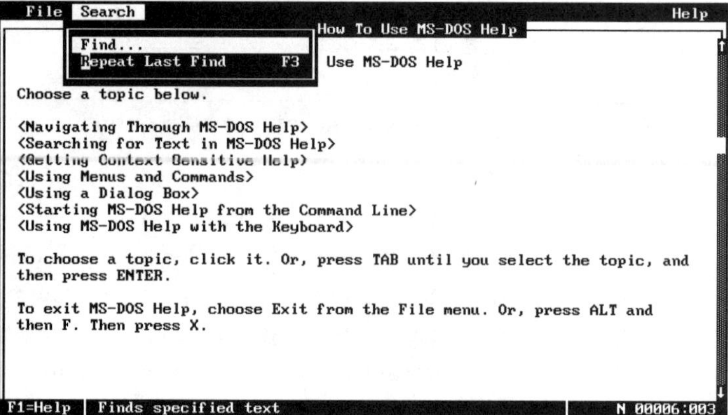

The Help utility Search menu.

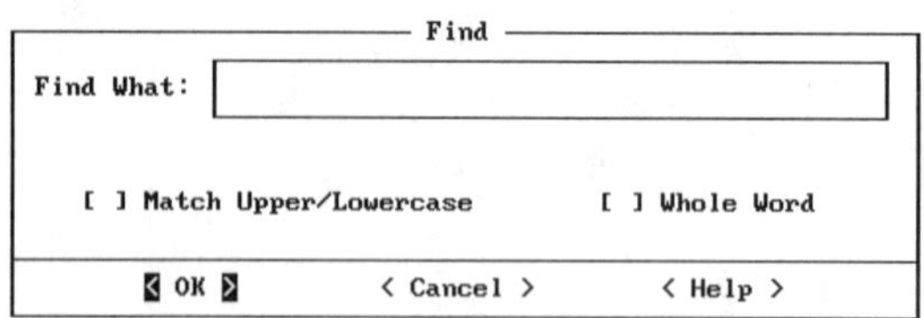

The Find dialog box.

2. In the Find What text box, type the DOS command for which you want help. Or you can type a word you want to search for in the Help text of a DOS command.

3. Choose OK.

   The Find command highlights the first occurrence of the command or word you typed.

4. If you want to repeat the last search, use the Repeat Last Find command on the Search menu or press F3.

The Help Menu

The Help utility's Help menu enables you to find advice on the operation of the Help utility. These steps describe how to use the Help menu:

1. Choose the How to Use MS-DOS Help command from the Help menu.

The Help utility's Help menu.

The screen shown in the following figure appears.

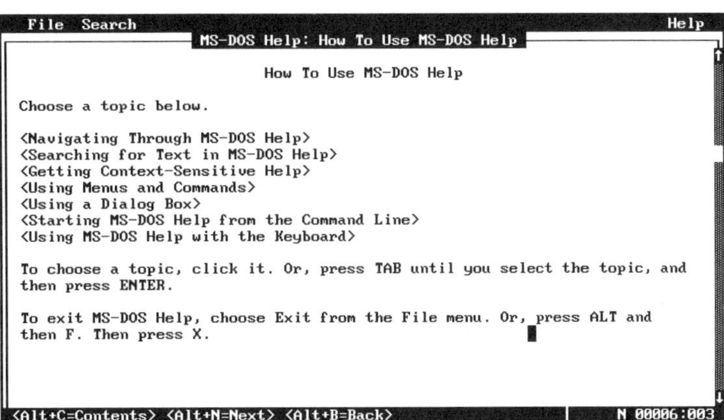

The Help utility's Help screen.

2. To make a selection on this screen, click the topic you want to examine. Or use the Tab key to move left to right and the arrow keys to move up and down to the topic you want to view.

3. Press the Enter key.

   Advice on the topic you selected appears on-screen.

Understanding DOS Command Syntax in Help

Syntax
The proper way to type a DOS command.

The way the Help utility explains DOS commands can be confusing for a newcomer to DOS. The Help utility uses brackets to separate parts of the command's *syntax*, and the utility uses words like *drive:* and *filename* and *path* to explain other parts of the command.

As an example, this section uses the DIR command covered earlier in this lesson. What you have already learned about the way the DIR command works will be helpful in understanding the material in this section. The following line is an entry from the Help utility on the DIR command:

```
DIR [drive:][path][filename]
[/P] [/W] [/A[[:]attributes]][/O[[:]sortorder]] [/S] [/B] [/L] [/C]
```

When you see square brackets in the syntax of a command, you do not type the square brackets. The brackets just show you how the parameters of the command are grouped. The following sections explain the various parts of the preceding syntax read-out.

Command Parameters and Switches

DIR—The exact characters you type to run the command. Entering the name of the command is always necessary to run the command.

Drive:—Indicates the drive on which you are executing the command, for example, A:, B:, C:, or D:. When you use this optional switch, you must always enter the drive letter *and* the colon.

Path—Indicates the directory on which you are executing the command. For example, if you are in the root directory C:\ and want a read-out of the C:\DOS directory, you enter the DIR command this way:

DIR C:\DOS

Filename—Indicates the file you want the command to affect. When using the [filename] switch, you must enter the name and extension. For example, if you want to run DIR on a file named TEST.DOC, you enter the command this way:

DIR TEST.DOC

If you enter only DIR TEST, you will not get the information you want on the file TEST.DOC.

Note: *You can use* wildcard *characters, or replacement characters, when working with the [filename] parameter with most DOS commands. The use of wildcards is covered in Lesson 4, "Working from the DOS Command Line."*

Square Brackets ([ ])

Square brackets indicate an additional part of the command or optional switch. Earlier in this lesson, you learned about the /P and /W switches on the DIR command. The Help utility represents these switches in this way:

```
[/P] [/W]
```

You may be confused when you see brackets enclosed within brackets. For example, the following line is part of the Help utilitys display of the DIR command syntax:

```
[/A[[:]attributes]]
```

Switches enclosed within brackets within other brackets mean that the switch is optional. The parameter after the optional switch is an *additional* parameter to the switch. For example, typing **DIR /A** produces a read-out of all the files in the current directory, even the files not shown when you enter DIR with no switches.

If this syntax still seems confusing, think of the command without brackets:

DIR */A:attributes*

The */A* switch and the word *attributes* are italic because they are optional to the DIR command. Attributes are covered in Lesson 6, "Maintaining Files."

The additional parameters enable you to fine-tune the way the command works. For example, when a word like *attributes* appears in square brackets, you replace the word with one of the optional parameters listed in the Help utility display. For the DIR command, the Help utility lists these parameters:

H	Hidden files
-H	Files that are not hidden
S	System files
-S	Files other than system files
D	Directories
-D	Files only (not directories)
A	Files ready for archiving (backup)
-A	Files that have not changed since the last backup
R	Read-only files
-R	Files that are not read-only

As an example, the command DIR /A:A uses additional parameters. This command displays only files whose archive bit is set (files ready for backup). Another example of the DIR command with optional parameters is DIR /A:D. This command causes the read-out to display only the directories within a directory, for example, the directories within the C:\ root directory of a disk.

Slashes (/)

A parameter preceded by a forward slash is used like the /P and /W switches covered previously in the section on the DIR command. As a reminder, /W causes the DIR command to display its read-out in a wide display and /P causes it to pause after a screenful until you press a key on your keyboard. Consider the Help utility's entry for the DIR command `[/O[[:]sortorder]] [/S] [/B] [/L] [/C]`. The switches that follow an optional parameter pertain only to the parameter that precedes them; in other words, the /S, /B, /L, and /C switches control the /O parameter.

If the way the Help utility displays syntax seems confusing, remember that the parameters for every common DOS command are explained in each topic of the Help utility, and additional help is available by choosing the Notes and Examples selections.

Parameters also are covered in the command references throughout this book, using clear syntax displays and examples.

2

Summary

To	Do This
Get a list of files	Use the DIR command
Get information on a file	Use the DIR command
Remove a file from disk	Use the ERASE or DEL command
Copy a file	Use the COPY command
Change directories	Use the CD command
Create a directory	Use the MD command
Prepare a floppy disk for use	Use the FORMAT command
Duplicate a floppy disk	Use the DISKCOPY command
Get help on DOS commands	Use the Help utility

On Your Own

Estimated time: 10 minutes

Use DOS commands and features.

1. Use the DIR command to view the files in the current directory.
2. Use the COPY command to make a copy of a file in the current directory.
3. Change from the current directory to another using the CD command.
4. Create a directory named TEST using the MD command. (You can remove the directory later using the RD command, which is covered in Lesson 4, "Working from the DOS Command Line.")
5. Format a new floppy disk using the FORMAT command. (Don't use a disk that contains data you want to save.)
6. Run the Help utility and select the COPY command. Also browse the information provided when you choose the Notes and Examples selections.

Lesson 3

Starting DOS

Booting
Starting your PC.

Cold boot
Starting your PC by turning on the power switch.

With early computers, operators started the computer by entering a binary program—called a *bootstrap loader*—and instructing the computer to run the program. The term *booting,* a derivation of *bootstrap,* comes from the expression "pulling yourself up by your bootstraps." To *boot* your PC means to turn on the computer (*cold boot*) or to instruct the computer to reset without your turning it off and then on again (*warm boot*).

This lesson helps you learn the following tasks:

- Perform cold and warm boots
- Display the directory tree
- Change directories and drives
- Issue commands at the DOS prompt
- Stop a command

Task: Cold Booting from the Hard Disk

If your computer already has DOS installed on the hard disk, booting the computer is a very easy process. Just turn on the computer; the system boots automatically. (If you don't have a hard disk or DOS isn't installed on your hard disk, you need working DOS disks to boot your computer. See Lesson 7, "Formatting Disks," for information on creating a boot disk, or see Appendix A for instructions on installing DOS on a system with only floppy disks.)

If you have a hard disk with the DOS bootup files installed, you rarely will need to boot the computer from a disk in the A: drive. However, you need to have a floppy disk available for booting, just in case. Problems with booting can occur if you have problems with your hard disk or if you make an error when you try to customize DOS by editing AUTOEXEC.BAT or CONFIG.SYS. (The editing of these files is covered in Lesson 11, "Customizing DOS.")

Task: Cold Booting from a Floppy Disk

Caution
If the disk doesn't go into the drive, make sure another disk isn't in the drive. Never force a disk because you could damage the disk, the drive, or both.

If you need to boot from a floppy disk, you start by inserting the floppy disk in the drive. You mount floppy drives horizontally or vertically; a properly inserted disk usually has its label facing left on vertical drives and up on horizontal units.

If you insert a 3 1/2-inch disk, push gently until you hear a click. If you insert a 5 1/4-inch disk, turn the latch clockwise or close the drive door. (On some newer computers, the 5 1/4-inch disk may click in, and you don't need to turn a latch or close a door.)

The following figures show how to insert floppy disks on a typical system.

Inserting a disk in a 5 1/4-inch drive.

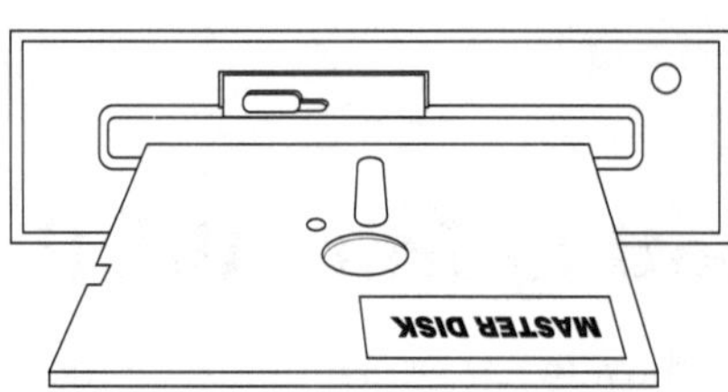

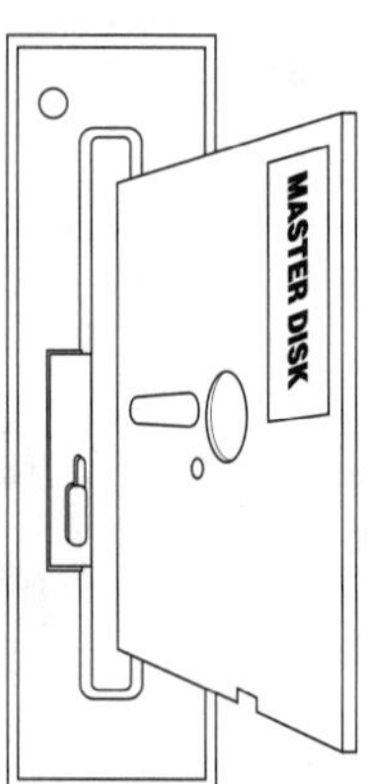

Inserting a disk in a 3 1/2-inch drive.

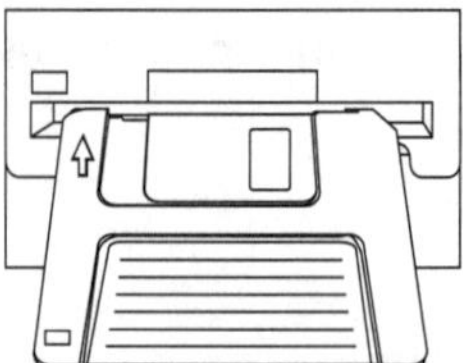

A floppy disk used to boot a computer is termed a *system disk*. The full installation package of DOS 6.2, which most often comes with a new computer, includes a system disk labeled *Startup* that you can use to boot your computer.

If you are using an earlier version of DOS, the boot disk may be labeled *Disk 1, System, Main,* or *DOS*. Check your manual if you are uncertain which disk is bootable, or ask your computer specialist for a bootable DOS system disk, or refer to Lesson 7, "Formatting Disks," for information on creating a system disk.

To cold boot with a floppy disk, follow these steps:

1. Insert the system disk into the A: drive. (Check your PC's system manual for the location of the A: drive and for disk-insertion instructions.)

2. If you have a lock on the front of the system unit and it is locked, unlock it.

3. If your monitor has a separate power switch, turn on the display. Some displays are powered by the system unit and do not have a switch.

4. Turn on the computer's power switch. On some computers, the power switch is on the right side and toward the rear of the system unit; on other units, the switch is conveniently located in the front.

At this point, the cold boot begins.

Reviewing the Booting Process

The instant you flip the power switch to turn on a computer, the computer begins a *Power-On Self-Test* (*POST*). The POST ensures that your PC's electronics are working properly. Completing the POST takes from a few seconds to several minutes.

Some computers enable you to watch the action of the POST. During the POST, you may see a description of the test or a blinking cursor on the display. The POST may run a memory check, for example, and you may see POST counting off the amount of random-access memory (RAM) installed on your system. After the POST ends, the computer beeps and drive A: spins.

Finally, the DOS bootstrap loader loads into RAM from the hard drive or the system disk. On most systems, the computer first looks for a system disk in the A: drive. If the A: drive contains a disk, the bootstrap loader tries to load DOS from the disk in the A: drive, even if you have a hard disk. If the disk in drive A: is not a system disk, you receive the following error message:

```
Non-System disk or disk error
Replace and press any key when ready
```

If drive A: does not contain a disk, the system then looks to the hard drive for the system files needed to boot the computer.

After DOS completes the bootup process, the DOS prompt appears, as described later in this lesson.

If you have problems...

If you have problems booting your system with DOS, first make sure that your system turns on. If it does not, check to see that the computer is plugged into the power socket on the wall. Then check to see that all cables are properly connected. If the computer seems to power on but you don't see anything on your monitor, make sure that the monitor is plugged into the power socket and turned on. If that step doesn't help, make sure that the monitor is properly connected to the computer. With 5 1/4-inch drives, you may accidentally insert a floppy disk upside down. Make sure that you insert the floppy disk properly and try again.

Task: Warm Booting

Warm boot
Restarting, or resetting, your PC by pressing Ctrl-Alt-Del rather than turning the power off and then on again.

The *warm boot* differs little from the cold boot. You generally use the warm boot, or *reboot*, to reset your system hardware after a program has malfunctioned and locked the computer. If the operating system isn't installed on your hard drive, the DOS system disk must be in drive A: to warm boot your computer.

To warm boot your system, follow these steps:

1. Press and hold down the Ctrl key.
2. As you hold down the Ctrl key, press and hold down the Alt key.
3. As you hold down the Ctrl and Alt keys, press Del.
4. Release all three keys.

The PC skips the preliminary tests and immediately loads DOS. Don't worry if nothing happens on the first try. With some systems that have been running programs, you may need to press Ctrl-Alt-Del twice.

Your computer also may have a *reset switch* you can use to restart your computer without having to turn it off. You can use the reset switch when a badly behaved program locks your computer and the Ctrl-Alt-Del warm boot does not work to restart DOS. To warm boot with the reset switch, just press the switch.

If you have problems...

If you have problems warm booting your system, make sure that you press and hold down the Ctrl key, the Alt key, and the Del key all at the same time. If you have a hardware reset button, make sure that you have pressed that button rather than another button on the front of your computer. Most modern computers have a turbo button alongside the reset button, and you can easily confuse the two.

Warm boot your computer only if your system locks from a malfunctioning program. Do not warm boot your system if a program still is running properly. Doing so may result in the loss of important data. Instead of warm booting your system, use the program's commands to save your data and then exit. After you return to the DOS prompt, you can restart your system if necessary.

Understanding the DOS Prompt

DOS prompt
The `C:\>` symbol or other characters that appear on-screen to indicate you must enter information before anything else can happen.

After the boot process is complete, the *DOS prompt* (also called *prompt, command-line prompt,* and *command prompt*) appears. The following DOS prompt appears by default when you are using DOS 6.2:

```
C:\>
```

You also may see a DOS prompt that looks like the following:

```
C>
```

The DOS prompt is the *user interface* of DOS. In other words, the DOS prompt indicates that DOS is waiting for you to enter a command or load programs.

The `C>` prompt, shown in the preceding example, indicates only the current (active) drive. The prompt doesn't display information about which directory you are in. Before DOS 6.2, this prompt appeared most often on systems with floppy drives only.

When the `C:\>` prompt appears by itself on-screen, you know you are in the *root directory* of the C: drive, the main directory on the hard disk. When you change directories, the prompt shows the directory you have changed to. For example, if you currently are in the DOS directory, the prompt appears as follows:

```
C:\DOS>
```

This detailed prompt tells you when you are in any directory or subdirectory. For example, if you are in the BOOKS directory, the DOS prompt looks like this:

```
C:\BOOKS>
```

Before DOS 6.2, commands issued in AUTOEXEC.BAT caused DOS to display the `C:\>` type of prompt. However, DOS 6.2 shows this detailed prompt by default.

Information displayed after the `C:\` is called the *directory path*. The directory path is a complete listing of the current drive and directory. For example, if you are in the SYSTEM subdirectory under the WINDOWS directory, the prompt looks like this:

```
C:\WINDOWS\SYSTEM>
```

You can see that the DOS 6.2 version of the DOS prompt is much more helpful than the plain C> prompt. The following section describes how to customize your DOS prompt; more details are described in Lesson 11, "Customizing DOS."

Task: Displaying the Directory Tree

Directory
An organized section of a disk in which you store files. A directory is like a file folder in a file cabinet.

Every *directory* can contain subdirectories (which is like having manila file folders within hanging file folders). But when you work with directories, you almost always work with a single directory at a time. The directory in which you are currently working is called the current directory. The directory path means the drive letter and all the subdirectories leading to that directory.

Directory tree
The representation of directories as a tree, with directories and sub-directories growing out of the root directory.

The complete list of all the directories on a disk is called the *directory tree*. To see what the directory tree of your drive looks like, follow these steps:

1. At the DOS prompt, type **TREE**.
2. Press Enter.

The following figure shows a partial directory tree on a typical hard drive.

Part of a typical directory tree.

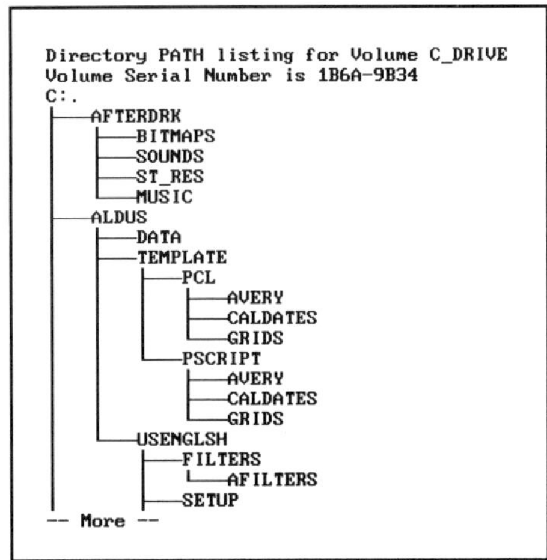

```
Directory PATH listing for Volume C_DRIVE
Volume Serial Number is 1B6A-9B34
C:.
├───AFTERDRK
│   ├───BITMAPS
│   ├───SOUNDS
│   ├───ST_RES
│   └───MUSIC
├───ALDUS
│   ├───DATA
│   ├───TEMPLATE
│   │   ├───PCL
│   │   │   ├───AVERY
│   │   │   ├───CALDATES
│   │   │   └───GRIDS
│   │   └───PSCRIPT
│   │       ├───AVERY
│   │       ├───CALDATES
│   │       └───GRIDS
│   └───USENGLSH
│       ├───FILTERS
│       │   └───AFILTERS
│       ├───SETUP
-- More --
```

The TREE command produces a readout that graphically displays directories and subdirectories as limbs growing out of the root directory. Instead of the root being at the bottom of the tree, however, the root directory in DOS is at the top of the TREE readout, with all directories appearing beneath the root and subdirectories growing off the main limbs.

On a drive with a large number of directories, the TREE command may display the directories on the drive too quickly for you to see them all. You can get an electronic copy of your directory tree by following these steps:

1. Make sure that you are in the root directory of your drive by entering the following command:

   CD

2. Enter the following command at the DOS prompt:

   TREE > TREE.TXT

   (The meaning of the > symbol is explained in Lesson 10, "Advanced DOS Commands.")

3. To view the electronic copy of your directory tree, use the MS-DOS Editor. Enter the following command:

   EDIT TREE.TXT

If you want, you can print the electronic copy of the tree by following these steps:

1. Open the MS-DOS Editor's File menu by clicking the File menu or pressing Alt-F.

2. Click Print or press P on your keyboard.

The tree will print out on your printer.

With the image from the TREE command fresh in your mind, you may be able to envision what happens when you use the CD (change directory) command. To make a different directory current, for example, you type CD and specify the name of the directory you want to make current. For example, to make BOOKS the current directory, follow these steps:

1. Type **CD\BOOKS** at the prompt.
2. Press Enter.

The prompt changes to `C:\BOOKS>`, which means you are in the BOOKS directory; the BOOKS directory is now the current directory.

You can continue changing directories and moving up and down the directory tree with the CD command. Notice that each directory change modifies the look of the DOS prompt, because the directory path changes to match your location. For example, if you type CD\WORD\DOCS, the DOS prompt looks like this: `C:\WORD\DOCS>`.

Try this example to change to the directory containing the DOS files:

1. Type **CD\DOS**
2. Press Enter. The prompt appears as `C:\DOS>`.

If you run Windows, you can change to the Windows directory this way:

1. Type **CD\WINDOWS**
2. Press Enter. The prompt appears as `C:\WINDOWS>`.

A subdirectory called SYSTEM is beneath the Windows directory. Try changing to the SYSTEM directory:

1. Type **CD\WINDOWS\SYSTEM**
2. Press Enter. The prompt appears as `C:\WINDOWS\SYSTEM>`.

If the concept of directories still seems strange to you, use the TREE command to reexamine the directory structure of your hard drive. You can see how directories and subdirectories are used to group together related files so you can find them easily.

Understanding Drive Letters

Drive letter
The designation used by DOS to keep track of disk drives, such as A:, B:, C:, D:, E:, and so on.

If you have a computer with one floppy drive and one hard drive, the floppy drive is always called the A: drive and the hard drive is almost always called the C: drive. The *drive letter* B is missing because DOS reserves the letters A and B for floppy drives. If you have only one floppy drive, letter B is held in reserve in case you later add a second floppy drive.

Task: Changing Drives

Logged drive
The drive in which you are currently working. Unless you specify otherwise, any DOS command you enter affects the logged drive.

After you learn the difference between drive names, you need to understand the concept of the current drive, or *logged drive*. The logged drive is the active drive, or the drive that responds to commands. For example, this prompt tells you that DOS is logged onto the A: drive:

```
A:\>
```

This example means that DOS is logged onto the B: drive:

```
B:\>
```

To switch drives, follow these steps:

1. Type the letter of the drive that you want to become active.
2. Type a colon.
3. Press Enter.

DOS reads the drive letter and colon as the disk drive's name. For example, if you have a computer with two floppy drives, you can change the logged drive from A: to B: this way:

1. Type **B:** at the `A:\>` prompt so the prompt appears as `A:\>B:`
2. Press Enter. The prompt appears as `B:\>`.

With this command, you have instructed your PC that you want to work with the disk in the B: drive.

Most commands automatically use the current drive and directory or other current information; you don't need to specify the current path in the command. However, if you want a command to act on a drive or directory other than the current one, you must specify a path.

If you have problems...

If you have problems logging to another drive, first make sure of the drive letters used by the drives on your system. If you have a hard drive, it is usually the C: drive. If you have one floppy drive, it is usually the A: drive. If you have two floppy drives, they are usually the A: drive and the B: drive.

When logging to another drive, remember that you must type not only the drive letter, but also the colon (A: not A). No space can be between the drive letter and colon. After you type the drive letter and colon, remember to press the Enter key to log to the other drive.

Learning How Commands Work

Command
An instruction you issue at the DOS prompt to perform a task.

Using DOS *commands* such as CD and DIR was discussed in Lesson 2, "Making a Quick Start with DOS 6.2." About 100 commands are available in DOS 6.2. You may use some of these commands quite often; many other commands you may never use. The commands described in Lesson 2 are among the most frequently used commands.

To execute a command from the DOS prompt, you type the command and press Enter. (If you correctly type the command and press Enter, the command executes. If you make an error, you receive an error message.) After you press Enter, COMMAND.COM, the command processor, steps in. COMMAND.COM's job is to find and *execute*, or *run*, the command you just typed.

The following example uses an imaginary command, DROP, to describe what happens when you execute a command. These steps show what DOS does, in precisely this order, after you enter the DROP command:

1. DOS looks in COMMAND.COM's own internal code to see if the DROP command is an *internal command*. Internal commands (such as DIR and DEL) are covered in more detail in Lesson 2, "Making a Quick Start with DOS 6.2." If the command is internal, DOS runs the command. If the command is not internal, DOS goes to the next step.
2. DOS looks for a file named DROP.COM. If DOS finds a file named DROP.COM, it executes the command. If it doesn't find DROP.COM, DOS goes to the next step.
3. DOS looks for a file named DROP.EXE. If DOS finds a file named DROP.EXE, it executes the command. If it doesn't find DROP.EXE, DOS goes to the next step.
4. DOS looks for a file named DROP.BAT. If a file named DROP.BAT exists, DOS executes the command. If DOS doesn't find DROP.BAT, it issues the following error message:

```
Bad command or file name
```

The way DOS searches for *executable* files (COM, EXE, and BAT files) is important. If you have two executable files named DROP in the same directory—for example, DROP.COM and DROP.BAT—DOS always runs DROP.COM rather than DROP.BAT unless you enter the full file name of DROP.BAT to run it. In other words, to run DROP.BAT you enter the following command:

DROP.BAT

To fully understand how DOS searches for COM, EXE, and BAT files, you need to know about the DOS path and the path statement in AUTOEXEC.BAT. The DOS path and the path statement are covered in Lesson 11, "Customizing DOS."

Task: Stopping the Computer

Occasionally, you may need to stop the computer from carrying out a command because a program may seem to go haywire, repeating the same action over and over even when you have not entered any command.

As a last resort, of course, you can use the Ctrl-Alt-Del combination described previously in this lesson, or if that method doesn't work, you can switch off power to the computer.

But before you try Ctrl-Alt-Del or turn off power, you should try three keystroke combinations that often can stop a command and restore control of your computer to you. These three combinations involve the use of the Ctrl key, and/or the Break key, and/or the C key, and/or the Esc key. When considering these keystrokes, remember that the hyphen between keys means you hold down the first key at the same time you press the second key. The following table describes these special keystrokes:

Key or Key Combination	Action
Ctrl-Break and Ctrl-C	Cancels the current process.
Ctrl-C	Stops the command and returns you to the DOS prompt. However, DOS carries out many commands too quickly for you to intervene with Ctrl-C.
Ctrl-S	Temporarily halts screen display until you press a key to resume it. For example, Ctrl-S is useful when the listing produced by the DIR command flashes by on-screen too quickly to be useful.
Esc	Stops the current operation in many application software programs, often reverting to the previous process.

These key sequences are panic buttons you can use to stop DOS. Don't worry if you need to use them to prevent disasters. Practice using these keys with a nondestructive command, such as DIR. If these commands fail, you can always press Ctrl-Alt-Del. And remember, many computers have a reset switch that reboots your system just like the Ctrl-Alt-Del keystroke combination.

3

You can try the Ctrl-C and Ctrl-S commands using the DIR command. To try Ctrl-C, use the following steps:

1. Change to a directory containing many files.
2. Type **DIR** at the DOS prompt.
3. Press the Enter key.
4. Quickly press **Ctrl-C**. The DIR command halts its operation and the following code appears on-screen:

```
^C
```

To resume display of files in the directory, you must re-enter the DIR command.

To see the effects of using Ctrl-S, use the following steps:

1. Change to a directory containing many files.
2. Type the **DIR** command.
3. Press Enter.
4. Quickly press **Ctrl-S**. The DIR listing halts immediately so you can read the listings.
5. To resume the DIR listing, press a key.

Refer to the documentation for your software applications before trying out the Esc key in an application.

If you have problems...

If you have problems stopping an operation in DOS, make sure that you press and hold down the Ctrl-C (or Ctrl-Break) keys at the same time. If you have a problem with stopping the screen readout, make sure that you press the Ctrl and S keys at the same time. To resume the display, press the Enter key (many other keys work, too).

Summary

To	Do This
Boot from the hard drive	Make sure that no disk is in drive A:
Boot from a floppy disk	Place a system disk in drive A: and restart your system
Cold boot your system	Turn off system power and then turn it on again
Warm boot your system	Press Ctrl-Alt-Del (or press the reset button if your system has one)
View your directory tree	Use the TREE command
Change directories	Use the CD command
Halt a DOS command	Press Ctrl-C (or Ctrl-Break)

On Your Own

Estimated time: 15 minutes

Boot your computer.

1. Find your system disk and boot from the floppy drive.
2. Practice cold-booting your system by turning off system power and then turning it on again. Before you cold boot, exit all application software or wait until the most recently executed DOS command has finished.
3. Practice warm-booting your system by pressing Ctrl-Alt-Del. Before you warm boot, exit all application software or wait until the most recently executed DOS command has finished.

Use DOS commands.

1. Use the TREE command to obtain a display of your directory tree.
2. Use the CD command to change to one of the directories on your drive.
3. Use the CD command to change to one of the subdirectories on the drive.
4. Place a disk in the A: drive and change (log) to that drive.

Lesson 4

Working from the DOS Command Line

The first few lessons of this book introduced you to the concept of entering DOS commands at the DOS prompt. In other words, previous lessons introduced you to the DOS *command line*. This lesson covers the DOS command line in detail. With the information in this lesson, you learn to do the following:

- Enter commands
- Use the correct syntax
- Use command parameters and switches
- Understand the search path
- Use wild-card characters in file names
- Get help on DOS commands

All DOS commands follow the same general rules for specifying paths and file names and for using parameters and switches as discussed in this lesson. You can find more detailed information about the use of various DOS commands in Lesson 8, "DOS Command Reference."

Understanding the Command Line

DOS prompt
The C:\> symbol that indicates DOS is ready for you to type a command. On drives other than C:, the prompt displays the appropriate drive letter—for example, A:\> or B:\>.

The DOS *prompt* is how DOS tells you that it is ready for your next command. For example, when you first boot your computer, the prompt is `C:\>`. This prompt also is known as the *command prompt*. The empty space after the prompt, where you type words or characters, is called the *command line*. The term command line also is frequently used to describe the words or characters you type to invoke a command.

To tell DOS what you want it to do, you enter DOS *commands*. Commands are letters, numbers, and acronyms separated by certain other characters known as *delimiters*. For example, to use the DIR command to view a wide file list for the current directory, you follow these steps:

Command line
Where you type and what you type after the DOS prompt to invoke a command.

1. At the DOS prompt, type the following command line:

   DIR /W

2. Press Enter.

Command
A collection of characters that tells the computer what you want it to do. Most commands are mnemonics of English words, with letters or numbers often added as optional instructions.

With DOS, you must be precise. DOS knows only what its developers programmed it to understand. When you type a command in its proper form—or *syntax*—at the DOS prompt, the DOS command and any additional parameters communicate your intent. Both the command and the parameters relay the action you want to perform and the object of that action.

Another way of looking at the DOS command line is that DOS is similar to a written instruction you might give to a work associate. People use interconnecting words and inferences that the human brain can grasp easily.

Delimiter
A character that separates the parts of a command. Common delimiters are the space and the slash (/).

If you want a sign on a bulletin board duplicated for posting on another bulletin board, you might instruct, "Make a copy of the no smoking sign on the hallway bulletin board and put it on the lunchroom bulletin board. Oh, and make sure you get it right." Stripped to its bare bones, your instructions really mean, "Copy sign A to sign B. Make sure that the copy is free of errors."

Syntax
The structure, order, and vocabulary in which you type the elements of the DOS command; in other words, the specific set of rules you follow when you issue commands.

Similarly, if you want DOS to duplicate all the data from a disk in the A: drive to a disk you have placed in the B: drive, and you want to verify that the copy is correct, use these steps:

1. At the DOS prompt, type the following command:

   DISKCOPY A: B: /V

2. Press Enter.

The instruction has no extra verbiage; it's simply a straightforward command that tells DOS what you want it to do: copy the data on the disk in A: to the disk in B:. DOS responds by making an exact duplicate of the disk. Adding the /V parameter tells DOS to check the copy to make sure it is an exact duplicate of the original.

To have DOS compare the copy with the original, follow these steps:

1. At the DOS prompt, type the following command:

   DISKCOMP A: B:

2. Press Enter.

When you use the DISKCOMP command, DOS provides an error message if the second disk is not an exact duplicate of the first.

The DISKCOPY and DISKCOMP commands are good examples of the way most DOS commands are named. You can understand clearly from the DISKCOPY command's name that DISKCOPY makes a duplicate of a disk. And the DISKCOMP command's name clearly indicates that DISKCOMP compares one disk with another. The parameters A: and B: indicate the disk drives you want DOS to use when the command is executed.

Command Name

You may think of the command name as only the first part of a DOS command. In addition to the name, though, many commands require or allow further directions. For example, if you enter the FORMAT command without parameters, DOS does not know which drive contains the disk you want formatted.

Parameter
Any additional information you type after the command name in the command syntax to refine what you want the DOS command to do.

When you add *parameters,* or directions for which drive contains the disk you want formatted, DOS knows what you want it to do. Parameters tell DOS where to apply the action or how to apply the action. Using DOS commands is quite easy if you follow the rules of order and use the correct parameters.

Command Syntax

Learning the ins and outs of issuing DOS commands takes practice. DOS commands follow a logical structure, but that structure is far more rigid than a casual conversation with a neighbor. Using proper syntax when you enter a DOS command is comparable to using the proper words when you speak. When you want coffee, you can't order tea. To carry out your command, DOS must clearly understand what you are typing.

The strength of DOS is that after you understand its rules, everything flows easily. Commands conform to standard rules. After you understand these basic concepts, you can use them with nearly any DOS command. To feel comfortable with DOS commands, remember these rules:

- DOS requires you to use a specific set of rules, or syntax, when you issue commands.
- Parameters, part of a command's syntax, modify, or fine-tune, the way DOS executes a command.
- *Switches,* also part of a command's syntax, turn on or off an optional instruction or function.

Switch
A part of the command that turns on or off an additional instruction or function.

Symbolic form
The use of a letter or name for illustrative purposes.

Many DOS manuals use *symbolic form* to illustrate the parameters and switches of DOS commands. For example, when the syntax for a command calls for you to enter the name of the file on which you want a DOS command to act, a symbolic file name like *example.com* may be used to illustrate the real file name. When you type the command, you substitute a real file name for the symbolic one.

Understanding symbolic form becomes more complex because it describes not only files, but also every parameter and switch that you can possibly enter on the command line. You cannot issue many DOS commands, however, to accept every possible option. Using all the options is like ordering a sandwich with white, rye, whole wheat, *and* cinnamon-raisin bread. The choice is usually either/or, rather than all. When you type a command, it should contain nothing more than what you want to instruct DOS to do.

The confusing part about many DOS manuals, and even the DOS Help utility, is that when they try to illustrate syntax, they present you with something that resembles a heavy algebra problem more than a basic command you enter at the DOS prompt. The following example is from the DOS 6.2 Help utility:

```
DIR [drive:][path][filename] [/P] [/W] [/A[[:]attributes]][/
O[[:]sortorder]] [/S] [/B] [/L] [/C]
```

Even a somewhat simplified symbolic representation of the DIR command might look like this:

```
DIR d:path\ filename.ext /W /P /A:attributes /O:order /S /B /L
```

On the other hand, a command you use in the real world might look like the following example:

DIR C: /W /P

As you can see, symbolic notation can confuse, rather than enlighten, until you understand the concept behind the form.

MS-DOS 6.2 QuickStart goes to considerable lengths to illustrate syntax in a simple manner, and this book provides actual examples of how you use commands and syntax.

Parameters and Switches

The term parameter, in most cases when used in this book, means an important part of a command you must enter before a DOS command will work. For example, the delete command (DEL) requires that, as a parameter, you enter the file name of the file you want to remove from a disk. For example, to remove a file named README.TXT, follow these steps:

1. Switch to the directory containing the README.TXT file.

   Do not delete the README.TXT file in your DOS directory. You will need this file later. Instead, delete a README.TXT file you have already read, or merely use this example as a reference without deleting anything.

2. At the DOS prompt, type the following line:

   DEL README.TXT

3. Press Enter.

The DIR command clearly illustrates the use of switches. Usually the DIR command displays a directory with one file listing per line. The date and time the file was created appear next to the file name. Sometimes a directory contains too many files to display on one screen. The /P and /W switches described in earlier lessons control the way directory information appears when you use the DIR command:

- When you use the /P switch, 23 lines of file names—approximately one full screen—are displayed. The display pauses when the screen fills. At the bottom of a paused directory listing, DOS prompts you to `Press any key to continue` to move to the next screen of files. The /P switch thus enables you to see all the files in the directory, one screen at a time.
- You can use the /W switch to display a wide directory of files that shows only file names and extensions and displays them in multiple columns across the screen. Often, the use of the /W switch allows you to view all the files in a directory without the use of the /P switch.

You can use the /P and the /W switches at the same time if you want both a wide listing of file names *and* you want the screen read out to pause when the screen fills up.

Note: *When DOS displays the* `Press any key to continue` *message, it means that you can press* almost *any key—A to Z, 1 to 0, plus most other keys. However, if you press the Shift, Alt, Caps Lock, Num Lock, or Scroll Lock keys, DOS ignores you. The easiest keys to press are the space bar and the Enter key.*

Syntax Example

This section breaks down the syntax of commands piece by piece, explaining each piece and the appropriate time to use each piece. For the sake of example, this section explains the DIR command. However, what you learn about syntax will be very useful when you see the syntax of other commands throughout this book. The following line is the syntax for the DIR command:

DIR *d:path\ filename.ext* /W /P /A:*attributes* /O:*order* /S /B /L

The following table describes each part of this syntax line.

Syntax part	Description of function and use
DIR	The command.
d:	The drive containing the directory listing. If the current drive is the drive you want, you don't need to specify a drive. If you want a directory listing of a different drive, type the appropriate drive letter.
path	The route DOS follows to find the directory that contains the files for which you want a directory listing. If you want a listing of the files in the current directory, you don't need a path.
filename.ext	The file name and its extension. You substitute your own file name in place of *filename.ext*.
/W	A switch that requests a wide, or horizontal, directory, rather than a single vertical listing.
/P	A switch that pauses the directory listing.
/A:*attributes*	A switch that lists only files with certain file attributes. You must use the colon (:) after /A and then the letter that indicates the type of files you want to view. A minus sign (-) before the attribute tells DOS not to list a file with that attribute. For information on attributes, see Lesson 8, "DOS Command Reference."
/O:*order*	A switch that specifies the sort order of the listing. A minus sign (-) before the sort order means to reverse the order. You must use the colon (:) after /O and before the letter designating sort order. The /O switch is covered in Lesson 10, "Advanced DOS Commands."
/S	A switch that lists the files in all subdirectories.
/B	A switch that lists only the file names, with no spaces between the name and the extension.
/L	A switch that displays the listing in lowercase letters rather than uppercase.

4

Among the many thousands of DIR command possibilities, you can type the DIR command in the following ways:

```
DIR
DIR /P
DIR /W
DIR /W /P
DIR A:
```

DIR A: /P

DIR /P /A:D

DIR /W /O:D

DIR /B

DIR /A:E /S

DIR /L

The following examples show the result of changing the switches for a command. When you issue the DIR command with no switches, a typical result looks like this example:

```
 Volume in drive D is D_DRIVE
 Volume Serial Number is 3A30-1DCE
 Directory of D:\MAJOR

.            <DIR>          01-09-94   8:38p
..           <DIR>          01-09-94   8:38p
CATALOG  EXE         28,715 08-03-93   1:00p
CONFIG   MS              23 01-08-94   1:32a
HS       MS1            209 01-08-94   1:32a
LICENSE  DOC          4,490 02-20-93   1:40p
MAJOR    EXE         84,217 02-20-93   1:40p
ORDER    FRM          3,321 08-03-93   1:00p
VOLUME1A MS1        890,061 02-20-93   1:40p
VOLUME1B MS1        989,752 02-20-93   1:40p
        10 file(s)      2,000,788 bytes
                      351,911,936 bytes free
```

Issuing the DIR command with the /P switch displays the directory listing page by page, with the message `Press any key to continue` at the bottom of the screen (the command itself scrolls off the screen):

```
Directory of D:\BSTONE

.            <DIR>          01-09-94   8:38p
..           <DIR>          01-09-94   8:38p
AUDIOHED BS1          1,280 12-01-93   1:00p
AUDIOT   BS1        162,268 12-01-93   1:00p
BS-HELP  EXE         12,203 12-01-93   1:00p
BSTONE   BAT            101 12-01-93   1:00p
BS_AOG   EXE        124,507 12-01-93   1:00p
CONFIG   BS1            744 01-10-94   7:07p
IANIM    BS1         18,977 12-01-93   1:00p
JAMERR   EXE         10,748 12-01-93   1:00p
JM_ERROR H            9,799 12-01-93   1:00p
MAPHEAD  BS1            834 12-01-93   1:00p
MAPTEMP  BS1         91,100 12-01-93   1:00p
ORDER    FRM          6,228 12-01-93   1:00p
SANIM    BS1        276,784 12-01-93   1:00p
SAVEGAM0 BS1         16,113 01-07-94   2:37p
SAVEGAM1 BS1         30,825 01-08-94   7:19p
SAVEGAM2 BS1         38,433 01-08-94   7:36p
```

```
SAVEGAM3 BS1         46,305 01-10-94   6:08p
Press any key to continue . . .
```

The command DIR /W displays the directory listing in a wide arrangement but doesn't display file size and date/time information about the files:

```
 Volume in drive D is D_DRIVE
 Volume Serial Number is 3A30-1DCE
 Directory of D:\BSTONE

[.]             [..]            AUDIOHED.BS1    AUDIOT.BS1      BS-HELP.EXE
BSTONE.BAT      BS_AOG.EXE      CONFIG.BS1      IANIM.BS1       JAMERR.EXE
JM_ERROR.H      MAPHEAD.BS1     MAPTEMP.BS1     ORDER.FRM       SANIM.BS1
SAVEGAM0.BS1    SAVEGAM1.BS1    SAVEGAM2.BS1    SAVEGAM3.BS1    SAVEGAM4.BS1
SAVEGAM5.BS1    VGADICT.BS1     VGAGRAPH.BS1    VGAHEAD.BS1     VSWAP.BS1
       25 file(s)      3,580,562 bytes
                     351,911,936 bytes free
```


The DIR /A:D command lists only the directories. Using this command produces the following kind of read out:

```
Volume in drive D is D_DRIVE
 Volume Serial Number is 3A30-1DCE
 Directory of D:\

ARCADE        <DIR>          01-09-94   8:38p
BASH          <DIR>          01-09-94   8:38p
BSTONE        <DIR>          01-09-94   8:38p
DESKSCAN      <DIR>          01-09-94   2:31p
FLIGHT        <DIR>          01-10-94  10:25a
MAJOR         <DIR>          01-09-94   8:38p
OPDIRECT      <DIR>          01-09-94  10:46p
PINBALL       <DIR>          01-10-94  12:16a
PSTYLER       <DIR>          12-20-93   7:41p
SHIHDAO       <DIR>          01-09-94   8:38p
SHOW          <DIR>          12-15-93  10:17p
SIERRA        <DIR>          01-09-94   8:38p
WINWORD       <DIR>          12-17-93  11:51p
WOLF3D        <DIR>          01-09-94   8:38p
ZIPSNEW       <DIR>          12-15-93  10:22p
       15 file(s)                0 bytes
                       351,911,936 bytes free
```

In the root directory of a bootable disk, DIR /A:S lists the DOS system files. These files normally do not appear on a directory listing. The following example is the kind of display produced with this command:

```
Volume in drive C is C_DRIVE
 Volume Serial Number is 1B6A-9B34
 Directory of C:\

IO       SYS       40,566 09-30-93   6:20a
MSDOS    SYS       38,138 09-30-93   6:20a
        2 file(s)          78,704 bytes
                      166,912,000 bytes free
```

Issuing Commands

If you make a mistake when typing a DOS command or one of its parameters, use the backspace key to erase what you have entered and type the command correctly. No command you type is executed until you press the Enter key.

As you gain experience, you will be able to use potentially dangerous commands like DEL and ERASE, and other commands that can be even more dangerous, in a routine manner.

Typing the Command Name

The command name is a key to DOS. When you type a command, enter the command name immediately after the prompt; in other words, don't leave a space after the DOS prompt's greater-than sign (>).

If the command has no parameters or switches, press the Enter key after you type the last letter of the command name. For example, type the directory command as DIR at the prompt and then press Enter.

Using Parameters

Parameters that aren't switches appear in this book in two ways: lowercase and uppercase. Uppercase switches mean that you enter letter-for-letter what you see. When you see lowercase text, you must substitute a value where the lowercase text appears. The lowercase letters are shorthand for the full names of the parts of a command. For example, earlier in this lesson you learned that when you read *filename.ext*, you type the name of the actual file on which you want the DOS command to act.

Remember that you delimit, or separate, parameters from the rest of the command. Most of the time the delimiter is a space, but other delimiters exist, such as the comma (,), the backslash (\), and the colon (:). Refer to the examples in this book to learn the correct delimiter.

If the example command has switches, you can recognize them by the preceding slash (/). Always enter the switch letter as shown. Remember to type the slash.

Executing a Command

The Enter key is the action key for DOS commands. Make a habit of pausing and reading what you have typed at the DOS prompt before you press Enter. After you press Enter, the computer carries out your command.

During the processing of the command, DOS doesn't display any keystrokes you type, but it does remember them. Be aware that the characters you type after a command begins to execute can end up in your next command.

Canceling a Command

When you are typing a DOS command, press Esc if you make a mistake and want to start again from the beginning. Don't worry if you mistype a command. Until you press Enter, DOS doesn't act on the command. As mentioned previously, you can correct a mistake by using the backspace key to reposition the cursor. You also can use the arrow keys to backtrack on a command. Pressing the Esc key clears the entry and gives you a new line to work with.

Just remember that these line-editing and canceling tips work *only* before you press the Enter key. If you make a mistake in typing and press the Enter key, you issue the mistaken command to DOS. Often when you make a mistake, DOS responds with the following message:

```
Bad command or file name
```

After commands have begun to execute, you can successfully stop some commands with the Ctrl-C or Ctrl-Break sequence, but checking that the command is typed correctly before you press Enter is always good practice.

Using DOS Editing Keys

Input buffer
A storage area in memory for commands you have typed at the DOS prompt.

When you type a command and press the Enter key, DOS copies the command into an *input buffer*, a storage area for commands. You can recall the last command from the buffer and use it again. This feature is helpful when you want to issue a command that is similar to your last command. The following table shows the keys you use to edit the input buffer.

DOS Command Line Editing Keys

Key	Action
Tab	Moves cursor to the next tab stop.
Esc	Cancels the current line and doesn't change the buffer if a previous command is stored there.
Ins	Enables you to insert characters in the line.
Del	Deletes a character from the line.
F1 or right arrow	Copies one character from the preceding command line.
F2	Copies all characters from the preceding command line up to the next character you type.
F3	Inserts the characters from the preceding command into your current command line.
F4	Deletes all characters from the preceding command line up to, but not including, the next character typed (opposite of F2).
F5	Moves the current line into the buffer but doesn't allow MS-DOS to execute the line.
F6	Produces an end-of-file marker when you copy from the console (keyboard) to a disk file.

Controlling Scrolling

Scrolling describes the way in which a screen fills with information. As the screen fills with information, the lines of the display *scroll off* the top of the screen and new information scrolls onto the bottom of the screen. To stop a scrolling screen, use these steps:

1. Press the key combination **Ctrl-S**.
2. Press any key to restart the scrolling.

   On most keyboards, you can press the Pause key as an alternative to Ctrl-S.

Specifying Other Directories

Most DOS commands act upon one or more files. When you issue a command that involves files, DOS acts on the files in the current directory as the default. To tell DOS to act on files in another directory, you must specify the path to the other directory. Because paths can be very important when you use the command line, this section reviews paths. (For more details, see Lesson 5, "Understanding and Using Directories.")

Specifying Paths

Path
A DOS command parameter that tells DOS where to find a file or where to carry out a command.

A *path* is a chain of directory names that tells DOS where to find the files you want. You must build complete path names when you use the prompt. Issuing the DOS TREE command produces a visual display of the paths on your drive.

To create a path name chain, you type the drive name, a directory name (or sequence of directory and subdirectory names), and the file name upon which you want the DOS command to act. Make sure that you separate directory names from each other with a backslash (\) character. Using symbolic notation, the path name looks like this example:

d:\directory\subdirectory\filename.ext

In this notation, *d* is the drive letter. If you do not specify a drive, DOS uses the current drive by default.

directory\subdirectory names the directories and subdirectories you want to search. You can add additional subdirectories to the chain by entering the subdirectory names (plus the backslash character to separate the subdirectory names). If you omit the directory specifier from the path name, DOS assumes that you want to use the current directory.

filename.ext is the name of the file. Notice that you use a backslash to separate directory names from the file name. The path name fully describes to DOS where to direct its search for the file. When you use the DIR command, if you do not specify directory names or a file name, DOS lists all files in the directory. With other commands, such as COPY, you must specify a file name. The following examples show the paths to specific directories.

To specify files in the DATA directory on the C: drive, the complete path is as follows:

C:\DATA

For files in the TAXES subdirectory of the DATA directory on the C: drive, the complete path is as follows:

```
C:\DATA\TAXES
```

If the C: drive is the current drive and you want to specify files on the C: drive, you do not need to include the drive letter. The path is as follows:

```
\DATA\TAXES
```

Therefore, to list all the files in the C:\DATA\TAXES directory, you can use the following command:

```
DIR C:\DATA\TAXES
```

Or you can use this command:

```
DIR \DATA\TAXES
```

Because the files are on the current drive (C:), using the DIR command either way produces the same result—a listing of the files in the directory C:\DATA\TAXES.

If your current directory is C:\DATA, you can tell DOS to start the search of the C:\DATA\TAXES subdirectory at the current directory and simplify the command to the following:

```
DIR TAXES
```

Notice that the preceding path does not start with a backslash, which means that the path starts in the current directory, C:\DATA.

When you change directories, the rules for directory paths are the same as those rules are for the DIR command. If you start the path with a backslash, the path starts at the root directory. If you omit the initial backslash, the path starts at the current directory. To change to the \DATA\TAXES directory, use the following command:

```
CD \DATA\TAXES
```

If your current directory is the \DATA directory, you can simplify the command:

```
CD TAXES
```

When the root directory is the current directory, you don't need to use the initial backslash. If you want to change to the directory C:\DATA\TAXES from the root directory, you can type the following command:

CD \DATA\TAXES

Or this command has the same effect:

CD DATA\TAXES

Understanding Path Errors

If you specify an invalid path name, one that is incomplete or incorrect, you get an error message. The error message you see when using a particular DOS command depends on the command you are using. For example, if you enter the command DIR TAXES, and the current directory does not contain a subdirectory named TAXES, the following message appears:

```
File not found
```


Using Wild Cards

Wild card
A character you substitute for another character or characters to broaden the list of files on which a DOS command will perform its function.

DOS allows the use of wild-card characters, usually simply called *wild cards*, as a substitute for parts of a file name in a command. The DOS wild card characters are the star (*) and the question mark (?).

The Star (*) Wild Card

You substitute the star wild-card character for a part of a *filename.ext* you want a command to act upon. For example, you can use the star wild card with the DIR command to search for all the files with the extension TXT in the current directory. To use this capability, follow these steps:

1. At the DOS prompt, type the following command line:

   DIR *.TXT

2. Press Enter.

In this example, because the * wild card is in the position where the 8-character name of the file is typed, the star substitutes for that part of the file name. The star character in this example causes DOS to display all files in the current directory with the extension TXT. For example, the list may contain files with names like README.TXT, NOTES.TXT, MYFILE.TXT, and YOURFILE.TXT. Files with other extensions are not displayed.

A similar way of using the star wild card, but a method that achieves a far different effect, is illustrated in the following command line:

```
DIR MARCH.*
```

In this example, the star is in the position of the extension. The command only displays files like MARCH.DOC, MARCH.TXT, and MARCH.TMP.

If you use wild cards on both sides of the period that separates file names and extensions, the DOS command you enter acts upon every file in the current directory:

```
DIR *.*
```

In the case of the DIR command, entering the command and *.* produces the same readout as simply entering DIR. However, with other commands, the result can be quite different. For example, issuing the DEL command with *.* deletes every file in the current directory (after a warning message). The following example shows exactly what you see on-screen after you enter the DEL command in the DOS directory with *.* as the DEL command parameter:

```
C:\DOS>DEL *.*

All files in directory will be deleted!

Are you sure (Y/N)?
```

If you want all files deleted, press the Y key for yes. After all files are deleted, DOS returns you to the prompt. If you made a mistake and do not want all files deleted, press N for no. DOS immediately halts the delete operation and returns you to the prompt.

Note: *Using wild cards in this way with the DEL command is an effective way of deleting all files from a directory prior to removing the directory. But the effect can be disastrous if you do not really intend to delete all files in the current directory. Use great caution when using the DEL command with *.* as its parameters.*

A little trick involving file names and the star wild card requires using similar extensions on similar types of files. For example, you can use the extension LET for all letters. Then when you want to search your word processor's DATA directory for letters, you can use the DIR command in the following manner:

DIR *.LET

If you use this trick to name memos (MEM) and reports (RPT) and billings (BIL), you can use the DIR command with the star wild card to easily keep track of your different kinds of files. This naming technique also enables you to hunt down a particular file if you don't remember its entire *filename.ext.*

4

You can use the * wild-card character to replace only part of a file name when you want to perform an operation on files with similar names. For example, you can copy files named MAY1.TXT, MAY2.TXT, and MAY3.TXT by entering the following command line:

COPY MAY*.TXT *destination*

The wild card in this example replaces only the number in the file name. The result is that all files with MAY as the first part of their file name are copied to the destination.

You could delete all files with the characters 02FIG in their file name by entering the following command line:

DEL 02FIG*.*

The Question Mark (?) Wild Card

The ? wild card differs from the * wild card. The ? wild card matches any character in precisely the same position in a *filename.ext.* For example, the command DIR MYFILE?.WK1 lists files such as MYFILE.WK1, MYFILE1.WK1 and MYFILE2.WK1, but not MYFILE10.WK1. These same rules apply to other commands that allow wild cards.

You can use the ? wild card to copy the 1990, 1991, 1992, and 1993 sales reports (assuming they are XLS files created in Excel) using the following command line:

COPY 199?.XLS *destination*

You also can use wild cards to copy all files with similar names, regardless of their extension, by using the following command line:

COPY 199?.* *destination*

This command line copies files with names like 1990, 1991, 1992, and 1993 regardless of their extension. In other words, the example command line would copy 1990.DOC, 1990.XLS, 1992.TXT, 1993.DOC, and all other files whose names begin with 199. Using wild-card characters can make using DOS commands quick and easy.

Getting Help

This section covers getting help on an individual DOS command. You can use one of two ways to get help on a specific DOS command. The first is to use help information stored in the command itself. The second is to use the Help utility. Both of these ways of getting help are covered in the following sections.

Getting Quick Help

The quickest way to get help on a particular DOS command is to use the help information stored in the DOS file itself. To take advantage of this function, you enter the name of the command followed by the /? parameter. For example, to get help on the COPY command, follow these steps:

1. At the DOS prompt, type this command:

   COPY /?

2. Press Enter.

The readout produced by the COPY command when you use the /? parameter is shown in the following figure.

The on-line help for the COPY command.

```
Win C:\DOS> copy /?
Copies one or more files to another location.

COPY [/A | /B] source [/A | /B] [+ source [/A | /B] [+ ...]] [destination
  [/A | /B]] [/V]

  source       Specifies the file or files to be copied.
  /A           Indicates an ASCII text file.
  /B           Indicates a binary file.
  destination  Specifies the directory and/or filename for the new file(s).
  /V           Verifies that new files are written correctly.

To append files, specify a single file for destination, but multiple files
for source (using wildcards or file1+file2+file3 format).

Win C:\DOS>
```

After you become familiar with a common DOS command, perhaps after using it just a few times, the quick help provided by the /? parameter may be all the help you need. With other commands, you may need to refer to this book, or you may decide to use the DOS Help utility.

Using the Help Utility

You can use the Help utility to browse the full range of DOS commands or to get quick help on a specific DOS command. If you type HELP without specifying a command, the program displays a command reference that lists all DOS commands, as these steps show:

1. Type **HELP** at the DOS prompt.
2. Press Enter.

A menu line extends across the top of the display, a status line across the bottom, and a scroll bar along the right side. You can use the keyboard or the mouse to choose items.

To use the Help utility for a specific command, at the DOS prompt enter the command HELP and the name of the DOS command you need help with. For example, if you want to display help information about the COPY command, use these steps:

1. At the DOS prompt, type the following line:

   HELP COPY

2. Press Enter. The following figure appears.

The Help utility for the COPY command.

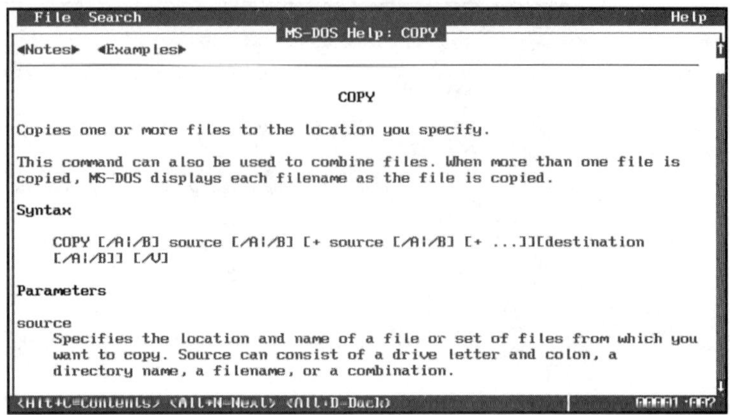

File Search Help
MS-DOS Help: COPY
◄Notes► ◄Examples►
COPY
Copies one or more files to the location you specify.
This command can also be used to combine files. When more than one file is copied, MS-DOS displays each filename as the file is copied.
Syntax
COPY [/A|/B] source [/A|/B] [+ source [/A|/B] [+ ...]][destination [/A|/B]] [/V]
Parameters
source
Specifies the location and name of a file or set of files from which you want to copy. Source can consist of a drive letter and colon, a directory name, a filename, or a combination.

DOS Help provides information about each command line parameter and switch you can use with a command. If you cannot figure out how to use a command with the syntax shown in the DOS Help utility, you can choose the Notes or Examples selections for more help. Choosing Notes displays suggestions on how to use the command. Choosing Examples produces examples for using the command. To access the Notes or Examples screens, move the cursor to the word *Notes* or *Examples* (or *Syntax*) at the top of the screen and press Enter, or click the word. To page forward and backward through the Help screens, press Alt-N and Alt-B or use the scroll bar or scroll arrows. To return to the command reference, press Alt-C.

Note: *Don't type the square brackets ([ ]) shown in the command line syntax.*

For general coverage of the DOS 6.2 Help utility, including how to use its menus and hotkeys, see Lesson 2, "Making a Quick Start with DOS 6.2."

Running Programs from the Command Line

To run a program, you enter the same kind of information on the command line that you do when you enter a DOS command. For example, to run Microsoft Word, a word processing program, you use these steps:

1. Change to the directory containing the Word program.
2. Type **WORD** at the DOS prompt.
3. Press Enter.

To run Word from the root directory, you add the path to the command. For this example, assume that Word is in the WORD directory under the root directory. You use this command:

C:\WORD\WORD

You can use the PATH command and batch files to make executing programs easier. This topic is covered in Lesson 11, "Customizing DOS."

Some programs enable you to specify a file name as a parameter when you run the program, which automatically loads the file. When you specify a file name on the command line, the program searches for that file in the current directory and if it finds the file, the program loads that file. For example, to run Word with the file MARCH.DOC already loaded, you use the following command line:

WORD MARCH.DOC

To determine if your application software enables you to load a data file by including its name as a command line parameter, refer to the software application's owners manual or other documentation.

Summary

To	Do this
Enter a command	Type the command at the DOS prompt
Make a command act in a specific way	Use command parameters and switches
Direct DOS to another directory	Type the correct path information
Act on more than one file	Use wild cards in the command line
Get quick help on a command	Type *command* /?

On Your Own

Estimated time: 10 minutes

Use variations of the DIR command.

1. Use the DIR command in the current directory to gain an understanding of entering commands.
2. Use the DIR /P and DIR /W commands to gain an understanding of using command switches.
3. Use the DIR *.TXT command in the DOS directory to gain an understanding of wild cards.
4. Change to the DOS directory and use the DIR README.* command to gain an understanding of wild cards.
5. Change to the root directory (C:\>) and enter the following DIR command to gain an understanding of using a path:

   DIR C:\DOS

Part II
Files and Directories

Lesson 5

Understanding and Using Directories

Directories often are described as electronic file folders in which you store files and application programs, and the root directory is like the file cabinet. This lesson focuses on the commands used to move from one directory to another and the ways to perform commands on one directory when you are in another. You also learn how to use DOS commands to organize your disk directories logically and how to use DOS to group and organize files. With the information in this lesson, you can accomplish the following tasks:

- Add and remove directories
- Organize directories and files logically
- Display directory listings
- Use correct path names
- Place files in appropriate directories

Understanding the Directory Structure

Directory
An area of the DOS file system that holds information about files and programs. The root directory is the highest directory of DOS's tree structure.

Some new computer users avoid learning about *directories* and *subdirectories* by putting all their files wherever they end up on the hard drive. This method is a mistake. The root directory of your hard drive (which is C:\ if you have only one hard drive) can hold a limited number of entries. After you reach that number, DOS does not allow you to put anything else in the root directory. Therefore, your hard drive becomes full, in effect, even though you may have many megabytes of space available on the drive.

Subdirectory
A directory created within another directory and subordinate to that directory.

Putting hundreds of unrelated files in the root directory (or any directory) makes keeping track of files nearly impossible. Your drive becomes a bewildering tangle of files. To take advantage of your hard drive space, you must use directories and subdirectories to group and organize your files.

Because the DOS directory structure enables you to put files in a specific place, you can keep files with similar names in separate directories. For example, you can have two files named README.TXT on your hard drive at the same time. (README is a common name for files that contain information not in the user manual for software applications. Two README files might exist, for example, because one file explains the use of WORD.EXE and the other explains MATH.EXE.) Without directories, you could not save both these files. You would need to erase the first file to save the second one.

The terms *directory* and *subdirectory* frequently are used interchangeably. For example, people might use the term *directory* when referring to the subdirectory C:\WORD\DOCS. Which term you use is not important, but in this lesson the term *directory* means it connects directly to the root, and *subdirectory* means it connects to a directory, not to the root directory.

Hierarchical Directory Structure

Hierarchical directory
An organizational structure used by DOS to segregate files into levels of subdirectories.

The DOS directory structure often is called *hierarchical*. This term means that one directory leads to another, which can lead to another, and so on. This multilevel file structure enables you to create a filing system. With a bit of foresight, you can logically group your files in directories so that you (and DOS) can locate your files more easily.

All DOS disks have at least one directory: the root directory. One directory often is adequate for a floppy disk because floppy disks have relatively small capacities. The number of files that fit on a floppy is limited. Although you can use DOS's multiple directory structure on floppy disks, this feature is more important for extending order to hard disks, which have very large storage capacities.

To understand how the root directory, directories, and subdirectories work together, think of the structure this way:

- *Root directory*. If the DOS directory structure were like a system of roads, the root directory would be the main street in town. The rest of the roads in town would connect with the main street or with roads that connect with it. The root directory of drive C: is represented as C:\, just as the main road through town might be called Main Street.

- *Directory*. Directories are the streets that connect directly with Main Street (to continue the analogy). Directories such as C:\BOOKS and C:\WORD, for example, connect directly to the root directory. The name of the directory (WORD) comes after the root directory name (C:\).

- *Subdirectory*. Subdirectories connect to directories, rather than to the root directory. In the street analogy, subdirectories are roads that feed into the streets that connect directly with Main Street. The name C:\WORD\DOCS consists of a subdirectory named DOCS connected to the directory C:\WORD.

Tree structure
A term applied to hierarchical directories that describes the concept in which directories *belong* to higher directories and *own* lower directories.

The term *tree structure* sometimes is used to describe the organization of files into hierarchical levels of directories. Try picturing the directory structure as an inverted tree as shown in the following figure. In this example, the term *root* stands for the root directory of the directory tree. The *D* markers show directories, and the *S* markers show subdirectories such as C:\WORD\DOCS. Directories and subdirectories have files attached to them like leaves.

5

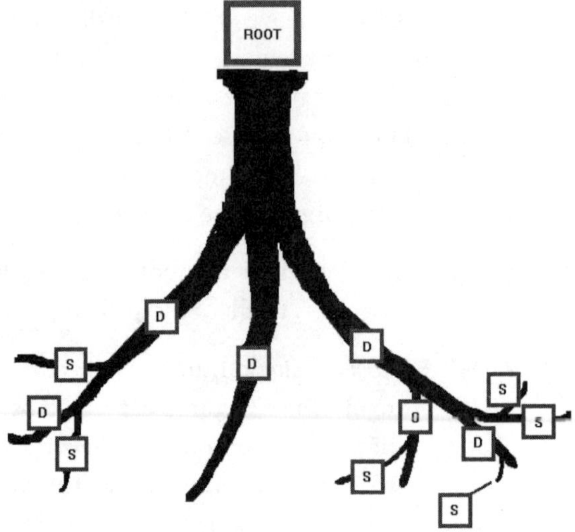

The inverted tree of the DOS directory structure.

Note: *Use the DIR command to obtain a list of files located in a directory or subdirectory. DIR is described in Lesson 2, "Making a Quick Start with DOS 6.2."*

Directories are frequently called *parent directories* and *child directories*. Each child of the parent can have children, or directories, of its own. In the directory hierarchy, each subdirectory's parent is the directory or subdirectory just above it.

Root Directory Capacity

When you format a disk, DOS creates the root directory for that disk. You cannot delete the root directory. The root directory can handle a preset number of files plus directories. The number depends on the disk's capacity. The following table lists the maximum entries (files plus directories) that can be present in the root directory of different capacity disks.

Size	Capacity	Maximum Number of Entries in Root Directory
5 1/4-inch	360K	112 entries
5 1/4-inch	1.2M	224 entries
3 1/2-inch	720K	112 entries
3 1/2-inch	1.4M	224 entries
Hard disks	any	512 entries (typically)

On any type of disk, you can have as many subdirectories as space permits. The only DOS limitation is the number of entries (files plus directories) in the root directory.

Directory Names

The names of directories indicate where you are working in the tree structure. An obvious example is that C:\BOOKS names the BOOKS directory on the C: drive. You should name subdirectories for the type of files they contain so you can remember what type of files each subdirectory contains. When the DOS 6.2 SETUP program installs DOS files, for example, it creates the C:\DOS directory to hold important DOS program files. You might install a word processing program in the directory C:\WORD. And to keep your word processing documents separate, you might want to save them in the subdirectory C:\WORD\DOCS.

Remember that when you are naming directories or subdirectories, the names must conform to the rules for naming DOS files. Directory and subdirectory names can be a maximum of eight characters, then a dot (or period), and then a three-character extension. For example, you can have a directory named C:\TEMP.DOC. But directory names normally do not have extensions because typing directory names with extensions can be confusing.

Directory Tree Display

Knowing the names of the directories and subdirectories on your hard drive is important. If you store data files in a subdirectory but forget the name of the subdirectory, you may have difficulty finding the data files. But you can obtain information about your disk's directories and subdirectories using the DIR command (as described in Lesson 2, "Making a Quick Start with DOS 6.2") or the TREE command (as described in Lesson 3, "Starting DOS"). For example, entering the DIR command when you are in the root directory displays the names of the directories under the root. To view the names of subdirectories under a directory, change to that directory and then enter the DIR command. To see a list of all directories within the current directory, use the TREE command.

Directory Specification Using DOS Commands

Directories do not share information about their contents with other directories, just as file folders hold only the files within them. In a way, each subdirectory acts as a disk within a bigger disk. DOS commands act on the contents of the current directory and leave other directories undisturbed. In other words, when you issue a command that specifies a file but not a directory, DOS looks for that file in the default, or current, directory.

Parameter
An option added to a command that directs DOS to perform the command in a certain way.

You can direct DOS commands to act on files in a directory or subdirectory other than the current directory by entering a path as a command line *parameter* to direct the DOS command to the directory you want to access. For example, regardless of the directory in which you currently are working, you can display the files in the C:\DOS directory by following these steps:

1. Type **DIR C:\DOS**
2. Press Enter.

In this example, you are using a directory name as a *parameter* to the DIR command, causing DOS to act in the specified directory rather than in the current directory.

By using command line parameters with other DOS commands, you can access any point in the tree structure while you remain in the current directory.

Paths and Path Names

Path name
Gives DOS the necessary directions to find the directory that contains the files you want. Also called *path* or *directory specifier.*

A *path name* is a chain of directory names that tells DOS how to find the file you want. In the command DIR C:\DOS, the path name is the command line parameter C:\DOS. The path name specifies to DOS the directory whose files you want the DIR command to affect. Before DOS can locate a file outside the current directory or subdirectory, DOS must know where to find the file.

Path Names and File Names

With most commands, DOS must know not only the path to act upon, but the name of the file. For example, the COPY command requires you to tell DOS the name of the file to copy and the path name of where you want the file copied.

When specifying the file upon which a command is to act, you must use the full file name. For example, to delete a file named APRIL.DOC, you must type the DEL command followed by the full file name, including the extension. The command DEL APRIL deletes only a file named APRIL without any extension. To delete APRIL.DOC, enter the following command:

DEL APRIL.DOC

DOS can be compared to an extremely strict order of command. All communications must go through the correct channels. If you want to act on a file in a subdirectory, you must direct DOS to that file by specifying not only the name of the subdirectory, but also the name of any higher directories. For example, when using a command to act on a file in the DOCS subdirectory of C:\WORD, you must specify the full path name where the file is located: C:\WORD\DOCS.

You can see the use of paths and file names in action by copying the file README.TXT from your DOS directory to your root directory. Follow these steps:

1. Change to your root directory if you are in a directory or subdirectory (type **CD** and press Enter).

2. At the DOS prompt, type the following line:

   COPY C:\DOS\README.TXT

3. Press Enter. DOS displays the following message:

   ```
   1 file(s) copied
   ```

You have copied the file README.TXT to your root directory. You can use the DIR command to confirm that the file copied:

1. Type **DIR** at the DOS prompt.

2. Press Enter.

The directory listing includes a line similar to the following:

```
README    TXT             76,705     09-30-93    6:20a
```

After you have tested the use of directories as parameters to the DIR command, don't forget to delete the unneeded copy of README.TXT from your root directory. Follow these steps:

5

1. At the DOS prompt, type the following line:

   DEL README.TXT

2. Press Enter. DOS deletes the file and returns you to the DOS prompt.

Path Names and Drives

Sometimes when using DOS commands, you must tell DOS not only the file name and directory that contains the file, but also the drive where the file is located. For example, to use the COPY command to copy the file APRIL.DOC from the C:\WORD\DOCS subdirectory to the A: drive, you use the following command:

COPY C:\WORD\DOCS\APRIL.DOC A:

To practice entering drives as parameters to DOS commands, you can copy the file README.TXT to the A: drive. Follow these steps:

1. Place a formatted floppy disk in the A: drive. Close the drive door, if the drive has one.

2. Change to the DOS directory if you are in the root directory or another directory. (Type **CD\DOS** and press Enter. The DOS prompt looks like `C:\DOS>`.)

3. At the DOS prompt, type the following line:

   COPY README.TXT A:

4. Press Enter. DOS displays the following message:

```
1 file(s) copied
```

You have copied the file README.TXT to the disk in your A: drive. You can use the DIR command to confirm that the file copied:

1. Type **DIR A:** at the DOS prompt.

2. Press Enter.

The directory listing includes a line similar to the following:

```
README   TXT        76,705    09-30-93   6:20a
```

Because you copied the file to A:, you have another opportunity to enter drive and path information as a parameter to a DOS command. You can delete the unneeded copy of README.TXT on the A: drive by following these steps:

1. At the DOS prompt, type the following line:

   DEL A:\README.TXT

2. Press Enter. DOS deletes the file and returns you to the DOS prompt.

You have used the path A:\ as a parameter to the DEL command to specify the location of the file on which you wanted the DEL command to act. You also specified the file on which you wanted the DEL command to act when you entered the full file name and extension of README.TXT.

The full drive name, path name, and file name for a file is sometimes known as the *path specifier.* In the command line, you type the disk drive, the directory name(s), and finally, the file name.

Path Names and the Backslash Character

Backslash (\)
The character used in commands to separate directory names from subdirectory names and file names. When used after a drive letter and colon, the backslash signifies the root directory.

The *backslash* (\) character is an important part of every command line that uses a path name. The backslash separates directory names from subdirectory names and also sets off the file name. When you specify a drive at the beginning of a command, a backslash also separates the drive letter and colon from the rest of the command line. (The drive letter, colon, and backslash represent the root directory. For example, C:\ is the root directory of the C: drive.)

To create a complete path name, you separate the following elements with a backslash (\):

- The drive name and colon
- The directory name (or sequence of directory and subdirectory names)
- The file name

For example, to create a complete path name for a file named TEST.DOC in the DOCS subdirectory of the WORD directory, you type the following line:

C:\WORD\DOCS\TEST.DOC

5

Using symbolic notation, the path name looks like the following line:

d:\directory\subdirectory\filename.ext

In this notation, *d:* is the drive letter. If you fail to specify the drive, DOS uses the currently logged drive. The notation *\directory\subdirectory* names the path of directories you want the command to use. You can add other directories to the *\directory\subdirectory* list by separating them with a backslash. If you omit the directory specifier from the path name, DOS assumes that you want to use the current directory.

Assume that a hard drive has a directory named LOTUS with a file named MYFILE.123. The complete path name for the MYFILE.123 file is the chain of directories that tells DOS how to find MYFILE.123. In this case, the chain consists of just two directories: the root (\) and LOTUS. The path name is as follows:

C:\LOTUS\MYFILE.123

The following figure breaks down the parts of the path name for the file MYFILE.123, including the backslashes, a directory name, and a file name. You can use this diagram as a quick reference any time to see the exact way to type the path name to any file.

A breakdown of the full path name for MYFILE.123.

Directory Display Shortcuts

You can save some typing and perhaps some time if you use a path name shortcut. For example, consider the following path name and file name for a budget file you created with the Lotus 1-2-3 spreadsheet program:

C:\LOTUS\DATA\BUDGET.WK3

Suppose that you want to see the directory where this file is stored. You normally use the following command line to give the DIR command its search parameters:

DIR C:\LOTUS\DATA\BUDGET.WK3

DOS begins by searching on the C: drive for the root directory, then it searches for the LOTUS directory, then it searches for the DATA subdirectory, and then it finds the BUDGET.WK3 file.

If you are already in the C:\LOTUS directory, you can save some keystrokes by typing the directory command line this way:

DIR DATA\BUDGET.WK3

Instead of beginning its search at the root directory, DOS begins the search in the current directory, then moves down to the DATA directory, and then moves to the file BUDGET.WK3. Entering the command in this manner works only if the subdirectory you want to search exists in the current directory (or subdirectory). In other words, if you were in the root directory, you would not find the file BUDGET.WK3 by entering this command:

DIR DATA\BUDGET.WK3

If the current directory doesn't lead to the subdirectory that contains the file, the following error message appears on-screen:

```
File not found
```


To find the file BUDGET.WK3, if you were not already in the C:\LOTUS directory, you need to enter the DIR command with the full path name:

DIR C:\LOTUS\DATA\BUDGET.WK3

If you have problems...

If you have problems using drives and directories to specify the location of the file on which you want a DOS command to work, remember the method for entering the path. First you enter the drive and the colon, then a backslash, then the chain of directories and subdirectories where the file is located (separate them with backslashes), and finally the file name and extension of the file on which you want the DOS command to work.

Make sure that you have not mistyped the DOS command you are using. Make sure that you have entered a valid drive letter and you use the colon. Don't forget to separate the directories and subdirectories from the file name using the backslash character. And make sure you have correctly typed the name and extension of the file on which you want the DOS command to operate.

Parent and Child Directories

The terms *parent directory* and *child directory* are sometimes used to refer to directories and subdirectories. Each subdirectory resides within a directory. The directory in which a subdirectory resides is known as the parent. For example, the directory C:\WORD is the parent directory for the subdirectory C:\WORD\DOCS. Of course, the child directory is the subdirectory C:\WORD\DOCS.

You can use a shortcut to move from a child directory back to the parent directory. If you want to move from the C:\WORD\DOCS subdirectory to its parent, C:\WORD, instead of entering the parent directory path as a parameter to the CD command, you can use the following steps:

1. Type the following at the child directory DOS prompt:

   CD ..

   (To type this command correctly, type **CD**, press the spacebar, then type two periods with no spaces between them.)

2. Press Enter. Your current directory now is the parent directory.

If you issue this command when you are in a parent directory, you return to the root directory, which is the parent of all directories on the drive.

This command can save you a lot of time when you are moving around in a complex directory structure.

Planning a Directory Structure

You can arrange your directory structure in a variety of ways. Although you may not know exactly what kind of directory organization you need, now is a good time to give some thought to this structure. This section provides some ideas that may prove useful in organizing your own hard drive. The command used to create directories, MD (Make Directory), is covered in Lesson 2, "Making a Quick Start with DOS 6.2."

Note: *If your computer is part of a network, check with the network administrator before you attempt to create new directories. You may not be able to create new directories because of security precautions on the network. Or you* *may be advised that new directories could interfere with the directory structure used by other people on the network.*

The following figure shows a typical hard drive directory structure. The directories ARCADE, BASH, BSTONE, MAJOR, SHIHDAO, and SIERRA have no subdirectories. Each of these directories contains all the files for the programs stored in the directory. The directory PSTYLER has subdirectories, each of which contains a different component for the program PhotoStyler. Subdirectories directly beneath the PSTYLER directory are COLORS, FILTERS, PALETTES, and PATTERNS. The subdirectory COLORS has subdirectories of its own: HUE, RAINBOW, SPECIAL, and SPREADS. The SHOW directory also has subdirectories, each containing graphics files.

A typical hard drive directory structure.

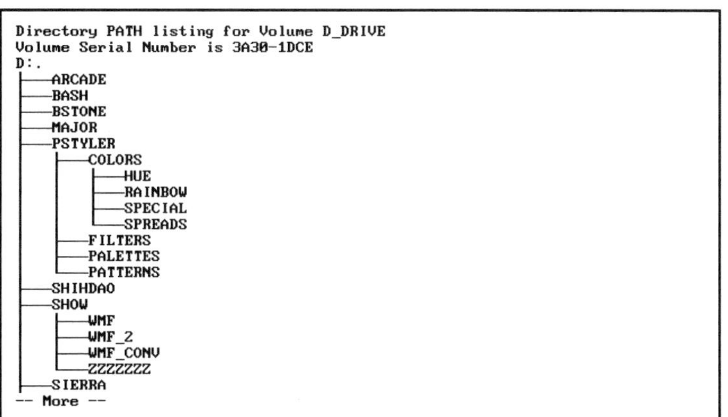

```
Directory PATH listing for Volume D_DRIVE
Volume Serial Number is 3A30-1DCE
D:.
├───ARCADE
├───BASH
├───BSTONE
├───MAJOR
├───PSTYLER
│   ├───COLORS
│   │   ├───HUE
│   │   ├───RAINBOW
│   │   ├───SPECIAL
│   │   └───SPREADS
│   ├───FILTERS
│   ├───PALETTES
│   └───PATTERNS
├───SHIHDAO
├───SHOW
│   ├───WMF
│   ├───WMF_2
│   ├───WMF_CONV
│   └───ZZZZZZZ
├───SIERRA
-- More --
```

Many times, a second level of subdirectories is useful, such as the subdirectories under the PSTYLER\COLORS subdirectory. You may want to group a series of related program directories under one directory name.

Suppose, for example, that you want to group together all the games on your disk into one directory. In the figure example, those files currently are in the directories ARCADE, BASH, BSTONE, MAJOR, SHIHDAO, SIERRA, and WOLF3D. Grouping these directories together as subdirectories of the GAMES directory gives you a listing like the one in the following figure. Such a directory structure would make keeping track of your games much easier.

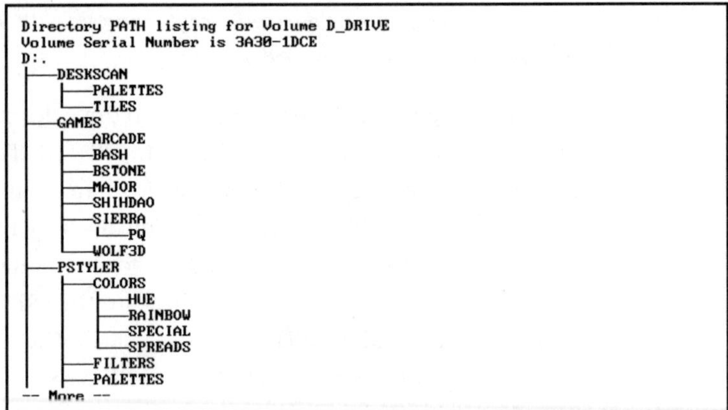

```
Directory PATH listing for Volume D_DRIVE
Volume Serial Number is 3A30-1DCE
D:.
├───DESKSCAN
│   ├───PALETTES
│   └───TILES
├───GAMES
│   ├───ARCADE
│   ├───BASH
│   ├───BSTONE
│   ├───MAJOR
│   ├───SHIHDAO
│   ├───SIERRA
│   │   └───PQ
│   └───WOLF3D
├───PSTYLER
│   ├───COLORS
│   │   ├───HUE
│   │   ├───RAINBOW
│   │   ├───SPECIAL
│   │   └───SPREADS
│   ├───FILTERS
│   ├───PALETTES
-- More --
```

Games installed in subdirectories beneath the GAMES directory.

In addition to grouping similar subdirectories under a main directory, you can organize your hard drive in other useful ways. You can group similar types of files, such as utilities or batch files, into directories that have recognizable names; then you can quickly use the CD command to get to these files. The directory ideas in the following sections can help you build a directory structure that makes sense for the way you use your computer.

Root Directory Files

The root directory is the default directory when you boot your system. Therefore, when you start or reboot your system, DOS presents the `C:\>` prompt (unless you have done some configuration work or altered the look of the DOS prompt).

The root directory of your first hard disk must contain the file COMMAND.COM, which processes commands. COMMAND.COM also must be on the root directory of any floppy disk you use to boot your computer. DOS expects to find COMMAND.COM in the root directory when you boot. If DOS cannot find COMMAND.COM in the root directory, DOS provides a warning message that says it cannot find the command interpreter and halts the system.

In addition to COMMAND.COM, the root directory almost always contains the files AUTOEXEC.BAT and CONFIG.SYS. When you boot the computer, DOS uses these files to set up your system hardware and otherwise configure your system so it runs the way you want. Lesson 11, "Customizing DOS," discusses these files. If you run Windows, you may need the file WINA20.386 in your root directory, as well as the Windows permanent swap file (386SPART.PAR) or temporary swap file (WIN386.SWP). You should find appropriate places for almost all other files in a directory or subdirectory other than the root directory, reserving the root directory for these essential files only.

C:\DOS Files

When you install DOS on your hard disk, the installation procedure creates the C:\DOS directory and copies the DOS files into this directory unless you specify otherwise.

You always should use the C:\DOS or C:\MSDOS directory for your DOS files. Then if your AUTOEXEC.BAT file doesn't set a path to your DOS files or if you use the F5 key to bypass your AUTOEXEC.BAT and CONFIG.SYS files when booting, DOS automatically sets the path to C:\DOS or C:\MSDOS. This feature will not work if you use another directory to store your DOS files. How and why the AUTOEXEC.BAT file sets the path to your DOS files is covered in Lesson 11, "Customizing DOS."

BAT Files

Batch files are text files that contain DOS commands to execute programs. Batch files are programs you can write yourself using a text editor. Most users keep their batch files in a separate \BAT or \BATCH directory. Lesson 11, "Customizing DOS," discusses batch files in more detail.

UTIL or UTILITY Files

Just as you keep all your DOS files in the DOS directory, you may want to keep utility programs in their own directory. Many users accumulate a variety of small utility programs such as a print spooler, file compression utility, disk utilities, and so on, and keep them in the \UTIL or \UTILITY directory. Most people do not like to place these utility programs in the \DOS directory because they do not want to get the two kinds of files mixed up. Also, if you put the utilities in the \DOS directory and later upgrade your version of DOS, the programs may no longer be available.

DATA Files

You probably create many different data files on your computer. Some people create a DATA subdirectory under each program directory. If you have a \LOTUS directory with 1-2-3 program files, for example, you may create a \LOTUS\DATA or \LOTUS\FILES directory for worksheet files.

Other users prefer a different structure. They may create a directory called DATA and then create subdirectories for each project or application. For example, you could put all the files related to your taxes in the \DATA\TAXES subdirectory. If you take a class in finance, you could put all the homework assignments in the subdirectory \DATA\FINCLASS. Or you could create a subdirectory called \DATA\MAY that contains worksheet files and word processing files, all related to activities during the month of May.

If you use a single \DATA directory as described in the preceding paragraph, you can easily back up your data files without also making a backup copy of your application programs. Creating backups is covered in Lesson 12, "Protecting Your PC's Data."

TEMP Files

Many application programs create temporary files and look for a directory named \TEMP in which to store these files. Although some application programs create the \TEMP directory when you run the application's SETUP or INSTALL program, other programs require you to create this directory. Check your software application documentation if you are unsure whether to create the \TEMP directory.

A better idea, however, is to create a \TEMP directory whether or not you know you have an application that needs this directory. Most users find that a directory to store temporary files is useful. You can copy files to \TEMP as a temporary storage place until you copy the files to a more appropriate directory. Do not use the \TEMP directory as a permanent home for a file, however. You should be able to erase all the files in this directory periodically so you can keep the \TEMP directory empty for use with temporary files.

If you are using Microsoft Windows, be careful when using a \TEMP directory. When you install Windows, the setup program creates a directory to store temporary files. The default for this directory is C:\WINDOWS\TEMP. Because Windows uses these files, never delete any files from the Windows temporary directory while Windows is running. If the Windows temporary directory is C:\WINDOWS\TEMP, you can use C:\TEMP for other files without causing any problems. Although the directories both have the name \TEMP, the two directories are unrelated because their full paths are different. If files are in the

C:\WINDOWS\TEMP directory after you exit Windows, you should delete them because they no longer are needed. Over time, unneeded files in the WINDOWS directory can use up valuable space.

Program Directories

Many application programs create their own directory structure when you install them on your hard disk. If a program doesn't create its own directory, or if the program leaves the directory name up to you, you should create a directory name that reminds you of the installed software. For example, if you use Lotus 1-2-3, you might name your spreadsheet directory LOTUS. You then can install 1-2-3's files to that directory.

If you work with multiple versions of the same program or you are upgrading from one version to another, you might keep multiple subdirectories under the main directory for that program. For example, you might add two subdirectories under C:\LOTUS: one directory called 123R24 for the 1-2-3 Release 2.4 program files, and one directory called 123R34 for the 1-2-3 Release 3.4 program files. If you have enough disk space, you should keep the old version and the new version of a program available for a while in case you have problems with the new version.

Task: Removing Unneeded Directories

Sometimes directories and subdirectories outlive their usefulness. Perhaps you no longer need a directory or the files in it. You should remove unused directories and their unneeded files so you don't waste the space on your hard disk. You use the DOS command RD (Remove Directory) to remove directories or subdirectories.

Before you can remove a directory, you first must delete all files from the unwanted directory. If you attempt to remove a directory that still contains files, DOS issues the following error message:

```
Invalid path, not directory,
or directory not empty
```

When you want to delete a single file, like the file NEW.TXT, you can issue the DEL command in the following way:

DEL NEW.TXT

However, if you want to delete *all* the files in a directory in preparation for removing the directory itself, using the DEL command, file by file, can take forever. A better way under these circumstances is to use special *wild-card characters* (instead of a file name) to tell the DEL command to operate on all files in the current directory. To delete all the files in a directory prior to removing the directory, follow these steps:

1. Change to the directory whose files you want to delete.

2. Type **DEL *.*** and press Enter. DOS displays this warning message:

   ```
   All files in directory will be deleted!
   Are you sure (Y/N)?
   ```

3. If you are sure you want to delete all files in the directory (as you must before you can remove the directory itself), type **Y** and press Enter. Otherwise, type **N** and press Enter. (Just pressing Enter causes DOS to redisplay the message.)

   If you press Y, DOS deletes the files. After the deletion process, you return to the DOS prompt in the directory whose files you just deleted.

4. Change to the parent directory of the directory or subdirectory you want to remove. For example, to delete a directory named C:\FILES, return to the root directory with this command:

   CD

   Or to delete a subdirectory named C:\FILES\NEW, return to the directory C:\FILES with this command:

   CD\FILES

5. Type this command to remove the subdirectory NEW from the directory C:\FILES\NEW:

   RD NEW

6. Press Enter.

To remove the directory C:\FILES, use preceding steps 1 through 3 to remove all the files in the directory, then use the following steps:

1. Type **CD**

2. Press Enter.

   You return to the root directory. You must exit a directory before you can remove it.

3. Type the following:

   RD FILES

4. Press Enter.

When you issue the RD command, so long as the directory or subdirectory you are removing contains no files, DOS removes the directory without any warning message.

If you try to use the RD command to remove a directory that has one or more files, or a directory that contains subdirectories, an error message appears, informing you that the directory is not empty. Before you can delete the directory, you must first delete all its files and all its subdirectories.

At times, DOS may not allow you to remove a file, or a file may exist whose name is not even displayed when you use the DIR command. You cannot use the DEL command to delete files whose attributes are Hidden, System, or Read-Only. You must first use the ATTRIB command to change the file's attributes and then use the DEL command to erase the file. Hidden, System, and Read-Only files are covered in Lesson 6, "Maintaining Files."

One helpful shortcut when removing directories is that instead of changing to the directory containing the files you want to delete, you can delete the files from the parent directory or root directory.

For example, from the root directory you can delete all the files in a directory named C:\FILES\NEW by using the following steps:

1. Type the following line:

   DEL FILES\NEW

   This command targets for erasure all files in the directory C:\FILES\NEW.

2. Press Enter. DOS displays this warning message:

```
All files in directory will be deleted!
Are you sure (Y/N)?
```

When you type **Y** for yes, DOS deletes all the files in the directory C:\FILES\NEW.

Caution
Take special care to identify the correct directory when deleting all the files in a directory or subdirectory. Deleting the files in the wrong directory can be a tremendous loss.

You can delete all the files in the C:\FILES directory using the following steps:

1. Type the following line at the DOS prompt:

   DEL FILES

2. Press Enter. DOS displays this warning message:

```
All files in directory will be deleted!
Are you sure (Y/N)?
```

When you type **Y** for yes, DOS deletes all the files in the directory C:\FILES.

If you have problems...

If you have problems with the RD command, make sure that you have removed all files and subdirectories from the directory. You cannot remove a directory without first removing all its files and subdirectories. If you have removed all subdirectories and the DIR command doesn't display any remaining files, refer to Lesson 6, "Maintaining Files," for information on hidden, system, and read-only files.

Make sure that you are properly typing the RD command and the name of the directory you want to remove. If you are trying to remove a directory with an unusual name, like a directory with both a name and an extension, you must type both the name and the extension when using the RD command.

Summary

To	Do This
Create a directory	Use the MD (Make Directory) command
Remove a directory	Use the RD (Remove Directory) command
Switch quickly between directories	Use the parent and child directory shortcuts
Direct DOS to a drive, directory, or file	Type the correct path name
Separate drives, directories, and file names	Use the backslash character
Organize files	Use a logical directory structure

On Your Own

Estimated time: 20 minutes

5

Create and work in a new directory.

1. Create the directory C:\EXAMPLE (be sure you are in the root directory before beginning the MD command).
2. Create the subdirectory C:\EXAMPLE\TEST.
3. Copy the file README.TXT from the C:\DOS directory to the subdirectory C:\EXAMPLE\TEST.
4. Remove the subdirectory C:\EXAMPLE\TEST (remember you must first delete the file README.TXT).
5. Remove the directory C:\EXAMPLE.

Lesson 6

Maintaining Files

Data and programs are stored as files, each with its own name. Over time, you may accumulate hundreds, perhaps thousands, of files. Without tools to manage these files, finding a particular file on your hard drive can become like trying to find your car in a mall parking lot during Christmas shopping season. In this lesson, you learn how to use DOS commands to perform these tasks:

- Copy a file so the copy has a different name than the original
- Copy a file or group of files between directories and disks
- Move files from one directory or drive to another
- Use parameters in the COPY command
- Copy the contents of one disk to another disk and compare them for accuracy
- Erase a file or group of files
- Rename an existing file or group of files

Many of the operations described in this lesson are used most often with floppy disks. As you work with your floppy disks, keep these important rules in mind:

- Always keep the stick-on labels on your disks current. Disks not labeled or labeled incorrectly are an invitation to lost data. If you don't label disks, you may mistake them for blank, unformatted disks.

- Use a felt-tipped pen to write on labels that are affixed to 5 1/4-inch floppy disks; never use a ball point pen. The jacket doesn't keep the pen point from possibly damaging the magnetic media and harming the disk.

Copying and Moving Files

Generally speaking, when you copy a file, you do so for one of several reasons: you need to work on the file on another computer, you want to share the file with another person, you want to make a backup copy to protect the original file, or you want to modify a copy of the original and keep the original intact after making your changes.

You also can use the COPY command to paste several files together to form one file. Pasting different files together is most often termed *combining* files. Using the COPY command to combine files can be somewhat hazardous, so if you want to use this capability, carefully study the information later on the plus (+) parameter.

The MOVE command places a duplicate of the original file in another location and then removes the original file. This command is useful if you decide that a file no longer belongs on a certain disk or in a certain directory and you want to put the file on another disk or drive. Sometimes you may use the MOVE command to put a file on a floppy disk to save as a backup.

Understanding the Principles of COPY and MOVE

Source
The disk or file from which you are copying or moving files.

Destination
The disk or file to which you are copying or moving files. Also known as the *target*.

Copying or moving a file or group of files is a relatively straightforward process. You have a *source* file you select to copy or move, which results in a *destination* file when the operation is complete. The destination is an important concept because when you use the COPY command, not only can you make a duplicate of a file in a different directory or disk, but the duplicate can have a different name.

Copying a file is different from moving a file. Copying a file gives you two identical files, each stored in a different place. The source file remains in its original location, and a duplicate of the file resides in a second location. If you copy the file more than one time, the file can reside in many locations. After you move a file, on the other hand, you still have only one copy of the file, and that copy is placed in the destination directory.

Note: *Avoid having multiple copies of the same file in many locations without a reason. If you have copies of a data file in multiple directories on your hard disk, you may update one copy and leave several out-of-date copies on the disk. Because all files have the same name, you may mistakenly use an old copy rather than an updated one. If you need to save old copies of files, a better method is to move the files to floppy disks.*

Task: Copying Files

One rule of DOS is that no two files in a single directory can have the same name. DOS cannot keep track of two files with identical names, plus you would not know which file contained the information you need.

For example, you cannot have two files named MEMO1229.DOC in the same directory. You can have one file named MEMO1229.DOC and another named MEMO1229.TXT. Although the root name (MEMO1229) is the same, DOS can differentiate between the two files because the file extensions are different; one is DOC and the other is TXT.

When you copy a file to the same directory, you must give the file a different name. Perhaps you have a file called EXPJAN94.WK4 that contains your expenses for January. Now you want to create a file with your expenses for February. If your expenses for each month are quite similar, rather than create a brand new file, you copy the file EXPJAN94.WK4, naming the new file EXPFEB94.WK4. You then can edit EXPFEB94.WK4 for the correct February expenses.

Copying a file or a group of files from one directory to another on a disk is just like copying a file or a group of files from one disk to another. The only difference is that the destination is another directory on the same disk instead of just another disk. Even though the source and destination are on the same disk, you don't need to worry about file names being the same if you copy to a different directory. Different directories on a disk are similar to different houses on the same block. Although each directory is on the same disk, each directory is a separate entity, much as each house has its own address.

Syntax
A symbolic representation of a DOS command and its parameters and switches.

The *syntax* of the COPY command is easy to understand. You issue the command, COPY, and as parameters to the command you name the source file (and the destination file if you want the file renamed during the copy process), and you provide path information so the COPY command knows where to place the copy. The following line shows the basic command syntax for the COPY command:

COPY source destination

Current directory
The directory in which you are currently working.

When you use the COPY command, you must specify both source and destination information. For example, you can copy a file in the *current directory* to the C:\TEMP directory by entering this command line:

COPY MARCH.TXT C:\TEMP

The result in this example is that the source, a file named MARCH.TXT in the current directory, is copied to a file of the same name in the directory C:\TEMP.

You can try the COPY command yourself by following these steps to copy the file README.TXT from the DOS directory to the root directory:

1. Change to the DOS directory (type **CD\DOS** and press Enter if necessary).
2. Enter the following command line:

   COPY README.TXT C:

   The file README.TXT is copied to your root directory. Make sure to delete the file after you have finished with this lesson because you should store only necessary files in the root directory.

If you have problems... If you have problems with the COPY command, refer to Lesson 2, "Making a Quick Start with DOS 6.2," which covers the COPY command in detail.

Task: Moving Files

The basic command syntax of the MOVE command is like the syntax of the COPY command:

MOVE source destination

For example, you can move a file in the current directory to the C:\TEMP directory by entering this command line:

MOVE MARCH.TXT C:\TEMP

In this example, the source is a file named MARCH.TXT in the current directory. As a result of the command, the file moves to the directory C:\TEMP.

You can try the MOVE command by using the copy of README.TXT you made in the root directory in the preceding example. As the target directory for the move, choose your TEMP directory or another directory in which you store temporary files. Follow these steps:

1. Change to the root directory (type **CD** and press Enter if necessary).

2. Enter the following command line:

   MOVE README.TXT C:\TEMP

   If you chose another destination directory, type its path instead of C:\TEMP.

The file README.TXT is moved to your TEMP directory or the directory you typed. You can delete the file after you have finished with this lesson.

If you have problems...

If you have problems with the MOVE command, change to the directory containing the file you want to move. Make sure that you correctly type MOVE at the DOS prompt, then press the space bar one time. Then correctly type the file name and extension of the file you want to move. Then type the target directory.

If you prefer, you can type the correct path information for the file you want to move, rather than changing to the directory containing the file. For example, if you are in the root directory and want to move the file README.TXT from the DOS directory to the TEMP directory, you type the following:

MOVE C:\DOS\README.TXT C:\TEMP

Task: Using COPY Parameters

The following line shows the COPY syntax in more detail, including the optional switches you can use to make the command perform in a specific way:

COPY /Y /-Y /A|/B ***source*** /A|/B + *source2* ***destination*** /A|/B /V

The following list covers each of the command line parameters for the COPY command and provides examples of how you can use these parameters:

Wild cards

The * and ? characters, which you can substitute for parts of a file name or extension.

- **COPY.** Invokes the COPY command.
- ***source.*** The *source* includes all information DOS needs to find the file. Enter the entire file name or use the * or ? *wild cards*. If the file you are copying is not in the current directory, the *source* must include the path to the file you are copying. The following examples show command lines that identify the *source* file to the COPY command:

  COPY MARCH.TXT *destination*

  COPY C:\TEMP\MARCH.TXT *destination*

  COPY MARCH.* *destination*

  In the last example, the asterisk (*) wild card indicates that all files named MARCH are copied. For example, if files named MARCH.TXT, MARCH.DOC, MARCH.RPT, and MARCH.MEM were all located in the current directory, all would be copied to the destination directory.

- ***destination.*** The *destination* must include all information DOS needs to put the file where you want it. If you are not placing the destination file in the current directory, the *destination* must include the path where you want the file to be copied. If you want the copy (the destination file) to have a different name than the original (the source file), you must specify the new name. If you do not specify a new name, the COPY command names the copy with the same name as the original. The following examples show command lines that identify the destination file to the COPY command:

COPY MARCH.TXT C:\SAVE

COPY MARCH.TXT MARCHOLD.TXT

COPY MARCH.TXT C:\SAVE\MARCHOLD.TXT

In the second example, MARCH.TXT is copied to the same directory, but the COPY command renames the copy with the name MARCHOLD.TXT. In the third example, the source file is copied to the directory C:\SAVE and the destination file is given the name MARCHOLD.TXT.

If you fail to specify both the source file and the destination or you attempt to copy a file to the same directory and give the file the same name as the source, the following error message appears:

```
File cannot be copied onto itself
0 file(s) copied
```

If you receive this error message, take a moment to think through what you want to do. Make sure that you know not only the source file but also the destination (where you want to copy the file and the name you want it to have). Then try the COPY command again with the proper command line parameters for source and destination.

- **+.** The plus sign (+) directs the COPY command to combine the files before and after the plus sign. In other words, if you invoke the COPY command with the following parameter, COPY combines the two files:

  COPY *file1.txt* + *file2.txt*

  When you use the plus sign in this way, the combined file has the same name as the first file. The combined file replaces the first file in the list.

You can specify a name for the combined file that is different from the first file's name, as the following example shows:

COPY *file1.txt* + *file2.txt* REPORT.TXT

The preceding command line creates the file REPORT.TXT by combining the two files *file1.txt* and *file2.txt*. The original first and second files remain unmodified on your disk.

Note: *Do not try to use the same name for a combined file as the second file in the list. Do not attempt to use the COPY command, for example, in the following way:*

COPY file1.txt + file2.txt file2.txt

Overwrite
To replace a file with a new file of the same name, writing over the old information so it cannot be recovered.

If you use file2.txt *as the name for the combined file, DOS* overwrites *the original* file2.txt *before the combine operation is complete, destroying the contents of* file2.txt. *The combined file must have either the same name as the first file in the list (*file1.txt *in this example) or a unique name.*

- /Y. This switch directs the COPY command to replace the existing file *without* prompting you for confirmation if the target directory contains a file of the same name. Unless you use this switch, specifying an existing file as the destination file causes COPY to ask if you want to overwrite the original.

- /-Y. This switch directs the COPY command to prompt you for confirmation before replacing an existing file. Use this switch if you have set the COPYCMD environment variable to automatically overwrite destination files (the COPYCMD environment variable is covered later in this section).

- /A. The /A switch indicates the file you are copying is an ASCII text file. In other words, the file contains no programming code or other binary information. By default, the COPY command treats files as ASCII text.

Placing the /A switch properly in the command line is very important. For example, if you place the /A switch following the source file name, the COPY command copies data that precedes the first end-of-file character but not the first end-of-file character or the remainder of the file. Because a file may have a stray end-of-file marker, the COPY process may copy only part of the file if you place the /A switch following the source file name. A more common use of the /A switch is to place it following the destination file name. That way, the COPY command copies all data in the file and then places an end-of-file marker at the end of the copied file.

- /B. The /B switch indicates the file you are copying is a binary file: it is programming code or contains other program instructions. The placement of the /B switch also is important. When you place the /B switch after the source file name, the COPY command copies the entire file, including any end-of-file character. When the /B switch follows the destination file name, COPY does not add an end-of-file character. The /B parameter causes COMMAND.COM to read the entire file, regardless of whether it contains an end-of-file marker.

  As if the rules for use of the /A and /B switches aren't complicated enough, still more rules apply when using the COPY command to combine files.

  When you place the /A switch on the command line prior to a list of file names to be combined, all files are treated as ASCII text files until the COPY command encounters a /B switch on the command line. Then the one file name *before* the /B switch is treated as a binary file. When the /A switch follows a file name in a list of file names to be combined, /A applies to the file *before* the /A switch and to all files *after* the /A switch until COPY encounters a /B switch. Then the /B switch applies to the one file *before* the /B switch.

- /V. The /V switch checks the source and destination files to ensure that they are identical after the COPY function is complete.

If you have problems...

If you have problems using the COPY command to combine two or more text files, try to keep the operation simple. Copy or move the files you want to combine into the current directory. Then decide which file you want at the beginning of the combined file, which file you want second in the combined file, and which file you want next. Use the following example as a guide in typing the command line:

COPY *file1.txt* + *file2.txt* + *file3.txt* COMBINED.TXT

Make sure that you press the space bar after typing COPY. Then correctly type the name of the first file you want to combine. Press the space bar. Type the + symbol. Press the space bar (and so on until all files are listed). After all files are listed, press the space bar and type the name you want to give the combined file.

The first few times you try to combine files, use the name COMBINED.TXT for the combined file so you don't risk overwriting or modifying any of the original files you are combining.

Task: Setting the COPYCMD Environment Variable

Environment variable
Information stored in the memory used by DOS that provides direction to a command on how to perform.

You can set the COPYCMD *environment variable* to customize the way the COPY command works when the command encounters a file with the same name you have specified for the destination file. By default, the COPY command warns you before overwriting a file with the same name as the file you are copying. You can set the COPYCMD environment variable so the COPY command never warns you before overwriting a file of the same name. To use this capability, type the following line in your AUTOEXEC.BAT file:

SET COPYCMD=/Y

Lesson 11, "Customizing DOS," covers editing the AUTOEXEC.BAT file. If you are a newcomer to DOS, refer to Lesson 11 before you attempt to use this environment variable or any other.

Copying Disks with DISKCOPY

You may encounter a number of situations where you want to make an exact copy of a floppy disk to another floppy disk. A common reason to copy disks is to make a backup copy of the installation disks for a newly purchased software application.

Note: *Never install software using the original disks. Always make backup copies of the disks and use the copies to install the software. Then your original disks are safe. If the installation copy becomes damaged, you can make a new installation copy from the original disks.*

You use the DOS command DISKCOPY to make a duplicate of a floppy disk. This command is much better than attempting to use the COPY command for this purpose.

The syntax of the DISKCOPY command is easy to understand:

DISKCOPY *source destination*

When you are using the DISKCOPY command, both the *source* and the *destination* refer to drive letters. The most important rule when you use the DISKCOPY command is that the floppy disk from which you are copying must be the same size and density as the disk to which you are copying. For example, you can duplicate a 360K 5 1/4-inch disk only onto a 360K 5 1/4-inch disk. You cannot make a copy of a 360K disk onto a 1.2M disk using DISKCOPY.

Note: *When you use DISKCOPY, any files on the destination disk are lost. So before you use the destination disk, make sure it does not contain valuable files.*

You can use DISKCOPY to duplicate a disk whether you have one floppy drive or two. DISKCOPY can duplicate a disk from one drive (A:, for example) to another drive (B:, for example) if both drives are the same size and handle the same density disks. Or DISKCOPY can copy the disk using a single drive (A:, for example).

Four types of floppy disk drives are commonly used:

- Low-capacity 5 1/4-inch drives (360K)
- High-capacity 5 1/4-inch drives (1.2M)
- Low-capacity 3 1/2-inch drives (720K)
- High-capacity 3 1/2-inch drives (1.44M)

High-capacity 5 1/4-inch drives (1.2M) can read and write 360K disks, but 360K drives cannot read or write 1.2M disks. Likewise, high-capacity 3 1/2-inch drives can read and write 720K disks, but 720K drives cannot read or write 1.44M disks.

Because of these limitations, you cannot use DISKCOPY to duplicate a 1.2M disk in a 360K drive, and you cannot use the command to duplicate a 1.44M disk in a 720K drive. In addition, you cannot use DISKCOPY to copy a disk in a 5 1/4-inch drive to a disk in a 3 1/2-inch drive, or vice versa.

Caution
If you duplicate a 360K disk in a 1.2M drive, you may not be able to read the duplicate in a 360K drive.

You can, however, use DISKCOPY to copy a 360K disk in a 1.2M drive, or a 720K disk in a 1.44M drive, because high-capacity drives are designed to handle lower-density disks of the same size.

When you run DISKCOPY, if the command detects drives or disks that are incompatible, the following error message appears and the copy operation stops:

```
Drive types or diskette types not compatible

Copy process ended

Copy another diskette (Y/N)?
```

The next section covers the process for duplicating a disk when you have two floppy drives that handle disks of the same size and density. The subsequent section covers using DISKCOPY to duplicate a disk when you have only one floppy drive or when you have two floppy drives but one is a 3 1/2-inch drive and the other is a 5 1/4-inch drive.

Task: Copying Disks Using Two Floppy Drives

If your system has two floppy drives the same size, you may be able to use both drives at the same time when running DISKCOPY. Using both drives depends on whether they are of the same density, for example, high-density. In such a case, using both drives at the same time speeds up the DISKCOPY process somewhat.

However, if you have a high-density and a low-density drive of the same size, you can use both drives at the same time only to duplicate lower-density disks. When using 5 1/4-inch 1.2M and 360K drives at the same time to run DISKCOPY, use the lower-capacity drive (the 360K drive) as the target drive. This procedure is not a DOS requirement, but if you use the high-capacity drive as the target drive, the disk may not be readable on some low-capacity drives on other computers.

If you have two drives the same size, you can copy a disk, based on the preceding requirements. The following example duplicates a disk in the A: drive (the source drive) to a disk in the B: drive (the target drive). You may need to substitute the correct letters for your drives.

1. Insert your source disk into the A: drive and a destination disk into the B: drive. Remember that DISKCOPY will overwrite any data on the destination disk. If the destination disk is not formatted, DOS will format the disk then continue the DISKCOPY operation.

2. At the prompt, type the following command:

   DISKCOPY A: B:

3. Press Enter.

   The following read out appears:

   ```
   Insert SOURCE diskette in drive A:

   Insert TARGET diskette in drive B:

   Press any key to continue . . .
   ```

4. Press any key.

   DISKCOPY reads the source disk to determine its density and produces a read out similar to the following:

   ```
   Copying 80 tracks, 15 sectors per track, 2 side(s)

   Reading from source diskette . . .
   ```

   After reading the entire disk, DISKCOPY begins the process of duplicating the source disk onto the destination disk. After the copy process is finished, the following message appears:

   ```
   Do you wish to write another duplicate of this disk (Y/N)?
   ```

5. To make another copy of the same disk, press **Y** for yes. If you do not want to make another copy of the disk, press **N** for no.

   After you finish making the copies you want of that disk, the COPY command displays the following message:

   ```
   Copy another diskette (Y/N)?
   ```

6. If you want to copy another disk, press **Y** for yes. (You will want to copy additional disks if, for example, you are making backup copies of a set of installation disks.) If you do not want to make additional copies, press **N** for no. The copy operation terminates.

If you have problems...

If you have problems using DISKCOPY to copy disks on a system with two drives, make sure that the drives are the same size (5 1/4- or 3 1/2-inch). Then make sure that the source disk and the target disk are the same density. Remember that you cannot use DISKCOPY to duplicate a 1.2M disk in a 360K drive, and you cannot use the command to duplicate a 1.44M disk in a 720K drive. In addition, you cannot use DISKCOPY to copy a disk in a 5 1/4-inch drive to a disk in a 3 1/2-inch drive, or vice versa.

Task: Copying Disks Using One Floppy Drive

This section covers using the DISKCOPY command when you must use a single floppy drive as both the source drive and target drive. When you use DISKCOPY to duplicate a disk using a single drive, DISKCOPY first reads the data on the disk from which you want to copy, then DISKCOPY prompts you to remove the original disk and insert the disk to which you want to copy.

You need to use a single drive as both the source and the target under these circumstances:

- You have only one floppy drive and want to duplicate a disk.
- You have two floppy drives but one is a 3 1/2-inch drive and the other is a 5 1/4-inch.
- You have two floppy drives of the same size, but one is a high-density drive and the other is a lower-density drive, and you want to duplicate a high-density disk.

Note: *Before using DISKCOPY to duplicate a disk using a single floppy drive, make sure that you write-protect the source disk. Then if you accidentally insert the source disk into the target drive, DISKCOPY will not overwrite your data. For information on write-protecting floppy disks, refer to Lesson 7, "Formatting Disks."*

When you need to use the same drive as both the source drive and the target drive, you specify the same drive letter as both the source and target drive. The following example shows you how to copy a disk of the same size and density using one floppy drive (the A: drive). You can substitute B: if that is the drive you are using.

1. Insert your source disk into the A: drive.
2. At the prompt, type the following command:

   COPY A: A:

3. Press Enter.

   DISKCOPY begins the copy process and produces the same read outs described in the preceding section. But after DISKCOPY finishes reading the data on the source disk, the following message appears:

   ```
   Insert TARGET diskette in drive A:

   Press any key to continue . . .
   ```

4. Take the source disk out of the drive and replace it with a disk onto which you want the data copied. Remember that DISKCOPY will overwrite any data on the destination disk. If the destination disk is not formatted, DOS will format the disk then continue with the DISKCOPY operation.
5. Press any key.

   When the duplication process is complete, DISKCOPY first asks whether you want to make another copy of the same disk and then whether you want to copy another disk.

6. To terminate the duplication process, press **N** for no at both prompts.

In versions of DOS before 6.2, DISKCOPY required you to swap disks several times when you used one drive to duplicate a disk. First you inserted the source disk, then the target disk, then you again inserted the source and finally the target again. However, DOS 6.2 performs the DISKCOPY process in one pass, which means that you do not remove the source disk from the drive until DISKCOPY has read the entire disk and is ready to write to the target disk.

If you have problems...

If you have problems using DISKCOPY to duplicate a disk using one drive, make sure that the source disk and the destination disk are of the same capacity. Make sure that you insert the source disk then correctly type DISKCOPY A: A: (if you are using the A: drive) or DISKCOPY B: B: (for the B: drive). After you type the source drive designator (A: or B:), press the space bar before typing the destination drive designator.

Verifying the Copy

Many times the disks you copy contain very important information. For example, your disk may contain documents concerning the incorporation of your business. When copying this disk, you want to be sure that the copy is as accurate as possible. You can instruct DISKCOPY to verify the copy, ensuring that the contents of the disk are protected. When you invoke the DISKCOPY command, simply add the /V switch, as the following command line shows:

```
DISKCOPY A: A: /V
```

Deleting Files

When you no longer need a file, you can remove the file from the disk. Erasing old files you no longer use is good computer housekeeping. Free space on disks, especially hard disks, gets scarce if you do not erase unneeded files. Deleting individual files is not a difficult task; the basics are covered in Lesson 2, "Making a Quick Start with DOS 6.2." This section briefly describes deleting groups of files.

Note: *Although this section describes the use of the DEL command, the syntax and use of the ERASE command is identical. If you prefer the ERASE command, invoke that command with the command line parameters shown in this section. The result is the same—unwanted files are deleted.*

Deleting Groups of Files with Wild Cards

You sometimes may want to delete groups of files from your hard drive to gain free space. For example, suppose that you have made backup copies of your 1992 reports and want to keep only 1993 and 1994 reports on disk. As long as the file names of the 1992 reports are different from the file names of the 1993 and 1994 reports, you can use wild cards to easily delete the unwanted documents.

For example, you may name reports with extensions like 92 for 1992 reports, 93 for 1993 reports, and 94 for 1994 reports. Using such a naming system allows you to give files quite descriptive names like 05.92 for the May 1992 report, 11.93 for the November 1993 report, and 02.94 for the February 1994 report. With file names like these, deleting just the 1992 reports is an easy matter.

Typing the following command deletes only the 1992 reports in the current directory:

```
DEL *.92
```

Suppose that you keep notes with the extension TXT along with README.TXT and other TXT files on your drive, but you decide you need to free up that space. Make a backup copy of all the files you may need later and use the following command line to delete the TXT files in the current directory:

```
DEL *.TXT
```

If you have problems...

If you have problems deleting groups of files using wild cards, make sure that you are attempting to delete files with names or extensions that are similar to one another, but different from the files you do not want to delete. For example, you can delete all files with the extension 92 by using DEL *.92. But if all files have an extension like TXT, you cannot use broadly acting wild cards. If you want to delete all files with MARCH in their file name, you can use DEL MARCH*.*.

If the files you want to delete do *not* have names or extensions that are similar to one another, but different from the files you want to keep, do not use wild cards with the DEL command. Delete the unwanted files one at a time.

Removing an Entire Directory of Files

If you decide to remove an entire directory of files, make a backup copy of the files you may need later. Then rather than changing to the directory you want to remove and issuing the command DEL *.*, change to its parent directory and enter the DEL command followed by the name of the directory you want to remove.

For example, to delete the files in the C:\TEMP directory prior to removing the directory, you use the following command line from the root directory:

```
DEL TEMP
```

The DEL command produces the following warning message:

```
All files in directory will be deleted!

Are you sure (Y/N)?
```

If you want the files deleted, press **Y** for yes. If you made a mistake and do not want the files deleted, press **N** for no.

After you have used the DEL command to clean out the directory you want to remove, use the RD (remove directory) command to complete your housekeeping task.

Renaming Files

From time to time, you may want to rename a file. If you created a file with the wrong name—such as TAXAS.WK4 rather than TAXES.WK4—you can rename the file to correct the spelling.

Suppose that you have a file called BUDGET.DOC that contains information about your current household budget. At the end of 1993, you want to start a new budget called BUDGET.DOC for 1994. You cannot have two files with the same name in the same directory, so you rename BUDGET.DOC to BUDGET93.DOC.

You use the REN command to rename files; its syntax is shown in the following line:

REN *d:path****source destination***

When you use the REN command, the *source* is the file name that already exists. The destination is the file name to which you want to rename the file. You do not need to specify a path if the file you are renaming is in the current directory. The following line is an example of renaming the file TAXAS.WK1 to TAXES.WK1:

REN TAXAS.WK1 TAXES.WK1

You can try the REN command by changing to your DOS directory and renaming the file README.TXT. Use the following steps:

1. Type the following command:

   REN README.TXT TEST.TXT

2. Press Enter.

The file README.TXT is renamed TEST.TXT. Remember to change the name back to README.TXT so you can find the file when you want it later.

Renaming a Directory

If you want to rename a directory, the REN command is useless. Instead, you use the MOVE command, with the following syntax:

MOVE *olddirectory newdirectory*

For example, to rename the directory C:\TEMP to C:\OLD, you enter the following command line:

MOVE C:\TEMP C:\OLD

The MOVE command renames the directory. The directory C:\TEMP no longer exists on the drive and the newly created directory C:\OLD now contains the files once stored in C:\TEMP.

Summary

To	Do This
Copy a file	Use the COPY command
Move a file	Use the MOVE command
Combine files	Use the COPY command with the plus (+) sign
Duplicate a disk	Use the DISKCOPY command
Delete a file	Use the DEL or ERASE command
Rename a file	Use the REN command
Rename a directory	Use the MOVE command

On Your Own

Estimated time: 5 minutes

Use commands with the README.TXT file.

1. Copy the file README.TXT from your \DOS directory to another directory on your system, for example, the C:\TEMP directory if you have one.
2. Change to the directory where you copied README.TXT and rename the file README1.TXT.
3. Move the file README1.TXT to your \DOS directory.
4. Delete the file README1.TXT from your \DOS directory.

Duplicate a floppy disk.

1. Write-protect a floppy disk to safeguard the contents against overwriting or mistaken reformatting.
2. Use DISKCOPY to make a duplicate of the write-protected floppy disk (remember that the target disk must not contain information you need to keep).

Part III
Using DOS Commands

Lesson 7

Formatting Disks

Before you can use a floppy disk, you must prepare it to receive data. This preparation is known as *formatting* the disk. This lesson teaches you how to format any DOS disk, hard or floppy, although you will not need to format a hard disk unless you install a new one that is fresh from the factory or you have a very serious problem with your computer. Therefore, this lesson focuses on floppy disks and helps you do the following tasks:

- Format different types of floppy disks
- Assign volume labels
- Transfer system files
- Understand the DOS safe format feature
- Use the quick format option
- Understand FORMAT command error messages
- Use the UNFORMAT command

Understanding Floppy Disks

Format
Initial preparation of a disk for data storage.

A floppy disk is a plastic disk in a plastic dust cover. The disk is covered with magnetic material similar to the metallic coating on recording tape. When you take them out of the box, disks usually aren't ready for you to use. You must *format* them first. Some stores carry preformatted disks that are ready for use, but they usually cost more. Your computer cannot use a disk until it is formatted.

The DOS FORMAT command prepares floppy disks to receive data. You enter the proper command line information, and FORMAT analyzes the disk for defects, creates a root directory, sets up a storage table (called a *file allocation table*), and alters other parts of the disk. You can compare formatted disks to the kind of paper that is divided into a grid, with horizontal lines subdivided by vertical lines (see following figure).

Paper divided into a grid.

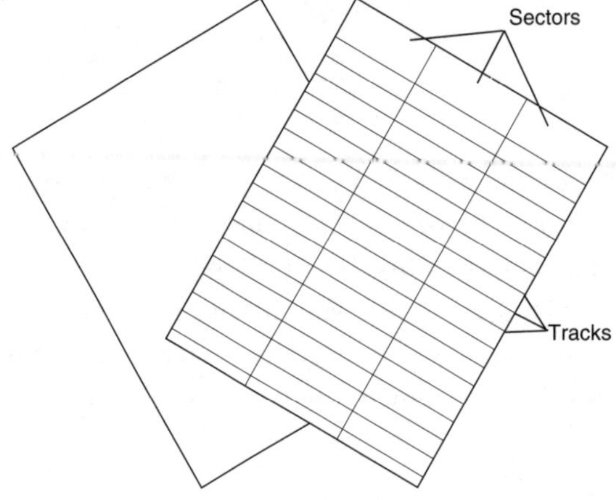

Track
A circular section of a disk's surface that holds data.

Sector
A sector of a track that acts as the disk's smallest storage unit.

Just as the gridlines on paper serve as guides for a writer, tracks and sectors on a disk are guides for the computer to store data. Because the storage medium of a spinning disk is circular, the premarked lines, or magnetic divisions called *tracks*, are placed in concentric circles. These tracks are further subdivided into areas called *sectors*. The following figure shows the tracks and sectors on a floppy disk after the FORMAT command has prepared the disk for use. After the disk is formatted, DOS stores data in these sectors and uses both the track and sector numbers to find and retrieve information.

The tracks and sectors on a floppy disk.

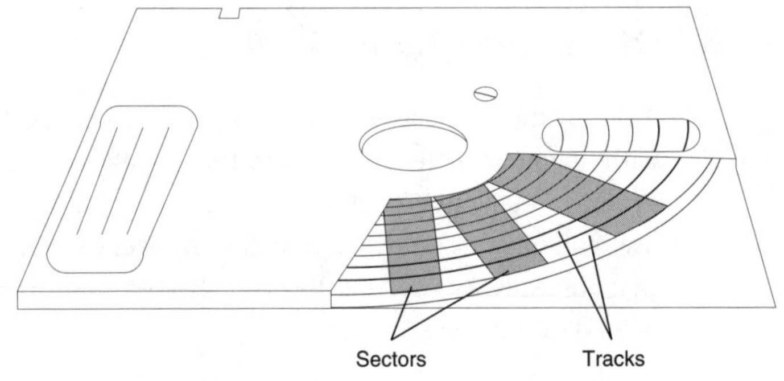

Properly formatting a floppy disk depends on the use of the proper parameters when you issue the FORMAT command. When you have entered the command properly, DOS positions the tracks and sectors correctly for the drive type you have and the capacity of the disk you are formatting.

Understanding Floppy Disk Types

Before you can buy the right disks for your computer, you must understand the different types of floppy disks available. Disks are described in many different ways. The information in the following sections helps you understand how to buy the different types of disks you may need.

Disk Size

Determining the disk size is the easy part of understanding floppy disks. Two sizes of floppy disks are available: 5 1/4-inch and 3 1/2-inch. The larger disks were available first and are more common. The smaller disks have a higher capacity, have rigid cases that protect the disk from damage, and are more reliable.

The size of the disks is clearly marked on the box and is easy to determine from the size of the box itself. You can use a 5 1/4-inch disk only if you have a 5 1/4-inch drive installed in your computer system. A 3 1\2-inch disk will fit only in a 3 1\2-inch drive.

Disk Capacity

Over the years, the maximum capacity of floppy disks has increased steadily. In 1981, a 5 1/4-inch floppy disk could hold 160K (kilobytes). Today, 360K, 720K, 1.2M (megabyte), and 1.44M disks are common, and 2.88M floppy disks are available.

Before you can use a disk of a particular capacity, your computer system must have a drive designed to handle that capacity disk. For example, you cannot use 2.88M disks in a computer with only 1.44M disk drives. The following table shows the capacities of 5 1\4-inch and 3 1\2-inch disks.

Disk Type	Sectors per Track	Tracks per Side	Capacity
5 1/4-inch Double-density	9	40	360K

7

Disk Type	Sectors per Track	Tracks per Side	Capacity
High-density	15	80	1.2M
3 1/2-inch Double-density	9	80	720K
High-density	18	80	1.44M
Extra-high density	36	80	2.88M

As long as you know the size and capacity of the floppy drive installed in your computer system, you can buy double-density, high-density, or extra high-density floppy disks for your machine. Just remember, you cannot use a 1.2M disk in a floppy drive with a maximum capacity of 360K. Likewise, you cannot use a 1.44M disk in a drive with a maximum capacity of 720K.

Double-sided
Floppy disks with storage capacity on both sides of the disk.

The term *double-sided* on a box of floppy disks means that the disks have tracks on both sides of the disk and, therefore, have twice the capacity of single-sided disks. Only double-sided disks are used in today's PCs. However, you can still find *single-sided floppy disks.* Some computer stores sell single-sided disks for very old computers. When you buy floppy disks, the box should be labeled *double-sided, two-sided, 2S,* or *DS.*

Make sure that you label every new floppy disk with its capacity before you use it the first time. That way, you will not later confuse a 1.2M 5 1/4-inch floppy as a 360K disk. However, the following explanation may help you sort out the capacity of different floppy disks if you did not label their capacity:

- **5 1/4-inch floppies.** 360K 5 1/4-inch floppies generally have a special ring on the disk itself that is used to help the drive mechanism center and grasp the disk. This ring is located around the hole in the center of the disk. 5 1/4-inch disks without this ring generally have a capacity of 1.2M.
- **3 1/2-inch floppies.** 1.44M 3 1/2-inch floppies have a special hole in the upper left corner, opposite the write-protect window. 3 1/2-inch floppies without this hole generally have a capacity of 720K.

Double-density Floppy disks with 360K or 720K of storage capacity.

High-density Floppy disks with 1.2M or 1.44M of storage capacity.

Extra high-density Floppy disks with 2.88M of storage capacity.

Floppy disks also come in different *densities—double-density, high-density,* or *extra high-density*. The density is a measure of how closely the bytes of information are placed on the disk. Single-density disks have never been used in PCs, but they have been used in older types of computers. Double-density disks usually are labeled *DD* or *2DD* (the *2* means double-sided), and high-density disks are labeled *HD* or *2HD*. Extra-high density disks are labeled *EHD* or Extra High-Density.

The box for 720K disks often is labeled *1M*, and 1.44M disks often are labeled *2M*. These numbers refer to the unformatted capacity of the disk and, unfortunately, such labeling merely helps create confusion about floppy disks. When you format a disk labeled 1M, it can hold 720K of data, and when you format a disk labeled 2M, it can hold 1.44M of data.

If you remember that you need to buy the proper disks for the capacity of your drive, and that you can find the capacity of your drive in your computer owner's manual, you don't need to remember all this information about floppy disks because the computer and DOS handle this information for you.

Matching Disks and Drives

Just as different types of floppy disks exist, different types of disk drives exist. The most obvious difference is the disk drive size. Drives can be either 5 1/4-inch or 3 1/2-inch. If you have only a 5 1/4-inch drive (or two of them), you cannot use 3 1/2-inch floppy disks, and vice versa. If you are lucky enough to have one drive of each size, you can read both sizes of disks.

Size is not the only consideration, however. Disk drives also have a maximum capacity. A 5 1/4-inch drive may be a standard (360K) drive or a high-capacity (1.2M) drive. A 1.2M drive can read and write 360K disks, but a 360K drive cannot read or write 1.2M disks. The 1.2M floppy disks fit in the drive, but you cannot use them.

Although you can use 360K floppy disks in 1.2M drives, the results can be unreliable at times. If you write to a 360K disk in a 1.2M drive, you should have no trouble reading that disk in the same drive. You may, however, have trouble reading the disk in a 360K drive. This problem occurs more often with older drives.

Keep this point in mind if you copy files onto a floppy disk to be read by another computer. The answer often is to format the disk in the system with the 360K floppy drive and then use the system with the 1.2M drive to copy the files onto the disk. You then should be able to read the files in the system with the 360K drive. Be forewarned that this little trick doesn't always work.

Just as you cannot read or write 1.2M disks in a 360K capacity 5 1/4-inch drive, you cannot use 3 1/2-inch 1.44M disks in a 720K capacity drive. If you have 1.44M drives, you can use both types of 3 1/2-inch floppy disks.

Formatting Floppy Disks

Formatting clears all information that a disk contains. When you format a new disk, of course, it contains no information, and therefore you need not worry. However, if you format a disk you used earlier, everything stored on that disk disappears. Be careful not to format disks that contain files you want to keep. Before you format a previously used disk, use the DIR command to check the list of files on the disk to ensure that you do not need to keep those files. Also be sure to put a label on your floppy disks with information about the disk's contents to safeguard against formatting a disk whose contents you may need later.

Note: *If you have two floppy drives, A: and B:, you can format disks in either drive; just remember not to insert a 3 1/2-inch disk in a 5 1/4-inch drive.*

Formatting disks takes time, so you may want to put some type of indicator on formatted disks to avoid mistaking them for unformatted disks. The indicator may be as simple as a dot, a check mark, or the letter *F* for *formatted*. When you buy floppy disks, adhesive labels are included. An easy method to keep track of formatted disks is to put a label on each disk that you format. Then you know that a disk without a label has never been formatted.

Note: *Never use a ballpoint pen or a pencil to write on labels already attached to floppy disks. Instead use a felt-tip pen. Pressing down too hard on a floppy disk label with a sharp pen or pencil can mangle the fragile disk, destroying any data already on the disk or rendering the disk useless for storing new data.*

Write-Protecting Disks

Write-protect
Protects the data on a floppy disk from being altered.

An important precaution to take with disks that hold important information is to *write-protect* them. This basic step keeps the FORMAT command from working on the disk and makes sure that you cannot copy new information to the disk. The way you write-protect 5 1/4-inch disks is different from the way you write-protect 3 1/2-inch disks:

- With a 5 1/4-inch disk, put a tape tab over the notch on the upper right corner of the disks dust cover. Usually when you buy 5 1/4-inch disks, the box contains tape tabs you can use for this purpose. Be careful when handling the floppy not to touch the shiny plastic disk inside the dust cover. The dust cover is the plastic material that covers the shiny disk itself. (Most disks are also enclosed in *dust jackets*, which are like envelopes that cover about half the disks dust cover.) The next figure shows a 5 1/4-inch floppy disk.

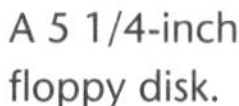

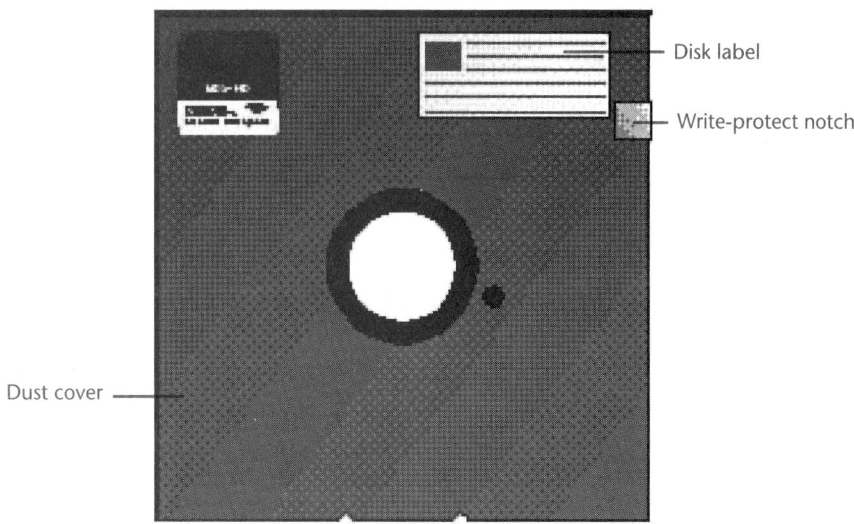

A 5 1/4-inch floppy disk.

- The 3 1/2-inch disks have a write-protect window with a sliding switch, rather than a notch, in the disk's upper right corner. To write-protect the disk, you slide the switch up so the window is open. When the window is closed, the disk is not write-protected and you can format the disk or copy data to it. The following figure shows a 3 1/2-inch floppy disk with its write-protect switch, disk label, and dust cover identified.

A 3 1/2-inch floppy disk.

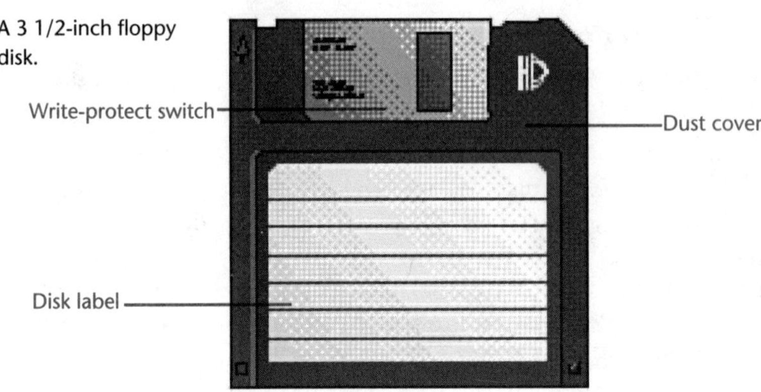

Understanding the Format Command Syntax

Volume label
An electronic label on the disk that identifies that particular disk when you use the DIR command.

The FORMAT command syntax is included in this section so you know what it is. But following sections show you in a much simpler way how to format each type of disk and how to format disks in different capacity drives. The following lines show the syntax of the FORMAT command:

FORMAT *drive*: /V:*label* /Q /U /F:*size* /B /S /C

FORMAT *drive*: /V:*label* /Q /U /T:*tracks* /N:*sectors* /B /S /C

FORMAT *drive*: /V:*label* /Q /U /1 /4 /B /S /C

FORMAT *drive*: /V:*label* /Q /U /1 /4 /8 /B /S /C

The following table describes the meaning of each of the parameters to the FORMAT command.

Parameter	Use
drive:	The drive containing the disk you want to format. If you fail to specify the drive to be formatted, the FORMAT command produces the error message `Required parameter missing -`.
/V:label	Adds the volume label you want encoded on the disk. You can view the volume label when you use the DIR command. A volume label can be a title or description of the files the disk contains. A volume label can contain as many as 11 characters. You can use the following characters in any order: ■ Letters A to Z in uppercase or lowercase ■ Numbers 0 to 9 ■ These special characters and symbols: ~ ! @ # $ ^ & ( ) - _ { } '

Parameter	Use
	If you try to enter too many characters, you hear a beep after the 11th character. If you enter an illegal character, you see an error message and a prompt to enter the volume label again. If you don't want to name the disk, press Enter without typing a name.
/Q	Performs a quick format. The quick format is covered later in this lesson.
/U	Performs an unconditional format. The unconditional format is covered later in this lesson.
/F:*size*	Specifies the size (or capacity) of the floppy disk to be formatted. Choices are 160, 180, 320, 360, 720, 1.2 (or 1220), 1.44 (or 1440), and 2.88 (or 2880).
/B	Allocates space on the formatted disk for system files (IO.SYS, MSDOS.SYS, and COMMAND.COM)
/S	Copies the system files to the formatted disk so you can use the disk to boot your computer.
/T:*tracks*	Specifies the number of tracks per disk side. Used to format odd-capacity disks or to force a drive to recognize a different capacity disk than what the drive currently detects.
/N:*sectors*	Specifies the number of sectors per track. Used to format odd-capacity disks or to force a drive to recognize a different capacity disk than what the drive currently detects.
/1	Formats a single side of a floppy disk.
/4	Formats a 360K floppy disk in a 5 1/4-inch high-density drive.
/8	Formats eight sectors per track.
/C	Tests clusters that are currently marked bad and if they are not actually unusable, returns the clusters to service.

The following sections provide the kind of information about the FORMAT command you can use every day, the kind of basic command line parameters you can write on a sticky note and put on your monitor. These sections also provide information about the DOS safe format feature, the UNFORMAT command, and creating a system disk with which you can boot your system.

Using the /F Switch

If you have a 1.44M drive and sometimes need to use 720K disks, or you have a 1.2M drive and sometimes use 360K disks, you need more command line parameters than if you format disks in a drive of the same capacity. The following lines serve as a quick reference to the exact command line you need to use for each type of disk. Replace the symbolic *drive:* with the correct designation (A: or B:) for the drive containing the disk you want to format.

FORMAT *drive*: /F:360 Formats a 360K disk in a 1.2M drive

FORMAT *drive*: /F:720 Formats a 720K disk in a 1.44M drive

You use similar command lines to force the FORMAT command to recognize the capacity of your drive and disk when the command misidentifies the drive.

FORMAT *drive*: /F:1200 Formats a 1.2M disk in a 1.2M drive

FORMAT *drive*: /F:1440 Formats a 1.44M disk in a 1.44M drive

FORMAT *drive*: /F:2880 Formats a 2.88M disk in a 2.88M drive

Although this explanation by no means covers all possible command line parameters to the FORMAT command, these commands can do the job for you most of the time unless you are formatting some very unusual disks.

The FORMAT command has additional /F parameters, some of which are for special purposes, like formatting a disk so it can be read on a computer that runs an old version of DOS. Other parameters are variations on the parameters covered in the preceding section. These additional /F parameters are covered in the following table.

Parameter	Use
/F:160	Formats 160K single-sided disk (DOS 1.x)
/F:180	Formats 180K single-sided disk
/F:320	Formats 320K double-sided disk (DOS 1.x)
/F:1.2	Formats 1.2M high-density disk
/F:1.44	Formats 1.44M high-density disk
/F:2.88	Formats 2.88M extra high-density disk

Using Safe Format

Safe format

During FORMAT, DOS saves key information so that if you act right away, you can use the UNFORMAT command to restore the disk to its original condition.

UNFORMAT

Restores a disk formatted by mistake to its original condition, if you use the UNFORMAT command before using the disk to store data.

When you format a disk, you tell DOS to completely clear the disk so you can use it again. When you format a new disk, FORMAT reads the disk, determines that data has never been written to the disk, and begins the format. But when the disk has been used, FORMAT reads the disk, finds the old format and any data remaining on the disk, and begins what is called a *safe format.*

The safe format gets its name from the fact that if you decide you didn't really want the disk formatted because it contains data you need to preserve, you can use the *UNFORMAT* command to restore the disk to its original condition. In formatting the disk, the safe format feature of the FORMAT command saves the information needed for the UNFORMAT command to work.

Safe format is automatic. When the FORMAT command detects that a previously used disk is about to be formatted, it produces the following display:

```
Checking existing disk format.

Saving UNFORMAT information.
```

Safe format is useful only when you realize right away that you formatted a disk in error. After you put any other files on the disk, you cannot use the UNFORMAT command to recover the original files.

In some cases, DOS cannot save the unformat information and warns you that the disk cannot be unformatted. When DOS cannot save unformat information, the FORMAT command produces the following read out:

```
This disk cannot be unformatted.

Proceed with Format (Y/N?)
```

When you see this message, stop and make sure that you will not need the data on the disk you are about to format. If you think you may need the data on the disk, press **N** (for no) to terminate the formatting process. If you are sure you *will not* need the data, press **Y** (for yes) to continue the format. The UNFORMAT command is covered later in this lesson.

Using Unconditional Format

Normally, DOS tries to perform a safe format and save the information needed to unformat the disk. You can use the /U switch to override the safe format and tell DOS not to save the unformat information. For example, you might use this switch to clear a disk of confidential data before you give the disk to someone else. The way to use this switch in formatting a disk in drive B: is shown in the following example:

FORMAT B: /U

When you use the /U switch, the UNFORMAT command will not be able to recover the data stored on the disk before you formatted it. If you really need the data that was on a disk before you used the /U switch, you need to consult an expert in data recovery.

Creating a System Disk

System disk
A disk containing the files needed to boot your system: IO.SYS, MSDOS.SYS, and COMMAND.COM.

The /S switch to the FORMAT command places the DOS system files on the formatted disk, which creates a *system disk* you can use to boot your computer. You cannot see two of the files transferred by command; IO.SYS and MSDOS.SYS are hidden, read only system files. But you can see COMMAND.COM, which also is transferred to the disk when you use the /S switch. The following line shows the proper use of the /S switch when you format a disk in the A: drive:

FORMAT A: /S

The following example shows a typical read out produced by the FORMAT command when you use the /S switch:

```
Insert new diskette for drive A:
and press ENTER when ready...

Formatting 1.2M
Format complete.
System transferred

Volume label (11 characters, ENTER for none)?

    1,213,952 bytes total disk space
      198,656 bytes used by system
    1,015,296 bytes available on disk

          512 bytes in each allocation unit.
        1,983 allocation units available on disk.

Volume Serial Number is 1B55-14CF
```

Even if you have a hard drive, your system is capable of booting from the A: drive. Always keep at least one floppy disk handy that contains the system files, in case you have trouble booting from your hard disk. You then can boot from the floppy disk to get to the hard disk and fix the problem.

Task: Formatting a Disk in the Same Capacity Drive

When you format a disk whose capacity is the same as your drive (a 360K disk in a 360K drive, for example), the FORMAT command is very basic. The following example shows formatting a 1.44M disk in a 1.44M drive. But the command works the same way if you format a 2.88M disk in a 2.88M drive, a 1.2M disk in a 1.2M drive, a 720K disk in a 720K drive, or a 360K disk in a 360K drive. Follow these steps to format a 1.44M disk in a 1.44M drive (the A: drive):

1. At the DOS prompt, type the following line:

   FORMAT A:

   DOS produces the following read out:

   ```
   Insert new diskette for drive A:

   and press ENTER when ready...
   ```

2. Insert the disk you want to format and press Enter.

   DOS produces the following read out:

   ```
   Checking existing disk format.

   Formatting 1.44M

     0 percent completed.
   ```

   The third line of this read out tells you how much of the disk DOS has formatted. The read out is updated in increments of three or four percent. When the format is complete, DOS produces the following display:

   ```
   Format complete.

   Volume label (11 characters, ENTER for none)?
   ```

3. Enter a volume label and press Enter. (Or skip this step by pressing Enter at the prompt.) DOS displays the following read out:

```
Volume Serial Number is 083E-11DC

Format another (Y/N)?
```

4. If you want to format another disk of the same capacity in the same drive, press **Y** for yes. If you want to terminate the FORMAT command, press **N** for no. If you want to format a disk of a different capacity than the first, or format a disk in another drive, you must terminate the formatting process and issue the command again for that disk or drive.

Task: Quick Formatting a Disk

Quick format
Quickly refreshes the format on a previously formatted disk without testing for bad sectors or rebuilding the track and sector grid.

If a floppy disk has been formatted before, you can clear the entire disk quickly by using the *quick format.* Normally when you format a disk, DOS lays out the sectors, checks every track for bad sectors, and builds the directory and file allocation table. If the disk has been formatted before, you can skip most of this work and just clear the directory and file allocation table in a few seconds. The following command shows how to use quick format on a disk in the B: drive:

FORMAT B: /Q

You do not need to specify the capacity of the disk in the drive because DOS can determine the disk type from the previous format. A quick format proceeds just like a regular format except that it takes only a few seconds.

Understanding FORMAT Messages

The error messages that occur during floppy disk formatting are rarely catastrophes. The messages usually are little more than statements suggesting that you did something wrong or that DOS had trouble carrying out the command. For example, if you reformat a completely full disk, no room remains to save the information that enables you to unformat the disk. You see a warning message that the disk cannot be unformatted. If you try to format a write-protected disk, you see a message that the format cannot be completed. The following sections describe some common formatting problems.

When the Drive Isn't Ready

If you respond to the FORMAT commands prompt `Press any key when ready` without placing a disk in the disk drive, or if the drive door is open, DOS displays the message:

```
Not ready

Format another (Y/N)?
```

Just insert the disk, close the door if necessary, press **Y,** then press Enter to start the format. If you specified the wrong disk drive, press **N** then Enter. Then execute the command again with the correct drive letter.

If the disk is in the drive, the drive door is closed, and you get this error, the disk is probably write-protected. Take the disk out and check the write-protect tab. To format a write-protected disk, remove the write-protect tape from a 5 1/4-inch disk or slide the tab on a 3 1/2-inch disk, reinsert the disk, and press **Y** then Enter at the prompt.

When the Disk Is Unusable

The worst disk-error mesage you can get when formatting a floppy disk is when DOS cannot initialize the first track of the disk media. When this problem occurs, the following error message appears:

```
Invalid media or Track 0 bad—disk unusable
```

This error message occurs when you are attempting to format a double-density disk as a high density disk—a 720K disk as a 1.44M disk, for example—or when the disk surface is damaged. Format the disk again with the /F:720 switch. If you are formatting the disk at the correct density, the disk likely has a scratched or damaged surface.

Note: *Never touch the shiny surface of the disk. Always handle floppy disks by the dust cover. If you do touch the disk surface, you almost always damage the disk, and this damage results in the* `disk unusable` *message.*

If you get the `disk unusable` error message on a new disk, take it back to your dealer. If the disk is old, throw it away. Disks are inexpensive and, in this case, should be discarded.

When FORMAT Detects Bad Sectors

After the format is complete and you type a volume label and press Enter, you see a report of the status of the disk. The report shows the total disk space and total bytes available on the disk. If FORMAT detects bad sectors on the disk, it marks them as unusable so that DOS does not later use them to store data. If DOS stored data in bad sectors, the data would be lost. The FORMAT command also reports how many bytes are unavailable because of bad sectors. The following example shows a screen display when a disk has bad sectors:

```
Formatting 1.2M
Format complete.

Volume label (11 characters, ENTER for none)?

    1,213,952 bytes total disk space
       46,080 bytes in bad sectors
    1,167,872 bytes available on disk

          512 bytes in each allocation unit.
        2,281 allocation units available on disk.

Volume Serial Number is 1E11-14DB
```

The `bytes in bad sectors` message means that DOS found bad sectors on the disk. DOS cannot use these sectors to hold information. The total amount of free space on the disk is reduced by the number of bytes in the bad sectors.

When the report contains bad sectors, try formatting the disk again. Sometimes the process of formatting revitalizes the electronic media and the sectors no longer are marked bad. If after you have formatted the disk again it still has bad sectors and is a new disk, have your dealer replace the disk. You should not use a floppy disk with bad sectors for storing important data.

Other information on the report includes how many bytes each *allocation unit* contains, how many allocation units are available on the disk for storage, and the volume serial number that DOS automatically assigns to every disk.

Allocation unit
A group of sectors DOS uses to keep track of where files are on a disk.

If you have problems using the FORMAT command, make sure that you have correctly typed the command and its parameters. Spelling mistakes, or leaving out the / character, keep the FORMAT command from functioning properly. Make sure that you use the proper capacity parameters for the disk you are attempting to format. For example, you cannot format a 1.44M disk as a 1.2M disk. Never attempt to format a 360K disk as a 1.2M disk or a 720K disk as a 1.44M disk.

Using UNFORMAT To Recover a Formatted Disk

When you format a disk that contains data, DOS saves the unformat information about the files on the disk before it clears the file allocation table and directory. If you format a disk in error and don't write any new files to the disk, you can use the UNFORMAT command to recover the files on the disk.

The syntax for the UNFORMAT command follows:

UNFORMAT *drive:*

Running the UNFORMAT command produces a series of dialog boxes, intended to ensure that the command functions properly and to inform you of its progress. To answer the questions in these dialog boxes, use the mouse to select the proper button or Tab to the box you want and press Enter. Run the UNFORMAT command this way:

1. At the DOS prompt, type **UNFORMAT** and press the space bar one time.

2. Type the name of the drive containing the disk you want to unformat.

3. Press Enter. The first dialog box you see contains the following read out (if you are unformatting the disk in the B: drive):

   ```
   Analyzing Drive B:
   ```

The UNFORMAT command then presents a dialog box in which you confirm whether you used MIRROR or the Norton Utilities' IMAGE program to save unformat information for the disk. The dialog box displays the following read out:

```
Did you previously use IMAGE.EXE or MIRROR.COM

        to save recovery info for drive B:?

        (If you're not sure, answer YES)
```

4. If you used the DOS 6.2 FORMAT command without the /U parameter, or the Norton Safe Format utility, choose the Yes button. If the answer is no, choose the No button. If you are unsure whether you used the safe format capability to format the disk, choose yes. If UNFORMAT doesn't find MIRROR or IMAGE information on the disk, it continues the operation as if you had chosen the No button (DOS uses information in the root directory and file allocation table to unformat the disk).

   The UNFORMAT command then prompts you in another dialog box for whether you want to continue the unformat operation:

   ```
   Are you sure you want to unformat drive B:?
   ```

5. If you want the UNFORMAT process to continue, choose the Yes button. If you want to cancel the operation, choose the No button.

   If you choose Yes, the UNFORMAT command produces a full-screen display that depicts the disk being unformatted. When a directory is unformatted, a D appears on-screen. Although UNFORMAT also restores files, the full-screen display doesn't show them unless you entered the UNFORMAT command with the /L switch (described in Lesson 8, "DOS Command Reference.")

   If you are running UNFORMAT without a MIRROR or IMAGE file, DOS prompts you to supply the first character in the file name of each file found on the disk. Type the necessary character.

If UNFORMAT finds a *fragmented* file (a file whose pieces are stored in separate places on the disk, rather than all together, or *contiguous*), UNFORMAT cannot recover the entire file. UNFORMAT then prompts you to confirm whether you want to recover only the part of the file UNFORMAT can locate or delete the file. If this problem occurs with a software application executable file or other file that contains program instructions, the application will not work correctly after UNFORMAT restores the file. In such a case, you need to reinstall the program from the original disks, or restore it from a backup.

6. After the UNFORMAT process is complete, check the disk to ensure that the data you need is intact.

Make sure that you unformat a disk immediately after you format the disk in error and before you write any files on the disk. After you write files on a disk, the information that used to be on the disk is lost. The UNFORMAT reference in Lesson 8, "DOS Command Reference," lists additional command line switches for the use of the UNFORMAT command.

If you have problems...

If you have problems using the UNFORMAT command, review steps 1 to 6. Make sure that you properly type the UNFORMAT command and that you enter the drive containing the disk you want to unformat. If prompted for the first letter of a file to be recovered, type the necessary letter.

Formatting Hard Disks

The hard disk is a valuable part of a computer system because of its speed and storage capacity. Just like a floppy disk, a hard disk must be formatted before you can use it. But *do not attempt to format your hard disk* unless you are familiar with the procedure. If you format your hard disk, you lose all data and application software installed on the disk.

Almost invariably, the hard disk in your system was formatted before you received the machine. Unless your hard disk is damaged, you will not need to re-do the format process. If you are installing a new hard drive in your system, you will need to format the disk, of course, but you should follow the installation instructions provided with the disk. Those directions likely include steps for not only formatting the disk, but also running the FDISK program, which is used to create a DOS partition or partitions on the disk and prepare the disk for the FORMAT command.

If you ever attempt to reformat your hard disk, first perform a complete backup. You also should have a bootable floppy disk ready that contains a copy of the DOS Backup program. Que's *Using MS-DOS 6.2*, Special Edition, devotes several pages to the steps for preparing and formatting a hard disk. If you must format your hard disk, consult that book or your computer's manual.

Remember that the FORMAT command erases all the data a disk contains. Always check the directory of the disk you want to format; it may hold data you need. Check the command line thoroughly when you use the FORMAT command.

Summary

To	Do This
Prepare a floppy disk for use	Use the FORMAT command
Buy the right floppy disks	Match disk size and capacity to the drive in your computer
Electronically label disks	Add a volume label
Quickly reformat a disk	Use the /Q switch
Format double-density disks in a high-density drive	Use the proper FORMAT command parameters
Create a bootable floppy disk	Use the FORMAT /S option
Rescue data on a reformatted disk	Use the UNFORMAT command

On Your Own

Estimated time: 15 minutes

Use FORMAT with different parameters.

1. Format a new floppy disk.
2. Use quick format on a previously used floppy disk that contains data you no longer need.
3. Add a volume label to the reformatted disk.
4. Create a bootable floppy disk.

Lesson 8

DOS Command Reference

This lesson is a command reference, encompassing the most frequently used DOS commands. The reference helps you become familiar with command syntax, the correct way to use commands, and when to use them. This lesson helps you do the following:

- Understand DOS command syntax
- Type commands correctly
- Determine which command to use
- Use the list as a handy reference

Command Presentation

Internal command
A command built into MS-DOS.

External command
A command that is a separate program located in the DOS directory.

This lesson presents each DOS command in the same format. The command name, such as COPY, appears first. The notation *Internal* or *External* follows the command name. The distinction between internal and external commands is important because internal commands execute more quickly than external commands, and you cannot find a COM or EXE file for an internal command.

The command entry then explains the command's purpose and shows the syntax required to invoke the command. After the syntax are step-by-step instructions for using the command.

Last are any cautions or notes about the command and often a brief comment indicating the emphasis you should place on mastering the command.

Command Syntax

Command syntax
Symbolic notation that shows the way you type a DOS command and its parameters.

The following example shows the *command syntax* for the FORMAT command.

FORMAT *d*: */switches*

In the command syntax used in this lesson, *d:* is the name of the disk drive on which you want a DOS command to act. The */switches* are optional or mandatory characters (depending on the command) that you enter to make the DOS command work the way you want.

Commands that use source and destination drive parameters use *sd:* for the source drive name and *dd:* for the destination (target) drive name. Some other commands also use the *s* and *d* parameters, as the next paragraph explains.

The *path* notation is the directory path to the file. The use of *spath* indicates the source path, or location of the file on which you are acting. The use of *dpath* indicates the destination path, or the directory into which you want to place the result of a command. The use of *path1* and *path2* indicates that you can enter a list of directories for the command to act upon.

A backslash (\) in the command syntax divides a drive and path from a file name. When a backslash is shown, you use it as part of the path. When a semicolon (;) is shown, you use it to separate the directories on which you want the command to act.

The notation *filename* indicates the root name of the file, and *.ext* is the file name extension. For example, with COMMAND.COM, the *filename* is COMMAND and the *.ext* is COM.

Ellipses (...) often are used to indicate that you can enter a list of files or directories.

If any elements described in this section do not appear in the command syntax, do not include the omitted part in the command. For example, the notation *d: filename.ext* indicates that you do not include path names in the command.

External Commands

You can issue DOS internal commands at any time and from any disk drive or directory. Issuing external commands, however, is a bit more complex. To issue an external command, you have three alternatives:

- Change to the directory that holds the external command. External commands are best kept in a subdirectory containing all other DOS files. On hard disks, the path is usually C:\DOS.
- Include the path name (disk drive and directory name, if necessary) every time you issue the command. This technique quickly becomes tedious.
- Add to your AUTOEXEC.BAT file a PATH statement that includes the subdirectory holding the DOS files. Then when you issue an external command, DOS can find and execute it no matter what directory is current.

If you issue a command and get a `Bad command or file name` message, you have not set the path with the PATH command, or the command is not in the default directory on the logged disk drive. Remember the following rules for issuing commands:

- If you do not specify a disk drive name for the command, DOS searches for the command on the current disk drive.
- If you do not specify a path, DOS searches for the command in the current directory of the current drive (or the current directory of the specified disk drive).

Common DOS Commands Listed by Purpose

Use the following list to determine which command to use for a specific task. Then refer to the command reference that follows the list for details about the use and syntax of that command.

To Perform This Function	Use This Command
Back up a hard disk	MSBACKUP or BACKUP (prior to DOS 6.0)
Copy or combine files	COPY
Change the current directory	CHDIR or CD
Change the current disk drive	Type the drive letter and colon (such as A:) and press Enter
Change the name of a file	RENAME or REN
Display the date	DATE
Change the system date	DATE
Display the system time	TIME
Change the system time	TIME
Clear the screen	CLS
Compare disks	DISKCOMP
Compare files	COMP or FC or MSBACKUP
Compress a hard disk	DBLSPACE
Copy files	COPY or XCOPY
Copy disks	DISKCOPY or COPY or XCOPY
Defragment a disk	DEFRAG
View a text file on-screen	TYPE or EDIT
Set display of batch file commands and text strings	ECHO
Display memory information	MEM
Display the files on a disk	DIR or CHKDSK
Display free space on a disk	DIR
Display Help text	HELP

To Perform This Function	Use This Command
Display the subdirectories on a disk	TREE or CHKDSK
Display the DOS version	VER
Display the volume label	VOL or DIR or CHKDSK
Erase command line character	Left arrow or backspace
Fix a file	SCANDISK or CHKDSK
Locate a string in a file	FIND
Make a new directory	MD or MKDIR
Move a file	MOVE
Optimize system memory	MEMMAKER
Pause the display	Pause key or Ctrl-S or MORE
Place DOS on the disk	FORMAT /S or SYS
Pipe output between programs	¦
Prepare a new disk	FORMAT
Prepare a hard disk	FDISK or FORMAT
Redirect program input	< or ¦
Redirect program output	> or >> or ¦
Remove a file	ERASE or DEL
Remove a directory	RD or RMDIR or DELTREE
Restore an erased disk	UNFORMAT
Restore DOS 6.2 backup	MSBACKUP
Restore earlier DOS backup	RESTORE
Check for software viruses	MSAV
Set the search path	PATH
Set checks on file writes	VERIFY
Set the system prompt	PROMPT
Sort a file	SORT
Undelete a file	UNDELETE
Use a new device driver	DEVICE= in CONFIG.SYS

APPEND

External

Use APPEND to do the following tasks:

- Open data files from a specified directory as if the data files were in the current directory.
- Start programs not in the current directory and not in the search directory specified by PATH.

Command Syntax

APPEND *d1:path1*;*d2:path2 ... /switches*

Steps

1. Type **APPEND** and press the space bar one time. You may need to precede the command with the drive and path for APPEND.EXE because APPEND is an external command.
2. Type the first search path, including the drive.
3. To search a second drive and path, type a semicolon (;) and then type the second drive and path. Repeat this step for additional search paths. The following line is a sample search path:

   C:\DOS;C:\DATA\WORDS;C:\DATA\ACCOUNTS

4. You may type any of the following switches

/E	Adds to the environment. Use this switch only the first time you use APPEND after starting the computer. Use this switch with no other parameters.
/X:ON	Enables searching the appended directories for program files.
/X:OFF	Disables searching the appended directories for program files.
/PATH:ON	Enables searching the append path if a program with a specified path is not found.
/PATH:OFF	Disables searching the append path if a program with a specified path is not found.

5. Press Enter.

6. To delete the search paths, type the command **APPEND ;**

7. Press Enter.

8. To view the appended directories, type the command **APPEND** without parameters.

Note: *Do not use APPEND to search for a program's data files if the program writes a new file when a data file is modified (as do most word processing programs). Use APPEND only if the program modifies an existing file (as do database programs). Do not use APPEND with Windows or when you are running the Windows Setup program.*

ASSIGN

External

Use ASSIGN to send the request for information from one drive to another drive.

Command Syntax

ASSIGN *d1:=d2:* /STATUS

Steps

1. Type **ASSIGN** and press the space bar one time. You may need to precede the command with the drive and path for ASSIGN.COM because ASSIGN is an external command.

2. Type the name of the drive you want to assign (such as A:).

3. Type an equal sign (=).

4. Type the drive to which you want to assign that drive (for example, C:).

5. Press Enter.

   The command ASSIGN A=C makes DOS read the C: drive when you specify the A: drive.

6. To view the current assignments, type **ASSIGN /STATUS** and press Enter.

7. To cancel the assignments, type **ASSIGN** and press Enter.

ATTRIB

External

Use ATTRIB to do the following tasks:

Attribute
Specifies whether a file is read-only, system, hidden, or has its archive bit set.

- Display a file's *attributes*.
- Change a file's attributes.

Command Syntax

ATTRIB *attribs d:path\filename.ext* /S

Steps

1. Type **ATTRIB** and press the space bar one time. You may need to precede the command with the drive and path for ATTRIB.EXE because ATTRIB is an external command.

2. Type any of the following attributes:

+R	Makes the file read-only so you cannot modify the file.
-R	Turns off the read-only attribute, enabling you to modify the file.
+A	Makes the file appear as if it were new or changed by turning on the archive attribute.
-A	Turns off the archive attribute.
+S	Makes the file a system file by turning on the system attribute.
-S	Turns off the system attribute.
+H	Hides the file.
-H	Turns off the hidden attribute.

Wild card
The characters * and ?, which you can use in place of parts of a file name or extension in a file name.

3. Press the space bar and then type the file name and extension of the file whose attribute you want to display or change. You may use the *wild cards* * and ? when you type the file name. (For example, type *.* to restore all files on a disk or subdirectory.)

4. You also may use the following switch with the ATTRIB command:

   /S Searches for files in subsequent directories.

5. Press Enter.

BACKUP

External

Use BACKUP with versions of DOS earlier than 6.2 to do the following tasks:

- Back up hard disk information to protect original programs and data in case of loss or damage.
- Back up files created or altered since a specific date or since the last backup.
- Copy files that are too long to store on one floppy disk.

Command Syntax

BACKUP ***sd:****spath\sfilename.ext* ***dd:*** */switches*

Steps

1. Type **BACKUP** and press the space bar one time. You may need to precede the command with a drive and path for BACKUP.COM because BACKUP is an external command.

2. Type the drive name (*sd:*) of the hard disk you want to back up (for example, C:).

3. To back up a directory or an individual file, type the path, file name, and extension; then press the space bar. You may use wild-card characters (* and ?) to designate groups of files.

4. Type the name of the drive (*dd:*) that will receive the backup files. (For example, to back up on a floppy disk in the A: drive, type A:.)

8

5. You may use any of the following switches:

/S	Backs up the subdirectories as well as the current directory. If you start at the root directory, DOS backs up all directories.

The following switches are for incremental backups:

/F:*size*	Formats the target floppy disk to the size you specify (360K, 720K, 1.44M, 2.88M).
/L:*d:path\logfile.ext*	Records the names of the backed up files to the file *logfile.ext*, located in *d:path*.
/A	Adds files to the files already on the backup disk.
/M	Backs up only those files that have changed since the last backup. Use the /A switch with the /M switch when restoring from the backup disks to avoid overwriting unmodified files.
/D:*mm-dd-yy*	Backs up files created or changed on or after the specified date.
/T:*hh:mm:ss*	Backs up files created or changed at or after the specified time.

6. Press Enter.

Note: *Use BACKUP only with versions of DOS prior to 6.2. With DOS 6.2, use MSBACKUP. To restore files backed up with the BACKUP command, use the RESTORE command.*

As you back up your files, remember to number the backup floppy disks. If you need to use the RESTORE command to restore lost files, you use the disks in numeric order.

Backing up your hard drive reduces the chance of losing valuable information. You do not need to memorize every step, but you should be familiar with BACKUP's basic command and switches.

CD or CHDIR

Internal

Use CD or CHDIR to do the following tasks:

- Change the current directory.
- Show the name of the current directory.

Command Syntax

CHDIR *d:path*

or

CD *d:path*

Steps

1. Type **CD** or **CHDIR**. This command is internal and does not require a path.
2. Press the space bar one time.
3. Type the drive name of the disk whose current directory you want to change (for example, A:, B:, or C:) and the name of the directory to which you want to change. If you don't specify a path, DOS displays the current path.
4. Press Enter.

CD (CHDIR) is very important and simple to use; it is one of the commands you need so you can navigate around your disk.

CHKDSK

External

Use CHKDSK to check the directory of the disk for disk and memory status. CHKDSK can display the following information:

- The number of files and directories on a disk.
- The bytes used and the space available on a disk.

- The presence of hidden files.
- Whether a floppy disk is bootable.
- The total RAM and available RAM.
- Whether files are fragmented (noncontiguous).

CHKDSK also can make minor repairs, but the SCANDISK command is better for making repairs. SCANDISK is covered in Lesson 2, "Making a Quick Start with DOS."

Command Syntax

CHKDSK *d:path\filename.ext /switches*

Steps

1. Type **CHKDSK** and press the space bar one time. You may need to precede the command with the drive and path, because CHKDSK is an external command.
2. To check a disk on another drive, type the drive name. For example, if your default is the C: drive and you want to check the B: drive, type CHKDSK B:.
3. You can use CHKDSK to determine the noncontiguous areas in an individual file by entering the path, file name, and extension. The file name and extension may contain wild cards.
4. You may type either of the following switches:

   /F Repairs errors (use with caution).

   /V (Verbose) Displays paths and file names.
5. Press Enter.

Note: *CHKDSK reports errors it finds. You can repair errors using the /F switch with the command. CHKDSK repairs the error, generally gathering fractured files and combining them into one special file in your root directory. However, a better alternative for checking and repairing files is SCANDISK.*

CLS

Internal

Use CLS to clear the screen whenever you are at the DOS prompt.

Command Syntax

CLS

Steps

1. Type **CLS**.

2. Press Enter. After DOS clears all messages on-screen, the DOS prompt and cursor reappear in the upper left corner.

You can use CLS to give your batch files a professional look.

COMP

External

Use COMP to compare two files to see whether they are the same.

Command Syntax

COMP *d1:path1****filename1.ext1*** *d2:path2****filename2.ext2*** / *switches*

Steps

1. Type **COMP** and press the space bar one time. You may need to precede the command with the drive and path for COMP.COM because COMP is an external command.

2. Type the file name and extension of the first file you want to compare. You may need to include the drive and path if that file is not in the current drive and directory.

3. Press the space bar one time.

4. Type the file name and extension of the second file you want to compare. You may need to include the drive and path if that file is not in the current drive and directory.

5. You may type any of the following switches and then press Enter:

/D	Displays any difference using decimal numbers (rather than the default hexadecimal numbers).
/A	Displays differences using ASCII characters.
/L	Displays the line number of any difference.
/N=*number*	Compares the specified number of lines in both files, starting at the beginning of each file.
/C	Performs a comparison that isn't case-sensitive.

If you do not specify file names, COMP prompts you for the file names and extensions of the first and second files you want to compare. After COMP finds 10 errors or differences between the two files, the comparison discontinues.

COPY

Internal

Use COPY to do the following tasks:

- Copy one or more files to another disk or directory, or copy a file to the same directory and change its name.
- Transfer information between DOS system devices.
- Send text to the printer.
- Create ASCII text files and batch files.

Command Syntax

The following line shows the most basic syntax for the COPY command:

COPY *sfilename.ext dfilename.ext*

When using the COPY command to copy a file, you must specify the source file name and extension and at least one of the following:

- Destination drive and/or directory for the copy.
- Destination file name for the copy.

The common syntax for the COPY command is shown in the following line:

COPY *sd:\spath**sfilename.ext dd:\dpath**\dfilename.ext /switches*

Steps

1. Type **COPY** and press the space bar one time.
2. Type the drive name and path of the source file (*sd:\spath*).
3. Type the file name and extension of the file you want to copy. You may use wild cards.
4. You may include the following switches for the source file:

   /A Treats the source file as an ASCII text file.

   /B Forces DOS to copy the entire file as though it were a program file (binary). Binary copying is the default.
5. Press the space bar.
6. Type the drive name, path, and file name of the target file (*dd:\dpath*). You may skip typing the file name and extension of the destination file if the file name is to remain the same as that of the source file.
7. You may include the following switches for the target file:

   /A Places an end-of-file character (Ctrl-Z) at the end of the copied file.

   /B Prevents an end-of-file character from appearing on a copied file.

   /V Specifies that COPY is to check and verify the accuracy of the COPY procedure.

   /Y Specifies that COPY is to replace existing files without prompting you for confirmation.

   /-Y Specifies that COPY is to prompt you for confirmation before replacing an existing file, which COPY does by default.
8. Press Enter.

Note: *COPY does exactly what you tell it to do. Before you use this command, make sure that you have planned well. When you copy to another directory or disk, the DOS 6.2 version of COPY prompts you before overwriting a file of the same name. But be sure to type the file names exactly, as well as the drive and directory names.*

COPY is a very flexible command that you should know well and use more than most other commands.

DATE

Internal

Use DATE to do the following tasks:

- Check the date currently entered in your system clock.
- Set the internal clock on a computer with a battery-backed clock.
- Enter or change the system date each time you start a computer without a battery-backed clock.
- Check the current date stamp for newly created and modified files.

Command Syntax

DATE *mm-dd-yy*

Steps

1. Type **DATE** and press the space bar one time.
2. Enter the date in one of the following formats:
   - *mm-dd-yy* (for North America; this format is the default)
   - *dd-mm-yy* (for Europe)
   - *yy-mm-dd* or *yyyy-mm-dd* (for East Asia)

   mm is a one- or two-digit number for the month (1 to 12).

   dd is a one- or two-digit number for the day (1 to 31).

   yy is a one- or two-digit number for the year (80 to 99). DOS assumes that the first two digits of the year are *19*.

   yyyy is a four-digit number for the year (1980 to 2099).

You can separate the entries with hyphens, periods, or slashes.

3. Press Enter.

If your PC doesn't have a built-in calendar clock, use this command every time you boot. Knowing when files were written or updated is good organizational strategy and aids you in being selective with MSBACKUP and XCOPY. Better still, cards containing battery-operated calendar clocks have become very inexpensive; you can purchase such a clock to eliminate typing the time and date every time you start your computer.

DBLSPACE

External

Use DBLSPACE to do the following tasks:

- Compress existing files on a disk.
- Install the device driver that manages compressed files.
- Display information about compressed drives.

Command Syntax

DBLSPACE Starts the DoubleSpace disk-compression program.

DBLSPACE *d:* Displays information about a compressed drive.

Steps

1. Type **DBLSPACE**. You may need to precede the command with the drive and path for DBLSPACE.EXE because DBLSPACE is an external command.
2. Press Enter.
3. Follow the instructions that the DBLSPACE program displays on-screen.

If you run Windows, the permanent swap file must be on the uncompressed drive. Lesson 13, "Using DoubleSpace SCANDISK, and DEFRAG," provides complete coverage of DoubleSpace and Windows.

Before you use DoubleSpace, refer to that lesson. If you require additional information about DoubleSpace, consult Que's *Using MS-DOS 6.2,* Special Edition.

Remember that DBLSPACE may take a long time. Use the command when you have finished all your other computer work for the day.

Note: *Do not run DBLSPACE if you use another disk compression program like Stacker. You can use only one such disk compression program at a time. You can, however, use file compression utilities like PKZIP at the same time you use DoubleSpace.*

DEFRAG

External

Use DEFRAG to reorganize the existing files on a disk to optimize disk performance.

Command Syntax

DEFRAG *d: /switches*

Steps

1. Type **DEFRAG**. You may need to precede the command with the drive and path for DEFRAG.EXE because DEFRAG is an external command.

2. Press the space bar one time and type the letter of the drive you want to defragment.

3. You may use any of the following switches:

/F	Defragments files and ensures that the disk contains no empty spaces between files.
/U	Defragments files and leaves existing empty spaces between files.
/S:*value*	Sorts the files according to the value entered. If you omit this switch, DEFRAG uses the current order on the disk. You may use any of the following values:

N	Sorts alphabetically by name A to Z.
N-	Sorts alphabetically by name Z to A.
E	Sorts alphabetically by file extension A to Z.
E-	Sorts alphabetically by file extension Z to A.
D	Sorts by date and time, earliest first.
D-	Sorts by date and time, latest first.
S	Sorts by size, smallest first.
S-	Sorts by size, largest first.

/B	Restarts your PC upon completion of defragmentation.
/SKIPHIGH	Loads DEFRAG into conventional memory rather than upper memory or extended memory.
/LCD	Starts DEFRAG using an LCD color scheme.
/BW	Starts DEFRAG using a black-and-white color scheme.
/G0	Disables the graphics mouse and graphics character set.
/H	Moves hidden files.

4. Press Enter.

5. Select whether you want to optimize the disk or configure the optimization.

6. When the optimization is complete, select Exit to return to DOS.

The DEFRAG program is a full-screen utility. You can use the keyboard or the mouse to make selections. Usually, the optimization method recommended by DEFRAG is sufficient to defragment the selected disk.

DEL

See ERASE.

DELTREE

External

Use DELTREE to delete a directory and all its files and subdirectories.

Command Syntax

DELTREE *d:path*

Steps

1. Type **DELTREE**.
2. Press the space bar.
3. Type the drive and path of the directory you want to delete. You may use wild cards.
4. If you want, you may add the /Y switch to suppress confirmation before DOS deletes the directory.
5. Press Enter.
6. If you are prompted to confirm the deletion, press **Y** and then press Enter to delete the directory and all the files and subdirectories in it. Or press **N** and then press Enter to abort the DELTREE command.

Caution
DELTREE deletes all files and subdirectories in the specified directory. Make absolutely certain the directory you type is the one you want to delete.

DEVICE

Use DEVICE in your CONFIG.SYS file to do the following tasks:

- Support add-on peripherals.
- Install a block-device driver.
- Install a virtual (RAM) disk.

Command Syntax

DEVICE=*d:path\devicedriver*

Steps

1. Using the MS-DOS Editor or another text editor, open your CONFIG.SYS file. See Lesson 11, "Customizing DOS," for information on the CONFIG.SYS file.

2. Type the following command on one line in your CONFIG.SYS file:

   DEVICE=*d:path\filename.ext*

   d:path is the drive and path to the device driver, and *filename.ext* is the file name of the device driver. If you have a mouse driver called MOUSE.SYS, for example, and it's located in the UTIL directory on the C: drive, you add the line DEVICE=C:\UTIL\MOUSE.SYS to your CONFIG.SYS file.

3. Repeat step 2 until you have all device drivers you want in your CONFIG.SYS file.

4. Restart your system.

Note: *Device drivers usually come with hardware you purchase. Check installation instructions for your device and driver.*

Sooner or later, you will add the DEVICE command to your CONFIG.SYS file. The most commonly used device driver is ANSI.SYS, which provides additional control over your display and keyboard. If ANSI.SYS resides in C:\DOS, include the command DEVICE=C:\DOS\ANSI.SYS in your CONFIG.SYS file.

DIR

Internal

Use DIR to do the following tasks:

- Display a list of files and subdirectories in a disk's directory.
- List a specified group of files within a directory.

- Examine the volume identification label of the disk.
- Determine the amount of available space on the disk.
- Check the size of individual files.
- Check the date the files were last modified.

Command Syntax

DIR *d:\path\filename.ext /switches*

Steps

1. Type **DIR** and press the space bar one time.
2. You may type one of the following parameters:
   - The drive name containing the disk on which you want the DIR command to display information.
   - The path name of the directory you want to display.
   - The file name, if you want to limit the number and types of files listed. You may use wild cards to list groups of files.
3. You may use any of the following switches:

   /P Displays the directory and pauses between screen pages. This switch prevents large directories from scrolling off the screen before you can read them.

   /W Displays the directory in a wide format of five columns across. The /W switch displays only the directory name and file names. For large listings, also include the /P switch.

   /A:*attrib* Displays those files that have certain attributes turned on or off. If you don't specify a particular attribute, DOS displays all files, including system and hidden files. The attributes are as follows:

   H Displays hidden files.

   S Displays system files.

D	Displays subdirectories.
A	Displays files that have changed since the last backup.
R	Displays read-only files.

-attrib Turns off the attribute.

/O:*sort* Displays files in sorted order. The sort options are as follows:

N	Sorts in alphabetical order by file name.
E	Sorts in alphabetical order by extension.
D	Sorts by date and time, earliest to latest.
S	Sorts by size, smallest to largest.
C	Sorts by compression ratio, lowest to highest.
G	Lists directories before file names.

-sort Sorts in reverse order.

/S Searches through subdirectories for files to display.

/B Displays file names in the format FILENAME.EXT.

/L Displays all file names and extensions in lowercase letters.

/C Sorts files according to their compression ratio—lowest to highest—if you are using DoubleSpace.

/-C Sorts files according to their compression ratio—highest to lowest—if you are using DoubleSpace.

4. Press Enter.

8

DISKCOMP

External

Use DISKCOMP to do the following tasks:

- Compare two floppy disks on a track-for-track, sector-for-sector basis to see whether their contents are identical.
- Verify the integrity of a DISKCOPY operation.

Command Syntax

DISKCOMP *sd: dd:* */switch*

Steps

1. Type **DISKCOMP** and press the space bar one time.
2. Type the name of the drive that holds the source disk (for example, type A:) and press the space bar again.
3. Type the name of the drive that holds the target disk (for example, B:). If you have only one floppy disk drive, type A: again.
4. You may use either of the following switches:

/1	Compares only single-sided floppy disks.
/8	Compares only eight-sectored floppy disks.

5. Press Enter. DOS instructs you to place the source disk into the A: drive and the target disk into the B: drive. If you have only one floppy disk drive, DOS instructs you to place the source disk into the A: drive.
6. Insert the floppy disks requested and press Enter. DISKCOMP compares all tracks and issues any necessary error messages, indicating the track number and side of the floppy disk on which errors occur. If you have only one floppy disk drive, DOS then instructs you to exchange the source disk with the target disk. When DISKCOMP is finished, DOS asks whether you want to compare more floppy disks.

7. To compare more disks, press **Y** and repeat steps 5 through 7; otherwise, press **N**.

Note: *You may rarely need this command because you also can use the /V switch to verify as you use DISKCOPY.*

DISKCOPY

External

Use DISKCOPY to secure data against loss by duplicating a floppy disk. Note that DISKCOPY works only when copying floppy disks of the same size and capacity. In other words, you cannot use DISKCOPY to copy a 1.2M disk in the A: drive to a 1.44M disk in the B: drive.

Command Syntax

DISKCOPY *sd: dd:* */switch*

Steps

1. Type **DISKCOPY** and press the space bar one time.
2. Type the name of the drive that holds the source disk (A:, for example). Press the space bar again.
3. Type the name of the drive that holds the target disk (B:, for example).

   If you are using DISKCOPY to copy a disk in the A: drive and the destination drive also is the A: drive, you use the following command:

   DISKCOPY A: A:

4. You may use either of the following switches:

   /1 Copies only one side of the floppy disk (use only with single-sided floppy disks).

   /V Verifies that the copy was performed correctly.

8

/M Specifies that DOS is to use *memory only*, not hard drive space, for making the copy. Using this switch requires you to swap the source and destination disks several times during the copy process.

5. Press Enter. Within a few seconds, DOS prompts you to place the source disk into the A: drive and the target disk into the B: drive. If you are using DISKCOPY to copy a disk in the A: drive to a target disk you also will place in the A: drive, DOS prompts you to place the source disk in the A: drive.

6. Insert the floppy disk and press Enter. If the source drive and target drive are the same (as in DISKCOPY A: A:), DOS prompts you to exchange the source disk with the target disk.

7. When the copy is complete, DOS asks whether you want to copy another floppy disk.

8. To copy another floppy disk, press **Y** and repeat steps 6 through 8; otherwise, press **N**.

Note: *DISKCOPY is for duplicating floppy disks, not hard disks. If a problem exists on the original (source) floppy disk, the same problem will appear on the duplicate floppy disk.*

DISKCOPY is one of the basic commands that you need to understand completely.

DOSKEY

External

Use DOSKEY to do the following tasks:

- Load the Doskey program, which enables you to recall and edit commands typed at the command line.
- Create custom commands (macros).
- View macros and commands.

Command Syntax

DOSKEY *macroname=text /switches*

Steps

1. Type **DOSKEY** and press the space bar one time. You may need to precede the command with the drive and path for DOSKEY.EXE because DOSKEY is an external command.

2. You may use any of the following parameters or switches:

macroname=text	Creates a macro that carries out one or more MS-DOS commands (a Doskey macro). *macroname* specifies the name you want to assign to the macro. *text* indicates characters you replace with the commands you want to record.
/REINSTALL	Installs a new copy of the Doskey program.
/BUFSIZE=*size*	Specifies the size of the buffer in which Doskey stores commands and Doskey macros. The default size is 512 bytes, but you can specify as little as 256 bytes.
/MACROS	Displays a list of all macros already created with Doskey.
/HISTORY	Displays a list of all commands that have been entered at the command line and stored in memory.
/INSERT	Inserts new text into old text instead of typing over it.
/OVERSTRIKE	Causes new text to overwrite old text instead of inserting it.

3. Press Enter.

You can use DOSKEY to create macros that carry out one or more commands.

To create macros, follow these steps:

1. Type **DOSKEY** and press the space bar. You may need to precede the command with the drive and path for DOSKEY.EXE because DOSKEY is an external command.

2. Type the name you want to assign the macro. For example, type **MACRO1**.

3. Type **=**.

Meta-string characters
A special code that is significant only when used in a Doskey macro or other special application.

4. Type the commands you want the macro to perform. You may use the following *meta-string characters*, preceded by a $, to further define the commands:

$G	Redirects output to a device or a file.
GG	Appends output to the end of a file.
$L	Redirects input to be read from a device or a file rather than from the keyboard.
$T	Separates commands.
$$	Specifies to include a dollar sign.
$1 to $9	Represents any command-line information you want to specify at the time you run the macro.
$*	Represents all command-line information you want to specify at the time you run the macro.

5. Press Enter.

For example, to create a macro called MACRO1 that will check a disk in any specified drive and then quick format a disk in any specified drive, type the following command:

DOSKEY MACRO1=CHKDSK 1TFORMAT/Q $2

To run the macro, type the macro name, followed by any information you want to specify. The following steps describe how to run the macro in the preceding example:

1. Type **MACRO1** and press the space bar one time.

2. Enter the drive on which you want to perform the disk check (such as B:) and press the space bar one time.

3. Enter the drive in which you want to quick format a disk (such as B:).

4. Press Enter.

DOSSHELL

External

Use DOSSHELL to do the following tasks:

- Perform DOS commands from menus.
- Manage files and directories.
- Manage and start programs.

Command Syntax

DOSSHELL */switches*

Steps

1. Type **DOSSHELL**. You may need to precede the command with the drive and path for DOSSHELL.COM because DOSSHELL is an external command.

2. You may use any of the following switches:

/T:*res*	Changes to a text display; *res* can be L, M, M1, M2, H, H1, or H2.
/G:*res*	Changes to a graphical display; *res* can be L, M, M1, M2, H, H1, or H2.
/B	Displays the DOS Shell in black and white rather than in color.

3. Press Enter.

Use the /T, /G, or /B switches to change the screen resolution or color scheme only when you start the DOS Shell. Generally, you do not need to reuse these switches because the DOS Shell remembers the last screen resolution you used.

ECHO

Internal

Use ECHO to do the following tasks:

- Display batch-file commands and text strings on-screen.
- Control video output to the screen.
- Debug batch files.

Command Syntax

ECHO OFF	Turns off the display of commands when you run batch files.
ECHO ON	Turns on the display of commands.
ECHO *message*	Displays a message.
ECHO.	Displays a blank line. Notice that the period is directly after ECHO with no space.

Note: *When using the ECHO OFF command, you can suppress the display of the ECHO OFF command itself by typing @ECHO OFF.*

ECHO is an excellent batch-file creation utility. If you understand how to use ECHO, you can have fun personalizing your PC's operation.

EDIT

External

Use EDIT to create or modify text files, such as a batch file or the CONFIG.SYS file.

Command Syntax

EDIT *d:path\filename.ext /switches*

Steps

1. Type **EDIT** and press the space bar one time. You may need to precede the command with the drive and path for EDIT.COM because EDIT is an external command.

2. Type the name of the file you want to edit, including the drive and path of the file (if the file is not in the current directory).

3. You may use any of the following switches:

/B	Makes EDIT display in black and white rather than in color.
/G	Makes a CGA monitor update faster
/H	Makes EDIT display in the maximum resolution of your video display.
/NOHI	Makes EDIT display in eight colors rather than the usual 16 colors.

4. Press Enter.

ERASE or DEL

Internal

Use ERASE or DEL to remove one or more files from the current disk or directory.

Command Syntax

ERASE *d:path**filename.ext*** */P*

or

DEL *d:path**filename.ext*** */P*

Steps

1. Type **ERASE** or **DEL** and press the space bar one time.

2. Type the drive name and path of the file you want to delete, unless the file is in the current directory.

8

3. Type the name of the file you want to delete.

4. You may use the following switch:

   /P Prompts `filename, Delete (Y/N)?` before deleting each file.

5. Press Enter. If you typed the /P switch, respond to the prompt by pressing **Y** to delete the file or **N** to cancel the command.

Note: *ERASE (DEL) is a deceptively simple command that can make your life easy or fill it with grief. Practice using this command and think carefully before pressing the Enter key. Be very careful when you use wild cards, or you may delete more files than you intend to delete. To learn how to recover an accidentally deleted file, see UNDELETE.*

FASTOPEN

External

Use FASTOPEN to mark the location of often-used files so DOS can access them quickly.

Command Syntax

FASTOPEN *d1:=n1* *d2:=n2 ... /X*

Steps

1. Type **FASTOPEN** and press the space bar one time. You may need to precede the command with the drive and path for FASTOPEN.EXE because FASTOPEN is an external command.

2. Type the letter of the drive containing the files you want DOS to remember (for example, A:).

3. Type **=**.

4. Type the number of files (*n1*) you want DOS to remember (type 40, for example, if you want DOS to remember the location of the last 40 files opened).

5. If you want DOS to remember additional files, press the space bar and repeat steps 2 to 4.

6. You may use the following switch:

   /X Places the storage area of often-used files in expanded memory.

7. Press Enter.

Caution
Do not use FASTOPEN when you are running Microsoft Windows. Do not run a defragmentation program when FASTOPEN is active.

If you use a program that opens the same files over and over again, such as a word processing or database program, FASTOPEN can speed up your program. If you use a program that reads files one at a time, such as a spreadsheet program, you get no benefit from the FASTOPEN command.

FC

External

Use FC to compare two files or sets of files to see whether they are the same.

Command Syntax

FC */switches d1:path1**filename1.ext1*** *d2:path2**filename2.ext2***

Steps

1. Type **FC** and press the space bar one time. You may need to precede the command with the drive and path for FC.EXE because FC is an external command.

2. You may use any of the following switches:

/A	Displays the first and last lines of the section of a file that is different, instead of displaying the entire section.
/B	Specifies that the files you are comparing are binary or program files, rather than text or ASCII files.
/L	Specifies that the files you are comparing are text or ASCII files, rather than binary or program files.
/C	Performs a comparison that isn't case-sensitive.
/LB*n*	Changes the internal buffer for *n* number of lines you want to compare in a file.

/N	Displays the line numbers of the differing lines when comparing text or ASCII files.
/T	Does not change an ASCII file's tabs to spaces for comparison.
/W	Condenses contiguous spaces and tabs into a single space during the comparison.
/*xxxx*	Tells FC the number of consecutive lines (*xxxx*) that must compare as equal before FC considers the two files to be back in sync after mismatches. The default number of consecutive lines is 2.

3. Type the file name and extension of the first file you want to compare. If the first file you want to compare is not in the current directory, precede the file name with the drive and path of the file. You may use the wild cards * and ? in the file name.

4. Press the space bar one time.

5. Type the file name and extension of the second file you want to compare. If the second file you want to compare is not in the current directory, precede the file name with the drive and path of the file. You may use the wild cards * and ? in the file name.

6. Press Enter.

FC is similar to COMP, but FC is more configurable using command line parameters.

FIND

External

String
A group of characters appearing in a document or file, such as the word *the* or the combination *ae*.

Use FIND to display lines that contain, or fail to contain, a certain group of characters, called a *string*.

Command Syntax

FIND */switches* ***"string"*** *d1:path1**filename1.ext1*** ...

Steps

1. Type **FIND** and press the space bar. You may need to precede the command with the drive and path if FIND is not in the root directory or in a path governed by the PATH command.

2. You may use any of the following switches:

   /C Counts the number of lines containing the search string.

   /N Displays the line number of each line containing the search string.

   /V Displays all lines that do not contain the search string.

   /I Performs a search that is not case-sensitive.

   Press the space bar after typing the switch.

3. Type the string, enclosed in quotation marks ("*string*"). The string is the character set you want to find. FIND is case-sensitive; if you want to find uppercase characters, for example, type the string in uppercase letters.

4. Press the space bar one time.

5. If the file is not in the current directory, type the drive name and path of the file you want to search.

6. Type the file name and extension of the file you want to search.

7. If you want FIND to search an additional file, press the space bar and repeat steps 5 and 6. You cannot use wild cards (? or *).

8. Press Enter.

FIND is a very convenient command, becoming particularly important as your hard drive fills with files and subdirectories.

FORMAT

External

Use FORMAT to initialize a floppy disk or hard disk to accept DOS information and files.

Command Syntax

FORMAT *d: /switches*

Steps

1. Type **FORMAT**. You may need to precede the command with the drive and path if FORMAT is not in the root directory or in a path governed by the PATH command.

2. Press the space bar one time.

3. Type the name of the drive holding the disk you want to format (for example, B:).

4. You may use any of the following switches:

/V:*label*	Gives the formatted disk an identifying volume label.
/S	Produces a bootable disk by placing the operating system on the formatted disk.
/4	Formats (on a high-capacity drive) a single- or double-sided floppy disk for use in computers that use double-density disks.
/1	Formats a floppy disk on one side. Use this switch to format floppy disks for older PCs and compatibles.
/8	Formats a floppy disk with eight sectors per track rather than the default value of nine sectors per track. Use this switch to format disks for older PCs and compatibles.
/B	Creates an eight-sector floppy disk that reserves space for the operating system.

/C	Retests bad clusters. By default, if a drive contains clusters that have been marked as "bad," FORMAT leaves them marked "bad" instead of retesting the clusters. Use the /C switch if you want FORMAT to retest all bad clusters on the drive. In previous versions of MS-DOS, FORMAT retested any bad clusters by default.
/F:*size*	Formats a floppy disk to a specific capacity, where *size* is one of the following values: 160K, 180K, 320K, 360K, 720K, 1.2M, 1.44M, or 2.88M.
/N:*xx*	Specifies the number of sectors (*xx*) per track on the disk. Always use this switch with the /T:*xx* switch.
/T:*xx*	Specifies the number of tracks (*xx*) on the disk. Use this switch with the /N:*xx* switch.
/Q	Performs a quick format on an already formatted disk.
/U	Performs an unconditional (nonsafe) format.

5. Press Enter.

   DOS now instructs you to place a floppy disk into the drive you named in step 3.

6. Insert the floppy disk you want to format and press Enter.

   In a few minutes, you see the message `Format complete` and a status report of the formatted floppy disk.

7. If you typed the /V switch, DOS asks you to enter the volume label, a name of up to 11 characters. Type the volume label and press Enter.

   DOS then asks whether you want to format another disk.

8. To format another disk, press **Y** and repeat steps 6 and 7; otherwise, press **N**.

Note: *If you format a 360K floppy disk in a 1.2M disk drive, the formatted disk may not be readable in a 360K drive. Also, a 1.2M disk may look exactly like a 360K floppy disk, but you cannot use the higher density 1.2M floppy disk in 360K disk drive.*

FORMAT is an absolute must to understand. This command is the heart of your disk maintenance system. If you accidentally format an already formatted disk, you may be able to recover the information using the UNFORMAT command.

HELP

External

Use HELP to display syntax help for a command.

Command Syntax

HELP *command*

Steps

1. Type **HELP** and press the space bar one time. You may need to precede the command with the drive and path for HELP.EXE because HELP is an external command.

2. You may use any of the following switches:

/B	Enables use of a monochrome monitor with a color graphics card.
/G	Provides the fastest update of a CGA screen.
/H	Displays the maximum number of lines possible for your hardware.
/NOHI	Enables the use of a monitor that is not capable of showing high-intensity text.

Press the space bar after typing the switch.

3. Type the command for which you want to get help (for example, FORMAT). If you do not enter a command name, HELP displays a complete command reference table of contents. You can select any command from the table of contents.

4. Press Enter.

Note: *The HELP program has its own shell. You can use the keyboard or the mouse to move through the Help screens.*

JOIN

External

Use JOIN to attach a drive to a directory on another drive.

Command Syntax

JOIN *d1: d2:path2*	Joins two drives.
JOIN *d1:* /D	Breaks two joined drives.
JOIN	Lists all currently joined drives.

The parameter *d1:* specifies the disk drive you want to attach, and *d2:* is the drive to which you want to attach the *d1:* drive. The parameter *path2* specifies the directory path on the host drive (*d2:*) where you want to attach the *d1:* drive. The /D switch cancels any previous JOIN commands for the specified drive (*d1:*).

Note: *The directory of the host drive must be empty and cannot be the root directory. If the directory of the host drive does not exist, JOIN creates the directory.*

Steps

Use the following steps to join a disk drive to an empty directory on another drive:

1. Type **JOIN** and press the space bar.

2. Type the drive designator of the drive you want to join. For example, type A: to join drive A: to a directory on another drive. Press the space bar.

3. Type the name of the drive and directory to which you want to join the drive in step 2.

4. Press Enter. If the directory does not exist, DOS creates it.

   For example, to join drive A: to the subdirectory C:\JOINED, type the following line:

   JOIN A: C:\JOINED

To use the files on the joined drive, access them as if they were a directory on the drive to which you joined their actual drive. For example, to access the files joined in step 3, from the root directory of the C: drive, follow these steps:

1. Type the following line:

   CD\JOINED

2. Press Enter.

LABEL

External

Use LABEL to change or remove the electronic label stored on a disk.

Command Syntax

LABEL *d:label*

Steps

1. Type **LABEL** and press the space bar one time. You may need to precede the command with the drive and path for LABEL.EXE because LABEL is an external command.

2. Type the drive for which you want to change the label, if that drive is not the current drive.

3. Type the new label. If you do not type a label on the command line, DOS prompts you for a label.

MEM

External

Use MEM to do the following tasks:

- Display available and used system memory.
- Display programs loaded into memory.

Command Syntax

MEM */switches*

Steps

1. Type **MEM** and press the space bar one time. You may need to precede the command with the drive and path for MEM.EXE because MEM is an external command.

2. You may use any of the following switches:

/FREE	Lists the free areas of conventional and upper memory. You can abbreviate as /F.
/MODULE *modulename*	Indicates how the specified module (*modulename*) is currently using memory. You can abbreviate as /M *modulename*.
/PAGE	Pauses after each full screen of output. You can abbreviate as /P.
/DEBUG	Displays programs and internal drivers loaded into memory, with the size and address if necessary. This switch also displays other programming information. You can abbreviate as /D.

/CLASSIFY	Displays programs loaded into memory, specifying whether they are in conventional memory or upper memory. This switch displays the size of each program with decimal and hexadecimal values. You can abbreviate as /C.

If you use MEM without any switches, DOS displays the status of your computer's memory.

3. Press Enter.

MD or MKDIR

Internal

Use MD (MKDIR) to create subdirectories to help organize your files.

Command Syntax

MD *d:path**directory***

or

MKDIR *d:path**directory***

Steps

1. Type **MD** or **MKDIR** and press the space bar one time.
2. Type the drive name and path of the new directory (if you are not in the drive and directory where you want to create the new directory).
3. Type the directory name.
4. Press Enter.

If you have a hard disk drive, you need to understand this command.

MEMMAKER

External

Use MEMMAKER to make more conventional memory available by moving device drivers and memory-resident programs to upper memory. MemMaker is covered in Lesson 10, "Advanced DOS Commands."

Command Syntax

MEMMAKER */switches*

Steps

1. Type **MEMMAKER** and press the space bar one time. You may need to precede the command with the drive and path for MEMMAKER.EXE because MEMMAKER is an external command.
2. You may use any of these switches:

/BATCH	Runs MemMaker in batch mode, which means that MemMaker takes the default action on all prompts.
/B	Displays MemMaker in black and white for monochrome monitors.
/SWAP:*d:*	Specifies the letter of the drive that originally was your startup disk drive, if your startup drive has changed since you started your computer. *d:* is the current drive.
/UNDO	Restores your original AUTOEXEC.BAT and CONFIG.SYS files.
/W:*size1,size2*	Specifies how much space to reserve in upper memory for Windows' transition buffers. The default is 12K for each region.
/T	Disables the detection of IBM token-ring networks.

3. Press Enter to start the MemMaker program.
4. Follow the on-screen instructions.

Caution
Do not use MemMaker while you are running Microsoft Windows. Exit Windows and then run MemMaker from the DOS prompt.

Note: *In most cases, the Express Setup successfully optimizes your system memory. Use Custom Setup only if you have a very strong understanding of your computer's memory configuration. You must have at least an 80386 processor to use MemMaker.*

MORE

External

Use MORE to display data one screen at a time.

Command Syntax

*d:path**filename.ext*** | **MORE**

Steps

1. Type the DOS command you want to execute (for example, DIR). Press the space bar one time.
2. Type | (the pipe symbol) and press the space bar.
3. Type **MORE** and press Enter.

   DOS displays one full screen (23 lines on most systems) at a time and displays the following message:

   ```
   --More--
   ```

4. Press any key to display the next 23 lines of data.

MORE is very convenient for reading files longer than one screen. You may need to precede the syntax with a program name that acts on the file name; for example, use the following syntax to display a text file one screen at a time:

TYPE *filename.ext* | MORE

MOVE

External

Use MOVE to do the following tasks:

- Move one or more files to another disk or directory.
- Rename a directory.

Command Syntax

MOVE /Y /-Y *d:\path**filename.ext dd:\dpath***\newname.ext*

Steps

To move a file:

1. Type **MOVE** and press the space bar one time.
2. You may add one of the following switches:

/Y	Specifies that MOVE is to replace existing files with the same name without prompting for confirmation.
/-Y	Specifies that MOVE is to prompt for confirmation before replacing existing files with the same name.

   Press the space bar after typing the switch.
3. Type the drive, path, and file name of the file you want to move. If the current directory contains the file you want to move, you may omit the drive and path information.
4. Press the space bar.
5. Type the destination drive and path. To rename the file when you move it, type the new file name after the drive and path.
6. Press Enter.

If the destination directory doesn't exist, DOS fails the MOVE command and produces the following error message:

`Cannot move` *filename.ext* `- Permission denied`

To rename a directory:

1. Type **MOVE** and press the space bar one time.
2. Type the drive, path, and directory name of the directory you want to rename.

Caution
When you move a file to another directory or disk, MOVE overwrites any file of the same name, so be sure to type the file names exactly (including directory names).

3. Press the space bar.

4. Type the new directory name.

5. Press Enter.

You can move more than one file at the same time to the same destination directory. Separate the file names with a comma. For example, to move the files TEXT.DOC and MEMO.DOC from the DOCS directory to the LETTERS directory, type the following line:

MOVE C:\DOCS\TEXT.DOC,MEMO.DOC C:\LETTERS

When you move more than one file, the destination must include a directory name.

MSAV

External

Use MSAV to do the following tasks:

- Start the Anti-Virus for DOS program.
- Scan your memory and drives for software viruses.
- Clean viruses from your system memory and drives.

Command Syntax

MSAV *d1:path1\filename1.ext1 d2:path2\filename2.ext2 è /switches*

Steps

1. Type **MSAV**. You may need to precede the command with the drive and path for MSAV.EXE because MSAV is an external command.

2. Type the drive or drives you want MSAV to scan (if you are not in the drive you want to scan), as well as the path to any particular files you want to scan.

3. You may use any of the following switches:

/S	Scans the specified drive but does not remove viruses.
/C	Scans the specified drive and removes viruses.
/R	Creates a report file called MSAV.RPT that lists the results of the scan.
/A	Scans all drives except the A: and B: drives.
/L	Scans all drives except network drives.
/N	Displays the contents of MSAV.TXT if this file exists and turns off the display of information during the scan.
/P	Displays a command-line interface rather than the graphical interface.
/F	Turns off the display of file names being scanned. Use this switch with /N or /P.
/VIDEO	Displays a list of switches that affect the way MSAV is displayed.
/25	Sets the screen display to 25 lines (default).
/28	Sets the screen display to 28 lines (VGA only).
/43	Sets the screen display to 43 lines (EGA and VGA).
/50	Sets the screen display to 50 lines (VGA).
/60	Sets the screen display to 60 lines (Video 7).
/IN	Uses a color scheme.
/BW	Uses a black-and-white color scheme.
/MONO	Uses a monochromatic color scheme.
/LCD	Uses an LCD color scheme.
/FF	Uses the fastest screen updating.
/BF	Uses the BIOS to display video.
/NF	Disables the use of alternate fonts.

/BT	Enables you to use a graphics mouse in Microsoft Windows.
/NGM	Uses the default mouse character rather than the graphics mouse character.
/LE	Exchanges the left and right mouse buttons.
/PS2	Resets the mouse.

4. Press Enter to start the Anti-Virus program.
5. In the Anti-Virus program, follow the on-screen instructions.

Anti-Virus is a full-screen utility. You can use the keyboard or the mouse to make selections and execute menu items. Anti-Virus is covered in Lesson 12, "Protecting Your PC's Data."

MSBACKUP

External

Use MSBACKUP to do the following tasks:

- Back up hard disk files to floppy disks.
- Restore backed up files to a hard disk.
- Compare backed up files to the original files.
- Configure the MS Backup program for your hardware system.

Command Syntax

MSBACKUP *setup file /switches*

Steps

1. Type **MSBACKUP**. You may need to precede the command with the drive and path for MSBACKUP.EXE because MSBACKUP is an external command.
2. Specify the setup file you want MS Backup to load. For example, type **MSBACKUP DATA.SET**. If you do not specify a setup file, MS Backup loads the default setup file.

3. You may use any of the following switches:

/BW	Specifies a black-and-white color scheme.
/LCD	Specifies a video mode compatible with laptop LCD displays.
/MDA	Uses a monochrome display adapter.

4. Press Enter to start the MS Backup for DOS program.

5. Select the function you want to perform: Backup, Restore, Compare, Configure.

6. Specify the files and disks you want to use for the current function.

7. Choose the Start button to start the function.

MS Backup is a full-screen utility. You can use the keyboard or the mouse to make selections and execute menu items. The first time you use the MSBACKUP command, DOS prompts you through configuration and a compatibility test. These features ensure that all the backup functions will work with your hardware system.

Note: *Remember to store your numbered disks in order. The restore operation can be crucial, and you do not want to create unnecessary complications in the middle of this procedure.*

MS Backup simplifies the task of backing up the files on your hard disk. The program also makes restoring your files much easier in case of an emergency. Becoming comfortable with the MS Backup program and establishing a regular backup routine are vital. Without backups, all your data is at risk. MS Backup is covered in Lesson 12, "Protecting Your PC's Data." Backup for Windows is covered in Lesson 14, "Configuring DOS 6.2 for Windows."

PATH

Internal

Use PATH to access files not in the default directory without changing directories. PATH tells DOS to search specified directories on specified drives if it does not find a program or batch file in the current directory.

Command Syntax

PATH *d1:\path1*;*d2:\path2;d3:\path3;...*

Steps

1. Type **PATH** and press the space bar one time.
2. Type the drive name you want to include in the search path (for example, A:, B:, or C:). If you include the drive name with the path, DOS finds your files even if you change default drives.
3. Type the directory path you want to search (for example, \KEEP).
4. To add another directory to the search path, type a semicolon (**;**), and then type the drive name and path of the additional directory.
5. Repeat steps 2 through 4 until you type all the directory paths you want DOS to search.
6. Press Enter.

PATH is an important navigational aid you should understand fully. If you don't understand PATH, you don't understand the directory concept.

PROMPT

Internal

Use PROMPT to do the following tasks:

- Customize the DOS system prompt.
- Display the drive and directory path.
- Display a message on the computer.
- Display the date and time or the DOS version number.

Command Syntax

PROMPT *promptstring*

Steps

1. Type **PROMPT** and press the space bar one time.

2. Type the text string and parameters you want to display.

   You may use these meta-string characters, preceded by $, with the PROMPT command to produce your own DOS prompt:

$D	Displays the current date.
$G	Displays the > character.
$L	Displays the < character.
$N	Displays the current disk drive name.
$P	Displays the current drive and path.
$Q	Displays the = character.
$T	Displays the system time.
$V	Displays the DOS version.
$$	Displays the dollar sign.
$B	Displays the | symbol.
$E	Displays a left arrow. Specifies the Esc code (ASCII 27) used with ANSI escape sequences.
$H	Moves the cursor back one space, erasing the preceding character.
$_	Moves the cursor to the beginning of the next line.

   DOS ignores any other character.

3. Press Enter.

After you place PROMPT in your AUTOEXEC.BAT file with the information you want, you may never need to refer to the PROMPT command again. PROMPT is used most frequently to extend the visual command line so it displays the path of your resident directory.

RD or RMDIR

Internal

Use RD or RMDIR to remove a directory.

Command Syntax

RD *d:path*

or

RMDIR *d:path*

Steps

1. Use the ERASE command to delete any files from the directory you want to remove. The directory can contain only the current (.) and parent (..) files.
2. Type **RMDIR** or **RD** and press the space bar one time.
3. Type the drive name of the directory you want to remove.
4. Type the full path and name of the directory you want to remove.
5. Press Enter.

RMDIR is another essential command for maintaining a logical hard disk drive subdirectory system.

REN or RENAME

Internal

Use REN or RENAME to change the name of a file or group of files.

Command Syntax

RENAME *d:path**oldfilename.ext newfilename.ext***

Steps

1. Type **RENAME** or **REN** and press the space bar one time.
2. Type the drive name and path of the file you want to rename if the file is not in the current drive and directory.

3. Type the name of the file you want to rename. You may use wild cards (* and ?) to specify groups of files.

4. Press the space bar.

5. Type the new name you want to assign the file and press Enter.

Note: *Avoid giving files in different directories the same file name. You may confuse these files and accidentally use or delete the wrong file.*

Practice this command. It has many uses and is essential for every DOS user.

REPLACE

External

Use REPLACE to do the following tasks:

- Replace files on a destination disk with the files of the same name from the source disk.
- Copy files from the source disk that do not already exist on the destination disk.
- Replace files on the destination disk with files from the source disk only if the source files have a later date than the destination files.

Command Syntax

REPLACE *sd:spath****sfilename.ext dd:dpath***\\ */switches*

Steps

1. Type **REPLACE** and press the space bar one time. You may need to precede the command with the drive and path for REPLACE.EXE because REPLACE is an external command.

2. Type the drive name and path of the source file (*sd:\spath*).

3. Type the name of the file you want to copy. You may use wild cards.

4. Press the space bar.

5. Type the drive name and path of the target location (*dd:\dpath*).

6. You may use any of the following switches:

   /A Copies files from the source disk that do not already exist in the destination directory.

   /R Replaces files on the destination disk even if the files have the read-only attribute turned on.

   /U Replaces files on the destination disk that are older than the files on the source disk.

   /P Prompts you before copying each file.

   /S Copies specified files from the current directory and from subdirectories of the current directory.

   /W Makes REPLACE wait before starting the copy so that you can insert the correct disks in the drive.

7. Press Enter.

RESTORE

External

Use RESTORE to retrieve one or more files from a backup disk made with a version of DOS prior to DOS 6.

Command Syntax

RESTORE ***sd:*** *dd:\dpath**dfilename.ext** /switches*

Steps

1. Type **RESTORE** and press the space bar one time.

2. Type the name of the source drive that contains the backed up files. (For example, to restore files from the A: drive, type A:.) Then press the space bar.

3. Type the name of the destination drive. (For example, to restore files to a hard disk in the C: drive, type C:.) If you omit the drive name, the current drive becomes the destination drive.

4. To restore files from only one directory, type the path.

5. Type the name and extension of the file or files you want to restore. You may use wild cards to designate a group of files.

   To restore a backup file named MARCH.DOC on the A: drive to the directory C:\DOCS, for example, you type the following command line:

   RESTORE A: C:\DOCS\MARCH.DOC

6. You may use any of the following switches:

/S	Restores all files in the current directory and subdirectories of the current directory, creating subdirectories when necessary.
/P	Displays a screen prompt that asks whether you want to restore files that have changed since the last backup or that are designated by the ATTRIB command as read-only.
/M	Restores only those files modified or deleted since the last backup.
/N	Restores only those files that no longer exist on the target disk.
/B:*mm-dd-yy*	Restores only those files modified on or before the specified date.
/A:*mm-dd-yy*	Restores only those files modified on or after the specified date.
/L:*hh:mm:ss*	Restores only those files that have changed at or later than the specified time.
/E:*hh:mm:ss*	Restores only those files that have changed at or earlier than the specified time.
/D	Displays the names of files to be restored, without actually restoring the files.

7. Press Enter. When prompted, place a backup disk into the source drive and press Enter again.

8. Repeat step 7 until all backup disks are processed.

Note: *You can use RESTORE only with data backed up with the BACKUP command prior to DOS 6.*

SORT

External

Use SORT to do the following tasks:

- Read input data, sort it, and write it to an output device.
- Sort and list directory information.
- Display, arrange, and sort data alphabetically in ascending or descending order.

Command Syntax

SORT *sfilename.ext dfilename.ext* */switch*

Steps

1. Type **SORT** and press the space bar one time.
2. Type the file name and extension of the file you want to sort (*sfilename.ext*). Press the space bar.
3. Type the file name and extension of the sorted file you want to produce with the SORT command (*dfilename.ext*). Press the space bar.
4. You may use either of the following switches:

   /R Sorts in reverse alphabetical order.

   /+*n* Sorts in alphabetical order, starting at column *n*.
5. Press Enter.

Consider the following command example:

SORT /R PRESORT.TXT POSTSORT.TXT

The SORT command sorts, in reverse alphabetical order, the contents of the file PRESORT.TXT and writes the sorted contents to the file POSTSORT.TXT.

SORT is not an essential command, but it is useful for visual control of data contained in lists of ASCII text.

SYS

External

Use SYS to transfer the operating system files to another disk. SYS enables the transfer of operating system files to a disk that holds an application's program if the disk has enough space.

Command Syntax

SYS *sd:* ***dd:***

Steps

1. Place the target disk (the disk to receive the operating system) into a disk drive.

2. Type **SYS** and press the space bar one time.

3. If the operating system you want to copy is on a disk other than the disk from which you booted, type the name of the drive containing the operating system (*sd:*). For example, type A:. Press the space bar.

4. Type the name of the drive holding the target disk (*dd:*). For example, type B:.

5. Press Enter. SYS transfers the operating system, including COMMAND.COM, to the floppy disk in the target drive. If you are using DoubleSpace, SYS also transfers the file DBLSPACE.BIN to the target drive so that this file is loaded in memory when you use the disk to boot your system.

Note: *You do not need to transfer the operating system to every floppy disk. Save disk storage space by transferring the operating system only to disks you want to use as boot disks.*

In earlier versions of DOS, the SYS command transferred the hidden system files to a floppy disk without copying COMMAND.COM. Since DOS 5, the SYS command transfers COMMAND.COM as well as the hidden system files.

TIME

Internal

Use TIME to do the following tasks:

- Enter or change the time used by the system.
- Set the automatic clock on a computer with a battery-backed clock.
- Establish the time that files were created or modified.
- Provide control for programs that require time information.

Command Syntax

TIME *hh:mm:ss.xx* A or P

Steps

1. Type **TIME** and press the space bar one time.
2. Enter the time in the format *hh:mm:ss:xx* (use colons to separate numbers) or *hh.mm.ss.xx* (use periods to separate numbers).

   For *hh*, type the hour, using one or two digits from 0 to 23. For *mm*, type the minutes, using one or two digits from 0 to 59. For *ss*, type the seconds, using one or two digits from 0 to 59. For *xx*, type the hundredths of a second, using one or two digits from 0 to 99. You don't need to include more than the hour and the minutes.
3. If you use the 12-hour clock when you enter the time, type **A** to represent AM hours or **P** to represent PM hours. For the 24-hour clock, omit these identifiers. (For example, to indicate 3:13 PM, type 3:13P for the 12-hour clock or 15:13 for the 24-hour clock.)
4. Press Enter.

Use TIME with the DATE command. Including the correct time in a file may not be as important as including the date, but don't get into poor management habits. Better still, think about getting a battery-powered clock card for your PC to save time.

TREE

External

Use TREE to do the following tasks:

- Display directory paths in hierarchical directories.
- List the available files in each directory.
- Find lost files within a maze of directories.

Command Syntax

TREE *d: /switch*

Steps

1. Type **TREE** and press the space bar one time.
2. Type the name of the drive whose directory paths you want to display. The TREE command lists information about this drive.
3. You may use either of the following switches:

   /F Lists the files in each directory.

   /A Uses the characters |, -, \, and + to display the subdirectory structure (instead of using graphic line characters).
4. Press Enter.

The TREE command is another way to monitor a hard disk drive's directory structure. As time goes on, you appreciate this command more.

TYPE

Internal

Use TYPE to do the following tasks:

- Display the contents of a text file on-screen.
- Send files to the printer.

Command Syntax

TYPE *d:path**filename.ext***

Steps

1. Type **TYPE** and press the space bar one time.
2. Type the drive name, path, and file name of the file you want to display.

   You must enter the file name and extension of the file you want to display using the TYPE command. You cannot use wild-card characters with this command.
3. Press Enter.

To send the typed output to a device such as the printer (PRN), use the redirection symbol >, as shown in this example:

TYPE TEST.TXT > PRN

TYPE enables you to read a file without opening it in a word processing program.

Note: *When using the TYPE command to display a file with too many lines to fit on your screen at one time, use the MORE command, which is covered earlier in this lesson. The MORE command pauses screen output after 23 lines, enabling you to examine the file contents.*

UNDELETE

External

Use UNDELETE to do the following tasks:

- Activate or deactivate deletion protection.
- List files that have been deleted but can be undeleted.
- Undelete files.
- Delete the contents of the SENTRY directory.

Command Syntax

To activate deletion protection:

UNDELETE */switches*

To undelete files:

UNDELETE *d:path**filename.ext*** */switches*

Steps

To activate delete protection:

1. Type **UNDELETE** and press the space bar. You may need to precede the command with a path for UNDELETE.EXE because UNDELETE is an external command.
2. You may type any of these switches:

/LOAD	Loads the UNDELETE program into memory.
/UNLOAD	Unloads the UNDELETE program from memory, completely disabling UNDELETE.
/S	Enables the Delete Sentry level of protection against deletion. Do not use the /S switch at the same time as the /T switch. If you do not specify /S or /T, UNDELETE defaults to the MS-DOS level of protection. You can add the following line to AUTOEXEC.BAT to enable Delete Sentry each time you start your system: **UNDELETE /S**

8

/T	Enables the Delete Tracking level of protection against deletion. Do not use the /T switch at the same time as the /S switch. If you do not specify /T or /S, UNDELETE defaults to the MS-DOS level of protection. You can add the following line to AUTOEXEC.BAT to enable Delete Tracking each time you start your system: **UNDELETE /T**
/PURGE	Deletes the contents of the SENTRY directory.
/STATUS	Displays the active level of protection.

3. Press Enter.

To undelete files:

1. Type **UNDELETE** and press the space bar. You may need to precede the command with a path for UNDELETE.EXE because UNDELETE is an external command.

2. Specify the drive, path, and file name of the file you want to undelete.

3. You may type any of these switches:

/LIST	Lists all deleted files but does not recover them. This setting is the default.
/ALL	Recovers all deleted files.
/DOS	Recovers files protected with the MS-DOS level of protection.
/DS	Recovers files protected with the Delete Sentry level of protection.
/DT	Recovers files protected with the Delete Tracking level of protection.

4. Press Enter.

5. Press **Y** for each file you want to undelete or **N** to cancel the process.

Undelete is covered in Lesson 12, "Protecting Your PC'S Data."

UNFORMAT

External

Use UNFORMAT to do the following tasks:

- Restore a disk that was erased using the FORMAT command.
- Rebuild a corrupted disk partition table on a hard disk drive.

Command Syntax

UNFORMAT *d: /switches*

Caution
UNFORMAT cannot restore a disk if you used the /U switch with the FORMAT command.

Steps

1. Type **UNFORMAT** and press the space bar. You may need to precede the command with a drive and path for the UNFORMAT.EXE file because UNFORMAT is an external command.

2. Type the drive on which you want the UNFORMAT command to operate.

3. You may type any of the following switches:

/L	Lists every file and directory found by UNFORMAT. If you do not specify this switch, UNFORMAT lists only fragmented directories and files.
/TEST	Shows how UNFORMAT would re-create the information on the disk, without actually going through with the unformat.
/P	Sends output messages to the printer connected to LPT1.
/J	Compares the disk with its mirror files to verify that they are up-to-date, without actually unformatting the disk.

/U	Unformats the disk without using its mirror files.
/PARTN	Restores partition tables.

4. Press Enter.

Note: *You cannot use UNFORMAT on network drives.*

VER

Internal

Use VER to display the DOS version number.

Command Syntax

VER

Steps

1. Type **VER**.
2. Press Enter. DOS displays the version number on-screen in a message such as the following:

```
MS-DOS Version 6.20
```

The VER command is infrequently used and has a single purpose.

VERIFY

Internal

Use VERIFY to do the following tasks:

- Set your computer to check the accuracy of data written to a disk.
- Show whether the data has been checked.

Command Syntax

To show whether VERIFY is on or off:

VERIFY

To set the verify status:

VERIFY ON

or

VERIFY OFF

Steps

1. Type **VERIFY** and press the space bar one time.
2. Type **ON** or **OFF** depending on whether you want VERIFY on to check for accuracy or off for fast disk-writing operation.
3. Press Enter.

Typing VERIFY without adding the ON or OFF parameters prompts the verify command to display the current status of the command, either `Verify is on` or `Verify is off`. VERIFY provides absolute peace of mind but requires twice as long to copy files. Many people are in the habit of using verification. If you have the time, you may find VERIFY worthwhile.

VOL

Internal

Use VOL to display the volume label of the specified drive.

Command Syntax

VOL *d:*

Steps:

1. Type **VOL** and press the space bar one time.
2. Type the drive name of the disk that has the volume name you want to examine (for example, A: or B:), if that drive is not already current.

3. Press Enter.

Some people never use this command, but in fact VOL is as important as labeling a disk.

XCOPY

External

Use XCOPY to do the following tasks:

- Copy files from multiple directories to another disk.
- Copy files with a specific date.
- Copy newly created or modified files.
- Copy subdirectories and files.

Command Syntax

XCOPY *sd:spath****sfilename.ext*** *dd:dpath\dfilename.ext /switches*

Steps

1. Type **XCOPY** and press the space bar one time. You may need to precede the command with the drive and path for XCOPY.EXE because XCOPY is an external command.
2. Type the drive name and path of the source file (*sd:\spath*).
3. Type the name of the file you want to copy. You may use wild cards.
4. Press the space bar.
5. Type the drive name, path, and file name of the target file (*dd:\dpath\dfilename.ext*). Skip this step if the file name is to remain the same as that of the source file.

6. You may use any of the following switches:

/A	Copies files with the archive attribute set on and does not change the archive attribute.
/M	Copies files with the archive attribute set on but shuts off the archive attribute.
/D:*date*	Copies files that were created or modified on or after the specified date.
/P	Prompts you before copying each file.
/S	Copies specified files from the current directory and from subdirectories of the current directory, creating directories on the destination disk when necessary.
/E	Copies empty subdirectories.
/V	Verifies each copied file.
/W	Makes XCOPY wait before starting the copy so you can insert the correct disks in the drive.
/Y	Specifies that XCOPY is to replace files with the same name as the files you are copying without prompting you for confirmation.
/-Y	Specifies that XCOPY is to prompt you for confirmation before replacing files with the same name as the files you are copying.

Caution
Before you use XCOPY, make sure that you have typed the correct information so you do not inadvertently copy over important files.

7. Press Enter.

Summary

To	Do This
Change directories	Use the CD command
Delete a file	Use the ERASE command
Copy a file	Use the COPY command
Copy a disk	Use the DISKCOPY command
Create a directory	Use the MD command
Set the system date	Use the DATE command
Set the system time	Use the TIME command
Clear the screen	Use the CLS command
Compress your drive	Use the DBLSPACE command
Backup your data	Use the MSBACKUP command

Lesson 9

Basic DOS Commands

9

Although DOS contains dozens of commands, some are more useful than others. Even long-time DOS users rarely exploit more than a fraction of the DOS commands. Earlier lessons cover the DOS commands most critical to your using the computer. This lesson looks at some other DOS commands that can make your life a little easier. In this lesson you learn how to:

- View file contents with the TYPE command
- Locate a file with the DIR command
- Get a report on available memory with the MEM command
- Clear your screen with the CLS command
- Determine the DOS version with the VER command
- Verify that a file is written with the VERIFY command
- Display the volume name of a disk with the VOL command
- Change a volume name with the LABEL command

You can get by without using these commands, but after you feel comfortable with the basics, you may find these commands to be handy helpers.

Task: Displaying File Contents with TYPE

To view the contents of a text file from the command line, use the TYPE command:

1. Change to the drive and directory that contains the file you want to view.
2. Type the following command, replacing *filename.ext* with the file name and extension of the file you want to view:

   TYPE filename.ext

3. Press Enter.

ASCII text
Pure text you can read using the TYPE command rather than a word processing program or other application program.

The TYPE command works only on *ASCII text* files. Using the TYPE command on a binary file shows nothing but gibberish. To view a binary file you can use the DOS Shell, which is covered in Appendix B. To view a word processing file, use the word processing program that created the file.

If you have problems...

If you have problems using the TYPE command, make sure that you correctly type the command at the DOS prompt. Press the space bar one time. Then type the name of the file you want to view. If your screen fills with gibberish, you need a software application, rather than the TYPE command, to view the file.

Task: Locating a File with DIR

A hard disk usually contains hundreds of files. You begin by organizing these files so you know where each file is located. Sometimes, however, you may not remember which subdirectory a file is in. You can use the DIR command to locate the file.

To search for a file from the command line, use the DIR command. For example, to try to find the file README.TXT in a directory full of files, follow these steps:

1. Type the following command at the DOS prompt:

   DIR README.TXT

2. Press Enter.

To have DOS search the current directory and any subdirectories, add the /S switch:

1. Type the following command:

   DIR README.TXT /S

2. Press Enter.

If you don't remember the name of the file you want but you know the extension, try using wild-card characters:

1. Type the following command:

   DIR *.TXT

2. Press Enter.

If you have little idea where you stored a file you want to find, the DIR command can help. For example, to find the file MOUSE.EXE, these steps may work:

1. Change to the root directory if you are in another directory or subdirectory (type **CD** and press Enter).

2. Type the following command:

   DIR MOUSE.EXE /S

3. Press Enter.

The read out for the DIR command when used in this way should be similar to the following:

```
Volume in drive C is C_DRIVE
 Volume Serial Number is 1B6A-9B34

Directory of C:\WINDOWS

MOUSE     EXE         93,316 03-31-93   9:00a
        1 file(s)         93,316 bytes

Total files listed:
        1 file(s)         93,316 bytes
                     119,676,928 bytes free
```

This result shows that the DIR command found MOUSE.EXE in the C:\WINDOWS directory.

Task: Getting a Memory Report with MEM

The MEM command reports the amount of system memory available for programs to load and run. The MEM command also tells you the types of memory available on your computer—conventional, extended, expanded, and upper—as well as free upper memory blocks (UMBs) and the size of the largest program you can execute. MEM also tells you whether DOS is using conventional memory or is loaded in the high memory area.

To run MEM, follow these steps:

1. Type **MEM** at the DOS prompt.
2. Press Enter.

The read out for the MEM command is similar to the following:

```
Memory Type          Total  =   Used  +   Free
-----------          -----      ----      ----
Conventional          640K       68K      572K
Upper                   0K        0K        0K
Reserved              384K      384K        0K
Extended (XMS)     31,744K   30,720K    1,024K
-----------          -----      ----      ----
Total memory       32,768K   31,172K    1,596K

Total under 1 MB      640K       68K      572K

Total Expanded (EMS)                 1,024K (1,048,576 bytes)
Free Expanded (EMS)                  1,024K (1,048,576 bytes)

Largest executable program size        572K (585,392 bytes)
Largest free upper memory block          0K       (0 bytes)
MS-DOS is resident in the high memory area.
```

Task: Clearing Your Screen with CLS

The CLS command erases or clears the display and positions the cursor at the top of the screen at the DOS prompt. Use CLS when the screen becomes too cluttered with the output of previous commands. CLS has no parameters; just follow these steps:

1. Type **CLS** at the DOS prompt.
2. Press Enter.

The main use for CLS is with batch files, which are covered in Lesson 11, "Customizing DOS."

Task: Determining the DOS Version with VER

Although you already know you are running DOS 6.2, if you are working on another computer, you may want to know the exact version of DOS that computer is using. The VER command reports the manufacturer's name and the version number of DOS. If you use the VER command on a computer that is running an earlier version of DOS, the report may look slightly different than the report shown for DOS 6.2. To run the VER command, follow these steps:

1. Type **VER** at the DOS prompt.
2. Press Enter.

Issuing this command before starting work at another person's computer is important so you can see which DOS commands are available. For example, if the other computer is running DOS 3.3, you know the SCANDISK command is not available to check problems on a floppy disk, because SCANDISK is new with DOS 6.2.

Task: Checking Data Storage Accuracy with VERIFY

The VERIFY command checks the accuracy of data written to disks. VERIFY can use only one of two parameters: ON or OFF. To use the VERIFY command, follow these steps:

1. Type the following at the DOS prompt:

   VERIFY ON

2. Press Enter.

After you type VERIFY ON at the prompt, DOS rereads all data byte-by-byte as it saves to disk to ensure that the data is recording correctly.

When VERIFY is set to ON, DOS operations are slower; therefore, you may want to use the command with only important data. To turn off verification, follow these steps:

1. Type the following at the DOS prompt:

   VERIFY OFF

2. Press Enter.

To display the status of VERIFY, follow these steps:

1. Type the following at the DOS prompt:

   VERIFY

2. Press Enter.

   The readout tells you whether VERIFY is on or off.

Task: Displaying the Disk Volume Name with VOL

Volume label
An electronic label that appears on-screen after you issue the DIR command.

When you format a disk, you can enter a *volume label* for the disk. Labeling a volume is useful for keeping track of your disks (labeling disks is discussed in the next section). You can use the VOL command to find out your disk's volume name.

To determine the volume label for a disk, follow these steps:

1. Type **VOL** at the DOS prompt.
2. Press Enter.

After you issue the VOL command, the volume name of the current disk appears if you entered a name when you formatted the disk. VOL also displays the volume serial number automatically assigned by DOS when you formatted the disk. If you add a drive letter after the command, DOS displays volume information for that drive.

Task: Changing a Volume Name with LABEL

After you format a disk, you can add to or change the volume label name with the LABEL command. You should change a disk's volume label name when you change the use for the disk. For example, when you first formatted a disk, you may have labeled it *TAX93*. Later, you want to use the disk to keep a backup copy of your 1994 business files, so you change the label name to *BUSINESS94*.

The following line shows the syntax for the LABEL command:

LABEL *d:* ***label***

The *d:* is the drive letter and *label* is the new label name. If you omit the drive letter, DOS uses the current drive. If you don't specify a label name, DOS displays the current volume label and prompts you to enter a new label. You cannot use any of the following characters in a volume label:

* ? / \ | . , ; : + = [ ] ( ) & ^ < > "

To add a volume named *BUSINESS94* to a disk, follow these steps:

1. Insert a spare floppy disk in the A: drive.
2. Type the following at the DOS prompt:

   LABEL A: BUSINESS94

3. Press Enter.

   DOS immediately changes the volume label if a previous label existed, or DOS gives the specified volume label to the disk if it had no label.

To remove a label from a disk in the A: drive, follow these steps:

1. Type the following at the DOS prompt:

   LABEL A:

   DOS displays the existing label with the following prompt:

   ```
   Volume label (11 characters, ENTER for none)?
   ```

2. Press Enter.

   DOS displays the following prompt:

   ```
   Delete current volume label (Y/N)?
   ```

3. Press **Y** for yes or **N** for no.

4. Press Enter.

Summary

To	Do This
View a text file	Use the TYPE command
Find a file	Use the DIR command
Get a memory report	Use the MEM command
Clear your screen	Use the CLS command
Determine the DOS version	Use the VER command
Ensure files are written correctly	Use the VERIFY command
Display the volume name of a disk	Use the VOL command
Change a volume name	Use the LABEL command

On Your Own

Estimated Time: 5 minutes

View text files and find files.

1. View your AUTOEXEC.BAT file by typing the following at the C:\> prompt and pressing Enter:

   TYPE AUTOEXEC.BAT

2. View your CONFIG.SYS file by typing the following at the C:\> prompt and pressing Enter:

   TYPE CONFIG.SYS

3. Find the file COMMAND.COM by typing the following at the C:\> prompt and pressing Enter:

   DIR COMMAND.COM

4. Find the file MSAV.EXE by typing the following at the C:\> prompt and pressing Enter:

   DIR MSAV.EXE /S

Use the MEM, CLS, and VER commands.

1. Get a memory report for your system by typing the following at the C:\> prompt and pressing Enter:

   MEM

2. Clear your screen by typing the following at the C:\> prompt and pressing Enter:

   CLS

3. Determine the DOS version by typing the following at the C:\> prompt and pressing Enter:

   VER

Use the VERIFY command.

1. Determine whether VERIFY is on or off by typing the following at the C:\> prompt and pressing Enter:

   VERIFY

2. Start the VERIFY command by typing the following at the C:\> prompt and pressing Enter:

   VERIFY ON

3. Turn off the VERIFY command by typing the following at the C:\> prompt and pressing Enter:

   VERIFY OFF

Display and change volume labels.

1. Display the volume name of your hard disk by typing the following at the C:\> prompt and pressing Enter:

   VOL

2. Place a floppy disk in drive A: and display its volume label by typing the following at the C:\> prompt and pressing Enter:

   VOL A:

3. Change the volume label on a floppy disk in drive A: to SPAREDISK by typing the following at the C:\> prompt and pressing Enter (be sure to use only a spare disk for this exercise):

   LABEL A: SPAREDISK

Lesson 10

Advanced DOS Commands

This lesson covers some of the more powerful capabilities of DOS 6.2. With the information in this lesson, you can learn how to do the following:

- Use the Doskey command line editor
- Understand DOS devices and redirection
- Work with pipes and filters

Using Doskey, the Command Line Editor

When you use the command line, you find that you repeat many commands over and over, sometimes with slight variations. With the Doskey command line editor, you can recall previous commands without retyping them. At times, you may type a long command and make an error. Whether you catch the error before or after you press Enter, Doskey enables you to correct the error without retyping the entire command.

Task: Running Doskey

To use Doskey's features, you must load it into memory. Follow these steps:

1. Type **DOSKEY** at the prompt.
2. Press Enter.

Buffer
A portion of memory where Doskey stores your commands.

Doskey is loaded into memory with a 512-byte *buffer*. As long as a command is in the buffer, you can recall the command without retyping it. After the buffer fills up, any new command you enter causes Doskey to delete the oldest command in the buffer.

You need to enter the DOSKEY command only one time per session. If you plan to use Doskey regularly, you can put the command in your AUTOEXEC.BAT file. The AUTOEXEC.BAT file is covered in Lesson 11, "Customizing DOS."

Task: Recalling Previous Commands with Doskey

After loading Doskey into memory, you can recall previous commands using these methods:

- Press the up-arrow key to recall the last command you entered.
- To recall an earlier command, continue to press the up-arrow key until DOS displays the command you want.
- If you press the up-arrow key too many times and go past the command you want, press the down-arrow key to cycle back through the commands in the buffer.
- Press the Esc key to clear the command line so you can enter a command from scratch.

Suppose, for example, that you enter the following commands:

C:

CD\DATA\TAXES

FORMAT A: /Q

COPY *.* A:

These commands make the DATA\TAXES directory the current directory, quick format a floppy disk in the A: drive, and then copy all the files from the DATA\TAXES directory to the floppy disk in the A: drive.

After the copy procedure is complete, DOS displays the DOS prompt. If you want to repeat this process for the DATA\DOCS directory, for example, you can retype each command or use Doskey to recall the commands, as these steps explain:

1. Press the up-arrow key one time to recall the last command entered:

```
COPY *.* A:
```

2. Press the up-arrow key three times to recall the third-from-the-last command entered:

```
CD\DATA\TAXES
```

3. Press the backspace key five times to erase the word TAXES.

4. Type **DOCS** and press Enter.

   DATA\DOCS becomes the current directory.

5. Press the up-arrow key to cycle through the previously issued commands until you see `FORMAT A: /Q`.

6. Because you do not want to change this command in any way, make sure you have a disk in the A: drive and press Enter.

7. After the format is complete, press the up-arrow key until you see `COPY *.* A:`.

8. Press Enter to copy all the files from the DATA\DOCS directory to the floppy disk.

Task: Using the Doskey Special Keys

To display and reuse the commands in the Doskey buffer, follow these steps:

1. Press F7 to display all the commands in the buffer. Each command is preceded by a number that indicates the order in which you used the commands. For example, if you had recently used the VER, CD\, and DIR commands, the read-out would look like the following:

```
1: ver
2: cd\
3: dir
C:\>
```

2. After DOS has displayed the entire list of commands, press F9.

3. Type the line number of the command you want to recall. For example, to recall the quick format command from the example in the preceding section, type **6**.

4. Press Enter. DOS recalls the command (for this example, the command at line number 6).

You have one more way to recall a command. Follow these steps:

1. Type one or more characters at the start of the command.

2. Press the F8 key.

   DOS searches the buffer, starting with the most recent command, for a command that starts with the characters you typed. If you type just the letter F and press Enter, DOS searches for the most recent command that starts with an F.

   If DOS finds a match when you use the F8 key, it recalls that command.

The following table shows the keys used with Doskey to recall previous commands:

Key	Action
Up arrow	Recalls the preceding command.
Down arrow	Recalls the next command.
Esc	Clears the command line.
PgUp	Recalls the oldest command.
PgDn	Recalls the most recent command.
F7	Lists all commands in the buffer.
F8	Searches the buffer for a command that starts with the text you specify.
F9	Recalls the command at the line number you specify.
Alt-F7	Clears the entire Doskey buffer.

Task: Editing Previous Commands with Doskey

After you recall a command, you can edit the command before you execute it. You already learned to use the backspace key to erase characters at the end of the command. Doskey provides additional keys that enable you to change any part of a command, although you can edit only one line. The following table shows the Doskey editing keys.

Key	Action
Home	Moves the cursor to the beginning of the command.
End	Moves the cursor to the end of the command.
Left arrow	Moves the cursor one character to the left.
Right arrow	Moves the cursor one character to the right.
Ctrl-left arrow	Moves the cursor one word to the left.
Ctrl-right arrow	Moves the cursor one word to the right.
Backspace	Deletes one character to the left of the cursor.
Del	Deletes one character at the cursor position.
Ctrl-End	Deletes all characters from the cursor to the end of the command.
Ctrl-Home	Deletes all characters from the cursor to the beginning of the command.
Ins	Toggles between Overtype and Insert modes. In Overtype mode, everything you type replaces existing characters. In Insert mode, the cursor changes from an underline to a square block, and everything you type inserts at the cursor.
Esc	Clears the command line.

Suppose, for example, that you execute the following command:

```
COPY *.DOC D:\BACKUP
```

You also want to copy all the files with a WK4 extension to the D:\BACKUP directory. Follow these steps:

1. Press the up-arrow key one time to recall the COPY command.

2. Press Home to move the cursor to the beginning of the command line.

3. Press the right-arrow key seven times to move the cursor to the D in DOC.

4. Type **WK4** in place of DOC.

5. Press Enter.

Doskey has other features that are beyond the scope of this book. You can find out more about Doskey in Que's *Using MS-DOS 6.2*, Special Edition.

If you have problems...

If you have problems running Doskey, make sure that you properly type the DOSKEY command and any parameters, and that you press the Enter key. If you have trouble reviewing previously issued commands, again study the previous information on recalling commands, special Doskey keys, and editing commands with Doskey.

Understanding DOS Devices

Devices
Extensions of the main unit of the computer that are used to send or receive input or output.

In DOS, the keyboard and display are the standard, or default, *devices* for input, messages, and prompts. Some devices are used only for input (keyboards) or only output (video displays or printers). Other devices send input and receive output. Disk drives are both input and output devices. Serial adapters (COM ports) can send output and receive input.

The computer screen (display) is the standard output device. The keyboard is the standard input device.

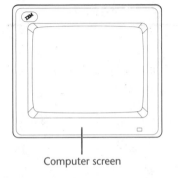

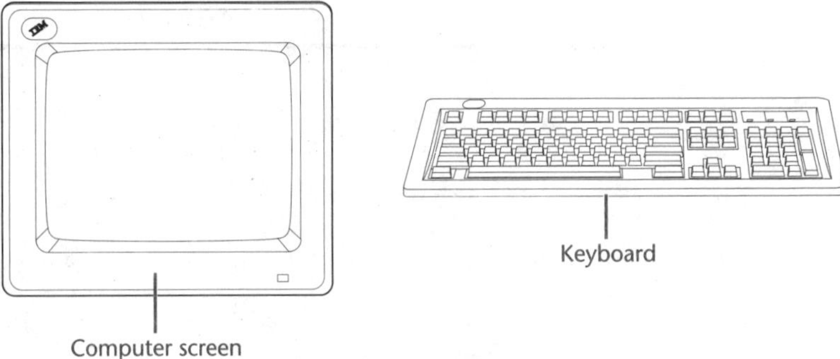

The system unit, a modem, and a disk drive both receive input and produce output. A printer is an output device.

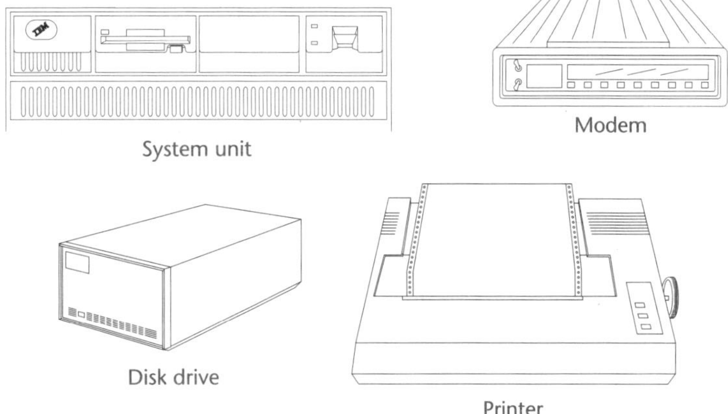

DOS treats devices as if they were files. Device names are three to four characters long and do not contain extensions. You cannot delete device names or use device names to name other files, but you can use device names in commands to perform some useful actions.

Reviewing DOS Device Names

DOS reserves the special names it uses for input and output devices. For example, you cannot name a file PRN because DOS reserves this name for output to the printer. The following table lists the reserved DOS device names.

Name	Device
CON	The console (the keyboard). The normal output device for the CON device is the display monitor.
AUX or COM1	The first asynchronous communications port, or serial port.
COM2	The second asynchronous port, or serial port.
COM3	The third asynchronous port, or serial port.
COM4	The fourth asynchronous port, or serial port.
PRN	The first parallel printer.
LPT1	The first parallel printer, an output device (sometimes also used for input to the computer).
LPT2	The second parallel printer (sometimes also used for input).
LPT3	The third parallel printer (sometimes also used for input).
NUL	A dummy device (for redirecting output to nowhere).

Task: Creating a File with the CON Device

CON
DOS's device name for the keyboard, which is an input (console) device.

A useful application for the *CON* device, and a quick way to gain understanding of the use of device names, is to create a file containing characters you enter directly from the keyboard. To do so, you use the familiar COPY command. This time, however, you copy data you input from CON.

In this case, suppose that you want to create a file named TEST.TXT. Follow these steps to send characters directly to the file:

1. At the DOS prompt, type the following command:

   COPY CON TEST.TXT

   This command specifies that you want DOS to copy data from the console and send the output to the TEST.TXT file.

   You can precede the file name and extension with the drive and directory where you want to create the file. For example, you can type the following command line:

   COPY CON C:\DOS\TEST.TXT

2. Press Enter. The cursor drops to the next line and no DOS prompt appears.

3. Begin typing characters as the input to the file. For example, type the following text:

   This is a file copied from a device to a disk file.

4. Press Enter. DOS writes the line that you typed in memory.

5. Type several lines, if you want, pressing Enter after each line.

6. After you finish typing text, press F6 or Ctrl-Z and press Enter. DOS recognizes either keystroke as the end-of-file character.

   DOS saves the information you typed as a new file and displays the message `1 File(s) copied`.

7. Press Enter.

You have just entered a text file into your computer by using a DOS command and a device name. Because you created the file as a test, you can delete it any time you want. However, the file will be useful in later sections of this lesson, so you probably do not want to delete it now.

You can create simple files quickly with this method. However, as the length of a file increases, COPY CON becomes more awkward to use. The MS-DOS Editor or another text editor is more reliable. With COPY CON, you cannot go back to a previous line and correct it after you press Enter. If you notice that you typed an error on a previous line, you have two options:

- Hold down the Ctrl key and press the Break key to end the COPY CON operation. You lose all the characters you typed.
- If you see an error after you saved the file, delete the file and start over, or use a text editor to correct the mistake.

Note: *Remember to close your file by pressing F6 or Ctrl-Z and then Enter. Until you close the file, DOS assumes that you are still typing characters into the file.*

To verify that the file is correct, use TYPE to view the file. You can follow these steps:

1. Change to the directory where you created the file.
2. Type the following line:

   TYPE TEST.TXT

   The TYPE command displays the contents of the file.

If you have problems...

If you have problems using COPY CON to create a text file, make sure that you carefully follow steps 1 through 7 in the previous directions. If you misspell something in a line, backspace over the mistake and correct it. To end each line, press the Enter key. To end the file, press Ctrl-Z or F6 then Enter.

Understanding Redirection

Redirection
Changing the source or destination normally used for input and output.

The standard source of input is the keyboard. The standard output location is the screen display. When you use the keyboard to type a command, COMMAND.COM carries the text and displays it on-screen. When you *redirect* output, you can use device names in some commands as you do file names.

Using Redirection Symbols

You must use special redirection symbols to tell DOS to use nondefault devices in a command. The following table lists the symbols DOS recognizes for redirection.

Symbol	Description
<	Redirects a program's input.
>	Redirects a program's output.
>>	Redirects a program's output to a text file but adds the text to an established file if it exists.

The < symbol points away from the device or file as a way of saying *take input from here*. The > symbol points toward the device or file as a way of saying *put output there*. The >> symbol redirects a program's output to a text file. When you issue a redirection command, place the redirection symbol after the DOS command but before the device name.

Task: Redirecting to a Printer

A practical use of redirection is to send output to the printer. For example, you can understand your directory tree structure more easily by redirecting the output of the TREE command to your printer. Follow these steps:

1. Make sure that the printer is turned on and connected to your computer.

2. Type the following command:

    TREE > PRN

3. Press Enter. The output of the TREE command goes to the printer.

You can keep such a printout near your computer so you can quickly view your directory structure. If you redirect the output of the DIR command to the printer, you can tuck the printout into the sleeve of a floppy disk to identify the contents of the disk.

If you created the TEST.TXT file mentioned earlier and your printer is ready, you can send the file to your printer from DOS. Follow these steps:

1. Type the following command:

    TYPE TEST.TXT > PRN

2. Press Enter.

You now have a printed copy of the TEST.TXT file.

A more efficient way to print a text file is to copy the file to the PRN device. Follow these steps:

1. Type this command:

    COPY TEST.TXT PRN

2. Press Enter.

Never try to redirect binary files to the printer. Redirecting binary data can result in paper-feed problems, beeps, meaningless graphic characters, and maybe a locked computer. If you get hung up, you can do a warm boot or turn the power switch off and then on again. If you must turn off your computer, wait approximately 15 seconds before turning it back on.

Task: Redirecting to a File

When you use commands, such as DIR or TREE, the result displays onscreen and then it is gone; the result isn't stored for future use. As you just learned, you can easily redirect a listing to a printer for a permanent printed record. You also can redirect the listing to a file for a record on your disk. To store a listing of all the directories on the C: drive in a file named TREE.TXT, follow these steps:

1. Type the following command:

    TREE C:\ > TREE.TXT

2. Press Enter.

You now have a permanent record of the structure of your hard disk at the time you created the file. To store a listing of all the directories and files on the C: drive in a file named TREEFILE.TXT, follow these steps:

1. Type the following command:

   TREE C:\ /F > TREEFILE.TXT

   The /F switch specifies that the TREE command is to list all files, directories, and subdirectories on the drive.

2. Press Enter.

After you practice with redirecting DOS commands, you will find many times that this capability is indispensable.

Working with Pipes and Filters

Pipe (|)
A symbol that enables you to use the output of one command as the input of another command.

Filter
A program that gets data from the standard input, changes the data, and then writes the modified data to the display.

Manipulating the input and output of DOS commands to use them with other commands is sometimes useful. Two common features that enable you to manipulate the output of DOS commands are *pipes* and *filters*. Together, pipes and filters give you a great deal of control over the results of basic DOS commands.

The pipe symbol (|) presents, or *pipes*, output from one command to another. For example, you can pipe the output, or result, of the DIR command so you can use the result as input for one of the filter commands. This example is shown in the following section.

To enter the pipe symbol, hold down the shift key and press the key that displays the backslash and pipe character.

Note: *Don't confuse the pipe symbol with the colon symbol. The pipe symbol is on the same key as the backslash. Books often print the pipe symbol as a solid vertical line (|), but on the keyboard and on your display the symbol appears as a broken vertical line.*

A filter enables you to change the way data from a standard input is displayed. The FIND, SORT, and MORE commands are filters that accept the output of a DOS command and do further processing on that output. This list describes how each filter works:

- FIND outputs lines that match characters given on the command line.
- SORT alphabetizes output.
- MORE displays a prompt when each screen of the output is full.

Task: Using the FIND Filter

One handy way of using the FIND filter is to display a directory listing showing only the files that contain certain characters in their file names. To list just the files that contain TAX in their file names, for example, follow these steps:

1. Change to the directory you want to search.
2. Type this command:

   DIR | FIND "TAX"

3. Press Enter.

The FIND command filters the output of this DIR command. FIND displays on-screen only the lines that contain the letters TAX. The | symbol pipes the output of DIR to FIND. The quotation marks specify the exact characters the FIND command is to display.

Task: Using the SORT Filter

The SORT command is a filter that alphabetizes input. In the following command, the output of the TYPE command, when used with a file containing a list of names, is piped to SORT:

```
TYPE NAMES.TXT | SORT
```

The listing filtered by SORT displays on-screen in alphabetical order.

The main use for the SORT filter with earlier versions of DOS was to sort a directory listing. With DOS 6, to sort a directory listing by file name, use the /ON switch as follows:

DIR /O*x*

You can replace the *x* character with one of the following letters:

N	By name (alphabetic)
S	By size (smallest to largest)
E	By extension (alphabetic)
D	By date and time (earliest to latest)
G	Group directories first
C	By compression ratio (smallest to largest)

Task: Using the MORE Filter

The MORE command stops the output of a command when the screen fills up. For example, if you have a directory containing dozens or hundreds of files and you use the DIR command, the list of files in the directory scrolls by so quickly you are unlikely to make any use of it. You can pause the display by pressing Ctrl-S or the Pause key on enhanced keyboards. But if you have a fast computer, pressing Ctrl-S or Pause at the right time may be very difficult, and information can scroll off the screen before you can read it. The MORE filter provides a better solution to this problem. MORE displays information one screen at a time, waiting until you press a key before displaying the next screen.

To see how MORE works, follow these steps:

1. Change to your DOS directory.
2. Type the following command:

   TYPE README.TXT | MORE

3. Press Enter.

   MORE displays 23 lines of text and then pauses, displaying the following message at the bottom of the screen.

   ```
   --More--
   ```

4. To continue displaying the README.TXT file, press any key. MORE displays the next screen of text.

If you want to read a long text file, using the MS-DOS Editor may be easier than using the MORE filter. With the Editor, you can use the PgUp and PgDn keys to scroll backward and forward through the text. With MORE, after a screenful of text scrolls off the screen, you cannot scroll back to see it again. Therefore, you should read or edit README.TXT using the following command:

```
EDIT README.TXT
```

If you have problems...

If you have problems using piping or redirection, or the FIND, SORT, or MORE filters, refer back to the section that covers the use of these powerful DOS tools.

When using redirection, make sure that you properly type the DOS command whose output you want to redirect, press the space bar, use the correct redirection symbol (< or >), and press Enter.

If you have problems using the SORT filter, make sure that you follow these steps:

1. Correctly type the SORT command.
2. Specify the file name and extension of the source file containing an ASCII text list you want to sort.
3. Specify an output file name and extension that will contain the result or the sort.
4. Press Enter.

If you have problems using the MORE filter, make sure that you follow these steps:

1. Correctly type the name of the DOS command whose output you want to control.
2. Press the space bar one time.
3. Type the pipe symbol (|).
4. Press the space bar.
5. Type **MORE**.
6. Press Enter.

Summary

<table>
<tr><th>To</th><th>Do This</th></tr>
<tr><td>Recall previous DOS commands</td><td>Use Doskey command line editor</td></tr>
<tr><td>Redirect command output</td><td>Use the > symbol</td></tr>
<tr><td>Redirect output into a command</td><td>Use the < symbol</td></tr>
<tr><td>Use a filter</td><td>Use the | symbol and the filter name</td></tr>
<tr><td>Find specific file name characters</td><td>Use the FIND filter</td></tr>
<tr><td>Pause output of a command</td><td>Use the MORE filter</td></tr>
<tr><td>Alphabetize file output</td><td>Use the SORT filter</td></tr>
</table>

On Your Own

Estimated time: 10 minutes

Use DOS device names, redirection commands, and filters.

1. Create a text file named TEST.TXT using the COPY CON command.
2. Send the output of TEST.TXT to your printer using the PRN device name.
3. Redirect the output of the DIR command to the printer using the redirection symbol.
4. Redirect the output of the DIR command to a file using the redirection symbol.
5. Change to the DOS directory, or another directory containing many files, and issue the DIR command using the MORE filter to control screen output.

Part IV
Customizing Your Setup

Lesson 11

Customizing DOS

Until now, the discussions in this book have been based on how DOS performs, especially on the command line. In this lesson you take control. You learn how to customize your DOS environment to meet your specific needs and construct your own commands so DOS works the way you want. This lesson helps you do the following:

- Create, edit, and back up AUTOEXEC.BAT and CONFIG.SYS
- Use the search path
- Customize the DOS prompt
- Create and change batch files
- Use the MS-DOS Editor
- Understand SmartDrive and HIMEM.SYS

Understanding the AUTOEXEC.BAT File

Batch file
A text file you can run, or execute, like a program because the file contains DOS commands.

AUTOEXEC.BAT
A batch file that executes automatically each time you boot your computer.

A *batch file* called *AUTOEXEC.BAT* has special significance to DOS. This file contains commands that make your computer work the way you want. (Batch files are covered in more detail later in this lesson.) DOS automatically searches for this file in the root directory when you boot your computer. If an AUTOEXEC.BAT file is present, DOS executes the commands contained in that file.

Technically, having an AUTOEXEC.BAT file is optional; however, every computer with a hard disk should have one. If for no other reason, you need an AUTOEXEC.BAT file so you can specify a path and prompt every time you boot your computer. You also probably want to use

AUTOEXEC.BAT to load your mouse driver software and other programs you want to run on your computer.

During the DOS 6.2 installation process, DOS creates, verifies, or changes your AUTOEXEC.BAT file to include a path to the \DOS directory plus any other commands it needs to run on your computer. Some application programs come with installation programs that create or modify AUTOEXEC.BAT as an installation step of the package's main program.

Most users and system managers put an AUTOEXEC.BAT file of their own design on their boot disk. Using a custom AUTOEXEC.BAT file enables you to benefit from commands that automatically specify operating parameters.

You can omit AUTOEXEC.BAT and manually enter the commands you might include in an AUTOEXEC.BAT file, thereby accomplishing the same result as an AUTOEXEC.BAT file. DOS, however, executes AUTOEXEC.BAT if it is there, so why not take advantage?

The following lines are from a sample AUTOEXEC.BAT file:

```
@ECHO OFF

PROMPT $P$G

PATH C:\DOS;C:\WORD;C:\WINDOWS;

MOUSE
```

The first line of this AUTOEXEC.BAT tells DOS not to display on-screen each line of AUTOEXEC.BAT as the line is executed.

The second line sets the type of prompt the screen will show (PG creates a prompt that shows the current directory).

The third line is the path statement that tells DOS to search the C:\DOS, C:\WORD, and C:\WINDOWS directories when you execute a command.

Search path
The directories specified in the PATH command in AUTOEXEC.BAT.

The last line loads a software driver that makes the mouse work in software applications (like the MS-DOS Editor) that support the mouse. This line is important to this example because it illustrates that you do not need to specify the path to the MOUSE program, so long as this piece of software is in one of the directories on the *search path*.

Using AUTOEXEC.BAT is an excellent way to set up system defaults. That is, AUTOEXEC.BAT is the place to put commands you want to enter every time you start your system. You can use AUTOEXEC.BAT, for example, to tell your computer to change to the directory that holds your most commonly used program and then start it. Used this way, AUTOEXEC.BAT runs your program as soon as you boot your computer. Some people who run Windows every day, for example, add the following command as the last line of their AUTOEXEC.BAT:


```
WIN
```

The following list covers some commands frequently included in basic AUTOEXEC.BAT files, plus a few other commands, to give you an idea of what you can add to your file.

Command	Function in the AUTOEXEC.BAT File
DATE	Sets the computer's clock to establish the correct date so DOS can accurately date-stamp new and modified files. Most computers have a built-in clock and do not need this command.
TIME	Sets the computer's clock to establish the correct time so DOS can accurately time-stamp new and modified files. The DATE and TIME commands also provide the actual date and time to programs that use the computer's internal clock. Most computers have a built-in clock and do not need this command.
PROMPT	Customizes the system prompt. The DOS prompt configuration can include information that makes navigating in directories easier. If you use the PROMPT command in the AUTOEXEC.BAT file, you don't need to enter the optional parameters each time you boot.
PATH	Tells DOS to search the named subdirectories for files that have EXE, COM, or BAT extensions.
SET TEMP	Stores temporary files. DOS, Windows, and other programs need a place on the hard disk to store temporary files. If you do not have a SET TEMP command in your AUTOEXEC.BAT file, DOS adds it during installation.
PAUSE	Pauses until you press a key so you have a chance to see the result of the preceding command before the next command executes.

Command	Function in the AUTOEXEC.BAT File
CD *path*	Changes the current path. For example, CD\DATA\DOCS changes to the \DATA\DOCS directory. If you have a data directory you use often, you may want to change to that directory each time you boot.
ECHO	Enables you to include a message as part of your startup. For example, you could include a message to remind yourself to back up your new data files.
@ECHO OFF	Keeps DOS from displaying all commands in your AUTOEXEC.BAT before they are executed. This command often is used in AUTOEXEC.BAT files because it makes the screen less busy during system boot.
DIR /O:D	Lists all files in the current directory in date order.
d:	Changes to another disk drive.
UNDELETE /S	Loads the Delete Sentry level of file deletion protection.

If you have doubts about which commands to include in your AUTOEXEC.BAT file, the following sections may give you some ideas. You can include any commands you want in the AUTOEXEC.BAT file.

Always back up your AUTOEXEC.BAT file before altering it. If you make a mistake in editing AUTOEXEC.BAT, your system may not start properly. If that is the case, reboot your system and when you see the words `Starting MS-DOS...`, press the F5 key. This action skips AUTOEXEC.BAT (and CONFIG.SYS). Then you can copy the backup of your original AUTOEXEC.BAT into your root directory (C:\). Your system will start properly and you again can edit AUTOEXEC.BAT, making sure to change commands correctly.

The AUTOEXEC.BAT file is a privileged batch file because DOS executes this file's batch of commands each time you boot your computer. In every other sense, however, AUTOEXEC.BAT is like any other batch file. The best way to create and modify an AUTOEXEC.BAT file is with the MS-DOS Editor, which is described in more detail later in the section "Using the MS-DOS Editor."

Because AUTOEXEC.BAT is like any other batch file, you could run AUTOEXEC.BAT by typing its name at the DOS prompt and pressing Enter. However, avoid using this technique. The commands listed in

AUTOEXEC.BAT already were executed when you booted your system. Executing the commands again could cause problems on your system. For example, if AUTOEXEC.BAT loaded the mouse driver when you booted your system, running AUTOEXEC.BAT again would attempt to reload the mouse driver. Depending on your mouse driver software, this step could load two copies of the driver into memory. At minimum, having two copies of the mouse driver loaded is a waste of memory.

Task: Viewing the AUTOEXEC.BAT File

You can see whether AUTOEXEC.BAT exists in your root directory or on your logged floppy disk. Follow these steps:

1. To change to the root directory, type **CD** and press Enter.
2. To look at the directory listing of all files with BAT extensions, enter this line:

   DIR *.BAT

3. Press Enter.
4. To view the contents of AUTOEXEC.BAT, type this line:

   TYP TOEXEC.BAT

5. Press Enter.

Use the MS-DOS Editor to read or print the contents of the AUTOEXEC.BAT file:

1. Type the following command at the DOS prompt:

   EDIT AUTOEXEC.BAT

2. Press Enter.

If you choose not to print a copy of your AUTOEXEC.BAT file, make sure that you write down the contents before you make any changes. Copy the syntax correctly. This copy serves as your worksheet. If you want to add or alter PROMPT or PATH commands, jot the additions or changes on your worksheet. Use your paper copy of the AUTOEXEC.BAT file to check for proper syntax in the lines you change or add before you commit the changes to disk.

Task: Backing Up the AUTOEXEC.BAT File

Always make a backup copy of your existing AUTOEXEC.BAT file before you make any changes to the file or install any programs. Some program-installation procedures automatically change AUTOEXEC.BAT. Before you run the installation program for new software, save the current version of AUTOEXEC.BAT by copying it to another directory or to a floppy disk. Then if a change keeps your system from operating properly, you can copy the backup of your AUTOEXEC.BAT file to your root directory (C:\).

Use the following procedure to make an archive copy of your AUTOEXEC.BAT file:

1. Type **CD** to change to the root directory.
2. Press Enter.
3. Copy AUTOEXEC.BAT to the directory C:\DOS or to a floppy disk in drive A: by typing one of the following commands:

    COPY AUTOEXEC.BAT C:\DOS

    or

    COPY AUTOEXEC.BAT A:

4. Press Enter.

Now you can change your AUTOEXEC.BAT file, and if something goes wrong, you still have a copy of the original file. If the new file has an error, restore the original by copying AUTOEXEC.BAT from the C:\DOS directory or from drive A: by using the following procedure:

1. Type **CD** to change to the root directory.
2. Press Enter.
3. Copy AUTOEXEC.BAT back to the root directory by typing one of the following commands:

    COPY C:\DOS\AUTOEXEC.BAT

    or

    COPY A:\AUTOEXEC.BAT

When you type this command, DOS detects that a copy of AUTOEXEC.BAT already exists in your root directory and prompts you, asking whether to overwrite this copy.

4. Because you need to restore your old AUTOEXEC.BAT file, press **Y** for yes. The backup copy replaces the version already in your root directory.

If you choose to save a backup copy of AUTOEXEC.BAT in your root directory, do not use BAK as a file extension. With some text editor programs, every time you save a file, the program saves the old file with a BAK extension. This action would cause the backup copy of the modified AUTOEXEC.BAT file to write over your archive copy of AUTOEXEC.BAT. Also, do not use OLD as a file extension because some program-installation procedures that change the AUTOEXEC.BAT file rename the existing file AUTOEXEC.OLD. This action would write over your archive copy of AUTOEXEC.BAT.

The safest way to back up your AUTOEXEC.BAT file is to save a copy on a floppy disk or in a directory on your hard drive. Storing this backup copy in the \DOS directory is good practice, because AUTOEXEC.BAT is a crucial file in DOS.

An error in your AUTOEXEC.BAT file can cause your computer to *hang*, or *freeze*, as soon as you boot it. You can prepare for this eventuality before you start making changes to the AUTOEXEC.BAT file by creating a bootable floppy disk containing your current AUTOEXEC.BAT and CONFIG.SYS. Follow these steps:

1. Insert a blank disk into the A: drive.

2. Type the following line at the DOS prompt:

   FORMAT A: /S

3. Follow the directions on-screen for formatting the disk.

4. Copy the AUTOEXEC.BAT and CONFIG.SYS files to the disk.

Keep this disk handy in case you cannot boot from your hard disk. Follow these steps to boot from the floppy disk:

1. Place the bootable disk in the A: drive.
2. Press **Ctrl-Alt-Del** (or turn the machine off and then on again).
3. After your system boots from the floppy, change to the C: drive and correct your AUTOEXEC.BAT file.
4. Take the disk out of the A: drive and try to boot normally from your hard disk.

Note: *Having a bootable disk containing your AUTOEXEC.BAT and CONFIG.SYS files is particularly important if you use DoubleSpace to compress your hard drive. DoubleSpace requires the special program DBLSPACE.BIN to be in the root directory of your boot drive; if this file on your C: drive is damaged, the copy placed on the floppy disk when you use FORMAT /S can enable you to access your C: drive.*

Task: Editing AUTOEXEC.BAT

The following list contains important rules you must follow for editing AUTOEXEC.BAT. If you do not follow these rules, your AUTOEXEC.BAT likely will not function properly when you start or reboot your system. Remember to make a backup copy of your AUTOEXEC.BAT file before you edit the original file in your root directory.

- Use a plain text editor, like the MS-DOS Editor, to make changes to the AUTOEXEC.BAT. Remember, the AUTOEXEC.BAT file is a pure text file. Never use a word processing program for editing AUTOEXEC.BAT because a word processing program may insert binary formatting codes that ruin AUTOEXEC.BAT.
- Each command in the AUTOEXEC.BAT must appear on its own line. In the sample AUTOEXEC.BAT shown earlier, the path statement and the directories specified in the path are on a line of their own. The command that loads the mouse is on a different line.
- When you edit AUTOEXEC.BAT, you must press the Enter key at the end of each line. For example, the list of directories in the path statement must end with a carriage return, which you insert at the end of the line when you press Enter. The carriage return causes DOS to execute that command, just as if you had typed the command at the DOS prompt and pressed Enter.

- The contents of the AUTOEXEC.BAT file must conform to the rules for creating any batch file.
- After you finish editing your AUTOEXEC.BAT, remember to save your changes. Use the editor's Save command.
- The full file name must be AUTOEXEC.BAT, and the file must reside in the root directory of the boot disk, normally the C: drive.
- Reboot your system so the changes to AUTOEXEC.BAT take effect.
- When executing AUTOEXEC.BAT after a boot, DOS does not prompt you automatically for the date and time. You must include the DATE and TIME commands in your AUTOEXEC.BAT file if computer does not have a built-in clock with a battery backup (onlythe oldest PCs lack a clock).

After you make an archive copy of your AUTOEXEC.BAT file and create a separate boot floppy disk, you can safely modify the file. Follow these steps:

1. Type **CD** to change to the root directory.
2. Press Enter.
3. Type the following line at the DOS prompt:

   EDIT AUTOEXEC.BAT

4. Press Enter.

   This action starts the MS-DOS Editor with AUTOEXEC.BAT on-screen.

5. Use the editor to add, delete, and change commands.
6. Save the file and exit the editor.
7. Reboot the computer to test the new file.

Task: Making Several Versions of AUTOEXEC.BAT

Technically speaking, you have only one AUTOEXEC.BAT file. You can benefit from having several versions on hand, however, by giving different extensions to files named AUTOEXEC. You then can activate an alternate version using the COPY command.

Having optional versions is handy if you want to include commands for special activities, for example, if you have a few days when you want to start the monthly spreadsheet automatically each time you boot your computer. After you finish the monthly work and you no longer need the spreadsheet each time you boot, you can restore your normal AUTOEXEC file.

In the extensions, you can use any character that DOS normally allows in file names. The extensions NEW, TMP, and 001 are just a few examples. By giving an AUTOEXEC file a unique name, such as AUTOEXEC.TMP, you can activate that AUTOEXEC file by copying it to AUTOEXEC.BAT. Making AUTOEXEC.TMP your current AUTOEXEC file is a two-step process:

1. Save your original AUTOEXEC.BAT to a different name by typing the following line:

   COPY AUTOEXEC.BAT AUTOEXEC.001

2. Press Enter.

3. Use the COPY command to save AUTOEXEC.TMP to AUTOEXEC.BAT by typing the following line:

   COPY AUTOEXEC.TMP AUTOEXEC.BAT

4. Press Enter.

Task: Bypassing the AUTOEXEC.BAT File

Clean boot
Bypassing the AUTOEXEC.BAT and CONFIG.SYS files when booting.

If you have problems booting your system after editing AUTOEXEC.BAT, or any other time, you can perform a *clean boot* by pressing the F5 key during system boot (immediately after you see the words `Starting MS-DOS` on-screen). Using F5 to bypass AUTOEXEC.BAT and CONFIG.SYS should allow you to access your hard drive to edit or restore your damaged AUTOEXEC.BAT.

To perform a clean boot, follow these steps:

1. Start your computer as you usually would.

2. Watch the screen as the computer performs its power-up routine.

3. When you see the message `Starting MS DOS...`, press F5.

   DOS skips the AUTOEXEC.BAT file and the CONFIG.SYS file and displays the DOS prompt C:\>.

Interactive boot
Boot method where you are prompted before DOS executes each line of CONFIG.SYS and optionally AUTOEXEC.BAT.

Alternatively, you can use the *interactive boot* to selectively execute the commands in AUTOEXEC.BAT. When you use an interactive boot, DOS first pauses before executing each line of CONFIG.SYS, asking whether you want to load each device driver and configuration command. Then DOS asks if you want to process AUTOEXEC.BAT in the same way. If you choose yes, DOS asks if you want to execute each command in AUTOEXEC.BAT.

To perform an interactive boot, follow these steps:

1. Start your computer as you usually do.
2. Watch the screen as the computer performs its power-up routine.
3. When you see the message `Starting MS DOS...`, press F8.

   DOS asks if you want to execute each command in CONFIG.SYS and then asks if you want to process AUTOEXEC.BAT.

4. Press **Y** for yes or **N** for no when prompted for whether to execute each line.

Customizing the Search Path

Path
A chain of directories and subdirectories. Also called the *search path.*

To tell DOS to execute a command in a directory other than the current directory, you use a *path* as a command parameter. This topic has been covered throughout this book. If you do not specify path information, DOS attempts to execute the command in the current directory. But you can use the DOS search path to instruct DOS to always search through the designated directory chain when it attempts to execute commands.

The search path, known more commonly as *the PATH,* is located in your AUTOEXEC.BAT, which was created on your hard drive when you installed DOS 6.2. When DOS 6.2 created your search path, it included one directory, C:\DOS. DOS added that one directory to the search path so you can execute DOS commands like FORMAT and SCANDISK at any time, whether or not you are in the DOS directory.

You can add to or change the search path designated in your AUTOEXEC.BAT. For example, if you want to be able to run a word processing program no matter which directory is the current directory, you add to the search path the directory that holds the word processing program. A typical search path might include the following directories:

C:\DOS

C:\WORD

C:\WINDOWS

Path statement
A list of directories, separated by semicolons, in the AUTOEXEC.BAT file.

The way you enter these three directories in your AUTOEXEC.BAT must take a specific form. This form is known as a *path statement.* The following line shows how a path statement looks for the three preceding directories:

PATH C:\DOS;C:\WORD;C:\WINDOWS;

Understanding How the Path Statement Works

When you execute the FORMAT command or another command, DOS must find the program on your disk. When you do not enter a path as a command-line parameter, DOS uses a specific method to search your system for the command:

1. DOS looks in the current directory for the command. If DOS cannot find the program in the current directory, then step 2 happens.
2. DOS looks in the directories specified in the path statement. Using the preceding path statement as an example, DOS first looks in C:\DOS; if the command is not found there, DOS looks in C:\WORD; if the command is not found there, DOS looks in C:\WINDOWS. If DOS finds the command, it executes the command. If DOS does not find the command, you receive the following error message:

   ```
   Bad command or file name
   ```

Task: Editing the Path Statement

Before you attempt to edit your path statement, make a backup copy of your current AUTOEXEC.BAT file, as described earlier in this lesson.

You should place the path statement at or near the top of the AUTOEXEC.BAT file so DOS can find the programs you instruct it to load in the rest of the lines of the AUTOEXEC.BAT file. A good place to put the path statement is immediately after the @ECHO OFF and PROMPT PG commands.

Use the following steps to add the directory C:\WORD to your path statement (assuming your path statement is PATH C:\DOS;):

1. Change to the root directory of your boot drive by typing **CD** and pressing Enter.

2. Type **EDIT AUTOEXEC.BAT** and press Enter.

   This action starts the MS-DOS Editor with AUTOEXEC.BAT loaded and ready to edit.

3. Locate the path statement in your AUTOEXEC.BAT. The PATH statement should look something like the following:

   PATH C:\DOS;

   Your path may list additional directories.

4. Position the MS-DOS Editors cursor at the end of the path statement (following the last semicolon).

5. Type the following line at the end of the path statement exactly as shown:

   C:\WORD;

   Your path statement now reads something like this line:

   PATH C:\DOS;C:\WORD;

6. Save the AUTOEXEC.BAT file.

7. Exit the MS-DOS Editor.

8. Press **Ctrl-Alt-Del** to reboot your system, or turn off the system, wait a few seconds, and turn it back on. The changes you made to AUTOEXEC.BAT take effect immediately when you reboot your system.

Follow these steps to see the effect of the change to your path statement:

1. From the root directory, type the name of the program contained in the directory you added to the path statement.

2. Press Enter.

   The program executes as if you had changed directories.

The maximum length for the path statement is 128 characters, an internal limit of DOS. Any entry after the 128th character is ignored.

DOS needs some time to search the directories in a search path for a program or batch file. Because DOS searches the directories in the order listed in the PATH command, you should list the directories in the order of most use. If you mostly use DOS commands, place the C:\DOS directory first in the path. As you become more experienced with batch files, you may find that you use batch files more than DOS commands. In that case, place the C:\BAT directory first in the path. Many Windows users place their Windows directory first in the path.

Task: Modifying the Path from the DOS Prompt

If you need to change the search path on your system quickly, you can modify the path from the DOS prompt. For example, to change the path so it includes only the DOS directory and the C:\LOTUS directory, follow these steps:

1. Type the following command at the DOS prompt:

   PATH C:\DOS;C:\LOTUS;

2. Press Enter.

Because you must specify a search path every time you boot your computer (or DOS defaults to PATH C:\DOS;), the PATH command is usually added to the AUTOEXEC.BAT file of every computer with a hard drive.

Creating an AUTOEXEC.BAT File

You may never need to create an AUTOEXEC.BAT file from scratch. The DOS 6.2 Setup program creates a basic AUTOEXEC.BAT file when you install DOS. After this AUTOEXEC.BAT file has been created, you should follow the directions in the section on backing up AUTOEXEC.BAT to keep a copy of this vital file safely where you can use it if you need it.

If you ever must create an AUTOEXEC.BAT file from scratch, follow these basic steps (use a piece of paper and a pencil for the first few steps):

1. Make a list of the directories you need to include in your path statement.

2. Make a list of the programs you need to load in AUTOEXEC.BAT, such as your mouse driver program.

3. Write down the path of the directory you use for your TEMP files, such as C:\TEMP.

4. Change to the root directory of your drive (if you are not already there) by typing **CD** and pressing Enter.

5. Type the following line:

   EDIT AUTOEXEC.BAT

   The MS-DOS Editor opens with a file tentatively named AUTOEXEC.BAT. The file of that name is stored on your drive only after you use the MS-DOS Editors Save command to save the file.

6. On the first line in the Editor, type the following line to suppress the display of commands as they are executed by AUTOEXEC.BAT:

   @ECHO OFF

   Press Enter to end the line and move to the next line in the MS-DOS Editor.

7. Type the following line to create a DOS prompt that displays the current directory:

   PROMPT PG

   Press Enter to end the command and move to the next line in the MS-DOS Editor.

8. Type the following line to create an environment variable that causes application programs to store their temporary files in your TEMP file directory (assuming your temp directory is C:\TEMP. Remember that you wrote down your temp directory path in step 3):

   SET TEMP=C:\TEMP

   Press Enter to end the command and move to the next line of AUTOEXEC.BAT.

9. Type the PATH command followed by the directories you want in your search path. For example, if you want the directories C:\DOS, C:\WORD, C:\WINDOWS, and C:\LOTUS in your search path, type the following line:

   PATH C:\DOS;C:\WORD;C:\WINDOWS;C:\LOTUS;

10. Press Enter after you have typed the semicolon following the last drectory path name.

11. Type the following line to add your mouse driver to AUTOEXEC.BAT so it loads each time you boot your system (assuming the mouse driver is located in the directory C:\MOUSE):

    C:\MOUSE\MOUSE

12. Press Enter.

13. Save your new AUTOEXEC.BAT file and exit the MS-DOS Editor.

14. Reboot your system for the changes to take effect.

The new AUTOEXEC.BAT file created in the preceding example looks like the following when viewed with the MS-DOS Editor or the TYPE command:

```
@ECHO OFF
PROMPT $P$G
SET TEMP=C:\TEMP
PATH C:\DOS;C:\WORD;C:\WINDOWS;C:\LOTUS;
C:\MOUSE\MOUSE
```

If you have problems...

Mistakes in AUTOEXEC.BAT can result in your system functioning in an erratic manner, or your system may fail to boot. If you have problems creating an AUTOEXEC.BAT file, or if it doesn't work correctly when you boot your system, carefully review the steps provided in the preceding example. You must enter each command correctly.

For example, unless your mouse driver software is in one of the directories specified in the search path, you must include full path information when typing the line that loads the mouse driver. If you load additional programs in AUTOEXEC.BAT, you must include path information for them, also, unless they are in one of the directories specified in the path.

When typing the PATH command and the directories to include in the search path, check the following elements carefully:

- Spell the PATH command correctly;
- Press the space bar after typing the PATH command;
- Each directory listing in the path statement should include the drive letter, the colon, the backslash, and the directory name, followed by a semicolon;
- No spaces can be between the semicolon that ends one directory and the listing for the next directory.

Changing the DOS Prompt

The DOS prompt is another visible part of your computer system you can customize. Unless you use the PROMPT command to establish a particular look for your prompt, DOS 6.2 automatically displays a prompt that tells you the current directory. For example, DOS 6.2 displays the following DOS prompt when you are in the root directory:

```
C:\>
```

When you are in the DOS directory, DOS 6.2 displays this prompt:

```
C:\DOS>
```

The default prompt, which shows you the current directory, has been the standard throughout this book.

By default, previous versions of DOS displayed a prompt that showed only the current drive followed by the greater-than sign: The prompt looked like the following:

```
A>
```

This prompt was adequate if you had only floppy disk drives, but the prompt is less than useful for todays systems, nearly all of which have hard drives with many directories to manage. To produce a DOS prompt that displayed the current directory, many people used the PROMPT command with the parameters shown in the following example:

```
PROMPT $P$G
```

Understanding the DOS Prompt

You can use the PROMPT command to customize the prompt. The following line shows the syntax for the PROMPT command:

PROMPT *text*

Meta-string
A special code DOS uses to determine the appearance of the DOS prompt.

You replace *text* with a combination of letters and special characters called *meta-string* characters. A meta-string consists of two characters, the first of which is the dollar sign ($); the second is a keyboard character. The dollar sign ($) tells DOS to use the following character to configure the DOS prompt.

DOS interprets meta-strings to mean something other than what you see when you enter them. For instance, the meta-string $T in the PROMPT command specifies that you want the DOS prompt to display the current time in the format HH:MM:SS.XX.

DOS recognizes the symbols > and < and the vertical bar (|) as special characters. These characters have meta-string equivalents, which you must substitute to cause the characters to appear in the prompt. Otherwise, DOS tries to act on the characters in its usual way.

The following table shows common meta-string characters and their use in the PROMPT command.

Character	Result
_ (underscore)	Moves the cursor to the next line
A	The & character
B	The pipe symbol (|)
C	The (character
D	The current date
E	The Esc character
F	The) character
G	The greater-than character (>)
H	Backspace; erases the preceding character
L	The less-than character (<)
N	The current disk drive letter
P	The current drive and path
Q	The = character
S	Blank space
T	The current time
V	The DOS version

You can type alphabetical characters in either uppercase or lowercase. The letters are shown here in uppercase for clarity.

Only the characters in this list are used as meta-string characters. DOS disregards other characters entered after the dollar sign. However, you can use other characters to change the DOS prompt display. Later examples show how you can customize the DOS prompt so it looks the way you want.

The standard prompt results from the following command:

```
PROMPT $P$G
```

The $P meta-string causes DOS to display the current path, including the drive. The $G meta-string causes DOS to display the greater-than (>) sign. DOS 6.2 uses the PG prompt by default.

Task: Customizing Your Prompt

You can use meta-string characters and phrases to produce your own DOS prompt. Experiment with different combinations by typing the PROMPT command with the meta-strings and phrases you want to try.

When you find a combination you like, you can edit the PROMPT command in your AUTOEXEC.BAT file (or add the command if necessary). Then each time you boot your computer, your custom prompt appears.

If you want your DOS prompt to tell you the current DOS path with words, not just symbols, follow these steps:

1. At the DOS prompt, type this line:

   PROMPT THE CURRENT PATH IS $P

2. Press Enter.

When you are in the DOS directory on the C: drive, for example, the preceding command produces the following prompt:

```
THE CURRENT PATH IS C:\DOS
```

Follow these steps to add the > character to the preceding prompt:

1. At the DOS prompt, type this line:

   PROMPT THE CURRENT PATH IS PG

2. Press Enter.

Now your DOS prompt appears as follows:

```
THE CURRENT PATH IS C:\DOS>
```

If you dont like the results of your experiment, you can restore the prompt to its default: the drive name, path, and greater-than sign. Follow these steps:

1. At the DOS prompt, type this line:

   PROMPT PG

2. Press Enter.

If you have problems...

If you have problems using the PROMPT command, review the list of meta-string characters you can use to modify the prompt, as well as the examples that show how you can add a phrase to your DOS prompt. Make sure that you correctly type the PROMPT command, press the space bar after you type the command, and use valid meta-string characters.

Using Batch Files

Batch files can execute DOS commands, execute programs, change the computer environment, or even provide special processing that is possible only in a batch file. You can add several commands to a single batch file. DOS executes these statements as if you had entered each one individually on the command line.

For example, you can create a batch file that uses the CLS command to clear your screen, uses the CD command to change directories, executes a command in that directory, and when the command is finished, returns you to the original directory. This single text file can do all this work because DOS executes the commands in a batch file one at a time, waiting until one command has finished before executing the next, as though you had entered the commands one at a time at the prompt.

The following example shows how the batch file described in the preceding paragraph looks in the MS-DOS Editor or another plain text editor:

```
CLS
CD C:\WORD
WORD
CD\
```

This batch file clears the screen, changes to the directory C:\WORD, executes the program WORD, and after you have finished with Word, returns you to the root directory of the C: drive.

Batch files can make using your computer easier and more pleasant. You can consider the batch file to be a non-programmers programming language. A batch file constitutes a limited yet powerful language. If advanced techniques in batch processing interest you, be sure to read about batch files in Que's *Using MS-DOS 6.2*, Special Edition.

Creating Batch Files

When you type a batch file name at the DOS prompt, *COMMAND.COM* searches in the current directory and then through the search path for a program or batch file with that file name. DOS then reads the batch file and executes the statements in that file. The whole process is almost automatic. You enter the batch file name, and DOS does the work. But you need to follow some guidelines, as noted in the following sections.

Format

ASCII text
Plain text you can view using the MS-DOS Editor or the TYPE command rather than a software application.

Batch files must contain plain text–*ASCII text* characters. DOS has an easy-to-use, full-screen text editor designed to produce only *ASCII text*. To learn about the editor, see the section "Using the MS-DOS Editor" later in this lesson.

Word processing programs save documents in a special format with codes for margins, indents, formats (such as boldface, type style, and size), and other information. Don't use a word processing program for creating batch files because these special codes make the batch file useless. Some word processing programs enable you to save text without formatting. The word processing program may call this format *unformatted, text,* or *ASCII.* But until you become quite knowledgeable about your word processing program, stick with the MS-DOS Editor for creating or editing batch files.

Contents

The batch file can contain any DOS command that you enter at the DOS prompt. You also can include in the batch file any program names you usually type at the DOS prompt, but remember to use only one command or program name per line in the batch file. When you are typing or editing a batch file, press the Enter key at the end of each line, including the last line. Pressing Enter at the end of a line in a batch file is like pressing Enter after typing a DOS command at the DOS prompt.

Names

The name of the batch file can be from one to eight characters long. The name must conform to the DOS rules for naming files. The file name must end with a period (.) followed by the BAT extension.

Use a unique file name for your batch file. The name shouldn't be the same as a program file name (a file with an EXE or COM extension) or an internal DOS command (such as COPY or DATE). Remember that when you type a name at the DOS prompt, DOS first looks for that name as an internal command built into COMMAND.COM. Then DOS looks for a COM file with the name you typed. Then DOS looks for an EXE file with the name you typed. Then, only if DOS found no internal command and no COM or EXE file with the name you typed, DOS looks for a BAT file that has the name you typed.

Running Batch Files

You start batch files by typing the batch file name at the DOS prompt. The following list summarizes the rules DOS follows when it loads and executes batch files:

- If you don't specify the disk drive name before the batch file name, DOS uses the current drive.
- If you don't specify a directory path, DOS searches the current directory and then the search path for the batch file.
- If a batch file has the same name as a program and both are in the same directory, DOS executes the program rather than the batch file. If the program and the batch file are in different directories, DOS executes the item it finds first in the search path.
- If DOS finds a syntax error in a batch file command line, DOS displays an error message, skips the errant command, and then executes the remaining commands in the batch file. Depending on the error, DOS may not pause at the error but flash an error message too fast to read, and then continue.

Note: *Do not assume that a batch file is correct because it seems to end normally. When you are editing a batch file, make sure that you type each command correctly. Then check to make sure that every command actually works correctly when you run the batch file.*

- You can stop a batch command by pressing Ctrl-C or Ctrl-Break. DOS prompts you to confirm that you want to terminate the batch file. If you answer no, DOS skips the current command (the one being carried out) and resumes execution with the next command in the batch file.

Note: *If you try to run a batch file and DOS displays an error message instead of running the batch file, you probably made a mistake when you typed the name, or the batch file is not on your search path.*

Task: Making a BAT Directory To Store Batch Files

The best place to store batch files is in a directory named \BAT or \BATCH. Don't put your batch files in the root directory or the DOS directory for the following reasons:

- The root directory probably is the most important directory on your hard disk because it contains the files needed to boot your computer, and it contains the first level of subdirectories, such as \DOS and your applications directories. When you view the files in the root directory, you don't want the file list to be complicated by other files.

- Don't put the batch files in the DOS directory, because this directory should contain only files that are part of DOS. For example, when you upgrade to another version of DOS, you do not want to sort through a directory that contains DOS files plus other files to determine the files you want to keep and those you want to upgrade.

To create a \BAT directory, you use the MD (make directory) command. Follow these steps:

1. Type **CD** to make the root directory current.
2. Press Enter.
3. Type the following line at the DOS prompt:

   MD BAT

4. Press Enter.

You just created the \BAT directory. Refer to the earlier section "Customizing the Search Path" to add the new \BAT directory to your path statement in AUTOEXEC.BAT. After you add the \BAT directory to your search path, you can run your batch files without regard to the directory in which you are currently working.

Using the MS-DOS Editor

If you have heard about the DOS line editor, EDLIN, from earlier versions of DOS, forget that EDLIN ever existed. EDLIN not only was difficult to use, but it enabled you to change only one line at a time. The MS-DOS 6.2 Editor program, on the other hand, is very easy to use and is great for creating and editing batch files. The following figures show how the Editor looks when you open the program.

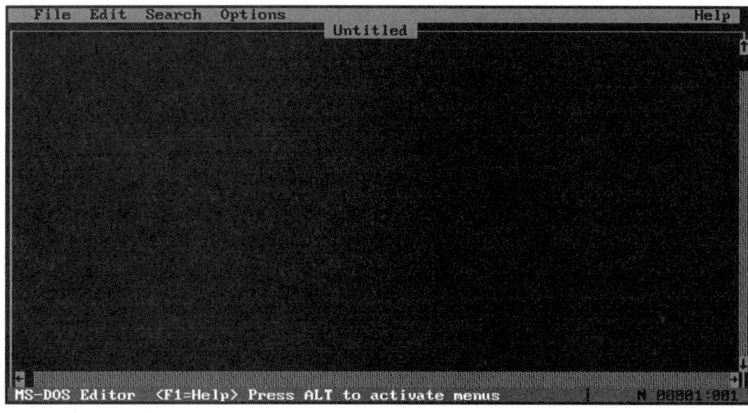

The blank screen in which you type text in the MS-DOS Editor.

The Editor with a text file loaded.

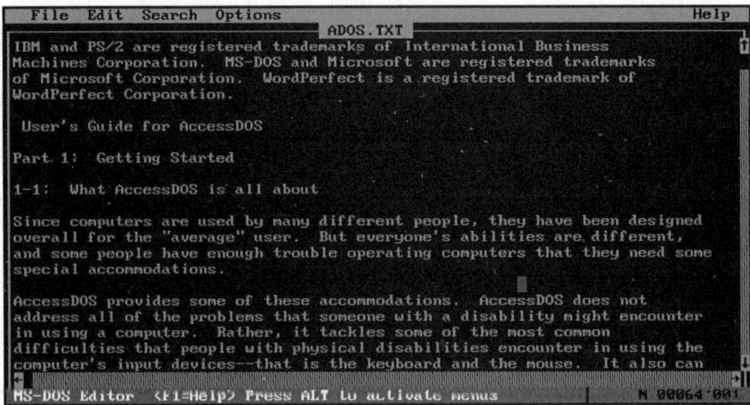

File Edit Search Options
Help
ADOS.TXT
IBM and PS/2 are registered trademarks of International Business
Machines Corporation. MS-DOS and Microsoft are registered trademarks
of Microsoft Corporation. WordPerfect is a registered trademark of
WordPerfect Corporation.
User's Guide for AccessDOS
Part 1: Getting Started
1-1: What AccessDOS is all about
Since computers are used by many different people, they have been designed
overall for the "average" user. But everyone's abilities are different,
and some people have enough trouble operating computers that they need some
special accommodations.
AccessDOS provides some of these accommodations. AccessDOS does not
address all of the problems that someone with a disability might encounter
in using a computer. Rather, it tackles some of the most common
difficulties that people with physical disabilities encounter in using the
computer's input devices--that is the keyboard and the mouse. It also can
MS-DOS Editor <F1=Help> Press ALT to activate menus

The following lists describe the menus you see after starting Editor (described in the next section).

The *File* menu contains most of the commands you use to create and change batch files:

- The New command clears the current file from memory. The file name changes to UNTITLED. Use this command after you save the current file and want to create a new file from scratch.
- The Open command reads a file into memory. Use this command after you save the current file and want to change another file.
- The Save command saves the current file (see following figure). Use this command after you change or create a file. If you have never saved the file, and file name is still UNTITLED, the Save command acts like Save As.

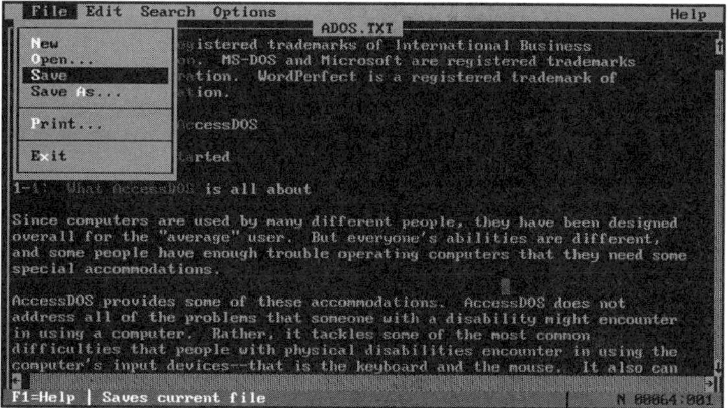

The Editors File menu, in which you save changes to a file.

- The Save As command saves the file but first asks you to supply a file name (see following figure). Use this command to save the file with a different name.

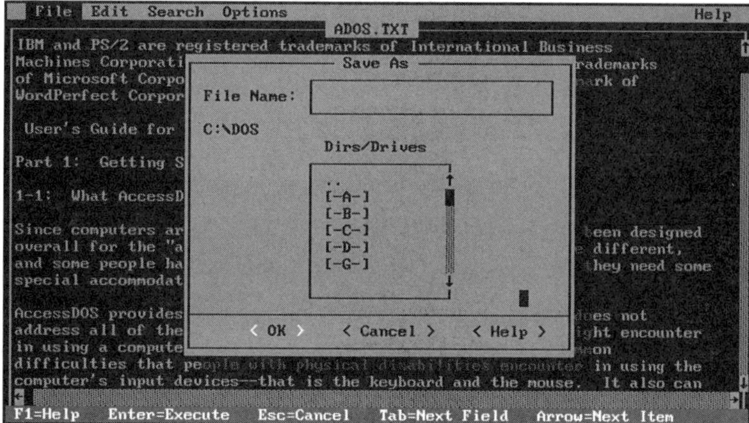

The Save As dialog box, in which you can give a file a new name.

- The Print command prints the file. Use this command to keep a printed copy of the file.
- The Exit command leaves the Editor.

The *Edit* menu contains commands you can use to work with blocks of type, rather than one character at a time. Practice selecting blocks of text as described in the section "Task: Selecting Text in a Batch File" later in this lesson before you use the commands in the Edit menu to work on an important file. This list describes the commands on the Edit menu:

- The Cut command deletes a selected block of text and copies it into memory so you can paste it into another place in your document.
- The Copy command copies a selected block of text into memory so you can paste it into another place in your document.
- The Paste command inserts cut or copied text at the current position of the blinking cursor.
- The Clear command deletes a selected block of text without copying it into memory.

The *Search* menu contains the commands you use to search for specific words or text strings and a command you can use to change all occurrences of a word or text string. The following list describes the Search menu commands:

- The Find command produces a dialog box in which you enter the word or text string you want to find.
- The Repeat Last Find command continues searching the document for the word or text string entered in the Find dialog box.
- The Change command produces a dialog box in which you enter the word or text string you want to find. You also enter the word or text string you want to replace the found word or text string.

The *Options* menu contains commands that enable you to change the colors used by the Editor and set the path to the Editors help files (usually C:\DOS):

- The Display command produces the Colors dialog box in which you can set the colors for the text in the Editor and for the background of the editing screen. You also can specify whether the Editor displays scroll bars and how many spaces to insert at the beginning of the line when you press the Tab key.

- The Help Path command produces the Help Path dialog box in which you can enter the path for the Editors help file. Usually this file is located in C:\DOS, the same directory as the Editor itself.

Task: Creating a New Batch File

To use the Editor to create a batch file, follow these steps:

1. Type **CD\BAT** and press Enter to make the C:\BAT directory current.

2. Type **EDIT**.

3. If you want, you can press the space bar and type the name of the file you want to create. For example, to create the file WORD.BAT, type the following command line:

   EDIT WORD.BAT

   You do not need to specify a file name at this time, however.

4. Press Enter.

   The Editor starts with a clean screen. If you specified a file name, the Editor assigns the specified name to the file you are creating.

5. Type DOS commands in Editor just as you would type them at the DOS prompt.

6. Press Enter at the end of each command.

   You can use the arrow keys to move the cursor and use the Delete key or backspace key to make corrections, much as you do in a word processing program.

7. Save the file after you have completed the batch file.

Saving your file is discussed in a later section, "Task: Saving a Batch File."

Task: Opening an Existing Batch File

You can open an existing file by specifying a file name when you type EDIT to start the Editor, as mentioned in the preceding section. If you don't specify a name, you can open a file using these steps:

1. Choose Open from the File menu.

   The Open dialog box opens. The default file name in the File Name box is *.TXT.

2. To see the list of batch files in the current directory, type ***.BAT** in the File Name box.

3. Press Enter.

4. If the name of the file you want isn't visible, use the scroll bar at the bottom of the Files list to scroll the list until you see the file you want.

5. Double-click the name of the file you want.

   or

   Use the cursor keys to select the file name and press Enter.

6. Edit the file as described in the preceding section.

Task: Selecting Text in a Batch File

To select a block of text in the Editor using the mouse, follow these steps:

1. Move the blinking cursor to where you want to begin marking text.

2. Hold down the left mouse button and drag the mouse to select the block of text (move the mouse across your desktop while you continue holding down the left button). The block of text changes color as you drag the mouse.

3. After you have selected the text you want, release the left mouse button.

To select a block of text using the keyboard, follow these steps:

1. Move the blinking cursor to where you want to begin marking text.

2. Hold down the Shift key and use the cursor keys to move the cursor. The block of text changes color as you move the cursor keys.

3. After you have selected the text you want, release the keys.

After you select the text, you can use the options on the menus to copy the text, cut-and-paste it elsewhere, or make other changes.

Task: Finding and Replacing Text in a Batch File

To have the Editor search for a particular word or other text string and replace that string with another, follow these steps:

1. Open the Search menu.
2. Choose the Change command to produce the Change dialog box.
3. In the Find What: text box, type the word or other text string for which you want to search.
4. In the Change To: text box, type the word or other text string with which you want to replace the found text string.
5. Choose the Find and Verify option if you want to review all changes before the Editor makes them.

   or

   Choose the Change All option to have the Editor make the changes without prompting you for confirmation before each change is made.
6. Mark the Match Upper/Lowercase check box if you want to make the search and replace operation case-sensitive.
7. Mark the Whole Word check box if you want to instruct the Editor to make a change only when it encounters an entire word that is identical to the text string you have entered, instead of changing words of which only part is the text string you entered.

   For example, entering *is* in the Find What: box and choosing Whole Word directs the Editor to look for only the word *is*. With the Whole Word option selected, the Editor will not stop when it encounters the word *this*, which contains the search string *is*. The Editor stops at *this* if you do not choose the Whole Word option.
8. Click OK to begin the search.

Task: Saving a Batch File

As mentioned earlier, you don't need to specify a file name at the command line when you start the MS-DOS Editor. If you don't include a file name, the Editor starts with an untitled file; you then can create a new file or open an existing file (as described in the preceding section). As you type and edit your batch file, save the file to disk by following these steps:

1. Open the File menu and choose Save. If the file has a name, the Editor saves the file and returns to the editing screen.

   If the file doesn't have a name, the Save dialog box appears.

2. Specify a name for the file in the File Name text box.

3. Choose OK or press Enter.

Task: Printing a Batch File

To print a batch file using the MS-DOS Editor, follow these steps:

1. Open the File menu.

2. Choose the Print command to produce the Print dialog box.

3. Choose Entire Document if you want to print the entire batch file.

   or

   Choose Selected Text Only if you have selected a block of text and want the Editor to print only the selected text.

4. Click OK.

Understanding the CONFIG.SYS File

CONFIG.SYS
A text file DOS uses on system start-up to help determine how your system will operate.

AUTOEXEC.BAT is not the only file DOS looks for when you boot your computer. Before DOS reads your AUTOEXEC.BAT file, it looks for the *CONFIG.SYS* file, the DOS system configuration file. CONFIG.SYS is a text file like AUTOEXEC.BAT that you can display on-screen or print out. You also can change the contents of CONFIG.SYS with the MS-DOS Editor.

As you know, DOS provides built-in services for disks and other hardware. But DOS also extends its services for add-on hardware like graphics scanners and CD-ROM drives. The additional instructions that enable you to use many of these hardware devices are included in the CONFIG.SYS file.

CONFIG.SYS also is the location for naming the values of DOS configuration items you can adjust, which means that you can enter different values that affect the way the items work, without changing their basic function. Files and buffers, discussed in the next section, are two such adjustable DOS items.

DOS does not execute CONFIG.SYS as it does AUTOEXEC.BAT. Instead, DOS reads the values in the file and configures your computer to agree with those values. Many software packages modify or add a CONFIG.SYS file to the root directory.

Note: *Before you install new software, make a backup copy of your CONFIG.SYS file and keep it in a safe place in case you need to restore the file later.*

The following example shows a typical CONFIG.SYS file:

```
FILES=30
BUFFERS=20
```

The range of possible values in the CONFIG.SYS file is wide, but some common values do exist.

Task: Specifying Files

When DOS moves data to and from disks, it does so in the most efficient manner possible. For each file that DOS acts on, an area of system RAM helps DOS track that file. The FILES command in CONFIG.SYS specifies how many open files DOS can track at one time. If a program tries to open more files than the FILES command setting allows, DOS tells you that too many files are open.

Do not be tempted to set your FILES command to a large number just so you always have room for more open files. The system memory you can use for running programs is reduced a small amount by each extra file included in FILES. As a rule of thumb, a safe compromise is 30 open files. To set the number of open files to 30, follow these steps:

1. Type **CD** to make the root directory current.
2. Press Enter.
3. Type the following line at the DOS prompt:

   EDIT CONFIG.SYS

4. Edit the FILES command so it reads this way:

   ```
   FILES=30
   ```

5. Save and exit the Editor.

The installation documentation for many programs tells you the minimum number you need to specify in the FILES command. Make sure that the FILES command is at least as large as the largest number a program requires. If one program requires 20 and another suggests 30, for example, use FILES=30. Do not add the numbers together and type FILES=50. However, some applications may need a FILES setting as high as 50.

Task: Specifying Buffers

Buffers
Holding areas in RAM that store information coming from or going to disk files.

The BUFFERS command in CONFIG.SYS is similar in some ways to the FILES command. To make disk operation more efficient, DOS stores disk information in RAM file *buffers* and then uses RAM, rather than the disk drives, for input and output whenever possible.

If the file information needed is not already in the buffer, new information is read into the buffer from the disk file. The information that DOS reads includes the needed information and as much additional file information as the buffer can hold. This buffer of information can help DOS avoid constant disk access. The principle is similar to the way a mechanic might use a small tool pouch. Holding frequently used tools in a small pouch relieves him of having to make repeated trips across the garage to get tools from his main tool chest.

As with the FILES command, however, setting the BUFFERS command too high takes needed RAM away from programs and dedicates it to the buffers. The optimum number of buffers depends on the size of your hard disk and the type of application. The following table provides some general guidelines.

Hard Disk Size	Number of Buffers
Less than 40M	20
40M to 79M	30
80M to 119M	40
120M or more	50

To set the number of buffers, use the MS-DOS Editor as described in the preceding section.

Task: Loading Device Drivers

Peripheral
A device connected to and controlled by the computer but external to the central processing unit (CPU).

Driver
A file containing information that a program needs to operate a peripheral.

As mentioned throughout this book, DOS works with *peripherals*, such as disk drives, printers, and displays. These peripherals also are called *devices*. DOS has built-in instructions, called *drivers*, to handle many hardware devices.

Some devices, such as a graphics scanner or CD-ROM drive, are foreign to DOS. DOS lacks the built-in capability of handling such devices. To issue directions to devices that DOS doesn't recognize, use the DEVICE command in the CONFIG.SYS file. The syntax for this command is as follows:

DEVICE=*d:path\filename*

You replace *d:path* with the drive and path name to the file containing the device driver; then replace *filename* with the name of the file containing the driver. The device driver for a mouse, for example, may be in a file called MOUSE.SYS in the \UTIL directory on the C: drive. As another example, suppose that you want DOS to access a Hewlett Packard ScanJet IIp graphics scanner; you would follow these steps:

1. Open the CONFIG.SYS file in the MS-DOS Editor.
2. Type the following command:

   DEVICE=C:\DESKSCAN\SJII.SYS

3. Press Enter.
4. Save and exit the Editor.

The DEVICE command tells DOS to find and load the driver program for the new device.

Many peripherals come with a disk that contains a device-driver file. This file contains the necessary instructions to control, or *drive*, the device. The device-driver disk usually contains a provision to modify your CONFIG.SYS file to include the proper DEVICE command.

Some device drivers also require additional parameters to work correctly on your computer. Always check your program and hardware manuals before experimenting with your system. Many installation programs provide prepared device drivers for you, but in some cases you need to enter the parameters yourself. For example, most mouse drivers are programs with the extension COM or EXE and are loaded in AUTOEXEC.BAT. But mouse drivers also may have the extension SYS. These drivers are loaded in CONFIG.SYS. A mouse set to use COM2, for example, may require a line similar to the following to configure the driver properly:

```
DEVICE=C:\UTIL\MOUSE.SYS /2
```

Note: *If you fail to use the proper parameters for a device driver loaded in CONFIG.SYS, the hardware device will not operate. Carefully follow the directions in the hardware device manual when you install any new device.*

Creating and Changing a CONFIG.SYS File

You should never need to create a CONFIG.SYS file from scratch. The DOS 6.2 Setup program creates a CONFIG.SYS file for you when you install DOS. Make a backup of your CONFIG.SYS at that time, and each time you or an automated installation program makes a change to CONFIG.SYS. Then, if your CONFIG.SYS file is damaged, you can restore the backup copy.

Because CONFIG.SYS is a text file, you can use the same methods to create, change, archive, and copy this file as with the AUTOEXEC.BAT file. Use the MS-DOS Editor to create and change the CONFIG.SYS file. Make sure that you have a backup copy and an extra copy on a floppy disk before making changes to your existing CONFIG.SYS file.

Errors in your CONFIG.SYS file cause your computer to hang more often than an error in the AUTOEXEC.BAT file. For this reason, having a floppy disk containing the system files is especially important before you start making changes to the CONFIG.SYS file. For tips on backing up your CONFIG.SYS file or using alternate copies of CONFIG.SYS, see the previous sections on AUTOEXEC.BAT.

If you must create a CONFIG.SYS file from scratch, use the following steps:

1. Change to the root directory by typing **CD** and pressing Enter.
2. Start the MS-DOS Editor by typing the following command line and pressing Enter:

   EDIT CONFIG.SYS

3. On the first line, type the following and then press Enter:

   FILES=30

4. On the second line, type the following and then press Enter:

   BUFFERS=20

5. Add any device drivers you need to the following lines. Remember to use the syntax demonstrated in the following line that loads ANSI.SYS:

   DEVICE=C:\DOS\ANSI.SYS

   Note: *You may need to search your system for the locations of device drivers you need. Make sure that you write down the correct spelling of the device driver and its extension. A typing mistake in a DEVICE= line can result in your system not booting properly.*

6. Remember to press Enter at the end of each line of CONFIG.SYS.
7. Save the CONFIG.SYS file after you have finished editing this file.
8. Reboot your system for the changes to take effect.

The CONFIG.SYS created in this example looks like the following when you view it with the MS-DOS Editor or the TYPE command:

```
FILES=30
BUFFERS=20
DEVICE=C:\DOS\ANSI.SYS
```

Note: *To avoid the tedious and difficult task of creating a CONFIG.SYS file from scratch, always back up your CONFIG.SYS after you or an automated installation program make any changes to this critically important file.*

Task: Bypassing the CONFIG.SYS File

To bypass the CONFIG.SYS file, you can use the same clean boot procedure you use to bypass the AUTOEXEC.BAT file. When the message Starting MS DOS... appears during startup, press F5 to bypass both CONFIG.SYS and AUTOEXEC.BAT. Or you can press F8 to use the interactive boot process. When you press F8, DOS pauses before loading each device driver in CONFIG.SYS, asking whether you want to load each device driver. DOS also asks if you want to process AUTOEXEC.BAT in the same manner.

To perform an interactive boot, follow these steps:

1. Start your computer as you usually do.
2. Watch the screen as the computer performs its power-up routine. When you see the message Starting MS DOS..., press F8.

   DOS skips the CONFIG.SYS file and prompts you to load each device driver individually. DOS then asks if you want to process AUTOEXEC.BAT in the same way.
3. Press **Y** for yes or **N** for no.

Understanding Advanced DOS Configuration Options

Extended memory
The memory beyond 1M on systems with additional memory installed.

Conventional memory
The first 640K of memory installed on your system; conventional memory runs most DOS programs.

A number of device drivers come with DOS. Some device drivers are added automatically to your CONFIG.SYS file during installation. These device drivers apply to the more advanced computers with a 286, 386, or 486 processor and *extended memory*. The normal memory that DOS and most programs use is called *conventional memory* and is limited to 640K. Extended memory is beyond the limit of conventional memory and can be used only in certain circumstances.

If you have a computer with a 386 or 486 processor and extended memory, you can configure your extended memory as *expanded memory* if an application program needs expanded memory. If you have a computer with extended memory, you can find more information in Que's *Using MS-DOS 6*, Special Edition.

Expanded memory
Memory beyond 640K that conforms to the LIM (Lotus, Intel, Microsoft)

If you have a computer with a 286 processor or higher and you have extended memory, the setup procedure when you installed DOS 6.2 added the following commands to CONFIG.SYS:

```
DEVICE=C:\DOS\HIMEM.SYS

DEVICE=C:\DOS\SMARTDRV.EXE nnn

DOS=HIGH
```


The file HIMEM.SYS is the DOS extended memory manager, which enables DOS and application programs to access extended memory. If HIMEM.SYS is loaded in CONFIG.SYS, it also tests all the memory on your system each time you start your computer to ensure no bad RAM chips exist.

The file SMARTDRV.EXE is the SmartDrive disk caching program that can speed up your disk operations, especially if you use database applications. A disk cache works a little like the BUFFERS command, but it can speed up disk access much more than the BUFFERS command. The *nnn* is the amount of extended memory in kilobytes that DOS reserves for the disk cache.

By default, the DOS 6.2 version of SmartDrive immediately writes all new data to your hard drive and holds in memory only information that it has read from your disk. The DOS 6.2 version of SmartDrive also caches data from CD-ROM drives, so long as MSCDEX.EXE is loaded in AUTOEXEC.BAT before SmartDrive.

The command DOS=HIGH tells DOS to load part of itself into extended memory and save more conventional memory for application programs. DOS 6.2 can load as much as 40K of itself into extended memory.

Summary

To	Do This
Edit AUTOEXEC.BAT and CONFIG.SYS	Use the MS-DOS Editor
Add a directory to the search path	Edit AUTOEXEC.BAT
Auto-load a program	Add the program to AUTOEXEC.BAT

To	Do This
Customize the DOS prompt	Use the PROMPT command
Automate commands	Use a batch file
Add a device driver	Edit CONFIG.SYS
Safeguard your configuration	Back up CONFIG.SYS and AUTOEXEC.BAT
Perform a clean boot	Press F5 at Starting MS DOS...
Perform an interactive boot	Press F8 at Starting MS DOS...
Access extended memory	Use HIMEM.SYS
Speed up your system	Use SmartDrive

On Your Own

Estimated time: 5 minutes

Use the PROMPT command.

1. Change your prompt by typing the following command at the DOS prompt and then pressing Enter:

   PROMPT THE CURRENT PATH IS PG

2. Return your DOS prompt to normal by typing the following com mand at the DOS prompt and then pressing Enter:

   PG

Manage AUTOEXEC.BAT and CONFIG.SYS files.

1. Make a backup of your AUTOEXEC.BAT and CONFIG.SYS files.
2. Print out your AUTOEXEC.BAT file and examine the printout to see how directories are listed in the path statement.
3. Print out your CONFIG.SYS file and examine the printout to see how the file is structured. Pay particular attention to the FILES=, BUFFERS=, and DEVICE= entries.

Lesson 12

Protecting Your PC's Data

Sooner or later, often when you can least afford it, disaster strikes—data on your hard drive is damaged or unusable. Your computer may malfunction. An electrical surge may destroy files. An aging disk may cause problems. Or you may make a mistake. The most common cause of data loss is human error. Any one of these problems can result in the loss of important data. This lesson discusses data protection and helps you perform the following tasks:

- Develop a data protection plan for your system
- Prevent hardware and software failures
- Protect your PC from viruses
- Use the Undelete program to recover lost data
- Use the Unformat program to recover from an unwanted disk format
- Use MS Backup to safeguard and restore data

Avoiding Data Loss

The reason you have a computer is to create files that contain valuable information. Because you are very careful and today's computers are very reliable, you may be tempted to trust that these files will be available when you need them. However, as an old computer saying goes, "There are two kinds of computer users: those who have lost files, and those who are going to lose files."

In this section, you learn three techniques to avoid data loss:

- Minimize the chances of loss by taking preventive measures.
- Learn and use DOS commands that often enable you to recover lost data.
- Maintain backup copies of your files on other disks that you can use to restore valuable data.

Restore
To copy to a hard disk the backup copies of files from floppy disks or other DOS-compatible devices, such as tape drives, to replace lost or damaged data.

Backup
Files from the hard disk copied to floppy disks or other DOS-compatible devices, such as tape drives, that you can use to restore lost or damaged data.

When you take preventive measures, you save yourself the aggravation of losing data and the time to recover it. When you recover data, you save yourself the time of finding and *restoring* the data from another copy. The first two techniques are not foolproof, however. The only way to ensure that data loss is not permanent is to have another copy available, a *backup* copy.

Taking Preventive Measures

The first way to avoid data loss is to prevent it before it happens. Unfortunately, no matter what you do, you have no guarantee that you will never lose data. You can minimize the risk, however, with preventive measures.

User Error

As you gain experience with your computer, you use it more. You create, copy, and erase more files. You also become a little less careful when you copy and erase files. One difference between a novice and an expert is that the expert makes many more mistakes and learns from them.

Commands such as COPY, ERASE, and FORMAT perform their jobs without regard to your intentions. DOS does not know when a technically correct command line will produce an unwanted effect. For this reason, always study the commands you enter before you execute them. Too easily, you can quickly enter a command that leads into ruin. Pressing Ctrl-C, Ctrl-Break, or Ctrl-Alt-Del may cancel a command before it does any harm, but you may not notice that the command is working improperly until it is too late.

Software Failure

The most common errors that cause data loss do not occur in DOS. Just as you must exercise care when you use DOS commands, you must be careful when you use commands in your application software. Most people spend much more time using application programs than they spend using DOS. You can lose data in your spreadsheet, word processing program, or database management system in many ways. For example, you can issue a command that erases a large part of your forecasting spreadsheet. Then, the next time you retrieve your spreadsheet, you may find that some of your data is gone. Make sure you have backup copies of your important files before you make changes to them.

Each software program you buy is a set of instructions for the microprocessor. Some software packages have mistakes called *bugs*, problems that the programmer was unaware of when the software was marketed. Software bugs are usually minor and rarely cause more than keyboard lockups or jumbled displays. However, sometimes bugs can mysteriously trash the data the software is designed to help you create. The only defense against a program with bugs, assuming you must continue using the program, is to make backups of all the data you produce using the program.

Sometimes utility programs, such as disk caches and partition utilities, can interfere with complex programs. A seriously faulty utility program can wipe out an entire hard disk. This occurrence is rare, but that fact is of little consolation when it happens to you. The best defense against such massive data loss is to have a full, current backup of your system at all times that you can use to restore your entire hard drive.

Bugs sometimes occur in the first releases of programs. Most software contains version numbers. Version 1 or 1.0 is the first version of a program. Version 1.1 is a minor upgrade, and Version 2.0 is a major upgrade. Many people try to avoid Version 1 of any program. Some people avoid Version x.0 of any program (such as 2.0 or 3.0), because a major upgrade is also likely to have bugs.

Perhaps the best way to avoid software errors is to talk to other people about a program before you buy or use it. Talk to friends and coworkers. You can meet people at computer user group meetings and find out about their experience with the program. If the program gets good reviews, the chances of serious software errors are minimal.

Hardware Failure

Today's personal computers are reliable and economical data-processing machines. The latest generation of PCs does the work of mainframe computers that only a fortunate few could access a decade ago. As with any machine, however, computer components can break down. By following the precautions presented in this section, you reduce the odds of losing time and information because of hardware failure.

Computers contain thousands of integrated circuits. Under ideal conditions, most of these circuits can last a century or more. However, disk drives incorporate precise moving parts with critical alignments, and although disk drives are very reliable, they are the component most prone to hardware failure. Other computer components are vulnerable to physical threats that include humidity, static discharge, excessive heat, and erratic electrical power. Dust and dirt also can stop your computer cold. Be vigilant about your computer's environment.

Surge suppresser
A protective device inserted between a power outlet and a computer's power plug to help block power surges—the sudden increases in voltage that often damage computer circuits.

Surge Suppressers

A surge protector is a good place to start when you begin considering how to protect your computer. Many *surge suppressers* are built into power strips like the one shown in the following figure. Power strips keep your cables neat and rid your work area of strings of extension cords.

A surge suppresser.

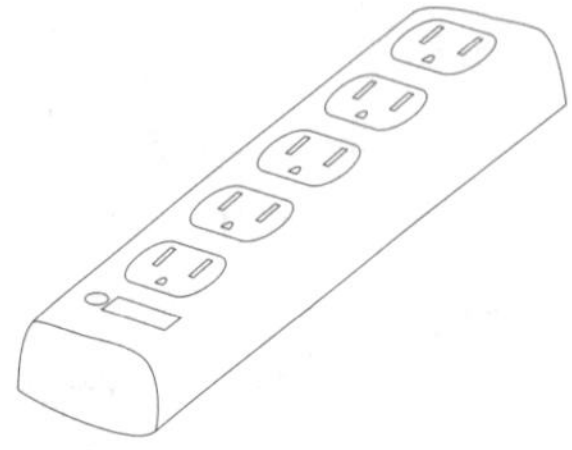

Surge suppressers constantly monitor the voltage that goes to your computer. If the voltage surges, or suddenly increases beyond what is safe for the computer, the surge suppresser opens the circuit. In other words, when the surge suppresser detects a dangerous power surge, it shuts down the computer before the surge can reach the computer's delicate circuitry.

Line Voltage Regulators

If the power in your office flutters and lights flicker, it means the current fluctuates. You probably need a line voltage regulator like the one shown in the next figure. Line voltage regulators remove dips and spikes in electric power lines.

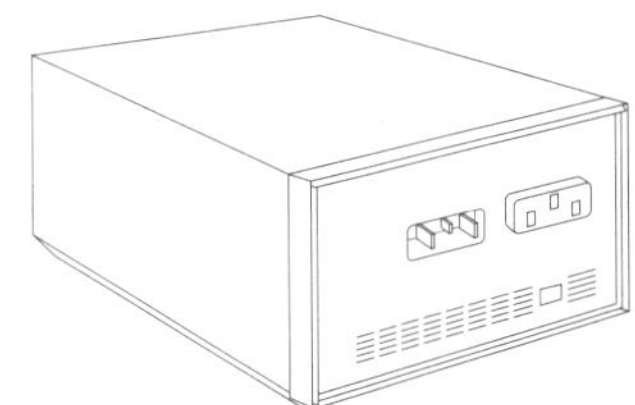

A line voltage regulator.

You also may be able to protect against fluctuating current by making sure your computer is away from any electrical appliances that pollute your power source. Connect your computer equipment to power sources not shared by copiers, TVs, fans, or other electrical equipment that contains a motor or uses a surge of power when it is turned on.

Static Electricity

Static electricity
An electrical charge that builds on an object and can discharge when it touches another object. Electronic circuits are easily damaged by static electricity discharges.

Your body generates *static electricity* when humidity is low, when you wear synthetic fabrics, or when you walk across carpet. Static electricity is harmless most of the time, but electronics are very sensitive to it. Just touching the keyboard while carrying a static charge can send an electrical charge through your computer, causing data loss or circuit failure.

You can avoid static problems by touching your grounded system unit's cabinet before touching the keyboard. If static electricity is a serious problem for you, a wide range of anti-static products are on the market, including anti-static pads you can touch when you sit down at the computer to dissipate any static build-up.

Computer Housekeeping

Your computer can become erratic when the temperature climbs. Circuits are not reliable when they overheat and can cause jumbled data. To ensure that your computer can function properly, keep it cool. If the fan on the back of your computer is choked with dust, heat collects quickly and can cause components to overheat or become loose in their sockets.

Your computer needs room to breathe. Frequently vacuum the dust build-up from your computer's breathing system; the fan on the back of your computer is the air-exhaust system for the computer's power supply. Cleaning the air-intake vents is particularly important if you, or someone in your office, smokes. This figure shows the places on the back of a computer you need to clean on a regular basis.

Parts to clean on the back of the system unit.

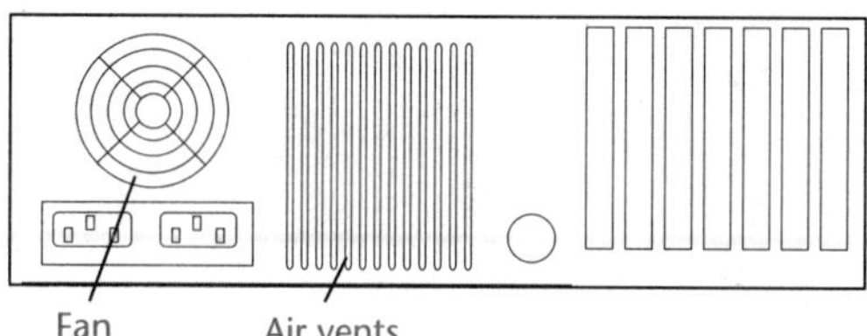

If the outside of your computer is dusty, the inside may be full of dust, too. Remove the cover occasionally and use a vacuum cleaner to clean the dust from the inside, making sure not to bang the vacuum cleaner into your computer's components while working inside the case.

Disk Drive Protection

Moving or shaking your computer can damage the disk drives. Never move your computer while the power is on. At all times while your system is turned on, the hard disk is rotating and the heads float a fraction of an inch above the disks. When you turn off your computer, the hard disk stops spinning and the heads settle onto the disks. With some hard drives, even with the power off, if you move or jostle your computer, the heads can move or bounce on the disks and damage the surface of the disks.

Self-parking heads
Heads on most newer disk drives that protect the disk from data loss by settling on a portion of the disk not used for data.

To prevent data loss, most hard disks have *self-parking heads*. When you turn off your computer, the heads move to a part of the disk not used for data. Even if the heads damage the disk surface, no data is lost. If your hard disk does not have self-parking heads, a *head-parking program* comes with your hard disk to park the heads manually. Always run the park program before you move your computer.

Head-parking program
A program that parks heads on a disk that does not have self-parking heads.

The heads on floppy disks can also be damaged when you move your computer. To protect them, insert a floppy disk that does not contain any data, and close the drive door before you move your computer.

Problem Prevention Checklist

Stopping small hardware problems before they become big ones takes a little planning and forethought. The following list describes a few simple, yet successful, preventive solutions for several hardware problems:

Static Electricity:

- Use anti-static touch pad on desk
- Use anti-static floor mat
- Use anti-static liquid or spray

Overheating:

- Clean clogged air vents
- Remove objects blocking vents
- Use air-conditioned room in summer

Hard Disk Damage:

- Don't move the computer while the disk is running
- Park the heads before you move the computer

Floppy Disk Damage:

- Store disks in a safe place
- Don't leave disks to be warped by sun
- Use protective dust jackets
- Avoid spilling liquid on disks
- Don't move the computer while the drive is running

Avoid magnetic fields from computer peripherals like printers and scanners. If possible, isolate these peripherals from your computer—just across the room is adequate. Also avoid placing your computer near appliances such as TVs and microwave ovens.

Protecting Your Computer from Viruses

Virus
A set of intentionally destructive instructions that duplicates itself inside computer programs to wreak havoc on your computer system.

One type of software problem that can cause serious data loss is a software *virus*. A computer virus is a set of instructions, hidden inside a program, that by duplicating itself can take over your computer and destroy all your programs and data files. Viruses are the work of computer vandals who destroy the property of others for enjoyment. Generally speaking, viruses infect executable files—files with the extension COM and EXE.

When you run a virus-infected program, the virus loads into memory. Some viruses immediately begin working to destroy data; others wait to wreak destruction. But viruses have a common trait: like biological viruses that spread human disease, computer viruses are designed to spread from computer to computer.

Viruses rarely infect the disks you receive when you purchase commercial software, although it has happened. Viruses usually are passed around on a floppy disk from one infected computer to another—by people who have no idea the floppy disk is infected. Viruses also can spread from computer to computer across networks, and sometimes viruses infect the software distributed through online services or electronic bulletin board systems (BBSs). Operators of most online services and bulletin board systems work very hard against viruses by testing the software they offer for distribution, but the risk is not completely eliminated.

To practice safe computing, never use a data disk or a program until you are absolutely sure it is not virus-infected. One precaution is to scan any data disk or program disk with an anti-virus program. Another precaution before you purchase new software or download software is to talk with other people who have used the program and make sure that they have had no problems.

Unfortunately, viruses are becoming all too common. Fortunately, DOS 6.2 includes programs you can use to detect and remove viruses from your computer. DOS 6.2 has two anti-virus programs that use different strategies to protect your data: Microsoft Anti-Virus and VSafe.

When you run MS Anti-Virus, it scans your PC's memory and the programs and other files on your disk drives to detect and clean viruses. MS Anti-Virus comes in two versions: one for DOS and one for Windows. MS Anti-Virus for DOS is discussed in the next section, and MS Anti-Virus for Windows is explained in Lesson 16, "DOS 6.2 Utilities for Windows."

Note: *MSAV installation is optional when you run the DOS 6.2 Setup program. If MSAV is not already installed, refer to Appendix A.*

Memory-resident program
A utility program that remains in memory after you run it, continuing to act on your system even while you run software applications. Also called terminate-and-stay-resident program.

VSafe is different from MSAV because VSafe is a *memory-resident program*, which means that after you run it, the program remains in memory, continuously monitoring your PC for viruses. (Another name for memory-resident is *terminate-and-stay-resident—TSR*.) If VSafe suspects that a virus is attempting to invade your system, a warning message appears. To install VSafe, follow these steps:

1. Type **VSAFE** at the DOS prompt.
2. Press Enter.

When you run VSafe, it remains in memory until you shut off your computer. To load VSafe each time you start your computer, add the VSAFE command to your AUTOEXEC.BAT file. Editing your AUTOEXEC.BAT file is discussed in Lesson 11, "Customizing DOS." The following figure shows the computer screen after VSafe detects a virus-infected program.

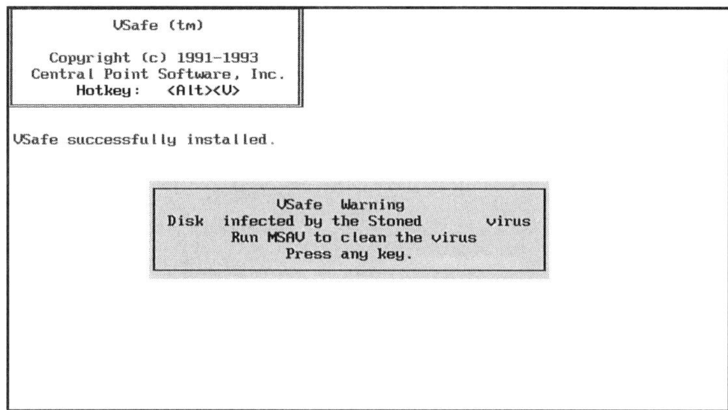

VSafe installation message and warning dialog box.

Task: Using MS Anti-Virus for DOS

You can run MSAV from the command line or add it to your AUTOEXEC.BAT file so it automatically scans your system for viruses each time you start your PC. To start MS Anti-Virus for DOS from the command line, follow these steps:

1. Type **MSAV** at the DOS prompt.
2. Press Enter.

The MS Anti-Virus Main Menu opens, as shown in the following figure.

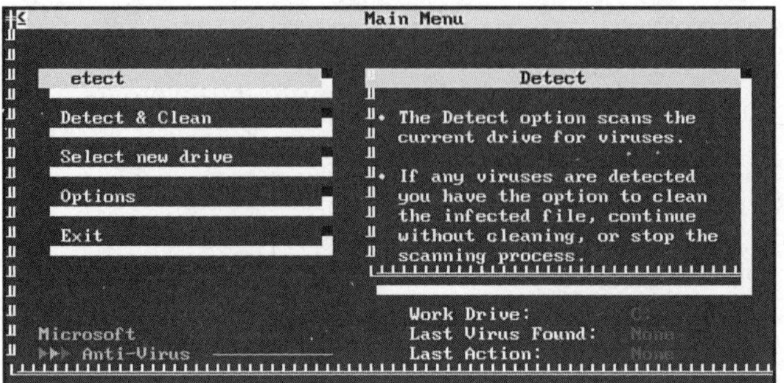

The MS Anti-Virus Main Menu.

MS Anti-Virus uses a full-screen interface. You can use the keyboard or the mouse to make selections from the Main Menu. In addition, the program displays a list of shortcut keys along the bottom of your screen. If you use a mouse, you can click the shortcut key to execute the associated command. For example, the shortcut key to exit MSAV is F3. If you click the word Exit, you can quickly return to the DOS prompt. To get help on MSAV, you press F1 or click the word Help.

The selections in the MSAV Main Menu are shown in the following list:

Selection	**Purpose**
Detect	Scans the current drive for viruses. If MSAV detects viruses, it presents you with the option to clean the file (remove the virus from the infected file), continue without cleaning, or stop the scanning process.
Detect & Clean	Scans the current drive for viruses and if viruses are found, MSAV automatically removes them from the infected file or files.
Select New Drive	Produces a dialog box in which you can select a drive to scan for viruses.
Options	Produces a dialog box in which you can change configuration options.
Exit	Returns you to the DOS prompt.

In some cases, MSAV can identify programs as having a virus infection when no infection exists. For example, if you update an application program, MSAV may mistake the updated program for an unknown virus. If you have recently updated an application program and MSAV identifies it as possibly virus-infected, do not be overly concerned. Run the program as normal and continue to regularly scan your system for viruses.

However, if MSAV later reports an occurrence of the same unknown virus in a second program file, it can be an indication of a virus and that it has spread. Treat both files as if they are virus infected—delete them.

After you have removed all infected files from your drive, you can reinstall all the software except the application that originally contained the virus (the program MSAV originally reported as containing an unknown virus). If possible, return the software containing the unknown virus to your dealer. You cannot reinstall the software infected with the unknown virus because it would reinfect your system. To scan the current drive for viruses, choose Detect from the Main Menu. To scan and clean the current drive, choose Detect & Clean. If you want to check a different drive, choose Select New Drive. Drive icons appear at the top of your screen. Choose the drive you want to scan.

As MS Anti-Virus scans a disk, it displays a status window showing you how much memory is being scanned, then how many directories and files are being scanned. The status window is shown in the following figure.

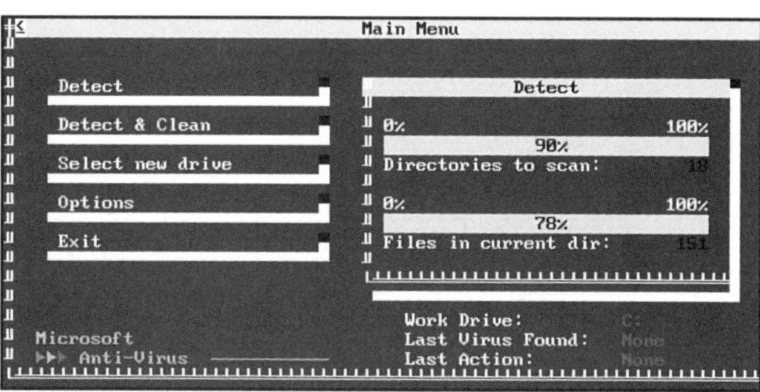

The MS Anti-Virus status window.

To interrupt the scan, press F3 or Esc, or click the word *Stop* at the bottom of your screen.

If MS Anti-Virus detects a known virus, or an unknown virus, it displays a warning. If MSAV detects an unknown virus, it displays the Verify Error dialog box shown in the next figure.

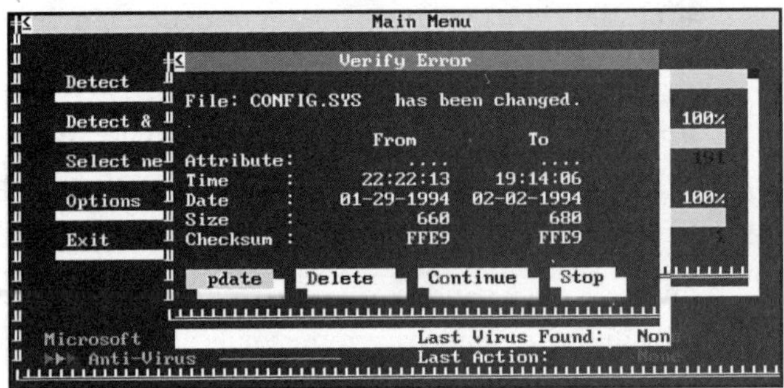

The Verify Error dialog box.

If MSAV detects a known virus, it produces an error message similar to the one shown in the following figure.

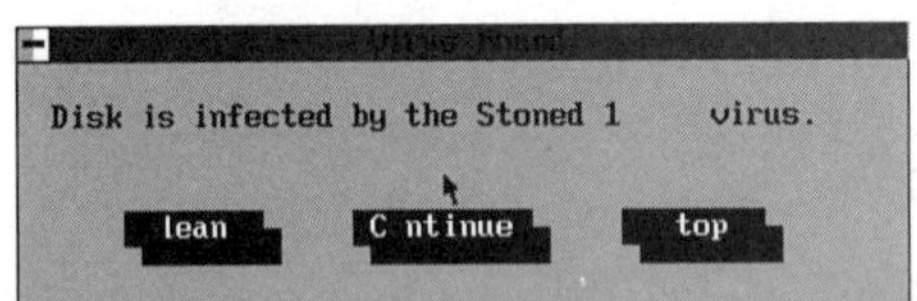

MSAV warning that a virus has been detected.

When the virus scan is complete, MS Anti-Virus displays the Viruses Detected and Cleaned report shown in the next figure, telling you the number of files scanned, the number of viruses detected, and the number of viruses cleaned. Choose OK to return to the Main Menu.

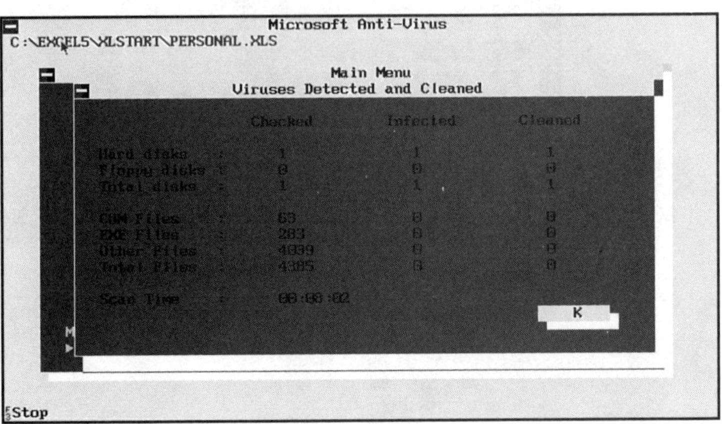

The Viruses Detected and Cleaned report.

When you finish using MS Anti-Virus for DOS, choose Exit and OK to return to the command line.

Viewing Known Viruses

MS Anti-Virus comes preset to scan your disks and memory for certain known viruses. In fact, MS Anti-Virus can detect more than 1,000 known viruses, including the best known and most dangerous viruses such as the Michelangelo virus and the AIDS virus.

You can see a list of the viruses and display or print information about each one. To see the list, follow these steps:

1. From the Main Menu, press F9 or click the word *List* at the bottom of your screen.

   A list of viruses appears.

2. To display information about a particular virus, click the name or select it and press Enter.

3. To print the virus list, click the Print button following step 1. The virus list is about 20 pages long.

Detecting Unknown Viruses

In addition to scanning for the known viruses, MS Anti-Virus scans for changes in executable files that may indicate an unknown virus. If the program detects a change, it displays a warning prompt. A change in an executable file is not proof that a virus is present. For example, updating an application program can change an executable file.

If an executable file has changed, MS Anti-Virus displays the Verify Error dialog box shown earlier. You must specify whether to update the file, delete the file, continue with the scan, or stop the scan.

If you have recently installed an updated version of a commercially marketed software application, a virus infection is unlikely, so you likely will want to continue the scan. Some chance exists that the file actually is infected with an unknown virus, so take special note of which file MS Anti-Virus identifies as potentially infected with an unknown virus. If, the next time you run MS Anti-Virus, additional files are identified as potentially infected, a real virus infection may exist and additional files may be infected.

Changing MS Anti-Virus Configuration Options

You can change the configuration options for MS Anti-Virus by turning the options settings on or off. To change the default options settings, follow these steps:

1. Choose the Options command from the Main Menu to produce the Options Setting dialog box (as shown in the following figure).

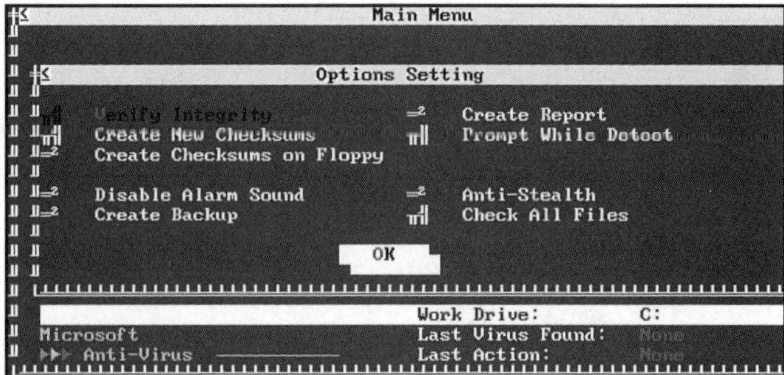

The Options Setting dialog box.

The settings that already are selected have check marks beside them.

2. To select an option, highlight it and click the left mouse button or press the space bar. A check mark appears.

3. To deselect an option, highlight that option and click the left mouse button or press the space bar. The check mark disappears.

4. Click OK after you finish selecting options.

The following list contains brief descriptions of each option.

Option	Purpose
Verify Integrity	Scans for changes in executable files. This selection is enabled by default.
Create New Checksums	Creates a *checksum* file for each directory scanned. If MS Anti-Virus detects changes in executable files, a warning message appears. This selection is enabled by default.
Create Checksums on Floppy	Creates the checklist files on floppy disks. This option enables you to have MSAV create checksums without taking up space on your hard drive.

Checksums
Small binary files that contain information MSAV uses to detect unknown viruses by determining if any file in a directory has changed.

Option	Purpose
Disable Alarm Sound	Turns off the audible alarm.
Create Backup	Creates a backup file of any file containing a virus before cleaning the file.
Create Report	Creates an ASCII text file of action taken during a scan.
Prompt While Detect	Displays a dialog box when MS Anti-Virus detects a virus, giving you the option of cleaning the file, continuing the scan, or stopping the scan. This selection is enabled by default.
Anti-Stealth	Activates a deeper level of virus detection that can protect against viruses that use advanced technology to escape detection while still infecting your system.
Check All Files	When on, scans all files. When off, scans only executable files. This selection is enabled by default. Turn off the option if you want a faster, less complete scan of your system.

If you have problems...

If you have problems running MSAV, make sure that you correctly type the MSAV command at the DOS prompt. If MSAV detects a known virus, in most cases you should have MSAV clean (remove) the virus. If MSAV detects an unknown virus, follow the directions outlined in the section titled, Task: Using MS Anti-Virus for DOS.

Recovering from Data Loss

Despite all your precautions, chances are you will experience data loss at some time. Earlier versions of DOS did not provide for recovering lost data. When you erased a file or formatted a disk, as far as DOS was concerned, the data was gone forever—even though in many cases the data still existed on the disk.

Many utility programs were written to recover this lost data. Some of the most well-known programs were part of Norton Utilities, Mace Utilities, and PC Tools. Microsoft incorporated some of the utilities from PC Tools

Deluxe into DOS 5 to provide recovery for lost data. These utilities include Unformat and Undelete. With these utilities, you can *undelete* a file you erased and *unformat* a disk you formatted in error. In DOS 6.2, Microsoft improves the utilities to make data recovery even easier and more reliable.

Data recovery is possible because of the way DOS stores files and information about these files. Every disk has at least one *file allocation table*. This table tells DOS which areas of the disk contain data and which are available for storing new data. The *directory structure* tells DOS information about a file, such as the file name and size.

The Unformat and Undelete programs can do their job because the ERASE and FORMAT commands do not really remove the files from the disk. After you erase a file or format a disk, all the files are still on the disk. The ERASE and FORMAT commands merely erase the file allocation table and the directory structure, leaving the data behind. The next time you create a file, DOS can write over the deleted files. Therefore, if you want to recover a file, do it immediately, before DOS uses the space to write another file.

You cannot recover some lost data. If you copy a file to a disk or subdirectory that already contains a file with that name, the old file is overwritten and is lost. If you save a file in an application program and save it under the same name as an existing file, the program may give you a warning message. If you override the warning and save the file, the old file is overwritten and is lost. Your only recourse is to restore a backup copy.

Using Undelete to Recover a Deleted File

If you delete a file or group of files in error, you need to act right away to recover the files by using the Undelete utility. The copying of Undelete to your DOS directory is optional when you run the DOS 6.2 Setup program. If Undelete is not present in your DOS directory, refer to Appendix A. Undelete comes in two versions, one for DOS and one for Windows. If you want to use Undelete for Windows, see Lesson 16, "DOS 6.2 Utilities for Windows."

As mentioned in previous sections of this lesson, Undelete offers three levels of file protection: Delete Sentry, the highest level of protection; Delete Tracker, the next level of protection; and a directory search method, which does not protect deleted files at all but can undelete them if you act promptly. Undelete can use only one level at a time.

To immediately recover a deleted file using the directory search method, follow these steps:

1. Change to the directory that contained the file you deleted.
2. Type **UNDELETE** at the DOS prompt.
3. Press Enter.

Undelete searches the current drive for files that have been deleted. When Undelete finds the file, it produces a read out similar to the following:

```
Delete Sentry control file not found.

    Deletion-tracking file not found.

    MS-DOS directory contains    2 deleted files.
    Of those,    2 files may be recovered.

Using the MS-DOS directory method.

      ?REVIEW  TMP     8347  1-19-94  2:12p  ...A  Undelete (Y/N)?
```

The last line in the read out displays the file Undelete found. The first character of the file name is missing, because that letter is erased when DOS deletes files. If you want to undelete that file, press the **Y** key for yes. DOS asks you to supply the first character of the file name. If you do not want to undelete that file, press **N** for no. If Undelete has found additional deleted files, it prompts you for whether to delete each of them. After you have been prompted for all deleted files, Undelete quits and you return to the DOS prompt.

When you are using the DOS directory level of Undelete, if the deleted file is fragmented or on the disk in sections, DOS can recover only the first section.

No matter which level of Undelete you install, the procedure for recovering a file is the same. You type **UNDELETE** at the DOS prompt. If you have Delete Sentry installed in memory, a read out similar to the following appears:

```
Directory: C:\
File Specifications: *.*

    Delete Sentry control file contains    2 deleted files.

    Deletion-tracking file not found.

    MS-DOS directory contains    3 deleted files.
    Of those,     1 files may be recovered.

Using the Delete Sentry method.

      SCREEN00 PCX    25596  1-19-94  2:12p  ...A  Deleted:
1-19-94  5:48p
This file can be 100% undeleted. Undelete (Y/N)?n

      SCREEN01 PCX     8347  1-19-94  2:12p  ...A  Deleted:
1-19-94  5:48p
This file can be 100% undeleted. Undelete (Y/N)?n
```

You can see from the read out that the Delete Sentry file contains two files you can undelete, SCREEN00.PCX and SCREEN01.PCX. Undelete's search of the DOS directory, on the other hand, found three deleted files, only one of which you can undelete. If the file you want to undelete is listed in the part of the read out for the Delete Sentry command, press **Y** for yes at the `(Y/N)?` prompt. Press **N** at the prompt for any files you do not want undeleted.

Generally speaking, any files found by Undelete's search of the DOS directory means these files were deleted before Delete Sentry was enabled. If you have used Delete Sentry every day for some time, chances are the files found in Undelete's DOS directory search are quite old. If you want to examine files deleted before Delete Sentry was enabled, use the /DOS parameter, as this example shows:

UNDELETE /DOS

Undelete Command Syntax

Unlike other DOS utilities, Undelete does not present a full-screen interface when you start the program, so you need to learn the program's command-line syntax to take advantage of its most powerful capabilities. The following example shows the Undelete command line syntax; details of each command line parameter are in the following list.

UNDELETE *d:\path filename* /DT (or) /DS (or) /DOS /LIST /ALL /PURGE_*d:* /STATUS /LOAD /UNLOAD /S_*d:* (or) /T_*d:* *-entries*

Parameter	Use
d:	Specifies the drive containing the files you want to undelete. If you do not specify a drive, Undelete searches the current drive.
path	Specifies the path to the directory containing the files you want to undelete. If you do not specify a path, Undelete searches the current directory.
filename	Specifies the file or files you want undeleted. For example, to undelete a file named WORK.DOC in the current directory you use the following command line: UNDELETE WORK.DOC You can use wild cards in the file name. For example, you can use the following command line to undelete all deleted batch files in the current directory: UNDELETE *.BAT If you do not specify a file name, Undelete searches for all files in the current directory that can be undeleted.
/DT	Recovers files protected by Delete Tracker.
/DS	Recovers files protected by Delete Sentry.
/DOS	Recovers files using the DOS directory search method.
/LIST	Lists the deleted files available for recovery.
/ALL	Recovers files without prompting for confirmation.
/PURGE *d:*	Purges all files in the Delete Sentry directory. The *d:* designation specifies the drive whose Delete Sentry directory is to be purged.
/STATUS	Displays the protection method in effect for each drive.
/LOAD	Loads Undelete into memory for delete protection.
/UNLOAD	Unloads Undelete from memory.

12

Parameter	Use
/S d:	Enables Delete Sentry method of protection. The *d:* designation specifies the drive for which you want to enable Delete Sentry protection.
/T d: -entries	Enables Delete Tracking method of protection. The *d:* designation specifies the drive for which you want to enable Delete Tracking protection. The *-entries* designation specifies the maximum number of deleted files Delete Tracking is to monitor. The value substituted for *-entries* must be 1 through 999. The following list shows the default number of files Delete Tracker monitors on a particular sized drive, and the size of the file used to keep delete tracking records (the *delete tracking file*).

Delete tracking file

A special file created by the Undelete program that DOS uses to make undeleting files easier and more reliable.

Disk Size	Files Tracked by Default	Tracking File Size
360K	25	5K
720K	50	9K
1.2M	75	14K
1.44M	75	14K
20M	101	18K
32M	202	36K
Larger than 32M	303	55K

Note: *You can remove Delete Sentry or Delete Tracker from memory by typing UNDELETE /U at the command line.*

Delete Sentry

Delete Sentry is the highest level of protection. When you run the Undelete program with the Delete Sentry parameter, Undelete remains memory-resident. After it is in memory, Delete Sentry creates a hidden directory called SENTRY, where deleted files are stored. Therefore, deleted files actually remain intact, protected, on the disk. DOS will not store a new file by replacing the first. If you use the Undelete utility to recover a protected file, the file returns to its original location on the disk. To install Delete Sentry in memory, follow these steps:

1. Type the following line at the DOS prompt:

   UNDELETE /S

2. Press Enter.

Undelete automatically purges the SENTRY directory after seven days so that a huge collection of deleted files does not accumulate on your disk, clogging it with files you don't need to keep any more. However, you can purge the directory using the /PURGE parameter described in the preceding section.

Delete Sentry can give you peace of mind when it comes to recovering deleted files. One minor drawback to consider is that Delete Sentry, as a memory-resident program, occupies memory, and the SENTRY directory occupies disk space. To load Delete Sentry into memory, type UNDELETE /S at the command line. DOS adds the command to your AUTOEXEC.BAT file so Delete Sentry loads each time you start your PC.

Delete Tracker

Delete Tracker is the middle level of protection. It also is a memory-resident program you must install from the command line. Delete Tracker records the location of deleted files in a hidden file called PCTRACKER.DEL, so Undelete can locate the file more easily. However, even with Delete Tracker installed, the file allocation table changes when you delete a file, enabling DOS to use the space on the disk to store a new file. Therefore, if you create a new file, you cannot recover the deleted file or you may be able to recover only part of it.

To load Delete Tracker into memory, follow these steps:

1. Type the following command at the DOS prompt:

   UNDELETE /T

2. Press Enter.

You can add the UNDELETE /T command line to your AUTOEXEC.BAT file so Delete Tracker loads each time you start your PC. For details on editing your AUTOEXEC.BAT file, see Lesson 11, "Customizing DOS."

If you have problems... If you have problems running Undelete, make sure that when you need to undelete a file, you do so immediately after deleting it. If you wait, chances are that DOS will use the disk space occupied by the deleted file, and you will not be able to recover the deleted file. If you run out of memory while using Delete Sentry or Delete Tracking, consider running MemMaker, which is covered in Lesson 14, "Configuring DOS 6.2 for Windows."

Using Unformat to Recover a Formatted Disk

If you format a disk in error and do not write any new files to the disk, you can use Unformat to recover the files on the disk. By default, when you use the FORMAT command to reformat a disk that contains data, DOS saves UNFORMAT information about the files on the disk before it clears the file allocation table and directory. The FORMAT command is covered in Lesson 7, "Formatting Disks." The following example shows the FORMAT command indicating it is saving UNFORMAT information.

```
C:\ >format A:
Insert new diskette for drive A:
and press ENTER when ready...

Checking existing disk format.
Saving UNFORMAT information.
Verifying 1.2M
Format complete.

Volume label (11 characters, ENTER for none)?

    1,213,952 bytes total disk space
    1,213,952 bytes available on disk

          512 bytes in each allocation unit.
        2,371 allocation units available on disk.

Volume Serial Number is 0872-19DF

Format another (Y/N)?
```

This process is called *safe formatting*. DOS uses a program called MIRROR to save the Unformat information. UNFORMAT then uses the MIRROR information to unformat the disk. The syntax for the UNFORMAT command follows:

UNFORMAT *d:*

The *d:* parameter specifies the drive you want to unformat. After you initiate the UNFORMAT command, you must confirm that you want to proceed; DOS then recovers the files on the formatted disk. Lesson 8, "DOS Command Reference," lists additional UNFORMAT options.

Make sure that you unformat a disk immediately after you format the disk in error and before you write any files on the disk. After you write files on a disk, the information that used to be on the disk is lost.

If you have problems...

If you have problems running Unformat, make sure that you correctly type the UNFORMAT command at the DOS prompt and then press Enter. Remember that you must unformat a disk immediately after you mistakenly format it. If you use the disk for new data, Unformat will not be able to unformat the disk.

Understanding Essential Data Protection Techniques

The most important data-protection measure you can take is learning to make backup copies of all your disk files. You can use Undelete and Unformat to recover from data loss, but these measures are not foolproof. The only way to avoid data loss is to make sure that you always have a backup copy of every file.

Develop a practice of using DISKCOPY to copy every disk that contains new software you buy *before* you install it on your hard disk. Then use the copy to install the software. Whenever you create or change a very important data file, copy it to a floppy disk. Then, if something goes wrong with the original disk or file, you can use the copy. Lesson 2, "Making a Quick Start with DOS 6.2," covers the COPY and DISKCOPY commands.

Using MS Backup to Protect Your Data

To back up all your installed programs and all the data stored on your hard drive, the MS Backup program included in DOS 6.2 is the best choice. MS Backup can copy all your files and your entire directory structure onto backup disks, and you also can use the program to restore these programs and data if you need them later.

Earlier versions of DOS used the BACKUP command to back up files. This command often got very confusing. You needed to know which command switches to set and which parameters to use to back up the files you wanted in the way you wanted. Then, you had to run the RESTORE program with its own parameters and switches if you needed to use the backup copies. MS Backup is a flexible, menu-driven program. You can select on-screen options and then save them in setup files you can use again and again.

MS Backup also has several advantages over COPY and DISKCOPY for backing up all your data:

- You can back up an entire disk or directory structure with one command.
- You can back up files that are larger than the capacity of a floppy disk.
- You can back up only those files created or changed since the last time you ran MS Backup.
- You need fewer floppy disks.

MS Backup simplifies the routine of backing up disks and directories. The rest of this lesson covers backup techniques, including how to restore the data from backup disks. With the examples in this lesson, you learn to back up and restore your entire hard disk or selective directories and files. You also learn the various options available for adapting MS Backup to your particular needs.

MS Backup can copy files from your hard disk to the destination floppy disk or to another DOS-compatible backup device, including network drives. The internal format of the backed-up file is different from that of normal files; therefore, you cannot use COPY to retrieve files stored on a backup disk. Your computer can use the files that MS Backup produces only after you use the MS Backup program to restore them.

MS Backup and its Restore feature are effective insurance against file loss. You can protect against the loss of hours or weeks of work through methodical use of MS Backup to make backup disks of your files. Of course, you also should master the Restore feature, which uses your backup disks to replace files lost from your hard disk.

If you have not yet tried to back up disk files, or if you are learning your way around DOS, the rest of this lesson is important. If you apply this information, you can avoid losing data.

Understanding MS Backup Basics

You use MS Backup to back up your hard disk files to floppy disks or to other DOS-compatible backup media such as network drives. When you use MS Backup, you create a backup set of disks that contains the files you selected to back up. You can use MS Backup to compare the backup sets to the original files or other files on the hard disk, and you can restore the backup sets to their original location on the disk or to a different location. You can even restore the files to a different computer.

Note: *MS Backup does not work with tape backup units. Even if you have a tape backup drive, you should know how to create and manipulate disk-based backups, in case you need to restore files to a computer that is not equipped with a tape backup.*

Using basic menu commands, you can back up an entire hard disk. You also can set up options for backups such as partial backups of the disk, selected files for backup, and for data verification. Basic menu commands also enable you to compare and restore the backed-up files.

Installation of MS Backup is optional when you run the DOS 6.2 Setup program, so if MS Backup is not installed on your PC, see Appendix A. MS Backup also has a version for Windows.

Understanding Backup Types

Every day you should ask yourself, "If my hard drive failed today, how much data would I lose? How much of that data can I *afford* to lose?" Performing a backup with MS Backup is much easier and cheaper than trying to reconstruct lost data or hiring a data recovery expert to reconstruct it for you. DOS does not prompt you to make backups. You need to remember to do a backup.

Three types of backup are available with MS Backup:

- A *full* backup makes backup copies of all the files you select before running MS Backup.

- An *incremental* backup makes backup copies of all files that have changed since the last time you ran a full or incremental backup. When you perform an incremental backup, the archive attribute, a signal that a file has not been backed up, is removed.
- A *differential* backup makes backup copies of all files that have changed since the last time you ran a full backup. When you perform a differential backup, the archive attribute is not removed, meaning that files backed up in a differential backup will be backed up next time you do an incremental backup.

Performing a full backup about one time a week is a good habit. An incremental backup at the end of the day keeps your backup data up-to-date. If you do not regularly schedule partial backups to copy your most important files, do a complete backup more often.

Starting MS Backup

Follow these steps to start MS Backup:

1. Type **MSBACKUP** at the DOS prompt.
2. Press Enter.

MS Backup's main program dialog box opens. Like Anti-Virus, MS Backup has its own shell, which makes the program easier to use. You choose items from dialog boxes and menus by using the keyboard or the mouse. You can display Help screens at any time by pressing F1.

The first time you run MS Backup, it prompts you for whether to run a compatibility test to ensure that MS Backup is properly configured to recognize your system hardware and that reliable backups can be made. If you do not run a compatibility test, the first screen you see when you start MS Backup is a warning, reminding you that without the compatibility test, reliable disk backups cannot be guaranteed. If you choose OK, DOS removes the warning and displays MS Backup's main program dialog box. From the main dialog box, you can perform a backup, restore backup files, compare backed-up files to the originals, or configure MS Backup. The compatibility test is covered in the next section.

Task: Configuring MS Backup

To configure MS Backup and perform the compatibility test, choose Configure from the main program dialog box. The MS Backup configuration is semi-automatic, meaning that the program checks your system and adjusts the configuration itself. To set the configuration, MS Backup runs through a series of tests on your video display, your mouse, and your MS Backup devices. The program tests your floppy drive configurations, your processor's speed, your hard disk's reading capability, and certain other performance indexes, and the results appear on-screen.

MS Backup displays your system configuration in the Configure dialog box. To change the configuration or see more details about a specific option, choose the option you want.

The compatibility test verifies whether MS Backup is correctly installed and configured to perform reliable file backups and restorations on your PC. The test consists of performing a small backup. You can skip the test, but then you cannot be sure whether MS Backup is working correctly. Also, each time you start MS Backup, it displays the warning screen.

Before you start the compatibility test, make sure that you have two blank disks available of the correct size and density for the drive you are going to use for the compatibility test. Then follow these steps:

1. Choose Compatibility Test from the Configure dialog box.

2. Choose Start Test. MS Backup starts the compatibility test and displays a dialog box when you are to insert the backup disk.

3. Insert the backup disk into the floppy drive. MS Backup backs up some files from your hard drive to the floppy disk. When the test is complete, a report screen appears.

4. Choose OK to continue. MS Backup then begins the process of comparing the data on the backup disks with the data on your hard drive to ensure they are identical.

5. Insert the backup disks when prompted by MSBACKUP and choose Continue. The comparison is made. When the comparison is complete, another report screen appears.

6. Choose OK to complete the compatibility test.

7. Choose OK again to return to the Configure dialog box.

8. Choose Save to save the configuration settings and return to MS Backup's main program dialog box.

Note: *If you ever change your hardware, reconfigure MS Backup by choosing Configure from the main program dialog box and running a compatibility test again.*

Task: Backing Up Files

The MS Backup program consists of a series of menu screens and dialog boxes. You can use the mouse or the keyboard to make selections. Every item also has a shortcut key, highlighted in a different color. The following sections describe how to perform a full or partial backup.

Performing a Full Backup

To perform a full backup, which is the default when you start MS Backup, follow these steps:

1. Choose Backup from MS Backup's main program dialog box. The Backup dialog box appears. The Backup dialog box enables you to choose the type of backup you want to perform, the source drive, the destination drive, and the files you want to include or exclude. If you accept the default settings, all the files on the C: drive will back up to floppies in the A: drive. The Backup dialog box displays the number of files selected for backup, the number of disks backup requires, and how long the backup will take.

2. Choose the source drive in the Backup From box. To back up all files on the C: drive, highlight the C: drive and press the space bar, or click the C: drive with the right mouse button.

3. Choose the Backup Type box, choose Full, and choose OK.

4. Verify that the destination drive in the Backup To box is the A: drive. If necessary, choose the Backup To box, choose the A: drive, and choose OK.

5. To verify the disk backup options, choose the Options button. The Disk Backup Options dialog box appears. Options include verifying data, compressing data, password protecting data, using error correction, and pausing to issue prompts. When options are the way you want them, choose OK.

6. Choose the Start Backup button to back up the selected files. MS Backup prompts you to insert a disk into the correct drive. During the backup procedure, MS Backup displays a status screen.

Always label your backup disks clearly, including the disk number, the files backed up, and the date you performed the backup. Put the backup disks in the proper sequence and store them in a safe place.

A full backup can take a long time, depending on the number of files and directories on your hard disk. When the backup is complete, MS Backup displays a status report. Choose OK to return to the main program dialog box.

Backing Up Selected Files

You do not need to back up every file each time you perform a backup. MS Backup is very flexible. For example, you can select only one file or several files in a directory, you can pick and choose files from different directories, or you can select all the files in entire directories. To back up selected files, follow these steps:

1. Choose Backup from MS Backup's main program dialog box. The Backup dialog box appears.
2. Select the source drive (the C: drive) in the Backup From box.
3. Choose the Select Files button. The Select Backup Files screen displays the files located on the source disk.
4. Select a directory or file by highlighting it and then pressing the space bar or by clicking the name with the right mouse button. Notice the check marks that appear beside the selected files. To deselect a directory or file, highlight it and press the space bar or click the name with the right mouse button.
5. To change the sort order of the listed files, choose the Display button at the bottom of the screen. The buttons at the bottom of the Select Backup Files screen enable you to specify by name the files you want to include or exclude from the backup.
6. You can use the Include and Exclude buttons to specify the path to individual files. Enter the path and file name and choose OK.
7. If you select the Special button, the Special Selections dialog box appears, enabling you to exclude files based on their attributes or the date they were created or modified.
8. After you select the files you want to back up, choose OK to return to the Backup dialog box.

9. Choose the Backup Type box, choose the backup type you want (such as Incremental), and then choose OK.

10. Select the destination drive (the A: drive) in the Backup To box.

11. Choose the Options button. The Disk Backup Options screen appears. Select the options you want and deselect the options you do not want.

12. Choose OK to return to the Backup dialog box. MS Backup displays the number of selected files, the number of disks you need, and how much time the backup will take.

13. Choose the Start Backup button. During the backup process, MS Backup displays status information. When the backup is complete, MS Backup displays a Backup Complete report.

14. Choose OK to return to the main program dialog box.

15. To return to the DOS prompt line, choose Quit from the MS Backup main program dialog box.

If you have problems...

If you have problems backing up files, make sure that you have run the compatibility test before beginning the backup. Carefully reread the section for the type of backup you are attempting to perform. Make sure that you correctly select in MS Backup the disk drive to which you want to perform the backup.

Setup file
A file used with MS Backup that includes favorite backup settings you can use for future backups.

Using Setup Files

The MS Backup menus and dialog boxes make it easy to set up any kind of backup, but DOS has included an even easier way. You can save your backup settings in a *setup file* you can use for future backups. That way, whenever you want to perform a particular type of backup, you can select a setup file instead of having to select individual options each time you run MS Backup. The default setup file that MS Backup uses is called DEFAULT.SET. You can save up to 50 different setup files for the different types of backups you commonly perform. To save the current backup settings in a setup file, follow these steps:

1. In the Backup dialog box, choose Save Setup As from the File pull-down menu. The Save Setup File dialog box opens.

2. In the File Name box, enter an eight character file name, such as DATAFILE. MS Backup automatically enters the extension SET.

3. In the Description box, enter a description of the backup settings. For example, enter \DATA files, verify, correct. MS Backup displays this information beside the file name in the Backup dialog box. If you have many setup files, the description helps you differentiate the files.

4. Choose the Save button.

After you have saved a setup file, you can easily use that file to run MS Backup. To select the setup file you want to use, follow these steps:

1. Choose the Setup File box from the Backup dialog box. A list of setup files appears.

2. Select the setup file you want to use and press the space bar, or click the setup file with the right mouse button. Notice the check mark beside the selected file name.

3. Choose the Open button. MS Backup displays the setup file information in the Backup dialog box.

4. Choose the Start Backup button to begin the backup procedure.

Using Catalog Files

Backup set catalog

A file created by MS Backup that contains information about the files and directories backed up and the setup file used.

Each time you perform a backup, MS Backup creates a *backup set catalog* file and stores it on your hard disk and on the last backup disk. The catalog contains information about the files and directories you backed up and the setup file you used. You use the catalog to compare backed up files to the originals and to select files you want to restore.

MS Backup uses a naming scheme for catalog files that helps you know what the file contains. Each name includes the first and last drives backed up in the set, the last digit of the year when the backup was performed, the month and day of the backup, the position of the backup in sequence if more than one backup was performed on the same day, and the backup type. For example, the catalog file for the first incremental backup from the C: drive on November 7, 1992, would be named CC21107A.INC. The catalog file name for a second full backup would be CC21107B.FUL.

Master catalog
A list of each backup set catalog file created using a particular setup file.

MS Backup also creates a *master catalog* file each time you back up. The master catalog contains a list of each backup set catalog file created using a particular setup file. A master catalog file has the same name as the setup file, with the extension CAT. For example, the name DATAFILE.CAT is the name given to the master catalog file for the setup file DATAFILE.SET.

If you delete a catalog from your hard disk, you can retrieve it from the backup set. If you cannot use the catalog on your hard disk, you can rebuild it. Catalog files are not necessary for comparing and restoring files, but they do make it easier, as explained in the next two sections.

Task: Comparing Files

You can use Compare to verify that a backup set of files is identical to the original files and that you can restore the backup. You also can use Compare to find out whether changes have been made to files on the hard disk since the last backup. You can compare one file, selected files, or all files in the backup set. Follow these steps to compare a backup set of files to the files on your hard disk:

1. Choose Compare from MS Backup's main program dialog box. The Compare dialog box opens. The catalog file for the most recently completed backup is loaded, but you can load the catalog file for the backup set you want to compare.

2. From the Backup Set Catalog box, select the catalog file you want and press the space bar, or click on the catalog file with the right mouse button. Then choose the Load button.

3. In the Compare From box, select the drive or device that contains the backup set.

4. In the Compare Files box, select the drives or files you want to compare. To select all files on a drive, press the space bar or click the right mouse button. To select individual files, choose the Select Files button.

5. To compare files to a drive or directory other than the original location, select that drive or directory in the Compare To box.

6. Choose the Options button to turn audible prompts off or on and to set MS Backup to exit after the comparison is complete. The Catalog button enables you to load, retrieve, or rebuild a master catalog file.

7. Choose the Start Compare button. The program prompts you to insert the disk containing the backup set into the correct drive.

   When the comparison is complete, the program displays a status report.

8. Choose OK to return to MS Backup's main program dialog box.

9. Choose Quit to return to the DOS prompt.

Task: Restoring Files with MS Backup

With MS Backup, you easily can restore files to a hard disk or to a different computer. Like Compare, Restore uses the backup set catalog files. The procedure for restoring files is similar to the procedure for comparing files. Follow these steps to restore a backup set of files to your hard disk:

1. Choose Restore from MS Backup's main program dialog box. The Restore dialog box opens.

2. Load the catalog file for the backup set you want to restore. The catalog file for the most recently completed backup is loaded. To load a different catalog file, select the file from the Backup Set Catalog box and press the space bar, or click the catalog file with the right mouse button. Then choose the Load button.

3. In the Restore From box, select the drive or device that contains the backup set.

4. To restore files to a drive or directory other than the original location, select the drive or directory in the Restore To box.

5. In the Restore Files box, select the drives or files you want to restore.

6. Choose the Options button to set restore options such as verification of data and whether you want the program to use prompts. The Catalog button enables you to load, retrieve, or rebuild master catalog files.

7. Choose the Start Restore button. The program prompts you to insert into the correct drive the disk containing the backup set.

   When the restoration is complete, the program displays a status report.

8. Choose OK to return to MS Backup's main program dialog box.

9. Choose Quit to return to the DOS prompt.

Restoring Files with RESTORE

If you have files that were backed up using the BACKUP command from a version of DOS earlier than DOS 6.2, you can restore those files by using the DOS 6.2 RESTORE command, which is in your DOS directory named RESTORE.EXE. The syntax for the RESTORE command is as follows:

RESTORE ***d: d:*** *path* /S

For example, to restore the files from a floppy disk in the A: drive to your hard drive (C:), follow these steps:

1. At the DOS prompt, type the following command:

   RESTORE A: C:*.* /S

2. Press Enter.

The /S switch causes DOS to restore all subdirectories and should be considered a mandatory switch unless the backup set does not include subdirectories. In the event that the backup set does not include subdirectories, use a command line that directs the RESTORE command where to place the restored files. For example, to restore the files on the A: drive to the C:\WORK directory, use the following command line:

RESTORE A: C:\WORK*.*

DOS prompts you to insert the backup disks into the correct drive.

Avoiding DOS Version Conflicts

Different versions of DOS use different methods for producing the contents of a backup disk. Versions 3.3 and later can restore files you backed up with previous versions of DOS. Versions earlier than 3.3, however, cannot restore backups made with versions 3.3, 4.x, or 5.x. No earlier versions can restore backups made with DOS 6.2. To avoid DOS version conflicts with backups, make sure that you use the same version of DOS (and that DOS versions RESTORE command) to restore a backup.

Be careful when you restore a backup to a computer running another version of DOS. Make sure that you do not copy any of the files in the /DOS directory. Each version of DOS has its own set of DOS files, and you cannot execute a command from one version of DOS on a computer running another version of DOS. If you have a computer running DOS 3.3, for example, and you copy the files from the /DOS directory of a computer that runs DOS 6.2, you get an error message every time you run an external command, such as CHKDSK. This problem occurs most often when you do a full backup on one computer and restore on another computer that runs a different version of DOS. This process results in a mismatch of DOS files, and you get errors when you try to run external DOS commands. To avoid this problem, install the later version of DOS on the second computer. Then you can safely restore the backup to that computer.

Summary

To	Do This
Protect against electrical problems	Use a surge suppresser
Discharge static electricity	Touch a grounded object
Detect software viruses	Use MS Anti-Virus
Prevent virus infection	Use VSafe
Recover deleted files	Use Undelete
Protect deleted files	Use Delete Sentry or Delete Tracking
Recover data from a formatted disk	Use Unformat
Safeguard your data	Perform frequent backups

On Your Own

Estimated Time: Varies

Protect against data loss.

1. If you do not have one, get a surge suppresser and use it.
2. Run MS Anti-Virus.
3. Configure Delete Sentry protection on your system (unless you have a critical shortage of system memory).
4. Back up your hard drive.
5. Design a backup plan for frequently backing up the data you cannot afford to lose.

Lesson 13

Using DoubleSpace, SCANDISK, and DEFRAG

Disk compression Software that automatically compresses each file on your hard drive, then when you need a file, automatically uncompresses it and loads it into memory.

DoubleSpace is a *disk compression* program. It stores the files on your hard drive (and on floppy disks) in less space than they require without DoubleSpace—roughly half the space. And unless you plan *never* to install additional software on your system, and you never use Microsoft Windows and Windows software (which gobble hard drive space), you need to learn about DoubleSpace.

In this lesson you learn to perform the following tasks:

- Install and use DoubleSpace
- Uninstall DoubleSpace
- Use DoubleSpace on floppy disks
- Bypass DoubleSpace during system boot-up
- Chεck how DoubleSpace is handling your data
- Use DEFRAG
- Understand CHKDSK versus SCANDISK

This lesson covers subjects that are related to the use of DoubleSpace. Some of these topics also relate to the everyday maintenance of your hard disk drive, whether or not you use DoubleSpace.

Determining When You Need DoubleSpace

There's an interesting saying about hard drive space: No matter how large your hard drive, the number of programs you want to install always increases to fill the available space on the drive. There is a bit of truth to the saying. Almost invariably, someone with a 40M, 60M, 80M, or even a 200M hard drive, finds that the hard drive eventually fills up. Program files, data files, and utilities need a lot of space.

Of course, one solution to a hard drive space shortage is to invest in a larger hard disk drive. But if that is not a possibility, DoubleSpace is the perfect answer when you run low on disk space.

Note: *DoubleSpace uses 33K to 50K of memory, so don't install DoubleSpace unless you need it. However, you can minimize the amount of conventional memory used by DoubleSpace by using the DOS utility MemMaker.*

Understanding DoubleSpace

DoubleSpace stores files in less space by compressing them. Without DoubleSpace, DOS stores files with no compression.

Token
A code used by DoubleSpace to replace recurring data in a file stored on disk.

When DoubleSpace compresses a drive, it looks for repeated data in each file. When DoubleSpace finds repeated data in a file, the word *the*, for example, it notes the first occurrence of this word and then replaces all other occurrences of the same word with a *token*. Such a token, for example, might be the @ character. DoubleSpace uses this token as a reference to the original data. The token and the cross-reference take less space than the original data.

If that seems complex, just imagine any text file. If the word *the* and the space after the word were replaced by the token @ every time *the* appears in the document, you would save hundreds, perhaps thousands, of bytes when you store the file on your hard drive.

The following sentence is an example of *the* replaced by tokens:

Today, @man and @dog spent @day in @field.

When you consider that DoubleSpace replaces all repeated data in the file with tokens, you can see why it may take less than half the hard drive space to store the compressed file.

DoubleSpace stores the file in a compressed state on your hard (or floppy) drive until you use the file. When the file is loaded into memory, DoubleSpace uncompresses the file so it returns to its original size, and contains the original data, so it can be used by your computer or application program. In other words, the @ tokens all are replaced by the original word they represent. When you finish using the file, DoubleSpace compresses it again and stores it on the drive.

DoubleSpace compresses some files more than others because some files have more repeated data than others. Text files usually compress quite a bit because they contain a lot of repeated data. Program files are usually compressed already, so DoubleSpace cannot compress them as much as text files. Files that were already compressed by compression utilities like PKZIP cannot be compressed further, so these files take the same amount of space on your hard drive whether or not DoubleSpace is used to compress the drive.

If your computer has a slow CPU, for example a 16MHz 386SX, you may notice a *reduction* in speed after compressing your drive. If you have a fast CPU—for example, a 66 MHz 486DX2—and a slow hard disk, DoubleSpace might improve your system's speed slightly because it takes less time to load compressed files into memory. If you have a computer with a fast CPU and a fast hard disk, you probably won't notice much difference in your system speed after installing DoubleSpace.

Compressing a Hard Drive with DoubleSpace

DoubleSpace uses at least 33K of memory, so before you use DoubleSpace to compress your hard drive you need to ensure you have enough memory available after installation to run your application software programs. You also should do a backup of all data on the drive so that you can restore your system if something goes wrong.

DoubleSpace cannot compress a disk that is completely full. To compress your startup hard disk drive, the drive must contain at least 1.2M of free space. Other hard disks and floppy disks must contain at least 1.1M of free space, therefore DoubleSpace cannot compress 360K or 720K floppy disks.

Task: Running the MEM Command

The first step is checking available memory prior to installing DoubleSpace. At the DOS prompt, enter the following command:

MEM

The DOS MEM (memory) utility provides a readout of the available memory on your system. The following is an example of the readout provided by the MEM utility, although your readout will be different because your system will be configured differently:

```
Memory Type         Total  =   Used  +   Free
----------------  -------    -------    -------
Conventional         640K       68K       572K
Upper                  0K        0K         0K
Reserved             384K      384K         0K
Extended (XMS)    31,744K   30,720K     1,024K
----------------  -------    -------    -------
Total memory      32,768K   31,172K     1,596K

Total under 1 MB     640K       68K       572K

Total Expanded (EMS)                1,024K (1,048,576 bytes)
Free Expanded (EMS)                 1,024K (1,048,576 bytes)

Largest executable program size       572K (585,392 bytes)
Largest free upper memory block         0K       (0 bytes)
MS-DOS is resident in the high memory area.
```

The MEM utility displays the amount of free conventional memory on your system in the column headed `Free`. Once you know the amount of free conventional memory on your system, you need to subtract from that total the 33K minimum that will be needed by DoubleSpace. The figure after the subtraction is the amount of conventional memory that will be free while you are using DoubleSpace.

Once you know the amount of conventional memory that will be free after DoubleSpace installation, check the memory requirements of your software applications. The conventional memory requirements of applications is provided in the owner's manual for each program.

If you have enough conventional memory free after installing DoubleSpace, proceed with the rest of this section, which describes

DoubleSpace installation. If you won't have enough free conventional memory after installing DoubleSpace (and you have a 386-, 486-, or Pentium-based system), you can free up conventional memory by running the MemMaker utility.

Backing Up Your System

Before running DoubleSpace, you should do a full backup of the programs and data on your system.

The DOS 6.2 utility MS Backup can be used to quickly and easily restore the information on your hard drive in the event that something goes wrong during DoubleSpace compression of your drive. If data is damaged during compression, you can restore that data from the backup. MS Backup is covered in Lesson 12, "Protecting Your PC's Data."

Understanding the DoubleSpace "Extra" Drive

Uncompressed drive
A drive on which DOS, not Double-Space, handles the storage of data. The files on an uncompressed drive are used to boot your system before DoubleSpace takes over.

When DoubleSpace compresses your hard drive, you will have a new drive letter on your system, usually drive H:. The additional drive is an *uncompressed drive* that is used to store files that must remain uncompressed, including IO.SYS, MSDOS.SYS, the Windows permanent swap file, DBLSPACE.BIN, DBLSPACE.INI, and DBLSPACE.000. These files are all read-only, hidden, system files.

Note: *Do not delete or tamper with the read-only, hidden, system files on the new drive. If you do, you might destroy your compressed drive and lose all the data and program files it contains.*

The way DoubleSpace assigns drive letters to compressed and uncompressed drives is interesting. If your computer has only drives A:, B:, and C:, DoubleSpace skips letters D, E, F, and G and assigns drive letter H to the new drive. However, if you have another drive, for example drive D:, and you compress that drive, DoubleSpace works backwards from the first drive letter it assigned so the uncompressed drive letter would be G:. If you have a CD-ROM drive, are on a network, have created drive letters by partitioning your hard drive with FDISK, use RAMDrive, or use installable device drivers that assign drive letters, DoubleSpace attempts to avoid drive-letter conflicts. However, if a drive-letter conflict does occur, DoubleSpace resolves the conflict by reassigning its own drive letters.

Choosing DoubleSpace Setup Modes

If you are running DoubleSpace for the first time, choose Express Setup. This setup mode is designed for the great majority of users and the widest range of systems. Most systems have only one hard drive, therefore Express Setup will handle these systems properly.

When you choose Express Setup, DoubleSpace compresses drive C:. If you want to compress another drive, you must use Custom Setup. Depending on the size of your drive, DoubleSpace Setup can take several hours to compress your files. The following provides more information on each setup mode:

- Express Setup is recommended for MS-DOS novices as well as those who are not yet knowledgeable about DoubleSpace. Express Setup automatically compresses your first hard drive (drive C: on most systems) using the DoubleSpace defaults. It creates drive H: as the uncompressed drive. Express Setup makes required changes to your system configuration files, CONFIG.SYS and AUTOEXEC.BAT.

- Custom Setup is for those who want to have a great deal of control over the way DoubleSpace compresses their drive, or for those who wish to compress a second or third hard drive, rather than the first.

Running DoubleSpace Setup

Running DoubleSpace to increase the amount of space available on your hard drive is straightforward. At the DOS prompt, type the following:

DBLSPACE

To use Setup, follow these steps:

1. When DoubleSpace starts, its opening screen informs you that you can press the Enter Key to continue, Press F1 for more information on DoubleSpace Setup, or press F3 to exit DoubleSpace Setup. To continue DoubleSpace Setup, press the Enter key.

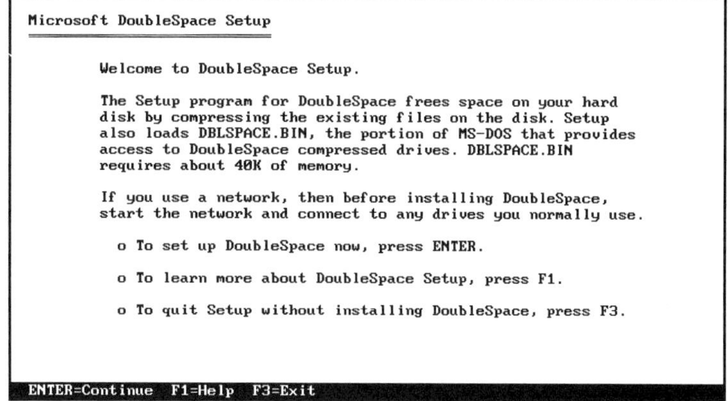
Microsoft DoubleSpace Setup

Welcome to DoubleSpace Setup.

The Setup program for DoubleSpace frees space on your hard disk by compressing the existing files on the disk. Setup also loads DBLSPACE.BIN, the portion of MS-DOS that provides access to DoubleSpace compressed drives. DBLSPACE.BIN requires about 40K of memory.

If you use a network, then before installing DoubleSpace, start the network and connect to any drives you normally use.

o To set up DoubleSpace now, press ENTER.

o To learn more about DoubleSpace Setup, press F1.

o To quit Setup without installing DoubleSpace, press F3.

ENTER=Continue F1=Help F3=Exit

The DoubleSpace opening screen.

2. Use the arrow keys to move the highlight to the setup mode you want to use and then press the Enter key.

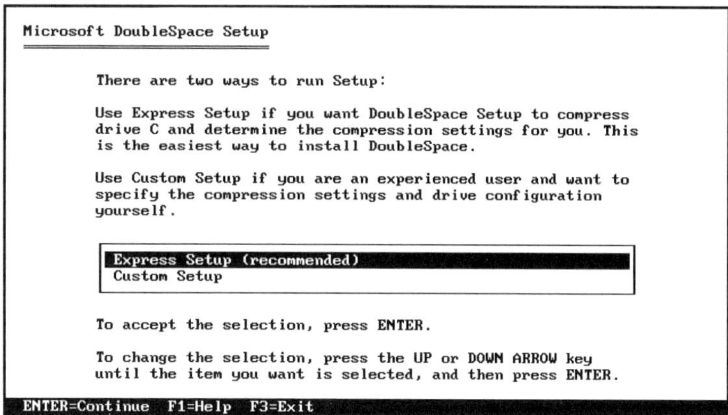
Microsoft DoubleSpace Setup

There are two ways to run Setup:

Use Express Setup if you want DoubleSpace Setup to compress drive C and determine the compression settings for you. This is the easiest way to install DoubleSpace.

Use Custom Setup if you are an experienced user and want to specify the compression settings and drive configuration yourself.

Express Setup (recommended)
Custom Setup

To accept the selection, press ENTER.

To change the selection, press the UP or DOWN ARROW key until the item you want is selected, and then press ENTER.

ENTER=Continue F1=Help F3=Exit

The DoubleSpace Setup mode selection screen.

After you choose a DoubleSpace Setup mode, your choices are specific to that mode. The following sections provide information about both Express Setup and Custom Setup.

Express Setup

To choose Express Setup, use the arrow keys to highlight the Express Setup option and press Enter. You are prompted once again for confirmation that you want to configure your system for DoubleSpace.

Setup warns you to backup your files before configuring your system for DoubleSpace (click the Continue button with the mouse or press C). To get help on DoubleSpace Setup, press F1. To quit DoubleSpace Setup, press F3.

SCANDISK
A DOS utility that tests your hard drive and repairs any problems that it finds.

DoubleSpace then runs *SCANDISK* to check your hard drive to ensure there are no errors in your file structure or in the physical media of the disk itself. Then DoubleSpace usually runs *DEFRAG* to defragment the files on your disk.

The Microsoft Defragmenter defragments your hard drive.

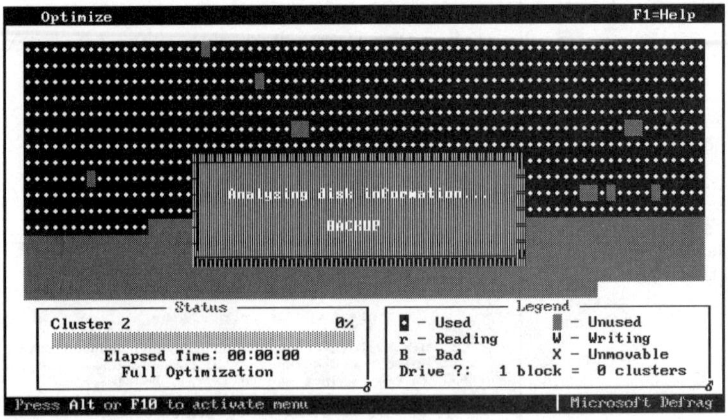

DEFRAG
The Microsoft Defragmenter, which makes sure all the parts of each file are stored together, and then moves files to the front of your disk to consolidate free space.

When SCANDISK and DEFRAG have finished preparing your drive, DoubleSpace compresses the files on the drive. The DoubleSpace screen keeps you informed of which file on your drive is currently being compressed and how much longer the compression process is expected to take.

Note: *While DoubleSpace is compressing your drive, do not attempt to use the system. DoubleSpace needs all the resources of your system to do its job. Since it can take several hours to compress a drive, if possible, secure the system so that a coworker does not mistakenly turn off the system. If your system is turned off, or if power goes out, you can simply restart your system. DoubleSpace will resume the compression process where it left off when the computer lost power.*

When DoubleSpace is finished compressing your drive, it displays information about the newly compressed drive, including the amount of space now available on the drive. To use your system, simply reboot as prompted by DoubleSpace. When your system boots, your CONFIG.SYS and AUTOEXEC.BAT files are processed normally and when that is finished, your system displays the DOS prompt. You can use your system just as you did before DoubleSpace compressed your files.

Custom Setup

To choose Custom Setup, use the arrow keys to highlight the Custom Setup option and press the Enter key. When you choose Custom Setup, you are presented with a variety of selections.

It is important for those who are new to DOS to note that even if you must run Custom Setup to compress a drive other than C:, after choosing the drive you can use the other default values presented by DoubleSpace.

Use the following steps to use Custom Setup:

1. Use the arrow keys to choose whether to compress an existing drive (C: or D:) or to create a new, empty compressed drive from the unused space on an existing drive. Press Enter when you have highlighted the correct choice.

   If you choose to create a new, empty compressed drive, the original drive (C: or D:) becomes the host and the new drive will be assigned a higher drive letter.

2. Use the arrow keys to highlight the drive you want to compress and press Enter.

   Custom Setup estimates the amount of free space that will be available on the drive when compression is complete.

   Setup then displays the default drive letter that will be assigned to the uncompressed drive and the amount of space that will be left uncompressed on that drive. If you want to change the default drive letter that will be assigned to the uncompressed drive or the amount of space that will be left uncompressed on that drive, use the arrow keys to highlight the option you want to change and press Enter. This produces a screen in which you can change the option you highlighted.

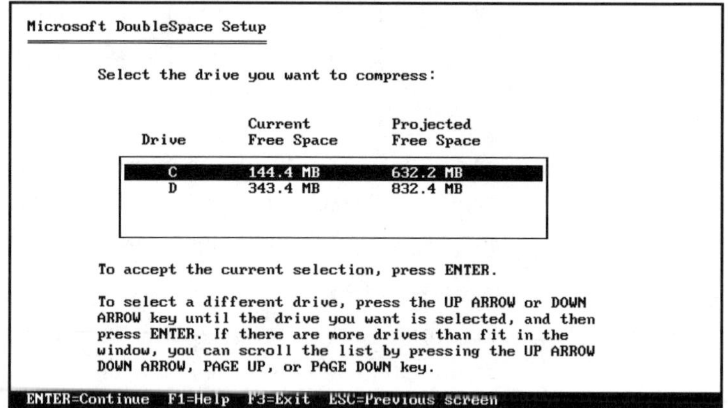

Choosing in Custom Setup the drive you want to compress.

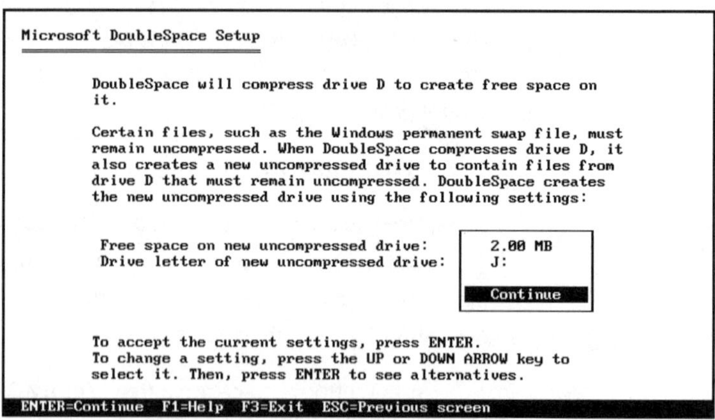

Microsoft DoubleSpace Setup
DoubleSpace will compress drive D to create free space on it.
Certain files, such as the Windows permanent swap file, must remain uncompressed. When DoubleSpace compresses drive D, it also creates a new uncompressed drive to contain files from drive D that must remain uncompressed. DoubleSpace creates the new uncompressed drive using the following settings:
Free space on new uncompressed drive: 2.00 MB
Drive letter of new uncompressed drive: J:
Continue
To accept the current settings, press ENTER.
To change a setting, press the UP or DOWN ARROW key to select it. Then, press ENTER to see alternatives.
ENTER=Continue F1=Help F3=Exit ESC=Previous screen

Choosing uncompressed drive letter and space options in Custom Setup.

3. To choose the drive letter, scroll through the list of available options. When you have chosen the drive letter, press the Enter key.

   By default, DoubleSpace usually chooses the drive letter H: for the uncompressed space on drive C:. However, you can choose another drive letter (such as D: if you have only one hard drive and no CD-ROM or other device driver that uses a drive letter). Choosing a drive letter that is sequential to the drives already on your system may make it easier to remember which drive letter is used by the uncompressed drive. Once you have chosen the drive letter you want to use, press the Enter key.

   or

   To increase or decrease the amount of uncompressed space, type in the number of megabytes (2.00, 3.00, 4.00, etc.) you want to remain uncompressed. Once you have specified the amount of space on the uncompressed drive, press the Enter key.

Choosing in Custom Setup the space on the uncompressed drive.

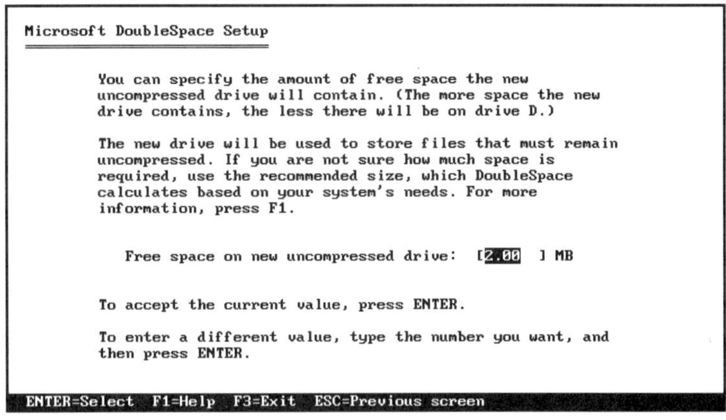

Microsoft DoubleSpace Setup

You can specify the amount of free space the new uncompressed drive will contain. (The more space the new drive contains, the less there will be on drive D.)

The new drive will be used to store files that must remain uncompressed. If you are not sure how much space is required, use the recommended size, which DoubleSpace calculates based on your system's needs. For more information, press F1.

Free space on new uncompressed drive: [2.00] MB

To accept the current value, press ENTER.

To enter a different value, type the number you want, and then press ENTER.

ENTER=Select F1=Help F3=Exit ESC=Previous screen

Choosing in Custom Setup the drive letter for the uncompressed drive.

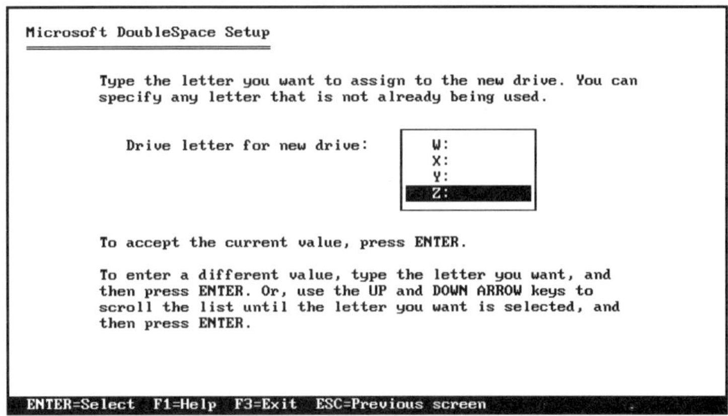

Microsoft DoubleSpace Setup

Type the letter you want to assign to the new drive. You can specify any letter that is not already being used.

Drive letter for new drive: W: X: Y: Z:

To accept the current value, press ENTER.

To enter a different value, type the letter you want, and then press ENTER. Or, use the UP and DOWN ARROW keys to scroll the list until the letter you want is selected, and then press ENTER.

ENTER=Select F1=Help F3=Exit ESC=Previous screen

4. Once you have specified the amount of space on the uncompressed drive and the drive letter the uncompressed drive will be assigned, press the Enter key to continue DoubleSpace Setup. Setup next presents you with a warning that you should back up your programs and data before configuring DoubleSpace.

5. Choose Continue to proceed. Choose Exit to quit DoubleSpace Setup. Choose Help to get help on DoubleSpace Setup.

   When you choose Continue, DoubleSpace prompts you one more time whether to continue compressing your files. To Continue, press the C key. To return to the previous menu screen, press Esc.

13

Once you choose Continue, DoubleSpace runs SCANDISK to check your hard drive to ensure there are no errors on your hard drive that would endanger your data or interfere with DoubleSpace Setup. When SCANDISK has completed testing your drive, DoubleSpace usually runs the Microsoft Defragmenter to defragment the files on your disk. Once SCANDISK and the Microsoft Defragmenter are finished with the drive, DoubleSpace compresses the files on the drive, keeping you informed of which file is currently being compressed and how much longer compression should take.

When DoubleSpace is finished compressing your drive, it provides details on the amount of space now available on the drive. When prompted by DoubleSpace, reboot your system, and then proceed to use it as usual. Your system should perform as it did before you compressed your files with the exception that you will have much more available hard drive space.

Managing Your Compressed Drive

Once your drive is compressed, there is one task you need to perform routinely to manage the compressed drive. And there are some other tasks you may want to undertake to manage your compressed drive more efficiently. This section covers the compressed drive management tasks you need to learn if you use DoubleSpace.

When you enter the command DBLSPACE alone at the DOS prompt, it starts the DoubleSpace Setup process. But when you use a command line parameter with the DBLSPACE command, DoubleSpace performs a compressed drive management task without displaying the screens described in the previous sections. This section details the parameters used with the DBLSPACE command to manage your compressed drive.

DBLSPACE Command Syntax

The basic syntax of the DBLSPACE compressed drive management commands is shown in the following:

DBLSPACE */parameter*

Each parameter to the DLBSPACE command may have its own switches. For example, you may need to enter the drive letter specifying the compressed drive on which you want the command to work. The following sections describe DBLSPACE command line parameters and the switches used with each parameter.

The /DEFRAGMENT Parameter

One of the most important of the compressed drive management tasks, one that you need to learn to perform even if you do not learn the others, is ensuring that your compressed drive, and the files on your compressed drive, do not become fragmented.

Fragmented files
Files whose data is scattered about your disk in numerous locations, rather than being stored together.

Not only do *fragmented files* slow down your system, but they also are difficult for DOS and DoubleSpace to keep track of. It is very important that you defragment your drive at least once a month, or more often if you frequently delete and create new files, move files from one directory to another, or install new software. Here is how to defragment your DoubleSpace drive:

1. Run the MS-DOS Defragmenter to ensure that all sectors of each file are end to end (contiguous). Type the following at the DOS prompt and press Enter:

    DEFRAG

2. When DEFRAG has finished, type the following at the DOS prompt and press the Enter key:

    DBLSPACE /DEFRAGMENT

Use of DEFRAG and the DBLSPACE /DEFRAGMENT command consolidates the data on the compressed drive and moves the compressed drive to one part of the physical hard disk platters.

If you are planning to reduce the size of a compressed drive, you should first use the Defragment command to consolidate the drive's free space. You can then make the drive smaller than you could if you did not first defragment it. This switch can be abbreviated as /DEF.

The basic syntax of the /DEFRAGMENT parameter is shown in the following:

DBLSPACE /DEFRAGMENT /F *d:*

Here is the use of the switches to the /DEFRAGMENT parameter:

Switch	Description
d:	Specifies the drive you want to defragment. This parameter is optional; if you do not specify a drive, DoubleSpace defragments the current drive.
/F	Enables the specified drive to be defragmented more fully. This switch is optional.

Microsoft recommends that to perform an especially thorough defragmentation of your hard drive, you follow this three-step process:

1. Run the DEFRAG utility.
2. Run DBLSPACE /DEFRAGMENT /F.
3. Run DBLSPACE /DEFRAGMENT (without the /F switch).

Note: *Running DEFRAG can take a long time, often several hours. It can take even longer to run DEFRAG, then DBLSPACE /DEFRAGMENT /F and then DBLSPACE /DEFRAMENT as described in the previous steps. You should defragment your hard drive when you will not need quick access to your computer, perhaps at the end of the day.*

The /INFO Parameter

The /INFO parameter causes DBLSPACE to display information about a compressed drive's free and used space, its actual and estimated compression, and the name of the compressed volume file. You can use the DBLSPACE /INFO command while Windows is running. The syntax of the /INFO parameter is shown in the following:

DBLSPACE /INFO *d:*

The *d:* switch specifies the drive about which you want information. This parameter is optional; if you do not specify a drive, DoubleSpace displays information about the current drive.

The /COMPRESS Parameter

The /COMPRESS parameter provides a method of compressing the files on an existing hard disk drive, floppy disk, or other removable media without the full screen display described in previous sections. When you use this parameter, you provide all the information on the command line that DoubleSpace needs to compress the drive, and DoubleSpace compresses the drive without further intervention. This option is most often used by those who are knowledgeable about configuring DoubleSpace.

If you use this option, you need to specify on the command line the letter designation of the drive you want to compress. Additional switches can be used to specify the drive letter for the uncompressed drive, and the amount of space to remain uncompressed. If you do not use these additional other switches, DoubleSpace uses default values. The /COMPRESS parameter can be abbreviated to /COM. The following is the command syntax for the /COMPRESS parameter:

DBLSPACE /COMPRESS *d:* /NEWDRIVE=*drive letter:* /RESERVE=*size* /F

The following explains the use of the switches to the /COMPRESS parameter:

Switch	Description
d:	Specifies the existing drive you want to compress. You must enter the identifier for an existing drive.
/NEWDRIVE=*drive letter:*	Specifies the drive letter you want assigned to the uncompressed (host) drive (you also type the colon). After DoubleSpace compresses an existing drive, your system will include both the existing drive (now compressed) and a new uncompressed drive. The /NEWDRIVE switch is optional; if you omit it, DoubleSpace assigns the next available drive letter to the new drive. This switch can be abbreviated to /NEW.
/RESERVE=*size*	Specifies the number of megabytes of space to leave uncompressed. It's a good idea to reserve some uncompressed space because some files, such as the Windows swap file, do not work properly when stored on a compressed drive. The uncompressed space will be located on the new uncompressed drive. (If the drive you are compressing contains a Windows permanent swap file, DoubleSpace moves the file to the new uncompressed drive.) This switch can be abbreviated to /RES.

Switch	Description
/F	Prevents DoubleSpace from displaying the final screen when compression is complete. The final screen shows the compression ratio of the compressed drive. If you use the /F switch, DoubleSpace immediately returns to the DOS prompt when compression is complete.

The /UNCOMPRESS Parameter

The /UNCOMPRESS parameter uncompresses a drive that was compressed by using DoubleSpace. When you uncompress all hard drives on a system, the /UNCOMPRESS parameter also frees up the 50K of system memory used by DBLSPACE.BIN, the portion of MS-DOS that provides access to compressed drives. The following is the syntax of the /UNCOMPRESS parameter:

DBLSPACE /UNCOMPRESS *d:*

The ***d:*** switch, a mandatory switch, specifies the drive you want to uncompress. You need to enter the drive designation letter for the drive you want to uncompress, for example C: or D:.

Note: *Before you use the /UNCOMPRESS parameter, ensure there is enough free space on your hard drive for the uncompressed files. You need roughly twice the space for the uncompressed files as they require in their compressed state.*

The /CREATE Parameter

The /CREATE parameter is used to create a new compressed drive in the free space on an existing drive while bypassing the DoubleSpace screens shown in the previous sections. This option is most often used by those who are knowledgeable about DoubleSpace Setup. This parameter can be abbreviated to /CR. The following is the syntax of the /CREATE parameter:

DBLSPACE /CREATE *d:* /NEWDRIVE=*drive letter:* /SIZE=*size* /RESERVE=*size*

The following details the switches to the /CREATE parameter:

Switch	Description
d:	Specifies the drive you want to compress. This is a mandatory switch. Examples include C: and D:.
/NEWDRIVE=*drive letter:*	Specifies the drive letter (you also type the colon) for the new compressed drive. The /NEWDRIVE switch is optional; if you omit it, DoubleSpace assigns the next available drive letter. This switch can be abbreviated to /N.
/RESERVE=*size*	Specifies the number of megabytes of free space DoubleSpace should leave on the uncompressed drive. To make the compressed drive as large as possible, specify a size of 0 (zero). The /RESERVE switch can be abbreviated as /RE. You can use either the /RESERVE switch or the /SIZE switch, but not both. If you omit both switches, DoubleSpace reserves 2M of free space.
/SIZE=*size*	Specifies the total size, in megabytes, of the uncompressed drive that you want to compress. You can use either the /RESERVE switch or the /SIZE switch, but not both. If you omit both switches, DoubleSpace reserves 2M of free space. The /SIZE switch can be abbreviated as /SI.

The /DELETE Parameter

The /DELETE parameter removes the selected compressed drive and erases all the files it contains. This can be a very dangerous command, and should be used only when you are absolutely sure you no longer want any of the data on a compressed drive, or once you have made a full backup of your system and you are prepared to restore your files once the /DELETE parameter removes the drive and its files. This switch can be abbreviated as /DEL.

The following is the syntax of the /DELETE parameter:

DBLSPACE /DELETE *d:*

The use of switches to the /DELETE parameter is detailed in the following:

d: Specifies the drive you want to delete.

DoubleSpace will not allow you to delete drive C. If your drive C: is compressed, and you wish to use it as an uncompressed drive, use the /UNCOMPRESS parameter rather than the /DELETE parameter.

Note: *Deleting a compressed drive erases the entire drive and all the files it contains. Use this command with great care, and only when you are sure you will not need the data on the compressed drive, or after you have made a full backup.*

The /LIST Parameter

The /LIST parameter briefly describes your computer's drives except CD-ROM and network drives. This switch can be abbreviated to /LI. The DBLSPACE /LIST command can be issued while Windows is running. The following is the syntax of the /LIST parameter:

DBLSPACE /LIST

The /LIST parameter also displays information on whether DoubleSpace's Automount and DoubleGuard features are enabled or disabled. Automount and DoubleGuard are covered later in this lesson.

The /RATIO Parameter

The /RATIO parameter changes the estimated compression ratio, a figure used internally by DoubleSpace when estimating how much free space the drive contains. You would want to change the estimated compression ratio only if you plan to store a large number of new files on the compressed drive that you are sure will compress more greatly than the current files. This switch can be abbreviated as /RA. The following is the syntax of the /RATIO parameter:

DBLSPACE /RATIO=*r.r d: /ALL*

The use of switches to the /RATIO parameter is detailed in the following:

Switch	Description
r.r	Specifies the ratio you want DoubleSpace to use when it is estimating free space. You can specify a ratio from 1.0 to 16.0. If you don't specify a ratio, DoubleSpace sets the drive's estimated compression ratio to the average actual compression ratio for all the files currently on the drive.
d:	Specifies the drive for which you want to change the estimated compression ratio. You can either specify a drive letter or use the /ALL switch, but not both. If you specify neither the drive nor the /ALL switch, DoubleSpace changes the estimated compression ratio for the current drive.
/ALL	Changes the estimated compression ratio of compressed drives. You cannot use this switch at the same time you enter a value for the *d:* (drive) switch.

The /SIZE Parameter

The /SIZE parameter is used to enlarge or reduce the size of a compressed drive. You might want to enlarge a compressed drive if its uncompressed host drive contains more free space than you need uncompressed. You might want to reduce the size of a compressed drive if you need more free space on the uncompressed drive, for example, if you need more room on the uncompressed drive for a Windows swapfile. This parameter can be abbreviated as /SI. The following is the syntax for the /SIZE parameter:

DBLSPACE /SIZE=*size* /RESERVE=*size d:*

Here is the meaning of the switches to the /SIZE parameter:

Switch	Description
d:	Specifies the drive you want to resize.
/SIZE=*size*	Changes the size of the specified drive. You can specify the new size of the drive in megabytes by using the /SIZE=*size* switch. The *size* of the drive is the number of megabytes of space used on the host (uncompressed) drive for the compressed drive. Rather than specifying the amount of space to use for the compressed drive, you can use the /RESERVE=*size* parameter to specify how much of the host drive will remain uncompressed. *You cannot use the /SIZE parameter and the /RESERVE parameter at the same time.* If you include neither the /SIZE nor the /RESERVE parameters, DoubleSpace makes the compressed drive as small as possible.
/RESERVE=*size*	Specifies how many megabytes of free space you want the uncompressed (host) drive to contain after DoubleSpace resizes the drive. The /RESERVE switch can be abbreviated as /RES. *You cannot use the /SIZE parameter and the /RESERVE parameter at the same time.* If you include neither the /SIZE nor the /RESERVE parameters, DoubleSpace makes the compressed drive as small as possible.

The /MOUNT Parameter

The /MOUNT parameter is used to establish connection between a compressed volume file and a drive letter so that you can use the files the compressed volume file contains. In other words, the /MOUNT parameter tells DoubleSpace to treat a drive as a DoubleSpace drive. You usually need the /MOUNT parameter only if you previously used the

/UNMOUNT parameter with a hard drive or on a floppy disk if Automount is disabled. Both the /UNMOUNT parameter and Automount are covered later in this lesson. The following is the syntax for the /MOUNT parameter:

DBLSPACE /MOUNT=*volext d:* /NEWDRIVE=*newdrive*:

The following covers the use of the switches to the /MOUNT parameter:

Switch	Description
/MOUNT=*volext*	Directs DoubleSpace to mount the compressed volume file with the filename extension specified by the *volext* parameter. Each DoubleSpace compressed drive is given a unique filename such as DBLSPACE.001. To mount a compressed volume file named DBLSPACE.001 you enter the following: **DBLSPACE /MOUNT=001 *d:*** If you omit the /MOUNT=*volext* parameter, by default DoubleSpace searches for and attempts to mount a compressed volume file named DBLSPACE.000. If that file is not found, DoubleSpace produces an error message. The /MOUNT switch can be abbreviated as /MO.
d:	Specifies the physical drive (A:, B:, C:, D:, etc.) that contains the compressed volume file you want to mount. You must specify a drive letter.
/NEWDRIVE=*newdrive*	Specifies the drive letter to assign to the new drive. This switch is optional. If you don't specify a drive letter, DoubleSpace assigns the new drive the next available drive letter. This switch can be abbreviated as /NEW.

The /UNMOUNT Parameter

The /UNMOUNT parameter breaks the connection between the selected drive's compressed volume file and its drive letter. In other words, issuing the /UNMOUNT parameter tells DoubleSpace to no longer keep track of a specified compressed volume. Unmounting a drive makes it temporarily unavailable. Because your DOS files, as well as hidden, read-only, and system files that keep your computer running, are on drive C:, you cannot unmount drive C:. The following is the syntax of the /UNMOUNT parameter:

DBLSPACE /UNMOUNT *d:*

The *d:* switch specifies the drive you want to unmount. This parameter is optional; if you omit it, DoubleSpace unmounts the current drive (except for drive C:, which cannot be unmounted).

Caution
You cannot unformat a drive that has been formatted by using DBLSPACE /FORMAT. All the files on the drive are lost when you use the DBLSPACE command with the /FORMAT parameter.

The /FORMAT Parameter

Just as formatting a floppy drive erases all the files previously stored on the drive, the /FORMAT parameter deletes all the files contained on a compressed drive.

The following is the syntax for the /FORMAT parameter:

DBLSPACE /FORMAT *d:*

The *d:* switch specifies the compressed drive you want to format. DoubleSpace will not allow you to format drive C.

Using DoubleSpace Automount

Automount
A DoubleSpace capability which enables your system to automatically read the data on a floppy disk or other removable media.

By default, DoubleSpace uses its *Automount* mode when handling removable media drives, such as floppy disks or Bernouli drives. The /AUTOMOUNT parameter of the DBLSPACE command modifies the current Automount setting, enabling you to shut off, or turn on, the Automount capability for specific drives. You may want to turn off Automount to save the memory required by DoubleSpace to continually check the system's removable media drives.

The /AUTOMOUNT setting is contained in the file DBLSPACE.INI. When you use the /AUTOMOUNT parameter, it modifies this file to update it with your selected values. For changes to Automount to take effect, you must restart your computer. The syntax of the /AUTOMOUNT parameter is shown in the following:

DBLSPACE /AUTOMOUNT=0 *(or)* **1** *d:*

The following covers the use of the /AUTOMOUNT switches:

Switch	Description
0	Prevents DoubleSpace from automatically mounting removable drives. (Cannot be used at the same time as the 1 switch.)
1	Directs DoubleSpace to automatically mount all removable drives. This is the default setting. (You cannot specify the 1 switch at the same time as the 0 switch.)
d:	Directs DoubleSpace to automatically mount the specified removable drives (A:, B:, C:, D:, etc.). You do not add a colon after the drive letter. For example, to have DoubleSpace automatically mount drives A, B, and G, you enter DBLSPACE /AUTOMOUNT=ABG at the DOS prompt.

Using DoubleGuard

DoubleGuard
DoubleSpace protection for the region of memory used to compress and uncompress files needed by your system and to keep track of compressed drives.

By default, DoubleSpace jealously guards the regions of memory it uses to keep track of your compressed drives and to uncompress your programs and data when they are needed in system memory. The capability that oversees these DoubleSpace memory regions is known as *DoubleGuard.*

When DoubleGuard is enabled, DoubleSpace constantly checks its memory for damage by some other program. If DoubleGuard detects any memory damage, DoubleSpace halts your computer to minimize damage to your data. You can restart your system and again try using the program that caused the problem. If the problem recurs, you should refrain from using the offending program until you check with its manufacturer to see if a bug fix is available that makes the program compatible with DoubleSpace, or uncompress your drives and uninstall DoubleSpace.

The /DOUBLEGUARD parameter can be used to switch off (or turn back on) DoubleGuard protection for your compressed drives. However, unless you are extremely short on memory, you should leave DoubleGuard enabled. It provides a great deal of protection for the data on your compressed drives. The following is the command line syntax for the /DOUBLEGUARD parameter.

DBLSPACE /DOUBLEGUARD=0 (or) **1**

The following covers the use of the switches to the /DOUBLEGUARD parameter:

Switch	Description
0	Prevents DoubleSpace from checking its memory for damage by other programs. Using this switch might speed up your system but could result in loss of data if a program violates the memory DoubleSpace is using.
1	Directs DoubleSpace to check its memory for damage by other programs. This is the default setting.

Enter the following to disable DoubleGuard protection:

DBLSPACE /DOUBLEGUARD 0

When you issue the **DBLSPACE /DOUBLEGUARD** command with a 0 or 1 as a switch, DoubleSpace modifies the DOUBLEGUARD setting in the DBLSPACE.INI file. You must restart your computer for this change to take effect.

Using DoubleSpace on Floppy Disks

The /COMPRESS parameter is used to compress the space on a floppy disk or other removable media. You issue the DBLSPACE /COMPRESS command, specifying the floppy drive you want to compress. The following is the command line syntax used to compress a floppy disk or other removable media:

DBLSPACE /COMPRESS *d:*

The d: switch designates the drive containing the floppy disk you want to compress. To compress a floppy disk in drive A:, enter the following command:

DBLSPACE /COMPRESS A:

You need to compress a floppy before using it to store data. DoubleSpace cannot compress a disk that is completely full. Floppy disks must contain at least 1.1M of free space at the time you create a compressed drive. Therefore, DoubleSpace cannot compress 360K or 720K floppy disks.

Once a floppy disk is compressed, DoubleSpace automatically mounts, or accesses, the disk when you attempt to use the drive. This DoubleSpace capability is named *Automount*. The /AUTOMOUNT parameter, which is used to turn on or shut off the Automount capability, is detailed in the section "The /AUTOMOUNT Parameter."

Bypassing DoubleSpace During System Boot-Up

There may be times when you need to bypass DoubleSpace when you start your system, although for most people these times will be rare. For example, you might need to bypass DoubleSpace to use a disk utility that directly tests the magnetic media of your hard drive for errors.

DOS 6.2 provides two different ways to bypass DoubleSpace and any other device driver or memory-resident program. Pressing the F5 key at the time your system displays the message `Starting MS-DOS` causes DOS to bypass both CONFIG.SYS and AUTOEXEC.BAT, giving you a clean boot. Pressing the F8 key at the message `Starting MS-DOS` results in an interactive boot in which you are prompted before each line of CONFIG.SYS and optionally AUTOEXEC.BAT is loaded.

- Pressing the F5 key bypasses all settings in your CONFIG.SYS and AUTOEXEC.BAT files; the DoubleSpace device driver DBLSPACE.SYS is not loaded.

- Pressing the F8 key enables you to step through the device drivers in your CONFIG.SYS file one at a time, confirming whether or not you want each device driver to be loaded. Once CONFIG.SYS has been processed, DOS 6.2 gives you the option of processing AUTOEXEC.BAT in the same manner.

When you use the F5 or F8 key to bypass the DoubleSpace device driver DBLSPACE.SYS, drive C: contains your normal startup files (IO.SYS, MSDOS.SYS, DBLSPACE.SYS, CONFIG.SYS, and AUTOEXEC.BAT), but all data stored in your compressed drive is contained in a single file, usually DBLSPACE.000.

Note: *Tinkering with your host (uncompressed) drive when DBLSPACE.SYS is not loaded can result in all the data in your compressed volume being damaged or lost. Before you use any utility that directly accesses your uncompressed drive, do a full backup of your system so you can restore your programs and data if your compressed drive is damaged.*

Maintaining Your DoubleSpace Drive

Using DoubleSpace does not create new hard drive maintenance requirements, but it does heighten the need to be vigilant about the old standbys. To get technical for a moment, instead of using the normal DOS file structure to store your data and programs, DoubleSpace stores data and programs as a single file, for example, DBLSPACE.000. Within that single compressed file, DoubleSpace keeps track of each program and data file using its own file structure.

Although DoubleSpace uses ingenious technology to nearly double the amount of data you can store on your hard drive, DoubleSpace depends on your hard drive to remain healthy. And using DoubleSpace means you need to take the necessary steps to safeguard your important data and programs. If something goes wrong on your hard drive when DOS stores your files, you probably lose one or two files. If something goes wrong on your hard drive when DoubleSpace handles your files, you can lose much more.

The following is a list of the common hard drive maintenance tasks which become all the more important when you use DoubleSpace:

1. Back up your data files regularly, at least once a week.

   Back up your programs when you have made configuration changes that took a lot of time and required a lot of work. For example, if you have configured Windows so it runs exactly the way you want, it would take much more time to reinstall Windows from floppy disks and then re-do all your configuration changes than it would take to make a backup of your Windows files. You can use either the DOS 6.2 MS Backup or the DOS 6.2 Backup for Windows.

2. Check your hard disk regularly for logical and physical errors.

   To check and repair a drive, use the SCANDISK program. SCANDISK is covered in the following section.

3. Check your computer's memory and hard disk for viruses.

   Viruses can damage your system so badly it can keep your system from running. Viruses also can destroy your programs and data. To check for viruses, use the DOS 6.2 MSAV (Microsoft Anti-Virus) utility or Anti-Virus for Windows. Check all compressed and uncompressed drives, and check floppy disks that have been used by others before you received them.

4. Defragment your hard disk drive and your compressed drive regularly. Defragmentation can take a long time, so you may want to do it at the end of the day. If your drive is not compressed, run the DEFRAG utility.

   Microsoft recommends that for a thorough defragmentation of your compressed hard drive, you take these steps:

   a. Run DEFRAG on your compressed hard drive.

   b. Run DBLSPACE /DEFRAGMENT /F

   c. Run DBLSPACE /DEFRAGMENT (without the /F switch).

5. Use the DOS 6.2 Undelete utility configured with either Delete Sentry or Delete Tracker enabled. These operating modes of the Undelete utility keep track of files so that you can reliably undelete them if you later discover you need an erased file. Delete Tracker and Delete Sentry are covered in Lesson 10, "Advanced DOS Commands."

Checking Disks with the SCANDISK Utility

Periodically you should check the file structure and the integrity of the data on your DoubleSpace drive. DOS 6.2 provides the SCANDISK utility for this purpose. The SCANDISK program can check and repair both uncompressed drives and DoubleSpace drives for file structure errors as well as errors in the magnetic media of the drive itself.

This section provides the kind of coverage of the SCANDISK utility you need to maintain your DoubleSpace drive. Lesson 2, "Making a Quick Start with DOS 6.2," provides additional coverage of the SCANDISK command and its role in protecting your system from data loss.

Note: *In DOS 6.2, DoubleSpace no longer recognizes the /CHKDSK parameter. Instead, use the new SCANDISK command to check your DoubleSpace drive. Although DOS 6.2 still includes the utility CHKDSK, you shouldn't waste your time using it. When you run CHKDSK, the utility itself advises you to use the SCANDISK utility instead. SCANDISK provides the same information about a drive as provided by CHKDSK, and a lot more, plus it carefully makes repairs when problems are found on your drive. The repairs made by CHKDSK when run with the /F parameter can cause as many problems as it solves.*

Running SCANDISK

To run SCANDISK, type the following at the DOS prompt and press the Enter key:

SCANDISK

SCANDISK is one of the DOS utilities that features a full-screen interface. The utility communicates in dialog boxes and you select its options in command buttons. You don't have to learn a lot of command line parameters to work with SCANDISK. When SCANDISK presents you with command buttons from which you can make a selection, you can make a choice using one of the following techniques:

1. Click the command button with the mouse.
2. Tab to the command button you want to select and press Enter.
3. Press the letter on your keyboard that corresponds to the command you want to choose. One letter on each command button is highlighted. Pressing this letter executes the command written on the button. For example, in a SCANDISK command button whose selection is Exit, the X is highlighted. When you press the X key, you choose the Exit selection.

The following is the command syntax for SCANDISK:

SCANDISK *d:*

The *d:* parameter designates the drive you want SCANDISK to test. In other words, to check a drive other than the current drive, type the drive letter after the SCANDISK command. For example, to check drive D:, type the following:

SCANDISK D:

If you do not specify a drive, SCANDISK tests the current drive. When you run SCANDISK, it tests the following parts of your disk:

- *Media descriptor.* SCANDISK checks for the code that identifies a drive as an MS-DOS drive. SCANDISK ensures that the proper media descriptor is in place. If the code is incorrect, SCANDISK will prompt you for whether to make a repair.

- *File allocation tables.* DOS keeps track of the location of every file on a drive in a record called the file allocation table, or FAT. DOS disks have one or more copies of the FAT. This redundancy is to ensure that if the main copy of the FAT is damaged, another can be used to recover it. SCANDISK ensures that all copies of the file allocation table match, and if they do not, prompts you for whether to make a repair.

- *Directory structure.* SCANDISK checks the drive's directory tree structure and each directory in the tree to ensure there are no errors in the DOS record of directories. Invalid directory entries can cause a wide range of problems on your drive, some of the more serious being data-threatening. If SCANDISK finds problems in the directory structure, it prompts you for whether to make a repair.

- *File system.* Disk space is made up of segments called *clusters. Sectors* are the minimum amount of space that can be used to store a file or any part of a file. Only one file should store information in each cluster, even if the file does not use the entire sector. When more than one file uses the same sector, these files are termed *cross-linked files.* Cross-linked files can cause data loss in either or both files. SCANDISK makes sure that each cluster is used by no more than one file. SCANDISK also checks for *lost clusters,* areas of a drive that contain data but are not linked to files. Lost clusters take up disk space that you could otherwise use. If SCANDISK detects cross-linked files or lost clusters you are prompted for whether to make a repair.

While these tests are running, you can pause SCANDISK, request additional information about a test, or stop the test and exit the program. At the bottom of the SCANDISK screen, three command buttons present the following choices:

```
< Pause > < More Info > < Exit >
```

Once the SCANDISK tests are complete, SCANDISK produces a dialog box that prompts you for confirmation before it performs a surface scan, which means it tests the electronic media of the disk itself. The surface scan can take a considerable amount of time, so you may want to run SCANDISK before you go to lunch. The test should be complete when you return. To have SCANDISK perform the surface scan, choose the Yes button (click it with the mouse, or Tab to the Yes button, or press the Y key). To have SCANDISK skip the surface scan, choose the No button (click it, or Tab to the No button and press the Enter key, or press the N key).

Note: *Most SCANDISK screens and dialogs include a* More Info *button. When you choose* More Info, *you are presented with another dialog box that provides more information. Usually the More Info selection provides additional technical details about the current SCANDISK operation. When SCANDISK informs you of a problem, the More Info selection displays information about the problem or about the affected files.*

Although you should run SCANDISK weekly to test the integrity of your disk, you do not need to run the surface scan every time. Instead, you may want to perform the surface scan every other time you use SCANDISK to test your disk. During a surface scan of an uncompressed drive, SCANDISK ensures that data can be reliably written and read from the drive being scanned. During a surface scan of a DoubleSpace drive, SCANDISK ensures that data can be reliably uncompressed.

When SCANDISK Finds Something Wrong

Most of the time, SCANDISK simply tests your drive, finds no problems, and when it completes, you Exit the utility. If SCANDISK finds a problem, it displays a Problem Found dialog box that briefly explains the problem and what will happen if you fix it. Most Problem Found dialog boxes present you with the following choices:

- Fix It
- Don't Fix It
- More Info

To have SCANDISK correct the problem, choose the Fix It button.

The SCANDISK Undo Disk

When SCANDISK finds a problem and you choose the Fix It selection, SCANDISK prompts you for whether to create an Undo disk, a floppy disk record of the problem, and what SCANDISK has done to repair the problem. You can later use the Undo Disk to restore your system to its previous condition so long as you haven't made changes to the tested disk since SCANDISK made repairs.

When you are prompted to create an Undo disk, use the following steps:

1. Insert a blank, formatted floppy disk in the A: or B: drive.
2. Choose the Drive A or Drive B option button in the SCANDISK dialog box.
3. Choose continue to create the Undo Disk.

Keep the Undo Disk in a safe location until you are sure you will not need it—for a few days, until you see that the repair made by SCANDISK has resolved the problem. To undo repairs you made previously, use the following syntax:

SCANDISK /UNDO *undo-drive:*

The switch *undo-drive:* specifies the floppy drive containing the Undo Disk. You enter A: or B:, depending on which drive contains the Undo Disk you created prior to SCANDISK making repairs on your system.

You normally would use the Undo Disk to reverse a repair made by SCANDISK only in the extremely rare event that SCANDISK's repair did not solve the problem, or made it worse. In such a case, before using the Undo Disk, you should determine if you would prefer working with the original problem or if you would rather work with the disk in the condition in which the SCANDISK repair left it. Some people might want to use the Undo Disk to return their disk to its original condition so they can try a third-party disk repair utility to see if such a utility can solve the problem.

Using SCANDISK with DoubleSpace Drives

When you run SCANDISK on a drive compressed with DoubleSpace, it prompts you for whether to check the host (physical) drive first. Almost invariably, you should allow SCANDISK to check both the host drive and the DoubleSpace drive. An error on the host drive could cause problems with the compressed drive.

To check an unmounted DoubleSpace compressed volume file for errors, use the following syntax:

SCANDISK *path* ***volume-name***

Each DoubleSpace drive on your system has a unique and specific volume name, such as DBLSPACE.000 or DBLSPACE.001. When checking an unmounted DoubleSpace drive, you use the DoubleSpace drive name in place of the *volume-name* parameter. The DoubleSpace volume must be in the root directory of a drive to use the *volume-name* parameter. You can use the root directory specifier (C:\ or D:\) as the path parameter to the SCANDISK command when you are also using the *volume-name* parameter.

The SCANDISK command also is useful when you already know you have problems in a compressed drive. SCANDISK will diagnose and repair these problems. For example, if DoubleSpace cannot mount your compressed drive C: because of problems with the drive, you diagnose and repair the problem by issuing the following command:

SCANDISK C:\DBLSPACE.000

Some of the other parameters to the SCANDISK command have special application on DoubleSpace drives, or you use a special syntax for these commands. You should take the time to become familiar with the other command-line parameters covered in the next section of this lesson.

Understanding SCANDISK Command Line Syntax

Although you should rarely need to issue the SCANDISK command with parameters, there are times when you might need to do so, or even want to. The following covers the SCANDISK command line parameters and switches. Here is the command line syntax for Scandisk:

> **SCANDISK** ***d:*** ... ***d:*** /ALL /CHECKONLY /AUTOFIX /NOSAVE /CUSTOM /SURFACE /MONO /NOSUMMARY

d: ... ***d:*** Specifies the drive or drives you want to check using SCANDISK. You can enter the following to check drives C: and D:

SCANDISK C: D:

A few SCANDISK parameters were covered in earlier sections of this lesson, mainly because you might need to use these parameters right away. This section covers the rest of the SCANDISK parameters that are useful for important tasks.

Parameter	Description
/ALL	Checks and repairs all local drives. The use of this parameter causes SCANDISK to test all your hard disk partitions, in addition to all mounted DoubleSpace drives.
/AUTOFIX	Repairs damage without prompting you first. For example, if you start SCANDISK with the /AUTOFIX parameter and SCANDISK finds lost clusters on your drive, it automatically saves the lost clusters as files in the drive's root directory. To have SCANDISK delete lost clusters, include the /NOSAVE parameter. If you use the /AUTOFIX switch and SCANDISK finds errors, it still prompts you for an Undo disk; to prevent this, include the /NOSUMMARY parameter. You cannot use the /AUTOFIX switch at the same time as the /CHECKONLY or /CUSTOM parameters.
/CHECKONLY	Tests a drive for errors but does not make any repairs. Instead, you are simply presented with a dialog box informing you of what SCANDISK has found. You cannot use the /CHECKONLY parameter at the same time as the /AUTOFIX or /CUSTOM parameters.

Parameter	Description
/CUSTOM	Runs SCANDISK using the settings you have entered in the [Custom] section of the SCANDISK.INI file. This parameter makes it easy to run SCANDISK from a batch file. You cannot use the /CUSTOM parameter at the same time as the /AUTOFIX or /CHECKONLY parameters. Editing the SCANDISK.INI file is covered in a later section of this lesson.
/MONO	Runs SCANDISK on a system with a monochrome display. Instead of using this parameter each time you run SCANDISK, you can edit SCANDISK.INI to include the following: **DISPLAY=MONO**
/NOSAVE	Causes SCANDISK to delete any lost clusters. You can use this parameter only when you also use the /AUTOFIX parameter. If you run SCANDISK with the /AUTOFIX parameter and do not use the /NOSAVE parameter, SCANDISK saves lost clusters as files in the root directory of the drive.
/NOSUMMARY	Prevents SCANDISK from displaying a full-screen summary of problems found and repairs made after operating on each drive. The /NOSUMMARY parameter also prevents SCANDISK from prompting you for whether to create an Undo disk if it finds errors.
/SURFACE	Automatically performs a surface scan after performing the other tests of a drive. When the /SURFACE parameter is used at the same time as the /CUSTOM parameter, the /SURFACE parameter overrides the Surface setting in the [Custom] section of SCANDISK.INI.
/FRAGMENT	Checks a file or files for fragmentation. The following syntax is used with the /FRAGMENT parameter: **SCANDISK /FRAGMENT** *d: path* ***filename.ext*** The switch *d: path* specifies the location of the file you want to test for fragmentation if the file is not on the current drive and directory. The switch *filename.ext* specifies the file you want to test. When working with a DoubleSpace drive, you specify the file you want to test on the host drive (for example DBLSPACE.000 or DBLSPACE.001). You can use DOS wildcards (* and ?) for the filename. An example of the use of this command is shown in the following: **SCANDISK /FRAGMENT H:\ DBLSPACE.000**

Most of the time, you will use SCANDISK without bothering with parameters and switches. However, there are times that you may want to perform a special operation. The preceding explanation of the SCANDISK parameters will help you greatly in maintaining your disk drives, as well as your DoubleSpace drives.

Editing the SCANDISK.INI File To Customize SCANDISK

When you start SCANDISK, it checks in a configuration file, SCANDISK.INI, to determine how it will behave. Some of these settings, the settings in the [ENVIRONMENT] section, are used to determine SCANDISK's startup configuration each time you start SCANDISK. For example, entries in the [ENVIRONMENT] section tell SCANDISK the type of display used on your system, whether or not you have a mouse installed, and how many times SCANDISK will test each sector during a surface scan.

Most of the settings in SCANDISK.INI determine how SCANDISK will behave only when you run SCANDISK with the /CUSTOM parameter. These settings are in SCANDISK.INI's [CUSTOM] section. For example, to prevent SCANDISK from prompting you for an Undo disk when you use the
/CUSTOM parameter, you edit the Undo setting in SCANDISK.INI's [CUSTOM] section to read as follows:

Undo=Never

This parameter by default reads `Undo=Prompt`, indicating you want to be prompted for whether to create an Undo Disk.

Note: *You should use the MS-DOS Editor, or another text editor that produces plain ASCII text, when editing SCANDISK.INI, which is an ASCII text file. Word processing programs can introduce formatting characters in SCANDISK.INI that can make the file useless, perhaps keeping SCANDISK from running at all. Before editing SCANDISK.INI, make a backup copy from your DOS directory to a floppy disk or another directory and keep the backup* *safe in case you make editing mistakes. Then, if the SCANDISK.INI file is damaged, you can replace the damaged copy with the backup.*

When you edit entries in SCANDISK.INI, SCANDISK ignores case; you can use uppercase or lowercase. The syntax for the settings in SCANDISK.INI follows a general rule: the setting name, such as Undo, is typed at the beginning of a line, then an equal sign (=), and then you type the replaceable parameter (Prompt or Never, for example). A line in SCANDISK.INI that determines a particular setting should look like the following:

Undo=Never

or

Undo = Never

If you use the MS-DOS Editor to open SCANDISK.INI, you will see that extra spaces are used in the line that determines a particular setting. SCANDISK ignores these extra spaces, which are included in the line to make the file easier to read and edit. You also will notice lines that are preceded by, or contain, a semi-colon (;). Any time a semi-colon precedes characters, SCANDISK ignores the semi-colon and everything that follows it. Semi-colons are used in SCANDISK.INI to differentiate comments or explanations from actual settings. For example, SCANDISK.INI contains the following explanation:

```
; The [ENVIRONMENT] section contains the following settings, which
; determine general aspects of SCANDISK's behavior:
```

Because a semi-colon precedes the explanation, SCANDISK ignores the comments that follow. If you make changes to SCANDISK.INI, you may want to add comments similar to the ones already in SCANDISK.INI reminding yourself of what you have done. Remember to precede these comments with a semi-colon.

The following sections cover the entries in SCANDISK.INI, as well as the options for each entry.

The [ENVIRONMENT] Section

The [ENVIRONMENT] section of SCANDISK.INI contains the settings that determine the general appearance of SCANDISK and other aspects of its behavior. The following shows a typical SCANDISK.INI [ENVIRONMENT] section:

```
[ENVIRONMENT]
   Display     = Auto    ; Auto, Mono, Color, Off
   Mouse       = On      ; On, Off
   ScanTimeOut = Off     ; On, Off
   NumPasses   = 1       ; 1 through 65,535 (anything over
                         ; 10 is slow)
   LabelCheck  = Off     ; On, Off
```

The [ENVIRONMENT] section settings are detailed in the following:

- *Display.* Configures SCANDISK to run with a particular type of display. The default display type is Auto (SCANDISK adjusts to the current display). You should need to change the Display setting only if SCANDISK mistakenly detects your display. The options for this setting are *Auto, Mono, Color,* and *Off.*

- *Mouse.* Enables or disables mouse support. The default value is On. Options for this setting are *On* and *Off.*

- *ScanTimeOut.* Determines whether SCANDISK should detect disk timeouts while performing a surface scan. The default value is Off. The options for this setting are *On* and *Off.*

- *NumPasses.* Determines how many times SCANDISK checks each cluster for errors during a surface scan. The default value is 1, which means SCANDISK will check each cluster once. Options for this setting are a range from 1 to 65,535 times. It is important to note that any setting higher than 10, although it thoroughly tests your drive, increases greatly the time it takes to run SCANDISK.

- *LabelCheck.* Determines whether SCANDISK should check volume labels for invalid characters. The default is Off. The options for this setting are *On* and *Off.*

The [CUSTOM] Section

The [CUSTOM] section of SCANDISK.INI determines SCANDISK's behavior only when SCANDISK is started using the /CUSTOM parameter. In effect, you use these settings to customize SCANDISK, for example, configuring it so it will run unattended. This capability can be especially useful when running SCANDISK from a batch file.

The following shows a typical SCANDISK.INI [CUSTOM] section:

```
[CUSTOM]
   DriveSummary  = Auto        ; Auto, On, Off
   AllSummary    = Auto        ; Auto, On, Off
   Surface       = Never       ; Never, Always, Prompt
   CheckHost     = Never       ; Never, Always, Prompt
   SaveLog       = Off         ; Off, Append, Overwrite
   Undo          = Prompt      ; Prompt, Never
```

The [CUSTOM] section settings are detailed in the following:

- *DriveSummary*. Specifies whether SCANDISK displays summary information after checking each drive. The default is Auto, which configures SCANDISK to display the summary only if it encounters errors on the drive. The options for this setting are *Auto, On,* and *Off*.

- *AllSummary*. Specifies whether SCANDISK displays summary information after checking all drives. The default is Auto, which configures SCANDISK to display the summary only if it encounters errors on any drive.

- *Surface*. Specifies whether SCANDISK performs a surface scan. The /SURFACE command-line parameter forces a surface scan regardless of this setting in SCANDISK.INI. The default for this setting is *Never*. The options for the Surface setting are detailed in the following:

  Never Does not perform a surface scan.

  Always Performs a surface scan without prompting first.

  Prompt Prompts before performing a surface scan.

- *CheckHost*. Specifies whether SCANDISK will first check a host drive before checking any compressed drives located on that drive. The default for this setting is *Never*. The options for this setting are detailed in the following:

13

Never	Does not check the host drive.
Always	Checks the host drive without prompting first.
Prompt	Prompts before checking the host drive.

- *SaveLog.* Specifies whether SCANDISK keeps a repair log file and if so how the log is kept. The default for this setting is *Off*. The options for this setting are detailed in the following:

Off	Does not save the repair log.
Append	Appends the log to the previous log, if any.
Overwrite	Replaces the previous log with the new log.

- *Undo.* Specifies whether SCANDISK creates an Undo floppy disk. The default for this setting is Never. The options for this setting are detailed in the following:

Never	Causes SCANDISK to skip creating an Undo disk.
Prompt	Causes SCANDISK to prompt you for a disk.

You also can use settings in the [CUSTOM] section of SCANDISK.INI to specify how SCANDISK (started with the /CUSTOM parameter) will handle specific errors when they are encountered.

- *DS_Header.* Indicates that SCANDISK has found a damaged DoubleSpace volume file header. The default for this setting is *Prompt*. The options for this setting are the following:

Prompt	Causes SCANDISK to prompt you before fixing this problem.
Fix	Causes SCANDISK to fix the problem without prompting you.
Quit	Causes SCANDISK to terminate if it encounters this problem.

- *FAT_Media.* Indicates that SCANDISK has found a missing or invalid FAT media byte. The default for this setting is Prompt. The options for this setting are *Prompt*, *Fix*, and *Quit*.

- *Okay_Entries.* Indicates that SCANDISK has found damaged, but repairable, directories or files. The default for this setting is *Prompt.* The options are *Prompt, Fix,* and *Quit.*

- *Bad_Chain.* Indicates that SCANDISK has found files or directories that should be truncated, or ended before DOS indicates that they do end. The default for this entry is *Prompt.* The options for this setting are *Prompt, Fix,* and *Quit.*

- *Crosslinks.* Indicates that SCANDISK has found crosslinked files recorded in the file allocation table. The default for this setting is *Prompt.* The options for this setting are *Prompt, Fix,* and *Quit.*

- *Boot_Sector.* Indicates that SCANDISK has found a damaged boot sector on the DoubleSpace drive. The default for this setting is *Prompt.* The options for this setting are *Prompt, Fix, Quit,* plus the following:

Skip	Causes SCANDISK to take no action on this problem, but continue testing the disk.

- *Invalid_MDFAT.* Indicates SCANDISK has found invalid entries in the file allocation table maintained by DoubleSpace. The default for this setting is *Prompt.* The options for this setting are *Prompt, Fix, Quit,* and *Skip.*

- *DS_Crosslinks.* Indicates SCANDISK has found crosslinked files within the DoubleSpace drive (MDFAT-level). The default for this setting is *Prompt.* The options for this setting are *Prompt, Fix, Quit,* and *Skip.*

- *DS_LostClust.* Indicates SCANDISK has found lost clusters files within the DoubleSpace drive. The default for this setting is *Prompt.* The options for this setting are *Prompt, Fix, Quit,* and *Skip.*

- *DS_Signatures.* Indicates SCANDISK has found missing DoubleSpace volume signatures. The default for this setting is *Prompt.* The options for this setting are *Prompt, Fix, Quit,* and *Skip.*

- *Mismatch_FAT.* Indicates SCANDISK has found mismatched file allocation tables on non-DoubleSpace drives. The default for this setting is *Prompt.* The options for this setting are *Prompt, Fix, Quit,* and *Skip.*
- *Bad_Clusters.* Indicates that SCANDISK has found physical damage to a drive or DoubleSpace decompression errors. The default for this setting is *Prompt.* The options for this setting are *Prompt, Fix, Quit,* and *Skip.*
- *Bad_Entries.* Indicates SCANDISK has found damaged and irreparable directories or files. The default for this setting is *Prompt.* The options for this setting are Prompt, Quit, and the following:

Delete	Causes SCANDISK to delete the damaged directory entries without prompting you first.

- *LostClust.* Indicates SCANDISK has found lost clusters. The default for this entry is Prompt. The options for this setting are Prompt, Delete, Quit, Skip, and the following:

Save	Causes SCANDISK to save the lost clusters as files in the root directory without prompting you first.

All these command line parameters and switches and options for the SCANDISK.INI file might make SCANDISK seem like a complicated, perhaps fearsome tool. It is not. You won't need to learn most of the command-line parameter or SCANDISK.INI settings until you actually need them.

Above all, use SCANDISK to test your hard drives frequently. If you catch errors in your hard drive structure, or in the magnetic media itself, before these errors have a chance to affect too many files, SCANDISK often can repair or reverse these problems without data loss.

Using the Defragmenter Utility (DEFRAG)

The DOS 6.2 DEFRAG utility reorganizes the files on a disk to optimize disk performance. This section covers the use of the DEFRAG utility.

Over time, the files on any hard drive become fragmented, meaning that one part of a file may be stored in a sector near the front of a drive and another might be stored in a sector at the rear of the drive. Since most files use more than two sectors, fragmentation can mean that the parts of a file are spread around the disk in what can be described as random order. Normal day-to-day use of a hard drive usually results in significant file fragmentation—with the individual parts of many files scattered about. The term *discontiguous* is often used to describe the situation when a file's parts are located in numerous different parts of a drive. When there is a great deal of fragmentation on a drive, it creates two problems:

1. Your hard drive read/write heads must work much harder to find the individual parts of files scattered around the disk in discontiguous sectors. Therefore, it can take much longer for the drive to locate and read a file. Over time, the performance of your hard drive, and therefore your system, can be seriously degraded by a seriously fragmented drive.

2. When many files are fragmented, it is somewhat more difficult for the record-keeping functions of DOS to keep track of files, perhaps resulting in lost clusters or invalid directory entries. Under some circumstances, severe fragmentation can contribute to cross-linked files, a condition in which more than one file is listed in the file allocation table as using the same sector on your drive. Your data can be threatened by cross-linked files.

Defragmenting your hard drive regularly is an important part of the routine maintenance you need to perform to protect your data and get the greatest speed possible out of your system.

Task: Running DEFRAG

When you run the DOS 6.2 Defragmenter utility it displays a full-screen menu-based interface, which means rather than needing to memorize a great number of command line parameters you can use the mouse or the keyboard to select DEFRAG options in the menus.

To make selections in the DEFRAG utility, you can click a command button or open a menu so you can make a selection. If you are using the keyboard, you can press the Tab to move between selections and once your choice is highlighted press the Enter key. To open the DEFRAG menu, press the Alt key or F10. To select from the menu, use the arrow keys to scroll up or down and once your choice is highlighted press the Enter key.

To run DEFRAG, enter the following at the DOS prompt:

DEFRAG

When DEFRAG starts, it produces a dialog box that informs you it is testing system memory. You are then presented with a dialog box in which you choose the drive you want to defragment. You can click the letter representing the drive you want to optimize or Tab to the drive selection box, use the arrow keys to select the drive you want to optimize, then press the Enter key to begin the optimization process.

Note: *When you are in the DEFRAG utility, you can get help at any time by pressing the F1 key.*

After you choose the drive to optimize, DEFRAG displays a graphical representation of your hard drive, with the areas that contain data displayed as white rectangles and areas that do not contain data in blue. This graphical representation of your drive shows how fragmented your drive has become.

At the same time DEFRAG first presents this graphical representation of your drive, it analyzes the drive and then produces a dialog box informing you of the level of fragmentation on the drive, finally recommending the type of defragmentation you should use. For example, on a drive that is not too badly fragmented, the following information would be displayed:

```
99% of drive C: is not fragmented
Recommended optimization method:
Unfragment Files Only
```

In the same dialog box in which DEFRAG presents its recommendation, there are two command buttons, *Optimize* and *Configure*. To choose one of these options, click it with the mouse or press the Tab key to highlight the desired command button and press the Enter key. The following is an explanation of these two selections:

- *Optimize*. Choosing the *Optimize* selection immediately begins optimizing your disk based on the recommendation made by DEFRAG for defragmenting your disk.

Caution
Do not run DEFRAG from within a multitasking environment like Windows 3.1 or DesqVIEW. If you start DEFRAG from within a multitasking program, you may lose data.

- *Configure*. Choosing the *Configure* selection enables you to control the type of optimization DEFRAG will do on your drive. When you choose the *Configure* selection, it opens a dialog box in which your choices are *Full Optimization* and *Unfragment Files Only*. The following provides information about these two different types of disk defragmentation:

  Selecting Full Optimization performs two actions, although both are done at the same time. The first action is that all files are made contiguous. In other words, all parts of each file are placed end-to-end on the disk so your hard drive does not have to work so hard to read the data contained in a file. Secondly, all the files on your hard drive are moved to the front of the drive so it is easier for your hard drive to read all the data and programs stored on the drive. When a new file is saved to your drive, chances are good that it will not be fragmented because all your empty space is contiguous and located toward the back of the drive.

  Selecting Unfragment Files Only makes all files contiguous. However, when you choose this optimization method your files are not all moved to the front of the drive, so your hard drive has to work harder to access data. This optimization method also leaves gaps between files. As DOS saves new files, or files whose size has changed, into these gaps, your files quickly become fragmented again. A Full Optimization is recommended unless you are terribly short on time. Depending on the size of your hard drive and your system CPU chip and speed, a full optimization can take a considerable period of time.

Using the mouse, click either *Full Optimization* or *Unfragment Files Only*. Then click the OK command button to continue with the optimization.

To use the keyboard to make your choice between *Full Optimization* or *Unfragment Files Only,* press the spacebar until the radio button next to your choice is filled.

The OK and Cancel selections, in the same dialog box as the *Full Optimization* and *Unfragment Files Only* selections, are the type of command button covered earlier. To select one of these command buttons, click it with the mouse, or press the Tab key until the command button is highlighted and then press the Enter key.

The OK selection continues the optimization process. The Cancel selection stops the optimization process.

Understanding the DEFRAG Screen

Whether you have accepted the suggestions of the DEFRAG utility for the type of optimization to be performed on your drive, or you have configured DEFRAG to perform the type of defragmentation you prefer, you next see DEFRAG at work in the graphic representation of your hard drive.

As DEFRAG works, it moves files (represented by white rectangles) from one area to another. At the bottom right corner of this screen is a legend that describes the meaning of certain codes in the graphic representation of your hard drive. You can stop the defragmentation of your drive at any time, but it is not recommended that you do so. Let DEFRAG do its work.

Once the optimization process is complete, DEFRAG produces a dialog box informing you that it is `Finished Condensing` your drive. This dialog box also contains the OK command button. Click OK or press Enter. DEFRAG then produces a dialog box in which you have three choices:

- Another Drive
- Configure
- Exit Defrag

Choosing Another Drive returns you to the drive selection dialog box described earlier in this section. The Configure selection returns you to the dialog box in which you choose between *Full Optimization* and *Unfragment Files Only*. The Exit Defrag button returns you to DOS. If you are using the mouse, click the button containing your choice. Using the keyboard, use the Tab key to move to your selection and then press the Enter key.

Understanding DEFRAG's Optimize Menu

DEFRAG has a single menu, the Optimize menu. To access the menu, click the Optimize selection at the top left of the DEFRAG screen or press the Alt or F10 key. The menu will open.

Most of the choices available in this menu are familiar to you already if you have spent time reading through the previous coverage of DEFRAG options. Nearly all the selections in the menu are presented in the dialog boxes DEFRAG presents when you start up the utility.

However, there is one DEFRAG option that you must use the menu to access—File Sort. This option enables you to configure DEFRAG so that, while your drive is being optimized, files are sorted by name, by extension, by date and time, or by size.

The following covers the selections in this DEFRAG menu:

- *Begin Optimization.* Immediately begins optimization of your drive based on the selection in the dialog box produces by choosing the menu's Optimization Method selection.

- *Drive.* Produces the drive selection dialog box described previously in this section. Use this dialog box to select the drive you want to optimize.

- *Optimization Method.* Enables you to choose between *Full Optimization* and *Unfragment Files Only,* which were described previously in this section. The selection when made in the DEFRAG menu controls the type of optimization that is performed when you choose Begin Optimization in the DEFRAG menu.

- *File Sort.* The File Sort selection enables you to determine the way files are sorted on your drive; in other words, the order in which they are listed when you use the DIR command. The selections presented when you choose the File Sort option are listed as follows:

Unsorted	Leaves files as they are on disk—no sort.
Name	Sorts files by the first letter of their name (the order A-Z or Z-A depends on your selecting Ascending or Descending, as described later in this section).

Extension	Sorts files by the first letter of their extension name (the order A-Z or Z-A depends on your selecting Ascending or Descending, as described later in this section).
Date & Time	Sorts files by date (the order earliest-latest or latest-earlier depends on your selecting Ascending or Descending, as described later in this section).
Size	Sorts files according to the number of bytes in the file (the order smallest-largest or largest-smallest depends on your selecting Ascending or Descending, as described later in this section).

When you select any of the sort options except Unsorted, you also are presented with the choices Ascending or Descending. When you select Ascending, files are sorted from A-Z, or earliest-latest in the case of date and time, or smallest-largest in the case of size. When you select Descending, the sort order is reversed.

- *Map Legend.* Displays the legend that explains which rectangles represent used parts of the disk, which represent available sections, and the meaning of the other symbols used in the display.
- *About Defrag.* Displays information about the DEFRAG utility.
- *Exit.* Exits DEFRAG immediately.

DEFRAG Command Line Syntax

Although most people will rarely use command parameters when they start the DEFRAG program, the use of command parameters comes in handy if you want to run DEFRAG from a batch file or if you want to simplify operation by specifying on the command line what you want done and having DEFRAG do it without intervention. The syntax of the DEFRAG command is shown in the following:

DEFRAG d: /F /S:*order* /B /SKIPHIGH /LCD /G0 /H

The DEFRAG command parameters are covered in the following table:

Parameter	Purpose
d:	Specifies the drive you want to defragment.
/F	Performs a full defragmentation, in other words defragments all files and moves all files to the front of the drive so there is no empty space between files.
/U	Defragments files, leaving empty spaces, if any, between files.
/S	Specifies how files are sorted in directories. If you omit this switch, DEFRAG performs no sorting, leaving files as they are on your drive. The following use of the /S parameter sorts files by name: DEFRAG /S:N
/B	Restarts your computer after your drive has been optimized.
/SKIPHIGH	Loads DEFRAG into conventional memory. By default, DEFRAG is loaded into upper memory, if upper memory is available.
/LCD	Starts DEFRAG using an LCD color scheme. (Should not be used at the same time as the /BW parameter.)
/BW	Starts DEFRAG using a black and white color scheme. (Should not be used at the same time as the /LCD parameter.)
/G0	Disables the graphics mouse and graphics character set. This parameter can be useful if your screen displays bizarre characters while DEFRAG is running.
/H	Moves hidden files. Rarely should you use the /H parameter. It enables DEFRAG to move files with the hidden property. Often, to function correctly, hidden files must be left in their original location.

The following list describes the switches representing each of the values you can use to sort files. You can use combinations of values, so long as they do not cancel one another out. Do not separate values with spaces.

N Alphabetical order by name

N- Reverse alphabetical order by name (Z through A)

E Alphabetical order by extension

E- Reverse alphabetical order by extension (Z through A)

D	By date and time, earliest to latest
D-	By date and time, latest to earliest
S	By size, smallest to largest
S-	By size, largest to smallest

Summary

To	Do This
Double hard drive storage	Use DoubleSpace
Double floppy drive storage	Use DoubleSpace
Ensure your drive safely stores data	Use SCANDISK
Diagnose drive problems	Use SCANDISK instead of CHKDSK
Speed up hard drive and protect data	Use DEFRAG

On Your Own

Estimated time: 30 minutes to 2 hours

1. Run SCANDISK to test your hard drive for errors.
2. Run DEFRAG on your hard drive to defragment your files.

Lesson 14

Configuring DOS 6.2 for Windows

This lesson covers advanced configuration of DOS for Windows users. Most of these configuration issues are important to anyone with a 386-, 486-, or Pentium-based computer. But the information is especially important to Windows users. The following topics are covered in this lesson:

- The Microsoft Diagnostic program (MSD)
- Conventional memory
- Upper Memory Blocks (UMBs)
- High memory
- Extended memory and XMS
- Expanded memory
- Managing memory with MemMaker
- Using SmartDrive with Windows
- Using a RAM disk with Windows
- Optimizing your hard drive for Windows

The Microsoft Diagnostic Program (MSD)

The Microsoft Diagnostic program (MSD) is one of the most important tools you have for configuring your system, whether you use Windows or want to take full advantage of other programs. Before you begin using advanced DOS configuration techniques to fine-tune your system, you must know precisely how your system is built. MSD is designed to give you the kind of information you need to manage memory and speed up your system.

Task: Running MSD from the DOS Prompt

The MSD program is located in your DOS directory. You can run MSD by following these steps:

1. Type **MSD** at the DOS prompt.
2. Press Enter.

The MSD program, like DEFRAG and other DOS 6.2 utilities, has a full-screen display. When you first start MSD, you see the screen shown in the following figure. On the bottom of the screen you see the message `MSD is examining your system`. During this startup period, MSD makes a wide range of tests to determine the hardware makeup of your system, as well as some important details about your DOS version, active device drivers, and memory-resident programs.

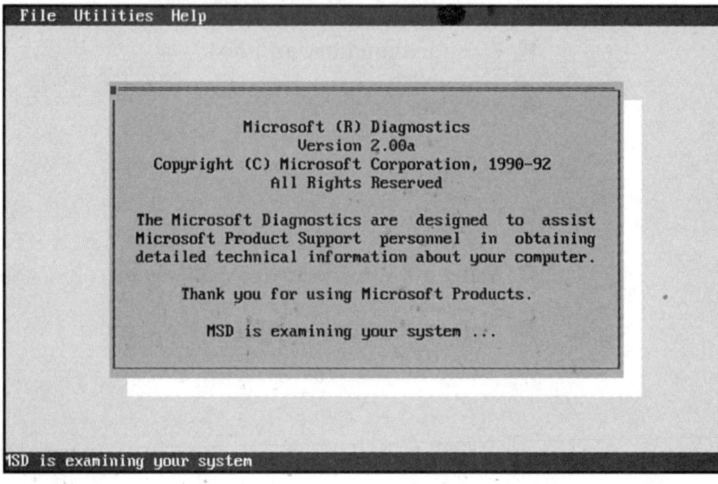

The MSD opening screen.

Understanding the MSD Information Screens

After MSD determines the basic makeup of your system, it displays the following screen.

The MSD basic information screen.

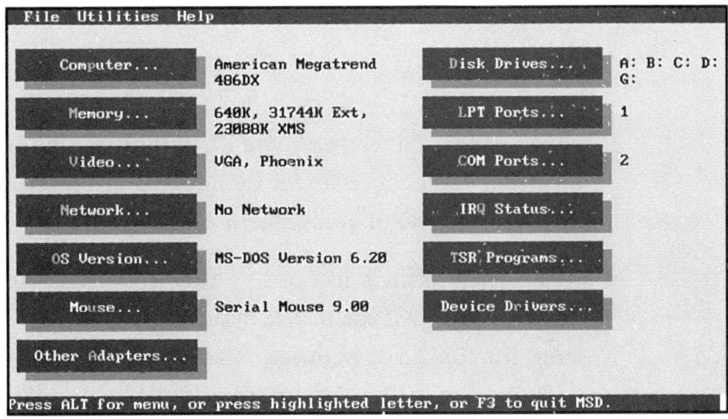

This screen provides the following information about your computer:

Computer	The type of central processing unit (CPU).
Memory	The amount of conventional and extended memory installed on your system and whether extended memory is configured as XMS or EMS.
Video	The video type.
Network	The network type, if any.
OS Version	The operating system used by your system.
Mouse	The type of mouse installed on your system, if any, and the version of the mouse driver software.
Other Adapters	Other installed adapters, such as a game card, if any.
Disk Drives	Installed disk drives.
LPT Ports	The number of LPT (parallel) ports.
COM Ports	The number of COM (serial) ports.

In addition, the following selections are shown on-screen with no information listed beside them:

IRQ Status

TSR Programs

Device Drivers

On the main MSD screen these three buttons do not display information, but when you choose any of them, MSD displays detailed information about that aspect of your system.

In fact, each of the selections on this screen is a selection button. When you choose any of the selection buttons, MSD displays more information about the topic. For example, when you choose the *Computer* button, MSD displays the kind of information shown in the next figure, which includes the CPU chip type (8088, 286, 386, 486, or Pentium) and the manufacturer of the system *BIOS* (the basic input/output system). This screen also contains information about the type of keyboard, the type of expansion bus on the system, whether a math coprocessor is installed, and other information.

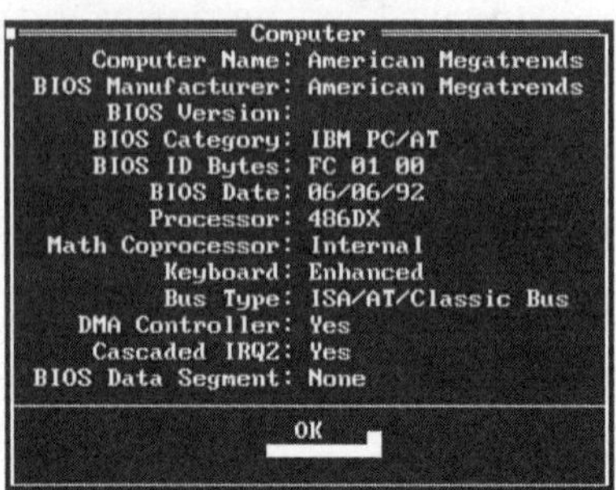

The MSD Computer information screen.

To choose one of the topic buttons in the main MSD screen, click the button with the mouse. If you would rather use the keyboard, notice that each of the buttons has a highlighted letter in the name of the command. Press this highlighted letter to choose the topic on which you want information.

Task: Printing an MSD Report

The top part of the MSD screen, which displays the words File, Utilities, and Help, is known as the *menu bar*. To open a menu you click its name with the mouse; or hold down the Alt key and then press the highlighted letter in the menu name.

To print an MSD report, do the following:

1. Open the **F**ile menu.

2. Choose **P**rint Report to produce the Report Information dialog box shown in the following figure.

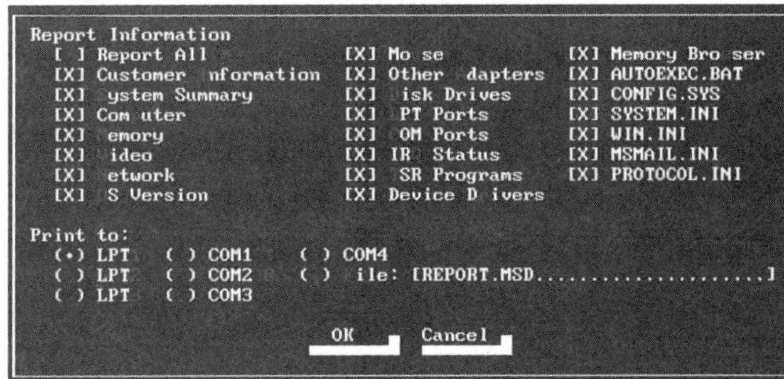

The Report Information dialog box.

3. Choose the type of report you want to print. The first time you print an MSD report, choose the Report All selection. Later you may want to print individual parts of the MSD report.

   Using the mouse, click your selection.

   or

   Using the keyboard, press the Tab key to move from selection to selection, then press the space bar to make a selection (an X appears in the selection box).

4. Choose the OK button when you are satisfied with your selection.

   Using the mouse, click the OK button.

   or

   Using the keyboard, Tab to the OK button, then press Enter.

Although you can use MSD to get quick information about a particular aspect of your system hardware, you should print out a detailed report of your system, at least the first time you use MSD.

Use this printed report to become familiar with crucial parts of your system, including the amount of memory installed on your system, the size of the hard drives installed on your system and the amount of available space, and the type of CPU chip on which your system is based. This information comes in handy when you begin to configure your system for Windows or when you optimize system memory.

Running MSD in Windows

You can run MSD in Windows, but doing so results in less accurate information than running MSD from the DOS prompt. In fact, virtually all the information displayed by MSD about your system may be inaccurate if you run this utility from within Windows.

When you run MSD in Windows, MSD produces an information dialog box that warns you are running Windows and provides details on the elements of your system configuration that MSD may improperly report if you use MSD in Windows. You can choose OK to continue using MSD in Windows or Cancel to quit MSD.

Memory and Windows

Memory
The electronic chips in which programs run and perform computations.

When you run Windows, the word *memory* seems more important than any other word. Although you do need a great deal of hard drive space to run Windows and the most powerful Windows applications, and although a fast video card is important when you use Windows, the one hardware component Windows craves more than any other is the *memory chip*.

The minimum amount of RAM (random-access memory) needed to run Windows, and accomplish real work, is 4M (megabytes). Many veteran Windows users wouldn't consider running Windows on a system with less than 8M. Future versions of Windows are likely to require at least 8M of memory and run far better with 16M. Keep that point in mind when you think about ways to configure your system for Windows and certainly when you consider the purchase of a new Windows system.

Because of the importance of system memory in Windows, most of this section focuses on optimizing your system memory. Memory management can be a very complex subject. This book covers only part of the topic of optimizing your computer's performance. You can find out more about memory management in Que's *Using MS-DOS 6.2*, Special Edition.

Task: Getting a Quick Picture of System Memory

You can get a quick idea of how your system currently is using memory by running the MEM command:

1. Type **MEM** at the DOS prompt.
2. Press Enter.

Your readout from the MEM command is similar to the following:

```
Memory Type        Total  =   Used  +   Free
---------          ---        ---       ---
Conventional        640K       68K      572K
Upper                 0K        0K        0K
Reserved            384K      384K        0K
Extended (XMS)    31,744K   30,720K   1,024K
---------          ---        ---       ---
Total memory      32,768K   31,172K   1,596K

Total under 1 MB    640K       68K      572K

Total Expanded (EMS)                  1,024K (1,048,576 bytes)
Free Expanded (EMS)                   1,024K (1,048,576 bytes)

Largest executable program size         572K (585,392 bytes)
Largest free upper memory block           0K       (0 bytes)
MS-DOS is resident in the high memory area.
```

The MEM command displays the total amount of each memory type—conventional, upper, reserved, and extended—and displays how much of each memory type is used and how much is free. Each memory type is covered in the following sections.

Conventional memory
The first 640K (kilobytes) of memory, the memory in which most DOS programs run and perform computations.

Understanding Conventional Memory

Conventional memory is another name for the main system memory used by DOS, most DOS utilities, and software applications written to run in DOS (rather than Windows, for example). The amount of conventional memory on a system commonly is 640K (kilobytes). But the amount of conventional memory actually available for running programs decreases by the amount of memory used by memory-resident programs and device drivers loaded in your AUTOEXEC.BAT and CONFIG.SYS files.

Memory-resident program
A program that after it is run remains in memory, even while you run other programs.

Memory-resident programs get their name because they remain in memory after you execute them, instead of performing an operation and then freeing the memory they had been using, as does the FORMAT command. Memory-resident programs, such as the mouse driver, MOUSE.COM or MOUSE.EXE, can be important to making your system work the way you want. Memory-resident programs also are called *terminate-and-stay-resident* programs, or TSRs.

Device driver
Software that serves as a connection, or interface, between DOS and your system hardware.

Device drivers are loaded in CONFIG.SYS and are used to give DOS control over system hardware that does not have built-in support in DOS. For example, ANSI.SYS enables DOS to display color text and backgrounds when you use a special code. These device drivers are loaded in memory when you start your computer and remain in memory as long as your computer is running.

In the era of computers based on the 8088 CPU chip, the primary way of managing memory was finding a way to load all the memory-resident programs and device drivers you needed and still have enough conventional memory left over to run programs. The solution to a memory shortage often was to stop using a much-needed memory-resident program or device driver. With a 386 or better, the solution to a conventional memory shortage is to run MemMaker, a DOS utility that frees up conventional memory.

Available conventional memory is important to Windows for two reasons:

1. Windows itself uses conventional memory to run. When you type WIN to start Windows, it loads first into conventional memory. Then, depending on your CPU type and numerous other factors, Windows uses memory beyond 640K.

2. The amount of conventional memory available when you first start Windows determines to a great extent the amount of memory that will be available when you attempt to run DOS programs from within Windows. When Windows runs a DOS program, Windows creates a block of memory for that program that approximates the amount of conventional memory available when Windows was started. If you have more conventional memory before Windows starts, you can run your more memory-demanding DOS programs in Windows.

For these reasons, you should make as much conventional memory available to Windows as possible. On systems based on a 386 CPU chip or higher, you can use MemMaker to free up conventional memory. MemMaker works by loading memory-resident programs and device drivers into upper memory and freeing up the conventional memory they used; you can use this extra conventional memory for other programs and for Windows. MemMaker is covered in detail later in this lesson.

Understanding Upper Memory, Reserved Memory, and UMBs

Upper memory
The 384K of memory just above conventional memory, normally used by hardware devices like the video card.

Upper memory is the memory between the end of conventional memory and the beginning of the second megabyte of memory (extended memory). Upper memory sometimes is also termed *reserved memory*. The upper memory region on 386 or better computers is 384K. Parts of upper memory are used by your computer hardware, for example, your video card. Although a 384K area is reserved, the computer does not use that entire area. The more adapter cards in your computer, the less upper memory is available.

Note: *Although the term* high memory *sometimes is used to refer to the reserved area of memory, high memory actually is the first 64K of extended memory. This memory region is technically known as the* high memory area (HMA).

Upper Memory Blocks
Available areas of upper memory that MemMaker can use to load memory-resident software and device drivers.

When you run MemMaker to free up conventional memory for Windows, MemMaker creates *Upper Memory Blocks* (*UMBs*) in the parts of the 384K of upper memory not used by the computer hardware. Then MemMaker loads memory-resident programs and device drivers into the UMBs, freeing up the conventional memory these memory-resident programs and device drivers had been using.

Task: Viewing the MSD Upper Memory Map

Choosing the Memory selection from the MSD main screen provides a map of how your system uses the area of memory between 640K and 1M. The following figure shows that your system has used some of the area between 640K and 1M (the light-colored and grainy areas are used). However, most of the area between 640K and 1M is available (black areas are unused).

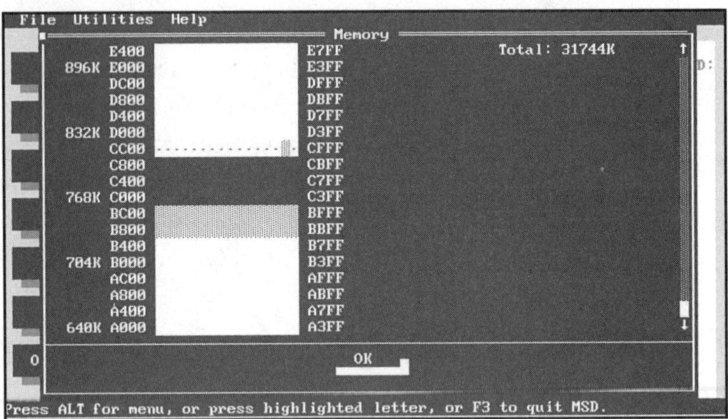

The MSD upper memory report.

To view the upper memory map on your system, use the following steps:

1. Run MSD by typing **MSD** at the DOS prompt.

2. Press Enter. The MSD main selection screen appears.

3. In the MSD main selection screen, choose Memory by clicking the Memory button or pressing the **M** key.

4. You can use the PgDn and PgUp keys to scroll through the MSD upper memory map. The legend at the top of the MSD memory map provides detail about how your system's upper memory region is used (see following list).

5. When you want to exit MSD, click the **F**ile menu and choose E**x**it, or press **Alt-F** and then **X**. Or press F3.

The following list describes the items shown on the legend at the top of the memory map:

Available — An unused area of upper memory.

RAM — An area of upper memory used as if it were conventional memory. Some programs, called *DOS extenders*, are capable of using upper memory as RAM, extending conventional memory beyond 640K.

ROM	Read-only memory. An area of upper memory used by your computer system or an adapter board such as a SCSI adapter. These areas are not available.
Possibly Available	MSD was unable to determine if the upper memory area currently was being used.
EMS Page Frame	The amount of upper memory, if any, that DOS uses to access expanded memory. (EMS stands for expanded memory specification.)
Used UMBs	The Upper Memory Blocks currently used by MemMaker or another memory manager to load memory-resident programs and device drivers into upper memory.
Free UMBs	Unused Upper Memory Blocks.
Free XMS UMBs	Unused Upper Memory Blocks in extended memory. (XMS stands for extended memory specification.)

Understanding Extended Memory and XMS

Extended memory
The memory above 1M, which can be used by only certain DOS programs, and by multi-tasking software like Windows to run more than one program at a time.

XMS memory
Memory configured by the DOS device driver HIMEM.SYS or other memory manager.

Extended memory is the generic name for any memory beyond the first megabyte. When a system has 4M of memory, the first megabyte is used as conventional and upper memory, and the last 3M are extended memory.

Windows and most other programs can use extended memory only after it has been configured as *XMS* (*extended memory specification*) memory. The generic term extended memory often is used to describe XMS-configured memory.

The DOS device driver *HIMEM.SYS* is used to configure extended memory as XMS memory. HIMEM.SYS is added to your CONFIG.SYS file when you install DOS 6.2, when you run Windows Setup, or when you run MemMaker. Or you can add the device to your system configuration by adding the following line to CONFIG.SYS:

```
DEVICE=C:\DOS\HIMEM.SYS
```

Note: *Although a version of HIMEM.SYS is installed with Windows 3.1, you should use the version that comes with DOS 6.2. The DOS 6.2 version of HIMEM.SYS provides services not available in previous versions. For example, each time you boot your computer, HIMEM.SYS tests all system memory for bad RAM chips.*

After HIMEM.SYS is loaded, Windows can use all your system memory for running programs, which means that on 386 or better computers, you can run several programs at the same time. Each program can continue to run and do its work, regardless of whether the program is designed to run in DOS or Windows. When your system memory is configured as XMS, Windows and DOS programs can run side by side in Windows.

Note: *If you add other device drivers to CONFIG.SYS that require extended memory, make sure that you place them after the line that loads HIMEM.SYS.*

Unless you load HIMEM.SYS or another XMS driver in CONFIG.SYS, any extended memory on your system is invisible to DOS and unavailable to programs. If you attempt to run Windows 3.1 without an XMS driver, Windows halts during start-up and displays an error message.

Understanding Expanded Memory

Expanded memory
Special memory above 1M configured by EMM386.EXE or another memory manager. EMS memory refers to expanded memory that conforms to the Expanded Memory Specification.

Expanded memory is a special type of memory also located beyond the first megabyte of memory. Some programs can use this memory, but it is not the type of memory best used by Windows, which uses extended (XMS) memory for running programs. The following figure shows the MSD memory map for a computer with Expanded Memory Specification *(EMS)* memory. The symbol P indicates the *EMS page frame*, the area of upper memory DOS uses to access the information in expanded memory.

Note: *Sometimes, expanded memory is located on a separate memory board rather than being installed on the motherboard. In such a case, if possible, you should reconfigure your expanded memory board so its memory is used as extended memory. Consult your system documentation for directions on reconfiguring an expanded memory board.*

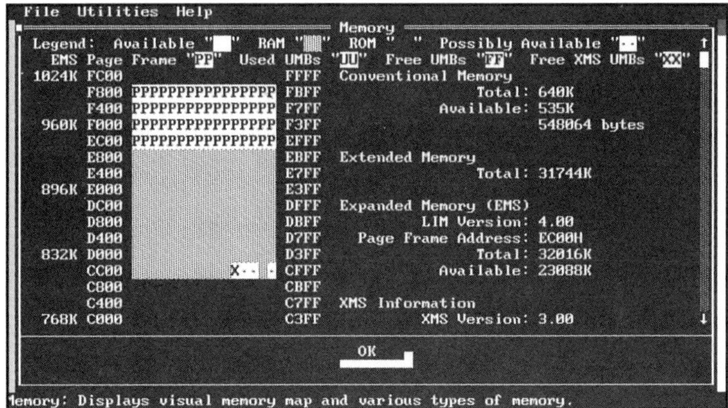

The MSD upper memory report showing EMS page frame.

If you need expanded memory for running a particular program, or programs, on 386 or better computers, MemMaker configures the program EMM386.EXE to provide expanded memory. After EMM386.EXE configures some of your extended memory as expanded memory, you can run programs in Windows that need expanded memory. Unless you load EMM386.EXE or another EMS driver in CONFIG.SYS, any expanded memory on your system is invisible to DOS and unavailable to programs. (EMM386.EXE is described further in a later section, "Using EMM386.EXE.")

Task: Configuring Memory for Windows with MemMaker

The DOS 6.2 MemMaker utility makes it easy to configure your system memory for Windows. The ideal way to configure your system memory is to load as many of your memory-resident programs and device drivers as possible into UMBs. DOS 6.2 also can load part of itself into high memory so, ideally, you can take advantage of this capability by freeing up still more conventional memory.

MemMaker takes care of all these details automatically. Plus, if you need expanded memory for DOS programs, MemMaker can configure your system to provide expanded memory for these programs.

To run MemMaker, take the following steps:

1. Type **MEMMAKER** at the DOS prompt.

2. Press Enter. The MemMaker opening screen appears, prompting you to choose whether to continue.

3. Choose Continue to have MemMaker configure your system memory for Windows.

4. From the next screen, choose one of these two options:

   - Express Setup, which uses the MemMaker defaults.

   - Custom Setup, which enables you to control more aspects of the MemMaker operation.

   Unless you are an expert on MemMaker, Express Setup is the better option. The rest of this section covers Express Setup. Choosing Express Setup produces a screen that prompts you for whether you run DOS programs that need expanded memory.

5. Press the space bar to toggle Yes or No. Then press Enter.

   If you are unsure, choose No. You later can run MemMaker and change this option if you discover you do run programs that need expanded memory. MemMaker then checks to see if you have Windows installed on your system.

6. Remove any disks from your floppy drives. MemMaker prompts you that it is about to reboot your system and begin configuring your system memory.

7. Press Enter.

   Your system reboots and MemMaker tests your system configuration and determines the best way to load your memory-resident programs and device drivers into upper memory. During this phase, do not interrupt MemMaker by pressing keys on your keyboard.

   MemMaker prompts you for confirmation to complete the memory optimization.

8. Press Enter. Your system reboots and your memory-resident programs and device drivers are loaded into upper memory.

MemMaker prompts you for whether your system appears to be working properly.

9. Use the space bar to toggle between Yes and No. Then press Enter.

   MemMaker then displays a table summarizing the changes to your memory configuration, including the amount of conventional memory available before and after you ran MemMaker. Your old AUTOEXEC.BAT and CONFIG.SYS files have been saved as AUTOEXEC.UMB and CONFIG.UMB.

MemMaker now has configured your system memory for optimal Windows operation. The following section provides information on some of the changes made to your system by MemMaker.

Reviewing MemMaker Changes

Running MemMaker makes important changes to your AUTOEXEC.BAT and CONFIG.SYS files. The following sections cover why MemMaker made some of the most common changes.

CONFIG.SYS after MemMaker

The following lines show a typical CONFIG.SYS file after MemMaker has optimized system memory for Windows on a system that requires no expanded (EMS) memory. The lines are numbered for reference:

1. `DEVICE=C:\DOS\HIMEM.SYS`
2. `DEVICE=C:\DOS\EMM386.EXE NOEMS`
3. `BUFFERS=15,0`
4. `FILES=8`
5. `DOS=UMB`
6. `DOS=HIGH`
7. `LASTDRIVE=E`
8. `FCBS=4,0`
9. `STACKS=9,256`
10. `SHELL=C:\COMMAND.COM C:\ /P`
11. `DEVICEHIGH=C:\DOS\ANSI.SYS`

14

The numbers in the following list refer to the lines in the preceding example. The descriptions explain why MemMaker added or changed the respective line in CONFIG.SYS:

1. Loads HIMEM.SYS. If you add other device drivers that require extended memory, make sure that you place them after the line that loads HIMEM.SYS.
2. Loads EMM386.EXE without expanded memory support.
3. Sets up 15 disk buffers (this small number is necessary because the system is running disk caching software.) The BUFFERS= entry is covered in Lesson 11, "Customizing DOS."
4. Specifies the number of files that a program can have open at one time. If the setting chosen by MemMaker proves inadequate, you can increase this value to 20 or 30. The FILES= entry is covered in Lesson 11, "Customizing DOS."
5. Creates UMBs in upper memory that MemMaker uses to move memory-resident programs and device drivers out of conventional memory.
6. Loads part of DOS into high memory.
7. Specifies the last drive on the system that DOS should look for. If you use DoubleSpace and have a system with only a CD-ROM drive or other device treated as a drive by DOS, this line may specify any drive letter up to Z. For example, `LASTDRIVE=Z:`.
8. Specifies the number of file control blocks, which are areas of memory DOS uses to store information about a file.
9. Creates 9 stacks of 256 bytes each, which helps make Windows more stable. A stack is an area of memory your system uses to keep track of hardware devices and enable them to access the CPU.
10. Specifies where DOS should look for COMMAND.COM.
11. Specifies that DOS should load the device driver following the equal sign (=) into UMBs.

AUTOEXEC.BAT after MemMaker

The following lines show a typical AUTOEXEC.BAT file after MemMaker has optimized system memory for Windows. The lines are numbered for reference:

1. `@ECHC OFF`
2. `PROMPT $P$G`
3. `PATH C:\DOS;C:\WINDOWS;C:\BAT;D:\NU;C:\UTILITY;`
4. `LH /L:0;1,45456 /S C:\DOS\SMARTDRV.EXE /X`
5. `LH /L:1,13984 C:\DOS\SHARE.EXE`
6. `SET MOUSE=C:\MOUSE`
7. `LH /L:0;1,23584 /S C:\MOUSE\MOUSE.EXE`

The numbers in the following list refer to the lines in the preceding example. The descriptions explain why MemMaker changed the respective line in AUTOEXEC.BAT (some lines did not change).

1. Standard first line in AUTOEXEC.BAT. Not changed by MemMaker. Suppresses the display of each line in AUTOEXEC.BAT as it is executed by DOS.
2. Creates standard C:\> DOS prompt. Not changed by MemMaker.
3. Path not changed by MemMaker.
4. Instructs DOS to load the memory-resident program following the LH command into UMBs. In this case, DOS is to load SMARTDRV.EXE into upper memory. The entry `/L:0;1,45456 /S` instructs DOS on the exact UMB in which to load SMARTDRV.EXE. The /X parameter specifies that SMARTDRV.EXE is not to use write-caching, which is covered later in this lesson.
5. Loads SHARE.EXE into extended memory.
6. Creates an entry in the system environment, a small amount of memory that programs can use as a scratchpad. In this case, the SET MOUSE=C:\MOUSE command provides information on the directory where MOUSE.EXE is stored.
7. Loads the mouse software driver into a UMB.

Using HIMEM.SYS on Certain Computers

If you have extended memory, DOS automatically adds the HIMEM.SYS device driver to your CONFIG.SYS file during installation. The standard statement is as follows:

```
DEVICE=C:\DOS\HIMEM.SYS
```

HIMEM.SYS machine code
Defines the computer to the DOS device driver, HIMEM.SYS.

Some computers need special handling to manage their extended memory. These computers need a special /MACHINE:*xxx* parameter to operate properly, where *xxx* is the HIMEM.SYS *machine code*. The following table shows the possible machine code values for different computers.

Machine code	Computer
AT	IBM AT
PS2	IBM PS/2
PT1CASCADE	Computer with a Phoenix Cascade BIOS
HPVECTRA	HP Classic Vectra
ATT6300PLUS	AT&T 6300 Plus
ACER1100	Acer 1100
TOSHIBA	Toshiba 1600 or 1200XE
WYSE	Wyse 12.5 MHz 286 with Micro Channel
TULIP	Tulip SX
ZENITH	Zenith ZBIOS
AT1	IBM PC/AT (alternative delay)
AT2	IBM PC/AT (alternative delay)
AT3	IBM PC/AT (alternative delay)
CSS	CSS Labs
PHILIPS	Philips
FASTHP	HP Vectra
IBM7552	IBM 7552 Industrial Computer
BULLMICRAL	Bull Micral 60
DELL	Dell XBIOS

If you don't include machine code, HIMEM.SYS defaults to AT, which applies to most 286, 386, 486, and Pentium computers. If your computer is one of those listed other than an AT, add the appropriate parameter to the HIMEM.SYS statement in your CONFIG.SYS file. For example, if you have an IBM PS/2, the HIMEM.SYS statement is as follows:

```
DEVICE=C:\DOS\HIMEM.SYS /MACHINE:PS2
```

Note: *If you have problems when you boot your computer with HIMEM.SYS, read the README.TXT file in your C:\DOS directory. This file may contain additional information regarding installation instructions for your computer.*

Using EMM386.EXE

If you have a 386 or 486 computer with extended memory, you can use the program EMM386.EXE, which MemMaker loads in your CONFIG.SYS, to help manage extended memory. You also can use EMM386.EXE to configure some or all of the extended memory as expanded memory. Although Windows does not make use of expanded memory to run programs, it automatically provides expanded memory for any program that needs it.

If you run a program outside of Windows that can use expanded memory, such as 1-2-3 Release 2.4, you can build much larger spreadsheets if you make some extended memory available to the program as expanded memory. The basic syntax to convert extended memory to expanded memory is shown in the following line:

DEVICE=C:\DOS\EMM386.EXE *nnnn*

The *nnnn* parameter is the number of kilobytes to convert to expanded memory. To convert 512K of extended memory to expanded memory, for example, the statement in your CONFIG.SYS file reads as follows:

```
DEVICE=C:\DOS\EMM386.EXE 512
```

Even when you do not need expanded memory, MemMaker configures EMM386.EXE on your system with the NO EMS parameter. This parameter enables EMM386.EXE to provide access to the upper memory area so you can run device drivers and memory-resident programs in upper memory.

Understanding the DOS=HIGH Statement

If you have extended memory, DOS automatically adds the following statement to your CONFIG.SYS file during installation:

```
DOS=HIGH
```

With part of DOS in extended memory, you have more conventional memory for Windows and other programs. HIGH refers to the high memory area, the first 64K of extended memory.

Using SmartDrive with Windows

Disk cache
A special area of memory where information is stored so it can be retrieved more quickly.

SmartDrive is a software utility that can speed up Windows operation greatly by holding in system memory information that the central processing unit (CPU) soon will need. SmartDrive improves Windows performance because your system can retrieve information from extremely fast memory, instead of having to search for it on your much slower hard drive. Software that holds information in memory until the CPU needs it is called a *disk cache.*

If you have extended memory, the DOS 6.2 Setup program automatically installs SmartDrive in your AUTOEXEC.BAT file with the following line:

```
C:\DOS\SMARTDRV.EXE
```

Accepting the Default Cache Sizes

InitCacheSize
The size of the SmartDrive disk cache while you are working in DOS or running a DOS program.

WinCacheSize
The size of the SmartDrive disk cache while you are running Windows.

When SmartDrive loads, by default it uses a certain amount of extended memory while you are running DOS programs; and SmartDrive automatically reconfigures itself to use less memory when you use Windows. For example, on a system with 2M of memory, SmartDrive uses 1M for a disk cache while you run a DOS program. When you load Windows, SmartDrive shrinks to 256K.

The amount of memory SmartDrive uses when you are running DOS programs is known as the *Initial Cache Size*, or *InitCacheSize*. The amount of memory used when you start Windows is known as the *Windows Cache Size*, or *WinCacheSize*.

When SMARTDRV.EXE is loaded without command line parameters, the utility uses its defaults to determine InitCacheSize and WinCacheSize. The defaults depend on the amount of extended memory installed on your system. The following list shows the SmartDrive defaults for InitCacheSize and WinCacheSize:

Extended Memory	WinCacheSize	InitCacheSize
Up to 1M	All extended	Zero (no caching)
Up to 2M	1M	256K
Up to 4M	1M	512K
Up to 6M	2M	1M
6M or more	2M	2M

These values work well on most systems. However, the next section covers changing the default SmartDrive values.

Task: Changing Cache Sizes

You can change the InitCacheSize and WinCacheSize for SmartDrive by entering command line parameters to the line in AUTOEXEC.BAT that starts SmartDrive. Working with these parameters is easy. You enter values in kilobytes for each setting. To specify an InitCacheSize of 1024K, or 1M, and a WinCacheSize of 512K, follow these steps:

1. Type **CD** to change to the root directory.
2. Press Enter.
3. From the DOS prompt, run the MS-DOS Editor with AUTOEXEC.BAT loaded by typing the following line:

   EDIT AUTOEXEC.BAT

4. Press Enter.
5. Edit the SMARTDRV command so it looks like the following line:

   SMARTDRV 1024 512

6. Save and exit MS-DOS Editor.

The first value on the SmartDrive command line is the InitCacheSize and the second value is the WinCacheSize. To create a 2M initial cache size and a 1M Windows cache size, repeat the preceding steps, editing the SMARTDRV command as follows:

```
SMARTDRV 2048 1024
```

Using Read-Caching Mode

Read-caching
The SmartDrive mode that reads additional information from a file that a program has accessed and holds this extra information in memory.

SmartDrive has two basic modes of operation—*read-caching* and *write-caching*. By default, when the DOS 6.2 version of SmartDrive is loaded, it is set to perform read-caching only. When a program reads part of the data in a file, SmartDrive reads additional information from that file and holds it in memory. Then, the next time the program needs information from that same file, the program can read it from memory rather than from the much slower disk.

Read-caching is SmartDrive's safest mode of operation because the only information held in memory is information that already is stored safely on disk. When new data is saved, SmartDrive in read-caching mode immediately writes the new data to disk.

Task: Changing to Write-Caching Mode

Write-caching
The SmartDrive mode that holds in memory the data to save to disk until a lull in disk activity occurs.

SmartDrive's second basic mode of operation is *write-caching*. When write-caching is enabled, SmartDrive speeds up system operation by holding new information in memory until other disk activity has slowed. For example, if you save a file in your word processor, SmartDrive may keep some or all of the new information in memory for a short period of time until a lull in disk activity occurs. When write-caching is enabled for a drive, SmartDrive continues to use its read-caching mode to read data from disk and hold it in memory until a program needs the data.

The increase in system speed with write-caching enabled may be considerable. However, using write-caching mode is not quite as safe as read-caching mode because data stored in the RAM chips of memory is not as secure as data stored on the magnetic disk. For example, if your system lost power before SmartDrive wrote newly saved data to disk, you would lose that information. However, when SmartDrive is in read-caching mode only, new data is immediately saved to disk, where a power loss commonly does not affect the data safety.

To start SmartDrive with write-caching enabled for a particular drive (like the C: drive) or to reconfigure SmartDrive when it already is running, follow these steps:

1. At the DOS prompt, type the following line:

   SMARTDRV C+

2. Press Enter.

You can enable write-caching every time you boot your computer by editing the line in AUTOEXEC.BAT. Follow these steps:

1. Type **CD** to change to the root directory.
2. Press Enter.
3. From the DOS prompt, run the MS-DOS Editor by typing the following line:

   EDIT AUTOEXEC.BAT

4. Press Enter.
5. Edit the SMARTDRV command so it looks like the following line:

   SMARTDRV C+

6. Save and exit MS-DOS Editor.

If you decide to use SmartDrive with write-caching enabled, you need to immediately become familiar with the /C parameter, which forces SmartDrive to immediately write all write-cached information to disk. To add this parameter to the SMARTDRV command, follow these steps:

1. At the DOS prompt, type the following command:

   SMARTDRV /C

2. Press Enter.

Use SMARTDRV /C whenever you want new data immediately saved to disk, particularly before you turn off your computer system or use your system reset switch. When you use the /C parameter, do not turn off your computer or use the reset switch until all hard drive activity has ended—SmartDrive may take a moment to write all data to disk.

Using the /C parameter is not necessary if you use Ctrl-Alt-Del to warm boot your computer, because SmartDrive detects this keystroke combination and writes all cached data to disk before your system reboots.

Setting SmartDrive Parameters

SmartDrive has additional configuration options that you enter from the command line. The syntax of the SmartDrive command is shown in the following:

> *d:path* **SMARTDRV** /X *d: + or -* /U /C *or* /R /F *or* /N /L /V *or* /Q *or* /S *InitCacheSize WinCacheSize* /E:*ElementSize* /B:*BufferSize*

Many SmartDrive command line parameters are for the advanced user, but the most common and useful parameters are described at the top of the following list:

d:	The drive where SMARTDRV.EXE is located.
path	The path to the directory where SMARTDRV.EXE is located.
/C	Immediately writes all write-cached information from memory to cached disks. This parameter is covered in the preceding section. Use this parameter when SmartDrive is already running. Begin to use this parameter right away if you enable write-caching with SmartDrive.
/R	Used only when SmartDrive has been running (instead of using in AUTOEXEC.BAT). This parameter immediately clears the contents of the existing cache, including writing all write-cached information to disk, and restarts SmartDrive.
/X	Disables write-caching for all drives. If you use this optional parameter, you still can enable write-caching for individual drives by using the *d:+* parameter.

/S	Displays additional information about the status of SmartDrive and its operation, including how efficiently SmartDrive is operating. This optional parameter frequently is useful.
d:+ or *d:*-	Replace the *d* with the letter of the disk drive for which you want to control caching. This parameter is optional. If you don't specify a drive letter, SmartDrive provides read-caching but not write-caching for floppy disk drives, CD-ROM drives, and drives created using Interlnk. Hard disk drives are read-cached and write-cached. Network drives are ignored, as are Microsoft Flash memory-card drives. If you specify a drive letter without a plus (+) or minus (-) sign, read-caching is enabled and write-caching is disabled. You can list multiple disk drives. The plus sign enables read-caching and write-caching for the specified drive. The minus sign disables read-caching and write-caching for the specified drive.
InitCacheSize	This optional parameter was covered in a previous section.
WinCacheSize	This optional parameter was covered in a previous section.
/U	Specifies that the CD-ROM caching module of SmartDrive is not loaded even if you have a CD-ROM drive. You cannot enable CD-ROM drive caching if SmartDrive is loaded with the /U switch. If SmartDrive is loaded without the /U switch, you can disable or enable caching for individual CD-ROM drives using the *d:*+ or *d:*- parameter. This parameter is optional.
/F	Writes cached data after each command completes. This is the default value.

/N	Writes cached data when the system is idle. When the command prompt returns, not all cached data may be written yet. To ensure that all the cached data is written, use the /C switch. This parameter is optional.
/L	Prevents SmartDrive from loading into upper memory blocks (UMBs), even if UMBs are available. You can use the /L switch if you want to reserve upper memory for program use. If you are using SmartDrive's double-buffering feature and your system appears to be running slowly, try adding the /L switch to the SmartDrive command in your AUTOEXEC.BAT file.
/V	Specifies that SmartDrive is to display status and error messages when it starts. By default, SmartDrive does not display messages unless the system has an error. You cannot use the /V switch at the same time as the /Q switch.
/Q	Instructs SmartDrive not to display status messages when it loads. By default, SmartDrive does not display messages when loading, but it does for most other operations. If SmartDrive encounters an error while starting, it displays an error message whether or not SmartDrive was loaded with the /Q switch. You cannot use the /Q switch at the same time as the /V switch.
/E:*ElementSize*	Specifies in bytes the amount of data moved into or out of the cache at one time. The default value is 8192. Valid values are 1024, 2048, 4096, and 8192. The larger the value, the more conventional memory SmartDrive uses.

/B:*BufferSize*	Specifies in bytes the size of the read-ahead buffer. A read-ahead buffer holds additional data that SmartDrive reads when an application calls for information from the hard disk. If an application reads 512K of information from a file, SmartDrive reads the amount of information specified in *BufferSize* and saves it in memory. The next time the application needs to read information from that file, it can read the information from memory rather than from the much slower disk. The default size of the read-ahead buffer is 16K. The buffer value can be any multiple of *ElementSize*. The larger the value of *buffersize*, the more conventional memory SmartDrive uses.

Including SmartDrive in CONFIG.SYS

DOS 6.2 Setup usually adds a SmartDrive line to your CONFIG.SYS that enables double-buffering, a special way of handling cached information with hard drive controllers. These controllers do not work with memory configured by EMM386.EXE or with Windows running in 386 Enhanced Mode. This line looks like the following:

```
DEVICE=C:\DOS\SMARTDRV.EXE /DOUBLE_BUFFER
```

If this line is present in your CONFIG.SYS, you can determine if your system really needs double-buffering by following these steps:

1. Load Windows in 386 Enhanced Mode by typing the following line at the DOS prompt:

   WIN /3

2. Press Enter.

3. Double-click the MS-DOS icon to shell to DOS.

14

4. Type **SMARTDRV** at the DOS prompt and press Enter.

   SmartDrive produces a display similar to the following:

```
Microsoft SMARTDrive Disk Cache version 5.0
Copyright 1991,1993 Microsoft Corp.

Cache size:  8,388,608 bytes
Cache size while running Windows:  8,388,608 bytes

            Disk Caching Status
drive   read cache   write cache   buffering
--------------------------------------------
  C:       yes           yes          no
  D:       yes           yes          no
  G:       yes           yes          no
Write behind data will not be committed before command prompt
returns.


For help, type "Smartdrv /?".
```

5. Look carefully at the screen display provided by SmartDrive. If all entries in the column headed `buffering` read `no`, you do not need double-buffering on your system and you can use the MS-DOS Editor to remove the double-buffering line from CONFIG.SYS.

6. To return to Windows, type **EXIT** at the DOS prompt.

7. Press Enter.

Task: Using a RAM Disk with Windows

RAM disk
A portion of system memory being used as an extremely fast hard drive.

The DOS file RAMDRIVE.SYS enables you to use a portion of your system memory as if it were an extremely fast hard drive. Such a disk in memory is known as a *RAM disk*. Because access to a RAM disk can be 20 or 30 times faster than a hard disk, a RAM disk can greatly speed up certain aspects of Windows performance. You can use a RAM disk to read and write files, just like you can with a real disk. A RAM disk is assigned a drive letter, just like a real disk.

Note: *Some dangers are associated with the use of a RAM disk. Data stored on a RAM disk is temporary. When you turn off your computer, reboot, or lose power to your system, you lose everything in the RAM disk.*

You can create a RAM disk in conventional, expanded, or extended memory. The best place for a RAM disk is extended memory. Conventional memory is best reserved for applications. You should have expanded memory only if applications need it.

To create a RAM disk, you add a line to CONFIG.SYS (after the HIMEM.SYS line) that loads RAMDRIVE.SYS. The syntax to create a RAM disk with the RAMDRIVE device driver is shown in the following line:

DEVICE=C:\DOS\RAMDRIVE.SYS *nnnn* /E or /A

or

DEVICEHIGH=C:\DOS\RAMDRIVE.SYS *nnnn* /E or /A

The *nnnn* indicates replaceable characters. You actually enter the size in bytes of the RAM disk you want (1024 creates a 1M RAM disk.) The /E parameter means to use extended memory. Use /A to store RAMDRIVE in expanded memory.

To create a RAM drive that uses 1M (1024K) of extended memory, add the following line to CONFIG.SYS:

C:\DOS\RAMDRIVE.SYS 1024 /E

14

DOS assigns RAMDRIVE the next available drive letter. For example, if your hard disk is the C: drive, the RAMDRIVE is the D: drive.

Many programs need a place to store temporary files. These temporary files may be written and read many times while the program operates. When you tell the program to store these temporary files in a RAM disk, the program runs much faster.

Note: *Never use a RAM drive as the location for the Windows swap file. Windows swaps programs out of memory when your system has a memory shortage. You only slow down your system if you attempt to solve a memory shortage by swapping to a RAM disk in memory, and this action may cause the system to stop.*

Programs that create temporary files often look for the TEMP parameter in the DOS environment to tell them where to store temporary files. The DOS environment is like a bulletin board that any program can read to get information. You can store information in the environment with the SET command. If the D: drive is your RAM disk, follow these steps to add the SET command to AUTOEXEC.BAT:

1. Type **CD** to change to the root directory.
2. Press Enter.
3. From the DOS prompt, run the MS-DOS Editor by typing the following line:

   EDIT AUTOEXEC.BAT

4. Press Enter.
5. Type the following line in the AUTOEXEC.BAT file:

   SET TEMP=D:

6. Save and exit MS-DOS Editor.

To find out how large your RAMDRIVE must be to hold all the temporary files for an application, check the documentation for the application.

Configuring Your Hard Drive for Windows

Swapping
A process in which Windows uses available hard drive space as if it were system memory.

When you are configuring your system for Windows, your hard drive should receive some attention. If you run out of system memory, Windows can use your hard drive as if it were actually system RAM by using a special process called *swapping*.

When Windows swaps programs to your hard drive, these programs can continue to run and do their work. However, before Windows can swap efficiently to your hard drive, you need available space on your drive. And this available space needs to be *contiguous*, or located all together without files or pieces of files breaking up available space into small blocks. For information on using swap files with Windows, see the Windows User Manual.

To prepare your hard drive for Windows, run the DEFRAG program before you create a Windows permanent swap file. Windows cannot create a permanent swap file unless it finds a large enough block of contiguous available space.

If you plan to use a temporary swap file, an extremely important point is to run DEFRAG frequently on your hard drive. If you do not set aside a permanent part of your hard drive for Windows, newly saved files and recently installed software can quickly make the available space on your hard drive discontiguous. Such discontiguous available space makes Windows work harder when you are using a temporary swap file. And breaking available space into too many small blocks can keep Windows from fully utilizing its swapping system.

The DEFRAG program is covered fully in Lesson 8, "DOS Command Reference." To load DEFRAG, follow these steps:

1. Type **DEFRAG** at the DOS prompt.

2. Press Enter.

Not only does Windows run faster when you use DEFRAG to frequently defragment the files on your hard drive, but your data is safer. DOS can keep track of a file more easily when all the sectors occupied by the file are contiguous, or together.

Summary

To	Do This
Use the Microsoft Diagnostic program	Type **MSD** at the DOS prompt and press Enter
Determine available conventional memory	Type **MEM** at the DOS prompt and press Enter
Determine amount of extended memory	Run MSD and choose the Memory option button
Enable XMS support	Load HIMEM.SYS in CONFIG.SYS
Create expanded memory	Load EMM386.EXE in CONFIG.SYS
Run MemMaker	Type **MEMMAKER** at the DOS prompt and press Enter
Optimize memory for Windows	Run MemMaker
Speed up Windows	Load SmartDrive in AUTOEXEC.BAT
Create a high-speed drive	Load RAMDRIVE.SYS in CONFIG.SYS
Optimize your hard drive or Windows	Use DEFRAG regularly

On Your Own

Estimated time: 35 minutes

Use the MSD program.

1. Run the Microsoft Diagnostic program and browse through the information provided by selecting each of the option buttons. Then browse through the menus.

2. Print an MSD report and determine from it your CPU chip type (386, 486, Pentium), the amount of installed system memory, and the memory types (conventional, extended, and expanded) present on your system.

Determine memory configuration and run DEFRAG.

1. Determine the amount of available conventional memory on your system by using the MEM command.
2. Use the MS-DOS Editor to determine whether DOS is loaded in high memory (look for the DOS=HIGH statement in CONFIG.SYS)
3. Use the MS-DOS Editor to determine whether memory-resident programs and device drivers are loaded into upper memory blocks (look for DEVICEHIGH and LOADHIGH or LH statements).
4. Run DEFRAG on your hard drive, choosing the Full Optimize option.

Part V
Appendix

Setup and Installation

Appendix

Setup and Installation

A

This appendix tells you how to install or upgrade to MS-DOS 6.2. If DOS 6.2 is already installed on your computer, you can skip this appendix. Go right to Lesson 1, "Understanding Hardware, Software, and DOS," and start to learn about DOS from the beginning. However, you may need the information in this appendix later to help you install some of the special utilities that come with DOS 6.2 or to replace DOS files that are accidentally deleted or become corrupted.

This lesson helps you perform the following tasks:

- Use the retail MS-DOS 6.2 Upgrade package
- Use the Step-Up upgrade that updates DOS 6.0 to 6.2
- Use the full install version of DOS 6.2
- Install DOS 6.2 on floppy disks
- Restore a previous version of DOS

Reviewing DOS 6.2 Requirements

DOS 6.2 can run on any PC with at least 256K of memory. Virtually every PC sold since 1983 has at least this much memory. Computers sold since 1986 usually have the maximum of 640K conventional memory.

If you plan to install MS-DOS 6.2 on a hard disk, you need at least 512K of memory and 4M of available disk space.

Understanding Different DOS 6.2 Packages

DOS 6.2 is available in three different and important packages:

1. The DOS 6.2 full install version, which most often is provided when you buy a new computer. You can use this version to install DOS on a hard drive that does not contain a version of DOS later than 2.11.

2. The MS-DOS 6.2 Upgrade package, which you can use to upgrade DOS versions 2.11 and later. You cannot use this package to install DOS on a hard drive without a previous version of DOS.

3. The MS-DOS 6.2 Step-Up version, which you can use only on systems already running DOS 6.0.

Note: *If the floppy drive capacity of your computer is 360K or 720K, you need to obtain 360K or 720K Setup disks from Microsoft before you can install DOS 6.2 on your system. Retail packages of DOS 6.2 include only 1.44M or 1.2M disks.*

Determining Non-Microsoft Versions of DOS

Certain computer brands require their own version of DOS 6.2. For example, Zenith, Compaq, and Toshiba systems use OEM (original equipment manufacturer) versions of DOS. If you are unsure whether your system needs an OEM version of DOS, consult your system documentation. If you already have DOS installed on the system, you can determine the version using these steps:

1. Type **VER** at the DOS prompt.

2. Press Enter.

If the readout says `MS-DOS Version x.xx`, your system is running MS-DOS rather than an OEM version, and you can almost certainly use the Microsoft version of DOS 6.2.

Task: Making Backup Copies of Your DOS 6.2 Disks

Your first step in installing DOS 6.2 is making backup copies of your new DOS 6.2 disks. If your computer has a previous version of DOS installed or you have another computer available with any version of DOS installed, use DISKCOPY to make the backup copies. Then install DOS 6.2 using the backup copies. Keep the original disks in a safe place.

If your computer does not already have a DOS version installed and you do not have access to another computer, you cannot make backup copies of the DOS disks. You may want to go ahead and use the original disks to install DOS 6.2. However, after you have DOS 6.2 installed, make a backup copy of the original DOS 6.2 disks.

Note: *If you cannot successfully complete the DOS 6.2 installation because you get errors reading the DOS disks, contact your dealer immediately.*

To make backup copies of the DOS 6.2 disks, you need five or six 5 1/4-inch, 1.2M floppy disks or three 3 1/2-inch, 1.44M disks. If you have two floppy disk drives that are the same size and capacity (for example, both drives have 1.44M capacity), follow these instructions:

1. At the DOS prompt, type the following line:

   DISKCOPY A: B: /V

2. Press Enter.

3. At the prompt `Insert the SOURCE disk in drive A:`, put the original DOS 6.2 disk labeled *Disk 1* in the A: drive.

4. You also are prompted to insert the TARGET disk in the B: drive.

   If you have two 5 1/4-inch 1.2M drives, put a blank 1.2M floppy disk in the B: drive, close the drive door, and press Enter. This disk does not need to be formatted.

   or

   If you have two 3 1/2-inch 1.44M drives, put a blank 1.44M disk in the B: drive and press Enter. This disk does not need to be formatted.

A

5. When the DISKCOPY process is complete, remove the disks from both drives and label the new disk *MS-DOS 6.2—Setup Disk 1.*

6. At the prompt `Copy another disk (Y/N)?`, press **Y**, press Enter, and repeat steps 3 through 5 for each original DOS 6.2 disk. Be sure to label the disks in the correct order.

7. After you complete the DISKCOPY for the last original DOS 6.2 disk, DOS asks whether you want to copy another disk. Press **N** and then press Enter.

If you have only one floppy disk drive or the A: drive and the B: drive are different sizes, follow these steps:

1. Type the following line at the DOS prompt:

   DISKCOPY A: A: /V

2. Press Enter.

3. At the prompt to `Insert the SOURCE disk in drive A:`, place the original DOS 6.2 disk labeled *Disk 1* in the A: drive and press Enter.

4. At the prompt to `Insert the TARGET disk in drive A:`, remove the original DOS 6.2 disk and insert a blank 1.2M or 1.44M disk into the A: drive and press Enter. This disk does not need to be formatted.

5. You may be prompted to remove the TARGET disk and insert the SOURCE disk again. You then are prompted to insert the TARGET disk again. Switch the same two disks as prompted until the DISKCOPY completes.

6. When the DISKCOPY process is complete, remove the disk from the A: drive and label the new disk *MS-DOS 6.2—Setup Disk 1.*

7. At the prompt `Copy another disk (Y/N)?`, press **Y**, press Enter, and repeat steps 3 through 6 for each original DOS 6.2 disk. Be sure to label the disks in the correct order.

8. When you complete the DISKCOPY for the last original DOS 6.2 disk, press **N** and then press Enter.

Note: *If the DISKCOPY fails, repeat the process using a different blank disk. If you cannot successfully DISKCOPY each original DOS 6.2 disk, contact your dealer for replacement disks.*

Store the original DOS 6.2 disks in a safe place and use the copies. If you get any errors using a copy of one of the DOS disks, repeat the DISKCOPY process to re-create that disk. If you cannot make a copy of the disk to use for the installation, contact your dealer for a replacement.

In all subsequent instructions, any reference to a DOS disk (or original DOS disk) refers to the copy of the original that you just made.

Upgrading to MS-DOS 6.2

If you are upgrading from a previous version of DOS, this section covers some important considerations.

Task: Determining Hard Drive Space

To determine the amount of available space on your hard disk, follow these steps:

1. Type **DIR** from your root directory.

2. Press Enter.

   The last line of the listing indicates the amount of hard drive space available.

3. If less than 4M is available, use COPY or BACKUP to copy some or all of the files on the hard disk to floppy disks.

4. Then delete enough files from the hard disk so that at least 4M is available. You can restore these copied files later.

Task: Backing Up Files if You Use Disk Compression

If your start-up drive (usually the C: drive) uses a disk-compression program like Stacker, DOS 6.2 will not be able to create an Uninstall disk for restoring your previous version of DOS if necessary. (Uninstall is covered later in this lesson.) If you use a disk-compression program, follow these steps:

1. Before you run Setup, back up all your data files using the MSBACKUP or COPY command.

2. Create a system disk by copying to a floppy disk the FDISK, FORMAT, and SYS commands as well as the system files of your current DOS version.

Task: Disabling Memory-Resident Programs

Memory-resident program
A program that remains in memory even while you run other software. The mouse software driver is a memory-resident program.

Some disk-caching, deletion-protection, and anti-virus programs may conflict with the DOS 6.2 Setup program. You must disable or remove the start-up commands for any of these *memory-resident programs* from your CONFIG.SYS and AUTOEXEC.BAT files before you start the upgrade procedure. Follow these steps:

1. In your CONFIG.SYS and AUTOEXEC.BAT files, type **REM** and press the space bar at the beginning of each command line that starts a disk-caching, delete-protection, or anti-virus program.

   For example, if the command C:\DOS\VSAFE.COM is in your AUTOEXEC.BAT file, type **REM** at the beginning of the line and press the space bar. The new command is REM C:\DOS\VSAFE.COM.

2. Save and exit the file.

3. Restart your computer before running Setup.

You can read about editing your AUTOEXEC.BAT and CONFIG.SYS files in Lesson 11, "Customizing DOS."

You also need to turn off automatic message services that print directly to your screen. For example, you must turn off network pop-up menus or printing notifications.

Using Spare Floppy Disks for Uninstall

Uninstall
Removes all traces of DOS 6.2 and restores the old version of DOS, along with your AUTOEXEC.BAT and CONFIG.SYS files.

During the Setup process you need one or more spare floppy disks so Setup can copy *Uninstall* information to them. If the installation fails or you cannot boot your system after installation of DOS 6.2, you can use these Uninstall disks to restore your system to its original condition. You then can retry the installation or contact Microsoft Corporation for troubleshooting help.

If you use 360K disks, you may need two disks; label them *Uninstall #1* and *Uninstall #2*. If you use disks with a capacity greater than 360K, you probably need only one disk; label it *Uninstall*. Uninstall disks can be formatted disks or unformatted disks. Setup destroys any existing data on the disks.

Ensuring Program and Data Safety

When you upgrade, you have data on your hard disk that you do not want to lose. The first part of the upgrade procedure is to use the MS Backup program to back up all the files on your hard disk and save your old version of DOS. Do not skip this step.

Even with software that is as well-behaved and bug-free as the DOS 6.2 Setup program, things can go wrong that destroy data. You are better safe than sorry. If something goes wrong with the upgrade, you can use the backup disks to completely restore your system.

Considering Other Upgrade Issues

If you are upgrading from a version of DOS prior to DOS 4.0, you may need to take special precautions before installing DOS 6.2 if either of the following conditions apply on your system:

- A nonstandard disk that requires special device drivers in CONFIG.SYS.
- A version of DOS prior to DOS 4.0 and a hard disk bigger than 32M.

If you are using a nonstandard disk that requires special device drivers in CONFIG.SYS, or you are using special partitioning software, consult the manufacturer of the drive or the partitioning software before attempting to upgrade to DOS 6.2. You must ensure that the device drivers for the drive or partitioning software are compatible with DOS 6.2. Your manufacturer also can tell you if you must take any special steps when upgrading your DOS version.

If your system is running a version of DOS prior to DOS 4.0 and you have a hard disk bigger than 32M, you may want to reformat your hard drive to take advantage of DOS 6.2's capability to access hard drive partitions greater than 32M.

If you want to use DOS 6.2 to create a hard drive partition larger than 32M, back up your entire hard drive and enable the DOS 6.2 Setup program to run FDISK to create the large hard drive. Setup then will FORMAT your hard drive. After DOS 6.2 is installed, you can restore all your data. For help on running FDISK or reformatting your drive, consult Que's *Using MS-DOS 6.2*, Special Edition, or the MS-DOS 6.2 manual for more detailed, technical information.

If you already have DOS Version 2.11 or greater installed on your hard disk, the upgrade consists of running the MS-DOS 6.2 Setup program. You can upgrade to DOS 6.2 without having to partition or format your hard disk.

Task: Upgrading to DOS 6.2 on a Hard Disk

To upgrade DOS on your hard disk, follow these steps:

1. Copy your AUTOEXEC.BAT and CONFIG.SYS files to a floppy disk. You may need them later.

2. Exit any shell programs or task-switching programs such as DOS Shell, Windows, DESQView, or Software Carousel.

3. Place Disk 1 in the A: drive and, if applicable, close the drive door.

4. Type **A:** and press Enter to change to the A: drive.

5. Type **SETUP** and press Enter. The Welcome screen appears. Press F1 for Help, F3 to exit Setup, or press Enter to continue.

6. After you press Enter, Setup prompts you to label the Uninstall disk. Press Enter when you are ready to continue.

   Setup prepares to install DOS 6.2. The program asks you to confirm the DOS Type, the DOS Path, and the Display Type.

Setup screen to confirm system settings.

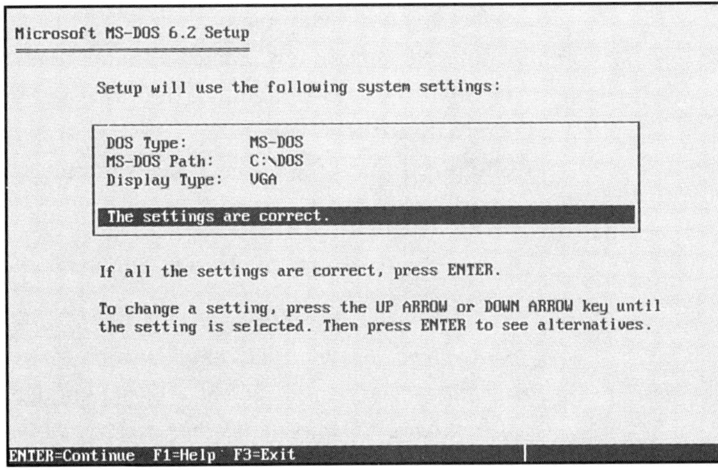
```
Microsoft MS-DOS 6.2 Setup

        Setup will use the following system settings:

         DOS Type:          MS-DOS
         MS-DOS Path:       C:\DOS
         Display Type:      VGA

         The settings are correct.

        If all the settings are correct, press ENTER.

        To change a setting, press the UP ARROW or DOWN ARROW key until
        the setting is selected. Then press ENTER to see alternatives.

ENTER=Continue  F1=Help  F3=Exit
```

7. To accept the displayed values, press Enter. To change a value, press the up- or down-arrow keys to highlight the value and press Enter to display alternative values. Use the up- or down-arrow keys to select an alternative and press Enter.

Setup screen to confirm installation of listed programs.

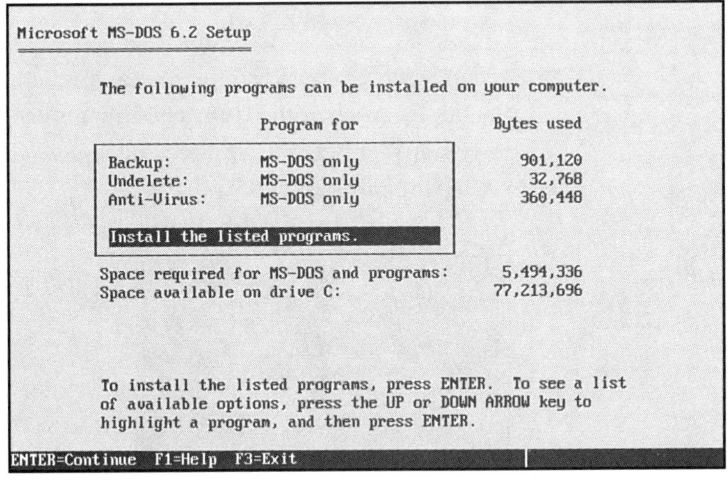
```
Microsoft MS-DOS 6.2 Setup

        The following programs can be installed on your computer.

                          Program for              Bytes used

         Backup:          MS-DOS only                901,120
         Undelete:        MS-DOS only                 32,768
         Anti-Virus:      MS-DOS only                360,448

         Install the listed programs.

        Space required for MS-DOS and programs:    5,494,336
        Space available on drive C:               77,213,696

        To install the listed programs, press ENTER.  To see a list
        of available options, press the UP or DOWN ARROW key to
        highlight a program, and then press ENTER.
ENTER=Continue  F1=Help  F3=Exit
```

A

8. Select any optional programs you want to install. To accept the displayed values, press Enter. To change a value, press the up- or down-arrow keys to highlight the value and press Enter to display alternative values. Use the up- or down-arrow keys to select an alternative and press Enter. When the values you want are displayed, press Enter.

   If you are installing only DOS programs, skip step 9 and go to step 10.

   Note: *If you do not install the optional programs now, you can do so in the future; however, you probably should install the programs now. If you do not have Windows at this time, you cannot install the program for Windows. When you get Windows, you can run Setup again and add the Windows program.*

9. If you are installing the Windows program, Setup asks you to verify the Windows directory. Press Enter to accept the directory that Setup displays or type the correct directory and press Enter.

10. Setup now is ready to upgrade to DOS 6.2. Press **Y** to begin the upgrade or press F3 to exit.

11. When Setup prompts you to insert a different installation disk in the floppy drive, or the Uninstall disk, remove the disk from the floppy drive, insert the requested disk, close the drive door if appropriate, and press Enter.

Setup prompt to insert Uninstall disk.

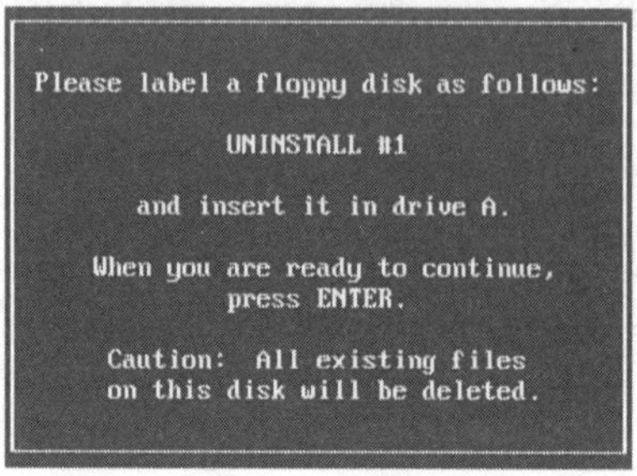

```
Please label a floppy disk as follows:

UNINSTALL #1

and insert it in drive A.

When you are ready to continue,
press ENTER.

Caution: All existing files
on this disk will be deleted.
```

If you insert the wrong DOS disk, DOS prompts you to insert the correct disk.

During the upgrade, Setup copies your previous DOS files to a directory named OLD_DOS.1 on your hard disk. (If you already have an OLD_DOS.1, Setup names the directory OLD_DOS.2, and so on.) Setup also copies your AUTOEXEC.BAT and CONFIG.SYS files to the Uninstall disks. The copies are named AUTOEXEC.DAT and CONFIG.DAT. Setup then copies the DOS 6.2 files to the hard disk.

As the upgrade proceeds, your screen shows a horizontal bar indicating what percentage of the total installation process is complete (see following figure). Setup describes the current activity in the lower right corner of the screen.

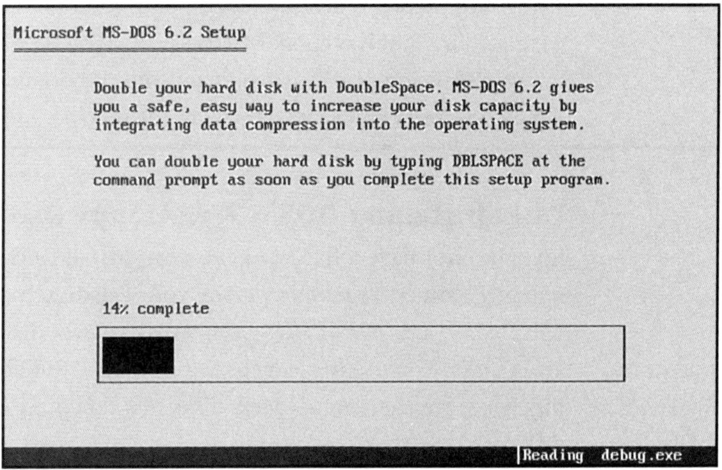

Microsoft MS-DOS 6.2 Setup
Double your hard disk with DoubleSpace. MS-DOS 6.2 gives you a safe, easy way to increase your disk capacity by integrating data compression into the operating system.
You can double your hard disk by typing DBLSPACE at the command prompt as soon as you complete this setup program.
14% complete
Reading debug.exe

Screen showing status of DOS 6.2 installation procedure.

After the install process is complete, DOS prompts you to remove all floppy disks from the disk drives and press Enter.

The completion screen shown in the following figure confirms that DOS 6.2 is installed on your hard disk. Press Enter to restart your computer with DOS 6.2.

MS-DOS 6.2 Setup completion screen.

```
MS-DOS Setup Complete

MS-DOS 6.2 is now installed on your computer.

Your original AUTOEXEC.BAT and CONFIG.SYS files,
if any, were saved on the UNINSTALL disk(s) as
AUTOEXEC.DAT and CONFIG.DAT.

  • To restart your computer with MS-DOS 6.2,
    press ENTER.

  • To learn more about new MS-DOS 6.2 features,
    type HELP WHATSNEW at the command prompt.
```

If you have problems...

If you have problems installing DOS 6.2 on your hard drive, carefully follow the directions in this section. Make sure that you have disabled disk-caching software, deletion-protection, and anti-virus programs, as well as any messaging programs that write directly to the screen.

Task: Installing DOS 6.2 on Floppy Disks

If you do not have a hard disk, you can install DOS 6.2 on floppy disks. Actually, you don't really upgrade your existing floppy disks to DOS 6.2; you create a new set of DOS floppy disks. These disks become your operating disks. You use these disks to run DOS. After you complete this process, store the original DOS disks in a safe place and use the operating disks.

If you plan to install DOS 6.2 on floppy disks, obtain a supply of blank disks that fit into the A: drive. If the A: drive is a 5 1/4-inch drive, for example, you need three 1.2M floppy disks during the installation process. If the A: drive is a 3 1/2-inch drive, you need three 1.44M disks. These disks can be unformatted; existing data on the disks will be destroyed. (If you are using the B: drive, substitute *A* for *B* in the following steps.)

DOS gives you the option to continue or cancel the installation throughout the installation process. If you cannot complete the installation for any reason, press F3. You can start from the beginning at a later time.

To install DOS on floppy disks, follow these steps:

1. Place your current DOS disk (not the DOS 6.2 disk) in the A: drive and turn on your computer. If your computer is already on, leave

your DOS disk in the A: drive and press Ctrl-Alt-Del. This action reboots, or restarts your computer with your current version of DOS.

2. Place the DOS 6.2 Disk 1 in the A: drive (or B: drive if that is appropriate for your system) and if applicable, close the drive door.

   Make sure the drive containing the Setup disk is the current drive.

3. Type **SETUP /F** and press Enter.

   The Setup program loads. Setup prepares to install MS-DOS 6.2. It checks your hardware configuration. Setup prompts you to label one or more floppy disks.

4. Press F1 for Help, F3 to exit Setup, or press Enter to continue.

5. Setup asks you to confirm the start-up drive and the Display Type. To accept the displayed values, press Enter. To change a value, press the up- or down-arrow keys to highlight the value and press Enter to display alternative values. Press the up- or down-arrow keys to select an alternative and press Enter. When the values you want are displayed, press Enter.

Setup screen to confirm system settings.

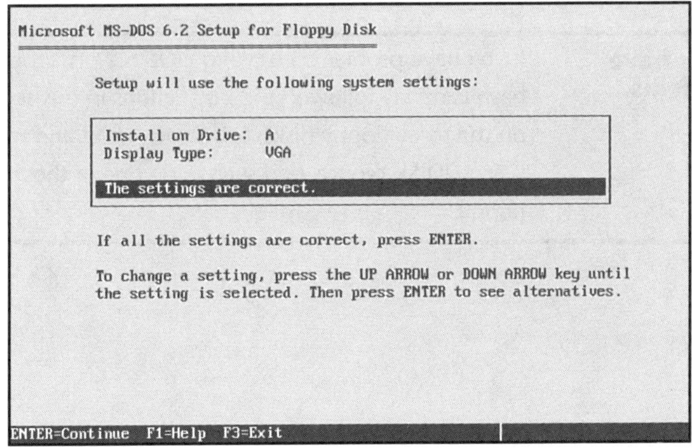

6. When Setup prompts you to insert a different disk in the floppy drive, remove the current disk from the floppy drive, insert the requested disk, close the drive door, if appropriate, and press Enter.

A

Setup prompt to insert a floppy disk.

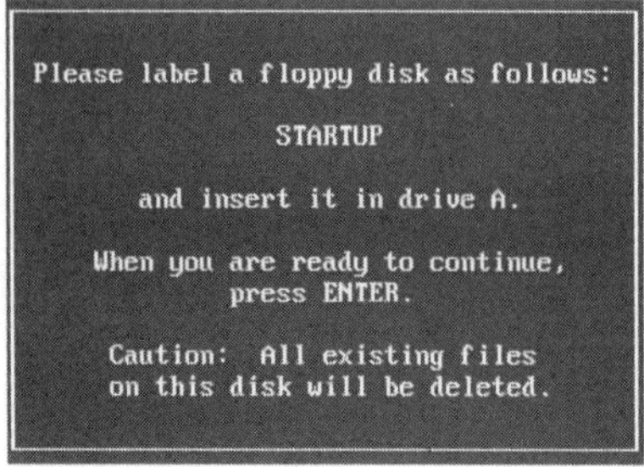

Please label a floppy disk as follows:
STARTUP
and insert it in drive A.
When you are ready to continue,
press ENTER.
Caution: All existing files
on this disk will be deleted.

If you insert the wrong DOS disk, DOS prompts you to insert the correct disk.

Setup proceeds to copy the DOS files onto the three floppy disks. The program displays a horizontal bar that shows what percentage of the total installation process is complete. Setup describes the current activity in the lower right corner of the screen.

7. When the installation process is complete, insert the Startup/Support disk in the A: drive and press Enter. This action reboots or restarts the computer by using the new working disk.

The installation process on floppy disks is complete.

If you have problems...

If you have problems installing DOS 6.2 on floppy disks, make sure that you have carefully followed the instructions in this section. Before installing DOS on the three floppy disks, format the disks and make sure they are error-free. If SCANDISK reports bad sectors on one of the floppies, do not use that floppy.

Task: Running the MS-DOS 6.2 Step-Up

To run the DOS 6.2 Step-Up to upgrade DOS 6.0 to DOS 6.2, use the following steps:

1. Place the Step-Up disk in the A: drive.
2. Type **A:** at the DOS prompt and press Enter to change to the A: drive.
3. Type **SETUP** at the DOS prompt and press Enter.

   The Setup program checks your system configuration. Press F1 to get help on running Setup. Press F3 to exit Setup. If you quit Setup, you can return later and start over.
4. Press Enter to continue with Setup. Setup prompts you to label the Uninstall disks.
5. Setup displays the detected system configuration. The program asks you to confirm the DOS Type, the DOS Path, and the Display Type. Press Enter to accept the displayed values. To change a value, press the up- or down-arrow keys to highlight the value and press Enter to display the options. Use the up- or down-arrow keys to highlight an option, then press Enter. When you are satisfied with your selections, use the down-arrow key to return to the selection `The settings are correct.`
6. Press Enter when you are ready to continue.

   Setup is now ready to upgrade to DOS 6.2. The program warns you not to interrupt Setup after this point.
7. To exit Setup at this time, press F3. To install DOS, press **Y** for yes.
8. Place Uninstall disk 1 in the A: drive when Setup prompts you.
9. Press Enter to continue.
10. When prompted, remove all floppy disks from your drives and press Enter to restart your computer with DOS 6.2.

The DOS 6.2 Startup program reloads, informing you that installation was successful. You are given the option of exiting and using DOS 6.2, or removing DOS 6.2 and returning to your previous DOS version.

11. Press **E** to exit Setup to reboot your system or **R** to remove DOS 6.2 and return to your previous DOS version.

Task: Running the Full Installation Version of DOS 6.2

The full installation version of DOS 6.2 is used to install DOS 6.2 on a hard drive that does not contain DOS (or that has DOS 2.11 or earlier). The full install version first determines your system configuration then proceeds to run FDISK on your hard drive, which creates a *partition table*. Then Setup formats your hard drive. To halt Setup at any time, press F3. If you quit Setup, you can return later and start over.

Running the Setup program from the full install disks is virtually automatic. Follow these steps:

1. Place Disk 1 in your floppy drive.
2. Turn on your system if it is not running.
3. Type **SETUP** at the DOS prompt and press Enter.

   Setup determines the hardware configuration of your system and then reboots your computer to begin installing DOS 6.2 on your hard drive and configuring DOS to work with your system.

4. When prompted to change disks, insert the requested disk and press Enter.
5. Select your preference when prompted for whether you want your hard drive partitioned as a single large hard drive or in smaller logical drives.

Setup runs FDISK to partition your hard drive and then runs FORMAT to format your hard drive. During the format, the system files IO.SYS and MSDOS.SYS are copied properly to your root directory, along with COMMAND.COM. When your hard drive is ready, Setup creates the directory C:\DOS and begins copying the DOS 6.2 files to this directory.

6. When Setup has finished copying the DOS 6.2 files to your hard drive, you are prompted to remove the disk from your A: drive and press Enter to reboot your computer.
7. Remove the disk and press the Enter key to reboot your computer with DOS 6.2.

Task: Creating a Rescue Disk

Rescue disk
A bootable floppy disk containing the DOS utilities you need to recover from a hard disk problem.

After DOS 6.2 installation is complete, you immediately create a *rescue disk*, a disk you can use in an emergency to boot your computer, diagnose problems with your hard drive, and make repairs when needed. A rescue disk is an essential set of tools to help you recover from a hard drive problem that keeps your system from booting.

After you have created a rescue disk, you should copy all the files from your DOS directory onto floppy disks and keep them in a safe place with your rescue disk in case you must reinstall one or more of your DOS files.

Bootable floppy disk
A disk containing the DOS system files, created by using the FORMAT /S or SYS commands.

The first step in creating a rescue disk is making a *bootable floppy disk*. Follow these steps:

1. Place a disk in the A: drive.
2. Type the following line at the DOS prompt:

   FORMAT A: /S

3. Press Enter.

4. After the disk formats, use the COPY command to place the following files on your new bootable floppy disk:

File	Purpose
SCANDISK.EXE	To test a malfunctioning hard drive
UNDELETE.EXE	To undelete important files
EDIT.COM	To change AUTOEXEC.BAT or CONFIG.SYS
QBASIC.EXE	Needed by EDIT.COM
SYS.COM	To replace the DOS system files (IO.SYS, MSDOS.SYS, and COMMAND.COM) on a damaged hard drive.
FORMAT.COM	To reformat your hard drive in case SCANDISK reports that reformatting is necessary.
FDISK.EXE	To redo your hard drive partition in case SCANDISK reports that repartitioning is necessary.

5. Use the XCOPY or COPY command to copy all the files from the C:\DOS directory onto floppy disks.

   Keep these disks in a safe place in case your DOS files are corrupted or accidentally deleted and you later need to restore them.

Task: Completing the Installation

In most cases, after you complete the installation or the upgrade, you are ready to use your computer. In some cases, however, you must do some additional work so you can improve the way DOS runs. For instance, you may need to modify the HIMEM.SYS command in CONFIG.SYS if you have one of the following computers:

- Abacus 386
- Chaplet
- Everex AT Plus 1800
- Everex Notebook ELX
- Excel Computer Systems

- OPT 386-25 Motherboard
- Pak 386SX
- PC Limited
- PC380/33C, PC350/33C, or PC300/33C BIOS revision 1.14

In the directory in which you installed DOS, such as C:\DOS, the README.TXT file contains additional information about DOS and the installation process. Read this file to see whether any of the information applies to your computer system.

To read the README.TXT file, use the following steps:

1. Type **CD \DOS** and press Enter.

2. Type the following line and press Enter:

   EDIT README.TXT

3. Use the up- and down-arrow keys to move through the document a line at a time. Use the PgUp or PgDn keys to move through the document a screen at a time.

   The README.TXT file contains technical information about the installation that is outside the scope of this book.

4. After you finish reading README.TXT, press the Alt key to activate the MS-DOS Editor menu bar, press **F** to open the **F**ile menu, then press **X** to E**x**it the MS-DOS Editor. These actions return you to the DOS prompt.

A

Task: Running Setup To Install the Optional Programs

If you did not install one of the optional programs when you originally installed DOS 6.2, or you want to change a program's setup, you can run Setup just for that purpose. For example, if you did not have Windows when you first installed DOS 6.2, you could not install Backup, Anti-Virus, or Undelete for Windows. If you now have Windows, you can run Setup to install those three optional programs.

To run Setup just to install the optional programs, follow these steps:

1. Insert Setup Disk 1 in the A: drive.
2. Type **A:** and press Enter.
3. Type **SETUP /E** and press Enter. The Welcome screen opens.
4. To begin installing the optional programs immediately, press Enter. To display Help information about the Setup program, press F1. To stop Setup, press F3.
5. Select the optional programs you want to install. To accept the displayed values, press Enter. To change a value, press the up- or down-arrow keys to highlight the value, and then press Enter to display alternative values. Use the up- or down-arrow keys to select an alternative, and then press Enter. When the values you want are displayed, press Enter.
6. If you are installing the Windows programs, Setup asks you to verify the Windows directory. Press Enter to accept the directory that Setup displays, or type the correct drive and directory and press Enter.
7. Setup prompts you to insert the other Setup disks in the A: drive. Insert the requested disk and press Enter to continue.
8. When the optional programs have been installed, Setup prompts you to press Enter to exit the Setup program.

Task: Restoring a Previous Version of DOS

If you upgrade to DOS 6.2 but cannot operate your computer, you can revert to your previous version of DOS by using the Uninstall disks created during Setup. You must use the most recently created Uninstall disk. If you try to use an Uninstall disk created during a previous installation, DOS prompts you for the most recent Uninstall disk.

To restore your previous version of DOS, follow these steps:

1. Insert into the A: drive the Uninstall disk (or Uninstall #1) that DOS created during the upgrade.
2. Restart your computer.
3. Uninstall tells you that if it can perform the restoration, it will remove the DOS 6.2 files and replace your original DOS files.
4. Press **R** to restore the original DOS. To stop the uninstall procedure, remove the disk from the A: drive and press **E**.

Under certain circumstances, you cannot restore your previous version of DOS. If, after installing DOS 6.2, you take any of the following steps, your Uninstall disk will not work:

- Repartition or reformat your hard disk.
- Delete or move either of the two hidden DOS system files (IO.SYS and MSDOS.SYS).
- Delete the OLD_DOS.*x* directory.
- Install DoubleSpace or any other disk-compression program.

Wait a few days after installing DOS 6.2 before deleting the OLD_DOS.*x* directory, installing disk compression, or repartitioning or reformatting your hard drive. After you are sure DOS 6.2 is running smoothly on your system, you can proceed with any of these actions.

Reinstalling DOS 6.2

At some point, you may need to uninstall or reinstall DOS 6.2, even if the installation was completed without error. With either of the following situations, you may find reinstalling DOS easier:

- You may have a marginal sector on your disk that goes bad, causing part of DOS to be unreadable. Reinstalling DOS and enabling Setup to reformat the drive should repair the problem. However, before you use this strategy, boot from a floppy disk and attempt to run SCANDISK on the drive.

- If you change your video display, such as from EGA to VGA, you can follow a complex procedure to upgrade the DOS installation without reinstalling. Reinstalling DOS 6.2 is much easier.

Task: Preserving DOS Shell Settings

If you changed the DOS Shell settings or added program groups, this information is stored in a file named DOSSHELL.INI. After you reinstall DOS 6.2 or install a future version of DOS 6.2, the DOSSHELL.INI file in the \DOS directory contains the original default settings. If the DOS Shell starts automatically when you boot DOS, you can see that you lose any customizing or program groups. To recover the custom settings, you must copy your customized DOSSHELL.INI file to the \DOS directory:

1. If you are in the DOS Shell, press F3 to cancel the Shell and return to the DOS command line.

2. Copy DOSSHELL.INI from the old DOS directory to the \DOS directory.

   In other words, if your old DOS directory was renamed OLD_DOS.2 during the upgrade and your new DOS directory is DOS, type the following command and press Enter:

   COPY \OLD_DOS.2\DOSSHELL.INI \DOS

   If your old DOS directory had a different name, substitute that name for OLD_DOS.2 in the command.

3. Type **DOSSHELL** to return to the DOS Shell.

4. Press Enter.

The DOS Shell now reflects the changes you made to the Shell in the previous installation of DOS 6.2.

Summary

To	Do This
Safeguard your data	Back up your system before upgrading to DOS 6.2
Prepare your computer	Make sure that 4M of hard disk space is available
Start the upgrade	Run SETUP on Disk 1
Install DOS 6.2 on floppy	Run SETUP /F
Upgrade from DOS 6.0 to 6.2	Run DOS 6.2 Step-Up
Make DOS restoration easy	Copy all DOS files to floppy
Guard against hard drive failure	Create a rescue disk
Restore your previous DOS version	Reboot with Uninstall Disk 1 in the A: drive

Index

Symbols

A

B

C

D

E

F

G–H

I

J–L

M

N

O

S

T

U

V

W

X–Y–Z

A Powerful Dose of DOS for the Everyday User!

Using WordPerfect Version 6 for DOS, Special Edition
Que Development Group

The complete tutorial and reference guide…ideal for users of all skill levels!

Version 6.0

$29.95 USA
1-56529-077-1, 1,200 pp., 7 3/8 X 9 1/8

Easy WordPerfect for Version 6
Shelley O'Hara

The revolutionary, 4-color introduction to the latest version of WordPerfect!

Version 6.0

$16.95 USA
1-56529-311-8, 256 pp., 8 X 10

Using 1-2-3, Release 3.4
Que Development Group

This comprehensive tutorial/reference covers all readers need to know to use 1-2-3!

Release 3.4

$29.95 USA
1-56529-004-6, 1,100 pp., 7 3/8 X 9 1/8

Que's Computer User's Dictionary, 4th Edition
Bryan Pfaffenberger

Completely revised and updated, with more terms than ever before!

All Computer Users

$12.95 USA
1-56529-604-4, 650 pp., 4 3/4 X 8

Quick & Dirty Harvard Graphics Presentations
Bob Benedict

A complete recipe book for a dazzling array of Harvard Graphics charts…plus advice on presentation!

Version 3

$24.95 USA
1-56529-089-5, 320 pp., 8 X 10

Upgrading & Repairing PCs, 2nd Edition
Scott Mueller, et al.

0-88022-856-3, 1,000 pp., 7 3/8 X 9 1/8
$34.95 USA

IBM PCs-Compatibles

Using Novell NetWare 3
Bill Lawrence

0-88022-756-7, 700 pp., 7 3/8 X 9 1/8
$29.95 USA

Through Version 3.11

Using dBASE IV 2.0, Special Edition
Steve Davis

1-56529-153-0, 1,100 pp., 7 3/8 X 9 1/8
$29.95 USA

Version 2.0

Using 1-2-3, Release 2.4, Special Edition
Que Development Group

0-88022-988-8, 1,000 pp., 7 3/8 X 9 1/8
$29.95 USA

Release 2.4

Using Paradox 4, Special Edition
Walter R. Bruce, III & Matthew Harris

0-88022-822-9, 900 pp., 7 3/8 X 9 1/8
$29.95 USA

Version 4

Using Quicken 6
Linda Flanders

1-56529-071-2, 750 pp., 7 3/8 X 9 1/8
$22.95 USA

Version 6

For more information or to place an order, call: 1-800-428-5331

Complete Computer Coverage

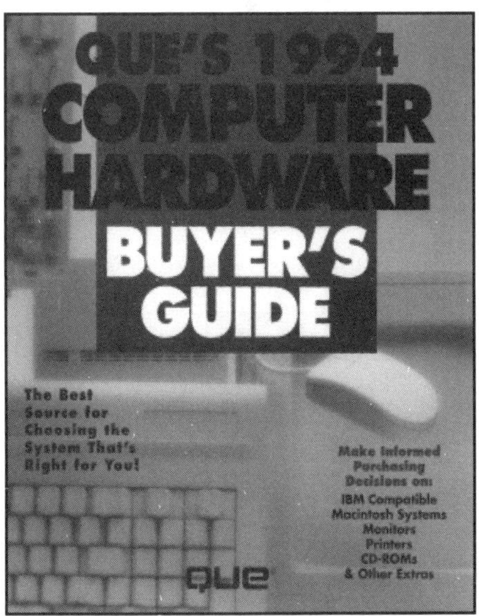

Que's 1994 Computer Hardware Buyer's Guide

Que Development Group

This absolute must-have guide packed with comparisons, recommendations, and tips for asking all the right questions familiarizes the reader with terms they will need to know. This book offers a complete analysis of both hardware and software products, and it's loaded with charts and tables of product comparisons.

IBM-compatibles, Apple, & Macintosh

$16.95 USA

1-56529-281-2, 480 pp., 8 x 10

Que's Computer User's Dictionary, 4th Edition

Bryan Pfaffenberger

This compact, practical reference contains hundreds of definitions, explanations, examples, and illustrations on topics from programming to desktop publishing. You can master the "language" of computers and learn how to make your personal computer more efficient and more powerful. Filled with tips and cautions, *Que's Computer User's Dictionary* is the perfect resource for anyone who uses a computer.

IBM, Macintosh, Apple, & Programming

$12.95 USA

1-56529-604-4, 650 pp., $4^{3}/_{4}$ x 8

To Order, Call: (800) 428-5331

MS-DOS 6.2 QuickStart DiskPack Order Form

Use this form to order the *MS-DOS 6.2 QuickStart DiskPack,* which contains approximately 30 pages of additional exercises that build on the examples presented in the chapters. These "hands-on" exercises enable you to further your learning of MS-DOS 6.2 by practicing with existing presentation pages (rather than creating new presentation pages from scratch). In addition, the *MS-DOS 6.2 QuickStart DiskPack* includes a 1.4M HD 3 1/2-inch disk that contains the following items:

- Sample files used in the chapters of *MS-DOS 6.2 QuickStart.* These files include the examples shown in the Visual Index at the beginning of *MS-DOS 6.2 QuickStart.*
- Practice files that you will use in the approximately 30 pages of additional exercises supplied with the *MS-DOS 6.2 QuickStart DiskPack.*

The easiest way to order your *MS-DOS 6.2 QuickStart DiskPack* is to pick up the phone and call

1-800-428-5331

between 9:00 a.m. and 5:00 p.m. EST.

For faster service, please have your credit card available.

ISBN	*Quantity*	*Item*	*Unit Cost*	*Total Cost*
1-56529-754-7D	_______	MS-DOS 6.2 QuickStart DiskPack	$7.99*	
			TOTAL	________

* The unit price *includes* the shipping and handling charges for domestic orders. For overseas shipping and handling, add $2.00 per disk pack. Price subject to change.

If you need to have it NOW, we can ship it to you so that you will receive the disk pack overnight or in two days for an additional charge of approximately $18.00.

Que Corporation
201 W. 103rd Street
Indianapolis, Indiana 46290

Orders: 1-800-428-5331 **Sales FAX:** 1-800-448-3804 **Customer Service:** 1-800-835-3202